WITHDRAWN

Thorstein Veblen ▨

Victorian Firebrand

ELIZABETH WATKINS JORGENSEN

HENRY IRVIN JORGENSEN

Thorstein Veblen

Victorian Firebrand

M.E. Sharpe

ARMONK, NEW YORK

LONDON, ENGLAND

Library of Congress Cataloging-in-Publication Data

Jorgensen, Elizabeth, 1917–
Thorstein Veblen : Victorian firebrand / Elizabeth and Henry Jorgensen.
p.   cm.
Includes bibliographical references and index.
ISBN 0-7656-0258-X (hardcover : alk. paper)
1. Veblen, Thorstein, 1857–1929.   2. Economists—United States—Biography.
3. Social reformers—United States—Biography.   4. Economics—
United States—History.   I. Jorgensen, Henry, 1915–   II. Title.
HB119.V4J67 1998
330′.092—dc21   98-20416
CIP

Printed in the United States of America

The paper used in this publication meets the minimum requirements of
American National Standard for Information Sciences—
Permanence of Paper for Printed Library Materials,
ANSI Z 39.48-1984.

MV (c)   10   9   8   7   6   5   4   3   2   1

Contents

Acknowledgments

In the Languedocien village of St. Cézaire de Gauzignan, too small to be in the Michelin Guide, too deprived to boast of a bistro, bar, boucherie, or church, we were surprised to find that our landlord's bookshelves contained a complete set of the works of Thorstein Veblen. This chance discovery started us thinking about Veblen again. So we have to thank our landlords, Mel and Ellie Leiman, for getting us going and pointing the way. It was Mel, economics professor from the New York State University at Binghamton, who told us that Sarah Dorfman had turned over what was left of her husband's remarkable collection of notes to Columbia in 1991. This also led to a pleasant afternoon tea with Mrs. Dorfman and an acquaintance with Solidelle Fortier Wasser, who later gave us information about her Parisian research into Laura Gagey's life in France.

We would also like to thank William Melton, heroic rescuer and restorer of the Veblen family homestead at Nerstrand, Minnesota. His meticulous research, guidance, and support have been invaluable. He read and carefully corrected our manuscript in one of its late stages. Eric Hilleman, archivist at Carleton College, has gone out of his way to be of service. Russell Bartley and Sylvia Yoneda Bartley have shared the results of their research with us.

Bernard Crystal and associates of the Rare Book and Manuscript Library of Columbia University, Richard Popp and Daniel Meyer of the University of Chicago Special Collections, Steve Cotham of the McClung Historical Collection, Knoxville, Tennessee, and Margaret Kimball of Stanford University's Department of Special Collections have been particularly helpful. Mr. Popp steered us to Chicago's newly acquired Sarah Hardy Gregory papers. The archives at Clark University; the Western Historical Collection at Columbia, Missouri; the Minnesota Historical Society; the Norwegian Historical Society; and The Bancroft

Library, University of California, Berkeley, have proven to be ready resources. We are grateful for their assistance and grant of permission for the use of their materials. We are also grateful for the inspiration provided by the International Veblen Association and Rick Tilman's suggestions.

It is amazing what the development of the inter-library loan system has done for researchers without constant access to a major university library. We have been particularly blessed to be able to rely on the expertise of Polly Archer, a research librarian at the Pacific Grove Library.

Invaluable assistance has been rendered by Thorstein Veblen's heirs, Esther Baran and Charles Sims, and by Brice Claggett, a McAdoo family descendant, who provided us with photos of Laura McAdoo Gagey.

Thorstein Veblen

Victorian Firebrand

1

Introduction

Thorstein Veblen, a dangerous man, challenged the *eternal verities* of America at the turn of the century. His *Theory of the Leisure Class,* which came out in 1899, is still in print and will be in print at the turn of another century. Although his ideas were shocking to the Victorian-era conscience, they are no less shocking to many today, because they undermine the consumerist values inherent in the great American rat race.

Albert Einstein said Veblen was the only contemporary scientific writer, other than Bertrand Russell, to whom he owed "innumerable happy hours."[1]

For a century America has been in denial about Veblen's ideas. They conflicted with the "American dream" of "winning" through perching atop a mountain of expensive possessions and becoming the envy of the neighbors. They conflicted with the American golden rule to love thy neighbor as thyself, although you may have to knife him to get to the top. Veblen's piercing insights were incompatible with the old-fashioned dream. It was easier to dismiss Veblen as a wacky eccentric, a womanizer, and a lecher.

Along with Mary Wollstonecraft, Henrik Ibsen, Edward Bellamy, Alexandre Dumas the younger, and John Stuart Mill, Veblen condemned the modern oppression of women. He scorned the idea that an upper-class woman's place was to be a parlor ornament and a clothes horse, to show off her rich husband's exemplary financial status. Like Ibsen, he understood women's desire to have absorbing work to do on their own. In fact, he felt that women were superior beings who had been unappreciated down through the ages. It is time that this part of Veblen's thinking be emphasized, as it has been largely overlooked.

Since he is a lost man, buried underneath a sanitary landfill of lies and half-truths, the information that has recently been made available about him in the archives of Columbia University, the University of Chicago, and Carleton College should be assessed.

These give us a new picture of Veblen. Yes, he was tall, muscular, and darkly handsome. Yes, he was extremely attractive to women. But was he the sexual adventurer portrayed by John dos Passos, and many of Veblen's modern followers, who seem to have accepted this version of his intimate life?[2] Or was he a Christ-like visionary pilloried and persecuted by an eccentric harpy who played by Victorian procrustean bed rules? Or, again, could he be more accurately likened to a hero in an old Norse myth—one who, as Edith Hamilton puts it in her book, *Mythology*, "laughs while his foes cut his heart out of his living flesh [and thus] shows himself superior over his conquerors." He says to them in effect, "You can do nothing to me, because I do not care what you do."

So perhaps the conventional economists have obliterated Veblen and his challenging ideas, but is he safely dead? Could he still be laughing at us somehow? Will his ideas continue to haunt us for another 100 years?

2

University of Chicago Beginnings

Thorstein Veblen, the Columbian Exposition, and the new University of Chicago were launched almost simultaneously.[1] The fair and the university were to usher "a new era into Chicago." Veblen eventually was to usher in a new era in thinking. The flamboyant exposition contrasted painfully with the somber university, which was built of grey limestone in the English Gothic style. The Divinity School was still being erected only a few hundred yards from the ferris wheel and the "Street in Cairo" with its gyrating belly-dancers. The tawdriness of the Midway contrasted strangely with the pristine grey towers symbolizing a medieval-like withdrawal from the world of the flesh.

The fair was popularly called "The White City" as most of the exhibition buildings were white and some were vast.

They showed, according to writers Robert Herrick and Theodore Dreiser, that America prized beauty as much as big money and raw power, and that if America put its mind to it, it could come out on top in the fields of art and architecture, too. The fair proved that American life did not have to be ugly, makeshift, and haphazard—America could darned well accomplish whatever it set its sights on![2]

One of the keynotes of the fair was the existence of the Woman Building, designed by women. It housed "evidences of women's abilities." "For the first time," it was said, "Woman publicly came into her own."[3] "Woman's hour has struck," as one speaker put it.[4]

How little the oratory was based on reality was shown by the fact that the University of Chicago, which opened "to six hundred students of both sexes, with an endowment of . . . seven millions of dollars" (founded by John D.

5

Rockefeller, who contributed $35 million to the university over a period of twenty years), had no dormitories at all for women students. "The Woman's Club [of Chicago] at once collected funds for the construction of a building which contain[ed] not only sleeping-rooms but parlors, a large hall, a dining room, library and gymnasium."[5] So much for the year of the woman!

Unfortunately, in 1893, Chicago was gripped by a deep depression. Never a clean or lovely site from the beginning, the city seemed disreputable and a shambles compared to the white walls and towers of the Columbian Exposition. Many visitors were, to say the least, unfavorably impressed.

After the fair closed, several thousand souvenir hunters vandalized the grounds. The next day, a large number of unemployed or homeless, who had been occupying some of the empty buildings, started a fire, whether by accident or design. It spread from building to building. "It was," the *Chicago Tribune* said, "the greatest pyrotechnic display of the Fair, lighting up the area like a midsummer's day at noon." Twenty thousand spectators stood around gaping and applauding, especially when statuary fell into the "icy lagoon . . . The statue of the Republic 'seemed to stand in the midst of it all like a giant silhouette, with uplifted arms as if appealing for help. The wind blew furiously, and now and then made great rifts in the smoky wall, revealing the blood red skeleton of arch and column.' "[6]

"Herrick wrote, 'The skeleton that had been heroically shoved into the closet all that summer, the skeleton of financial panic, now stalked forth. There were unemployed men by the hundreds of thousands in the cold streets that cold winter and even the prosperous citizens were quaking in the throes of 'hard times.' "[7] Homeless people were sleeping on the steps of the city hall and the floors of the police stations.

In 1894, Coxey's Army marched on Washington, DC. These jobless troops from all over the West were composed, some said, of hoboes, tramps, radicals, and foreign immigrants. Thirteen of the "armies" started out for Washington. On top of this there was the Pullman strike. George Pullman, president of the Pullman Palace Car Company, had reduced wages to 75 percent of the previously paid amount, but had not decreased the rents paid by the workers in his company housing. The strike cut the number of unobstructed rail lines entering Chicago from twenty-four to six. Chicago trade was in deadlock.

With all this going on, the university students were looking for answers, or at least some new way to solve old problems. Maude Radford Warren, later a well-known novelist, described a university scene that contrasted markedly with the turmoil downtown: "I remember . . . the first time I saw him. I was an undergraduate, walking along Cottage Grove Avenue with a friend who said, 'There is Veblen.' Mr. Veblen was walking in the center of a body of six students and I'll never forget those silhouettes: they were all poking their heads forward, eager to lose not a word."[8]

The younger instructors became instant Veblenites, and "the older ones [also became Veblenites] as fast as they could adjust themselves."[9] "We thought he had hidden resources," a woman student wrote, "too precious for everyday life—but no one got very near to him . . . manifestly, he knew his power."[10]

One student in Veblen's Chicago classroom described the effect his lectures had on him:

> Although his genius was largely ill-expended on my then 18-year-old immaturity, I distinctly recall that [the student next to me] used to commonly nudge me in class hours at the time of a particularly telling thrust (and they were rapier-like) that Veblen had just delivered, and [my classmate] would whisper usually: "Isn't he a keen boy?" or something to that effect.
>
> Professor Veblen (we never called him doctor, as I recall it) then looked the part of a thorough-bred scholastic. He looked as if he had an odor to him of his subject. He was steeped in it. He droned in his speech and never rocked from an even keel of steady and easy discourse. He was a master mind. In appearance he was lean, brown and bearded to an almost Van Dyke style. There was nothing studied in his make up. His charm lay in a natural grace. He had vigor without effort, ease without languor . . . He lounged in his chair on a raised platform in front of our class of 3 or more students and seemed to coin his words as they came, nothing from memory, no cut and dried fossilized jewels of economic lore from some other master of economic laws. He discovered *his* as he went along.
>
> . . . I sat in class in rapt . . . attention. His periods and demeanor were not to be lost by gluing one's eyes to his notebook in transcription. He was not oratorical, far from bombastic, nothing of a so-called radical and never dreamed of sensationalism . . . He was always a star and his light will never dim.[11]

Another student was delighted, because Veblen would come to class looking wan and dragged out from a long night's work, heave a weighty tome of some obscure German text on the desk, and turn the pages

> with nervous yellow fingers. In a low croaking tone he began a recital of village economy among the early Germans. Presently he came upon some unjust legal fiction imposed by rising nobles and sanctioned by the clergy. A sardonic smile twisted his lips, blue devils leaped in his eyes. With mordant sarcasm, he dissected the tortuous assumption that the wish of aristocrats is the will of God. He showed similar implications in modern institutions. He chuckled quietly. Then, returning to history, he continued the exposition.[12]

Veblen had become a "character," a wonderful campus character, and as such, among the students, was beloved and cherished.

This was his first job teaching in a college. When the new president of the rich, new university raided the eastern colleges to set up a faculty that would give Chicago instant status as a rival of the best of the Ivy League, he grabbed, among others, J. Laurence Laughlin, head of the Economics Department at Cornell. Laughlin, who recognized talent when he saw it, even though coming from one who listened to a different drummer, brought along his promising student, Veblen, starting him out on the lowest academic rung at less than $600 a year. Soon, however, Laughlin decided that, with all the controversy arising over day-to-day economic events on the labor front, his department should have a course on socialism, and he assigned Veblen the job of teaching it. It was later said that Veblen was "the only man who would be permitted to lecture on socialism at the University of Chicago."

"This was partly a joke," said ex-student Harriet Bement, "but not entirely so, for Dr. Veblen was 'safe' in that he expressed himself with the greatest impartiality on any radical economic doctrine, in class, certainly, and I do not recall it differently in private conversation. He represented both sides and argued both sides and left you to make your *choice*."[13] His course on socialism was as concerned with anthropology, prehistoric man and woman, Icelanders, Vikings, medieval history, and Darwin's theories as it was with the present day.

Later, an ex-Missouri student, Isador Lubin, said: "Regarding Veblen's economic philosophy . . . I never saw evidence of animus or personal dislike of the economic system or of the people who ran the system . . . Capitalism to him was a system which he was trying to analyze as a scientist would analyze a rock of a certain geologic age, or a doctor or physiologist would analyze the human body to see how it functioned."[14] In analyzing socialism he had a similarly detached attitude.

A Chicago student wrote:

> The one statement which he emphasized very strongly, and which is not found in any of his books, was that socialism was impossible until the desire for the common good could be substituted in the mind of the common man (which is everyone) for the desire for private advantage at the expense of whomever it might concern. I also remember his stating that at the present rate of progress he thought at least a thousand years would be required to make the substitution."[15]

Still, there were those who felt that this pesky new socialism should be ignored until it went away, such as the president of the university, William Rainey Harper. The tone at Chicago was somewhat Baptist, as one-third of the board of trustees were Baptists and the university was supposedly a continuation of the old "Baptist University of Chicago."[16] Harper was head of the theology department as well as being head of the entire college and soon became a wary enemy of Veblen. He was a boomer and a Baptist and a devout supporter of Rockefeller, Rockefeller generosity, and Rockefeller pelf.

But Laughlin had confidence in Veblen because, while a student at Cornell, Thorstein had published two notes in the *Quarterly Journal of Economics*, which, according to Joseph Dorfman, very ably "defended Laughlin's common-sense point of view" in discussing articles by Eugen von Böhm-Bawerk and Uriel Crocker.[17] Laughlin thought so highly of Veblen's capabilities that he wanted Veblen to be free to analyze whatever he wished. He also gave him the thankless task of acting as managing editor of the *Journal of Political Economy* with no raise in salary. Thorstein was "virtually in entire charge" of the journal and gained a considerable amount of prestige from this among the nation's economists. His scholarly drive stood him in good stead in such a responsible, if unpaid, position.

This sophisticated and erudite young instructor had a Ph.D. in philosophy from Yale University, plus two years of graduate work in economics at Cornell. In addition, his wife, Ellen, was the niece of a college president, the niece of a former president of the Atchison, Topeka, and Santa Fe Railroad, and the daughter of a prominent Kansas City businessman.

Yet, he was the son of a Norwegian immigrant who signed his name with an "X."[18]

3

The Immigrants

Thorstein Veblen's mother, Kari Thorsteinsdatter Bunde Veblen, had a brain that was "the fastest machine that God ever made," according to John Edward, Thorstein's younger brother, generally called Ed. "There was something about her that always made me think of lightning," Ed said. "She would decide questions in the fraction of a second, while father [Thomas Anderson Veblen] took days and weeks and often years, but both [however] always arrived at a solution of any problem that came up." Ed felt that Thorstein got his brains and personality from her.[1]

Thorstein's older brother, Andrew, however, was highly indignant that his father was pictured this way:

> He was a man of few words, but (like Coolidge) he could talk, and did talk, readily and convincingly, and expressed himself with great facility. I wrote many a letter from his dictation, and I have all along marvelled at the rich diction of those letters. When he talked everyone "sat up and took notice." He was not *slow,* as we knew well enough. His brain was nimble and precise, as many a man found out if anyone tried to get the better of him. It was father, especially, that was the driving force to get us schooled . . . You are wrong about his requiring days, weeks, years to solve his problems. I don't know of any important step in the affairs of our family that did not start with his initiative.[2]

Thorstein told Henry Waldgrave Stuart, a student of his at the University of Chicago (and later a professor of philosophy at Stanford at the same time Veblen taught there), that the basic ideas in *The Theory of the Leisure Class* came from boyhood talks with his father, who was a deep thinker.[3]

Kari was a model pioneer woman, staggeringly competent, talented in many directions, and the patient bearer of twelve children, three of whom died in infancy. Although she was sometimes brought to childbed under primitive conditions, she did not die while giving birth on the wind-swept prairie. She was a survivor, who, although her husband was a few years older than she, lived beyond him, unusual for those days. He died at age eighty-eight, she lived on for a few months.

She was the "most beautiful girl" in the Valdris valley of Norway, still a teenager when she was courted by Thomas, a powerfully built, taciturn, unflappable carpenter, seven years her senior. On May 2, 1847, they departed for America, via what was supposed to be a short stopover in Hamburg, and were married shortly before they emigrated.[4]

Both Kari's and Thomas's parents had been dispossessed of their farms, one by legal trickery, another by financial trickery.[5] The younger Veblens felt this keenly. In Norway owning land or even leasing farmland, no matter how meager, gave one status. Thomas was a skillful carpenter and cabinetmaker; times were hard; and when they heard of the opportunities for acquiring property in the midwestern part of the United States, they determined to go there.

Over the years Thomas had saved money for the passage. They prepaid their way on a sailing ship. Two other couples from Valdris were to accompany them. Unfortunately, their only child—a little boy, one and a half years old—died on the eve of their embarkation for America, and the grief-stricken couple stayed behind for the funeral, while the others went on ahead.

After the service, they sailed, with many others, to Hamburg. There they were left stranded by the greedy captain, who, once he had their money in his pocket, had no intention of fulfilling his bargain. They were rescued, however, by the captain of a sealing and whaling vessel who agreed to take them to America in his sturdy ship. But first they had to spend four weeks scouring and cleansing it of blubber, and making it habitable for their little company.

Because it was the first ice-breaker ever built, the little "tub" was not comfortable as a passenger ship. It pitched and tossed miserably. They ran out of food and—what was more crucial—water. Everyone became deathly sick, and all children under the age of six died on the trip. The captain did his best to help them out with some of his own supplies and medicines.

They landed briefly in Quebec. Thomas had just undergone a siege of fever; he was barely able to walk. Would he pass muster with the inspecting physician? Captain Foyn told him to cleanse his tongue, rub "his face with brandy to overcome his pallor," and advised Kari to steady him as they walked by the doctor.[6]

The total trip from Norway to Milwaukee had taken them four and a half months. It was already mid-September, and they were down to their last two or three dollars. Thomas forced himself to tramp twenty-five miles to get in touch with a friend from the old country. Kari followed in a dray with the luggage.

Their countryman found them both jobs, but they felt too ill and worn out to do very much.

Thomas proved too weak to function at the fanning mill (where they separate the wheat from the chaff), and Kari was unable to force herself to work as a housemaid for longer than two weeks. They would have been in a bad spot if their countryman had not hired them to move onto, and look out for, some property while he went to Europe. That way they were able to rest, and he paid them $30.

The next decade or two was a time of great effort, as Thomas and his brother, Haldor, who had come over two years later, sold one piece of land after another and bought better ones. They whittled superior axe handles at night to raise money. The first time they moved, they had to drive the animals they had acquired (a cow and a calf and "probably pigs") to their new home. The wagon that carried their goods was drawn by oxen. In order not to weigh down the wagon, they walked beside it, taking turns carrying a new baby—for twenty-four long miles.[7]

Sheboygan County, Wisconsin, did not prove satisfactory, however. Two babies later they moved to Manitowoc County, Wisconsin. At first, they had to live in an unfinished house, adjacent to the property they had acquired there. It was "so badly built and so open to the weather that my mother had a hard time keeping the children [Andrew, Betsey, and Orson] warm that winter," wrote Thorstein's sister Emily.[8] Kari used to put them to bed in mittens, and when they woke up, likely as not, snow had drifted across the counterpane. In this bleak, unfinished house Emily was born. Thorstein was born, July 30, 1857, in their own, snugly built new house. He was named after Kari's father, and according to his brothers Ed and Andrew, Thorstein was probably her favorite son.[9]

Near their Manitowoc house there were deep woods. Emily wrote:

> The forest had been cleared away to make fields, but, in whatever direction you looked, there was always the background of woods beyond the clearings. Hidden in the woods there was the river (mysterious to us children), which ran in a half circle, from three quarters to a half a mile away from our house, to the west and north. The trees in these woods were no ordinary ones. When we children [picked] flowers in the spring, or berries later, and we looked upwards to the tops of the trees they seemed so tall they touched the sky. I'll never forget the wonderful . . . hepaticas and other spring flowers . . . we found there . . . The blackberries we picked and ate . . . at the edge of the wood were delicious.[10]

Thorstein's intense interest in botany and biology may have been inspired by the study of plants and animals in these woods.[11]

But there were elements of danger as well. Feral dogs ran loose in the neighborhood; bears lurked in the depth of the forest. During his adolescence Thorstein, like many a farm boy, was enamored of guns. His brother Ed said, "He had a little pistol. I think it was a muzzle loader and [he] always talked hunting and shooting, etc. . . . He . . . had a twenty-two cartridge pistol, and kept trading until [when he was a teenager] he owned a twenty-two six-shooter, and I'll never forget how glad and proud I was when he showed it to me and swore me to secrecy as to his having it."[12]

In Manitowoc County they had friendly Irish and German neighbors with plenty of children to play with, and the Veblen offspring attended schools taught in English.[13] Thorstein attended school there from age five to eight. During the winter, a lot of the older boys attended, and there was a male schoolteacher. During the summer, the older boys worked on the farms, and the girls and younger children attended with a female teacher. Emily wrote:

> One of the lady summer teachers I remember especially. She was the incarnation of refinement and beauty . . . Her complexion did not need any powder, it was so white and velvety . . . Her dark hair, almost black, hung in long curls all around her head, down to her shoulders or . . . lower. Her eyes were large and dark, quite like those of a fawn. She wore hoop skirts and a wide-brimmed hat over which was thrown a veil . . . No ray of sun could tan her fair face when it was thus protected. No wonder her complexion was adorable.[14]

As Thorstein started to school when he was so young, he no doubt had the benefit of summer lessons from this adorable teacher. But he also attended all the winter sessions with the older boys. "Most of the lady teachers [and many of the men] did not have much more than the ordinary elementary school training," said a chronicler of early times.[15] Andrew, for example, the oldest Veblen boy, taught school for three months with only a grammar school education, and later taught seven more months with a smattering of high school learning, which he had picked up during fourteen weeks at Faribault High School.[16]

Emily wrote:

> Speaking of pictures retained in my mind from this . . . time, I must mention that of my mother. She had a light colored print dress, white ground with tiny rose buds scattered over it, which was one of her "best dresses." When she had this dress on, I thought her the handsomest lady I had ever seen. She was very fair, with color in her cheeks, very blue eyes and wavy golden brown hair. It is too bad there is no photograph of her from that time.[17]

"In the earliest times in Wisconsin," Emily wrote, "we had a large open fireplace in our living room instead of a heating stove, as we had later. Sitting around the fireplace on a winter evening, there were many stories told, especially about what had happened in Norway. The children were all ears, of course."

There were stories about imps and elves "that plagued people in tricky ways," there were fairy tales and many ghost stories. "My parents did not believe in the truth of these stories, of course, but there were some [boarders or guests] who told them who believed in them, more or less."[18]

It was in 1864, toward the end of the Civil War, that Thorstein's father decided to move for the final time, in search of better land, to Rice County, Minnesota.

Even though Kari's relatives lived in Minnesota, this was the only time she expressed reluctance to move. "Mother was not so willing to 'pull up stakes' and leave the comfortable home they had established in Wisconsin," Emily said, "but finally agreed to go." Now a middle-aged woman with seven children, one a baby, she understandably did not look forward to starting all over again under pioneer conditions.

Emily wrote:

> I remember seeing my father receive payment from the buyer of the Wisconsin place. He emptied out, from some receptacle, a pile of shining gold and silver coins on to a table—the biggest pile of money I had ever seen, or ever expect to see . . . Everybody got busy! For one thing, we all had to have new clothes. And didn't we look fine in our new outfits! I was old enough to wear a hoopskirt, which I loved. Our route of travel was: by team to Manitowoc City, by boat on Lake Michigan to Milwaukee, by rail to La Crosse, by boat on the Mississippi north to Hastings, Minnesota, and by team to Rice County (because the train had not yet reached Northfield, we had to take this circuitous route).[19]

The first year in Minnesota (1865), they lived in a makeshift log cabin on their new property. And it was a handsome property—two hundred acres of fertile soil and ninety acres of partially cultivated, but mostly wild, woods. The youngest child, barely a year and a half old, died soon after they arrived. Meanwhile, the men went ahead, building stables and quarrying limestone, so that, the year after, they could live in the limestone basement of the fine new house they were constructing. Thomas and his brother Haldor had erected a temporary roof over the basement, with plenty of storage space under it. There the Veblen family huddled together, cooked, washed clothes, bathed, and took care of the eight children. A new baby, John Edward, had been born on October 18, 1866, in the log cabin, immediately before they moved in.20 Although it was a commodious basement, with two sizable windows that looked out on a gently sloping hillside, it was heated only by a huge fireplace and Kari's cookstove. In one corner there may have been a large sunken cistern that gathered rainwater for washing; in another corner was a deep well.21 "It was as good living quarters as could be found for many miles around on the prairie," insisted Andrew, Thorstein's older brother.22

Thorstein's sister Emily said, "It is easy to understand that we were quite crowded this first winter when we lived in the basement." And crowded as they were, the ever-unselfish, forty-year-old mother took in yet another immigrant.

"She was a queer character," according to Emily, "an old woman whose relatives had helped her come to America, but who was unable to find shelter when winter came. Her work, whereby she made her living, was to spin woolen yarn. My mother let the poor old woman come and stay with us all winter. She prepared her meals on my mother's cook stove, and slept on a cot-bed in one corner. Her spinning wheel hummed lustily all day and evening."[23]

But better days were ahead. The house, when it reached its full two stories plus a large attic, was a marvel of craftsmanship.

They had fulfilled their destiny. The fierce will to regain farm-owning status had carried them through. Also, they were happily settled in a Norwegian community among relatives and friends. But, "We early became very patriotic Americans and were glad we were born in America," wrote Emily.[24]

"All the settlers who could find room in their houses for newcomers were obliged to give them shelter [and food] until they could find homes for themselves," Andrew said. "As father had built a fairly large house on his arrival in the settlement, . . . we housed newcomers those first years to the capacity of the house."[25] As Ed noted, they came "out of a race and a family who [made] of family loyalty and solidarity a religion."[26]

Certain of the mother's close relatives lived with them for years.[27] Some of her cousins and one of their daughters were also aboard for lengthy stays. Another young female relative "was early with us and was a most helpful girl," Andrew wrote. Three more were with them "for quite a time . . . A sister of some neighbors . . . was with us one of the first years or two, and was a very strong and industrious woman . . . Toward the time of the [Civil] war came an old chum of mother's . . . and her nearly-grown son . . . Three or four years before the war came [a] widowed mother and her eight children, ranging from young manhood to six years." For the latter they were able to find an unoccupied cabin. However, "Several of these young people got houseroom and employment at our house . . . All of these . . . mentioned were constantly attached to us, as much as three or four years in some cases."

Andrew continued: "But there were many others. [A young man], who was hare-lipped, cleared land one winter." Another young man named Erik:

> was with us a year, perhaps, . . . others . . . got jobs clearing land during the winter and staid [*sic*] with us, often for months at a time. Then there were other house guests, often for a week or two. Such was my tutor, Berge, who returned each winter for a somewhat prolonged stay . . . Captain Rode [a retired sea captain] . . . was always good for at least two weeks [and] a student and distant relative . . . spent a vacation with us while he was studying. [A] theological student . . . invariably staid [*sic*] a while . . . He sometimes preached. Once, he . . . gave the audience their choice of hearing about heaven or hell . . . they voted for hell, and he gave them all they wanted of it.[28]

With this large work force, Thomas was able to pay off his mortgage of $1,000 on the west farm, and $1,800 on the main farm, in less than five years.[29]

But Kari, with the aid of her household help, was obliged to serve banquet-sized meals, at least during harvest time.

The Veblens provided meat, milk, and eggs from their own cows, pigs, chickens, ducks, and geese, vegetables from their own fields, clothing from their own sheared sheep and dried-out flax plants (cotton had to be bought). A shoemaker came periodically to make shoes from their own hides, a laborious process. It required scraping the hides, boiling them, drying them, working them over until they were supple, making the lasts, cutting the leather and sewing it. Andrew helped the shoemaker, and learned how to make shoes himself. Soles had to be bought.[30]

Kari not only wove, carded, spun, cut out, and sewed all their clothes, but actually sheared the sheep as well. And two years later had another baby, this time a girl. The next and last child was born when she was forty-five, but he died within eight months. Ed wrote: "Mother was a midwife and a natural nurse, so that, at one time, she was the only doctor the neighborhood had any use for . . . no one ever came to her for help . . . but that she tried something, and no one ever sent for her but that she went and stayed until there was a change."[31] "Doctors were far away; Northfield was twelve miles, Faribault fourteen," wrote Emily.

Kari wove her special woolen cloth, which was much in demand (at higher prices than was asked in the stores), and Thomas bought a small threshing machine that he could pull into a barn to avoid stormy weather. He could be threshing away for his neighbors as late as December or January, while the larger commercial rigs had to stop during the long Minnesota winters.[32]

Often, his work for his neighbors would be paid back with labor in the Veblen fields, but it was not entirely a barter system, and the prodigious Thomas, with his arms as stout as tree trunks, and the indefatigable Kari, at her spinning wheel and loom, made their family very prosperous. Five years after they settled in Minnesota they were the richest farmers in the Township of Cato, according to the 1870 census.[33] And how rich they must have felt when they remembered the Norwegian farms, 98 percent of which had less than fifty acres and nearly one-third of which had less than one-half acre.[34]

Later on, when his children and grandchildren visited Norway, Thomas Veblen would insist that life was unbearably hard there, stating, "I don't ever want to go back!"[35]

There had been two Sioux uprisings in Minnesota in 1862 and 1863, only two years before the Veblens moved there, and Norwegians had been killed.[36] At the end of the Civil War, when Thorstein was almost eight, the Wisconsin settlers had become alarmed about the local Indians and spread stories that they were burning houses and murdering settlers only a few miles away. Men had arrived at a meeting carrying guns, axes and pitchforks. Thomas, whose "middle name should have been Poise," did not get carried away by this propaganda. "He never got excited, mad or tired,"[37] but did think it wise to stock a wagon ready with provisions, in case the Indians actually came. "The horses were harnessed and stood ready in the barn. [Emily] secretly brought out [her] best doll with a china head and a stuffed body made by [her] mother, and hid her in the back of the wagon."[38] Nothing came of it.

Thorstein, however, took the side of the Indians. His brother Ed "noticed [that Thorstein] was always on the side opposite to all the others . . . shortly after the close of the Civil War . . . he took the part of the South . . . I remember many arguments on that subject between him and the older children."[39]

He was three when the Civil War broke out. Their father had luckily missed being taken in the first draft, and when the second draft was made, Thomas had just passed the forty-five-year age limit. They all rejoiced, because they could not imagine what would have happened to them or the farm without him.

Thorstein read whatever he could get his hands on, sometimes finding nothing better than old almanacs, old newspapers, and "some old novels that had been acquired as premiums with the newspapers."[40] "The folks were too thrifty to destroy the papers, but let them accumulate in the attic," said Ed, "and then 'Tosten'[41] could be found reading those old papers when he should be hoeing corn or potatoes. I can remember once. He must have been about thirteen or fourteen. He made a very hasty and precipitate exit from his attic study. He came down the stairs very fast. The reason being that Mother was after him with a switch."[42]

Their immigrant neighbors and friends "were a rather proud and domineering people," according to Ed:

> Those people had the nerve to pick up and leave their native land and take up the awful task of creating a new country for themselves. They were adventurous, ambitious, unafraid, strong people. And in the case of the Norwegians, descendants of that irrepressible race called the Vikings—people with brains, physique . . . fearless and proud. They built temporary log cabins, and even sod houses, but their ambition was to have white houses, and red barns, and fat cattle, and splendid horses, and churches, and school houses, and they soon had them. They had no use for the man who was satisfied to remain poor, where wealth and independence could be dug out of the ground.[43]

It was not long before the senior Veblens had their own white house, red barn, fat cattle, and splendid horses, along with the best of them. As a builder, Thorstein's father Thomas "was no slouch"; the Veblen house still stands as a National Historic Landmark. William Melton, who is restoring the property, said: "The house is more modern than any Victorian-era house I have ever seen. It is very sunny, even in the basement [and it] has walk-in closets." Jonathan Larson, author of *Elegant Technology,* who has been carefully observing the restoration, believed: "When Veblen talked about the instinct of workmanship, . . . he was talking about his father . . . The house is a gem of careful craftsmanship, with hardwood floors, wainscoting, paneled walls, planked pine ceilings, large windows, a . . . dining room with a built-in pass-through to the kitchen, an indoor water supply . . . an upstairs family room [used as a workroom for Kari for weaving cloth and quilting], and a double deck porch."[44]

But Thomas was not just a farmer or master carpenter. He also venerated men of learning.[45] "The group that gathered about [their] dinner table . . . discussed everything: books, politics, public affairs, the tariff, economics, current events." Thomas "never learned to read English, although he spoke it well, but he was a great reader [in Norwegian] . . . All the family were interested in Norway's scholars and literary men, and [Thorstein] was well acquainted with Norwegian literature before he went to college."[46]

Thomas was a kindly and totally fearless man, who never physically punished any of his children.[47] He was abstemious and disliked the free-flowing whiskey and boisterous merriment at local social gatherings and so tried to avoid them. Tobacco was not to be found in any form in the Veblen household. Yet, Thomas was not religious, but somewhat skeptical. He was simply and strongly gripped by the work ethic, a desire to protect and further the interests of his family, and a delight in good craftsmanship.

All but two of his children attended the Carleton preparatory school. Three graduated from the college.[48] Some attended college, but did not graduate. Betsy and Mary did not attend college. One boy was killed in an accident in his junior year. One took work at the University of Minnesota.

Brother Ed's opinion was that "the female members of the family [were] really wonderful, much better stuff than the male contingent." John Bates Clark, a professor at Columbia University (formerly of Carleton College), "considered Emily the 'smartest in the family . . . What a wonderful scholar!' "[49]

Only Thorstein was "queer." Brother Ed said, "He is queer, and has always been queer." His queerness seemed to consist in the fact that he did not hold the same get-ahead philosophy as the others. He also had the liability of genius. To Ed, however, he was "lazy" and "a loafer." By this, Ed meant that he tried to avoid doing his full quota of farm chores. "At that early childhood age he seemed to be better posted on almost any subject than grown-ups, including the old preacher and the school masters, but he was always different, queer," Ed insisted. Nonetheless, "from my earliest recollections I thought he knew everything. I could ask him any question, and he would tell me about it in great detail."[50]

The rest of the family was sober and industrious but, as a child, Thorstein was involved in many pranks. According to his sister-in-law, Florence:

> When a neighbor's dog was allowed to harry and torment his father's cattle, Thorstein deliberately shot the dog; the same dog had several times bitten and frightened his horse. This act of reprisal having produced further irritation and aggression, he next wrote anathemas in Greek on the neighbor's fence. Since nobody but the minister could read them, and that worthy man was, himself, greatly astonished, they created a sensation. It is amusing to note that the effect of the Greek anathemas was much more compelling than the sacrifice of the dog. There was no further trouble.

"That brother of yours is a very remarkable boy," said the minister to Orson.[51] Besides being queer, Ed admitted, Thorstein was also funny:

Everyone who was acquainted with him knew it. They would begin to laugh at his stories and sayings before he opened his mouth. An old man who had been our neighbor and moved away came to visit us. It was, I think, in '85, when Tosten was loafing. He met Tosten, and asked him which one of those Veblen boys he might be, and Tosten told him. "Then," the man said, "you are the one who took the prize." "No," answered Tosten, "they neglected to take me to the fair, so I did not take any prize."[52]

The Veblen family came from the race of Vikings, and "the men in the family," as Andrew wrote, "were all very strong and could generally lift much heavier weights than most men can."[53] Physically, compared to the others, Thorstein did not quite measure up. Although he was more muscular and adept than the average American male, his "laziness" and periods of "loafing," according to his stepdaughter Becky, masked a heart insufficiency, of which he was only partially aware at the time and which he evidently tried to hide.[54] So he early learned to do things with the greatest economy of effort, such as enlisting the aid of the dog "Passup" to take food to the men in the fields while riding on his back at the same time. His brains would carry him far, but his health was always a problem.

4

Carleton

I n 1874 young Thorstein Veblen first learned that he was to leave home when a buggy stopped near the field where he was working, and one of the farmhands came to fetch him. He was seventeen years old. His luggage was in the buggy, and he was not told his destination until he arrived at Carleton Preparatory School.

Thomas, his father, was not high-handed or domineering, but simply a man of the soil who was not given to much conversation or explaining. Thomas once happened to meet his son in their small Minnesota town on market day and passed him by without a nod or a word of recognition. They had nothing to talk about at that time, Thorstein later indicated to Robert L. Duffus, so any sort of salutation was unnecessary.[1]

Thorstein's canny father had taken advantage of the presence of the new Carleton College and Preparatory School, only ten miles away from the farm, to take care of his children's higher education. He had bought a lot near the campus in the little town of Northfield and built "a little square two-story cottage," where his children could sleep, study, and cook for themselves.[2] It was located on a pleasant wooded lot, with a stream running through it. A wagon load of provisions was brought in from the farm regularly.

Thorstein took studying seriously and would put up with no nonsense. He worked in a low-ceilinged upstairs room, on an unpainted pine table, lighted by an oil lamp, and heated by the stove pipe from below. According to a fellow student:

> One evening, some of the young men gathered at the house for jollification, and in the course of the evening, owing to the exuberance of youthful (or otherwise) spirits, became rather boisterous in their demonstrations. T.B. [as

Thorstein was known at Carleton] stuck his head through the trap door, and with a gun in hand proceeded to shoot up the house. Whether he used blanks or bullets he did not state . . . but the boys thought it was time to go home.[3]

After graduating from the preparatory school in three years instead of four, Thorstein went on to finish Carleton College (part of the same campus), also in only three years. He won the Athens prize of $80 for the best college entrance examination (as his brother Andrew had done before him) and was rated, by "at least one of his professors, as the most brilliant man the college had graduated."[4]

The majority of the institutions of the day were strictly religious. Sunday church service was compulsory and noses were counted. "An instructor was considered capable of teaching any subject, as long as 'the light of Godly example' was shown in his life and work."[5] Perhaps reflecting the attitude of a free-thinking father, Thorstein was irreligious. (He later said, "if there is a difference between religion and magic I have never seen it."[6]) Nonetheless he was careful to avoid sensational confrontations with his college mentors. The Carleton faculty, composed mostly of devout Congregational ministers, may have suspected the presence of a heretic among them but only expressed themselves as being somewhat repelled by Thorstein's originality and his "keen, cold mentality which held him aloof from friendship with others."[7]

At Carleton, drinking, smoking, and swearing were forbidden, as was all mingling of the sexes in the evenings or on Sundays, "except by special permission." Dancing was of course tabooed. Smoking was grounds for expulsion. Independent-minded Thorstein took up smoking at Carleton, nonetheless, and from then on, in his free time, was rarely seen without a long self-rolled cigarette of dark, strongly flavored Perique tobacco in his hands. Grown in Louisiana, Perique was cured in its own juices to give it a stronger flavor, and was usually used only in small quantities as part of a blend. A fellow student commented that Perique "would ruin the nerves of a marble statue" and called its use "dangerous."[8]

The college president was even more devout than the Congregationalist professors. James W. Strong wore a long grey beard and a long frock coat, and took himself very seriously: "A self-imposed style forbade him to appear with parcel in hand on Northfield streets."[9] "As he walked the streets he was a very imposing and dignified gentleman," but there were very few streets to walk.[10] Northfield was a tiny country town.

The story goes that Thorstein, when asked to what church he belonged, answered "The Moravian"—a church so far out of town it would be impractical to attend it.[11] Such impishness did not endear him to the stodgy faculty, nor to ultra-pious President Strong.

Thorstein cheekily defended cannibalism and mocked the then-popular phrenology by claiming he was classifying men by the size and shape of their noses. He surprised everybody by his agility at reading Kant in the original German. For his required graduation speech, he launched an attack against the so-called

"Common Sense" philosophers, whose common sense was that nobody could inquire into morals or divinities, because that was "a given," and a condition that was unknowable. Thorstein's speech was too baffling and complicated to be understood by his clerical audience—a learned discussion of John Stuart Mill's attack on Sir William Hamilton, the leading Common Senser.[12]

Thorstein had an instant critic, the first of a long line. This was a man who always prayed aloud before he taught his mathematics class.[13] The pious instructor, perhaps angry because the speech was over his head, exploded to Thorstein's brother Andrew, who was sitting next to him: "Thorstein is a fraud. He was never any good in my classes."[14] But his parents sat proudly in the audience, no doubt marveling at the brain that their union had produced. Such a subversive intellect was not only disturbing to the faculty. The more tractable coeds did not find him terribly attractive.

Victorian educational institutions were limited in scope and had their drawbacks. Still, Carleton was a most unusual college for the 1870s and 1880s, because it was coeducational. Only a handful of colleges were, and farm girls were fortunate if, like the girl of the Limberlost, in the novel by Gene Stratton Porter, they were allowed even to attend high school. At that time Oberlin and Antioch College were coeducational, as were Cornell and Swarthmore and the universities of California, Indiana, and Michigan, but the women who attended were special people, avid to get an education in order to "make something of themselves."

At Carleton the sexes were rigidly separated; nevertheless, on the few occasions of minimum mingling, Thorstein and one Ellen Rolfe, not a tractable girl, were usually seen whispering together in a corner. Outsiders and rebels, "neither was popular, both were gifted and admired."[15] Ellen was, as previously mentioned, the niece of President Strong and the niece of the president of the Atchison, Topeka, and Santa Fe Railroad. Her father, a wealthy Kansas City businessman, was also vice president of the railroad. She was the smartest girl in her small class, and thought of as "a princess," or alternately as "a genius."

Although Thorstein's wry comments attracted Ellen, her rebellion had taken a divergent path. She was a fervid follower of John Ruskin, the devoutly Christian, quintessential Minever Cheevy of the Victorian era. Ruskin sounded very much like a radical, saying: "The art of making yourself rich is the art of keeping your neighbor poor." He despised America's "Lust for wealth and trust in it, vulgar faith in magnitude and multitude instead of nobleness." He believed the present social system should be replaced "by a feudal society, brought up to date and purged of its blemishes."

Ruskin had a lifelong scorn for universal suffrage. Suffrage for women would have been beyond his comprehension. He wrote, "So far from wishing to extend parliamentary suffrage, I would take it from most of those who possess it." He was also against labor unions and opposed the emancipation of negro slaves.[16]

Ellen was ambitious to be "somebody"—a poet, perhaps, or at least a writer.

Long after she had left college she wrote: "I want most of all to be a poet of the new time—a mighty poet . . . a poet could save this people if he could reach them with the new truths."[17]

She was "dreamy, introspective, disinclined to active physical effort [and] lacking in physical fortitude. The painstaking operations of everyday life seemed to interest her less than the smallest details of life far removed."[18]

The majority of her classmates frankly admitted that they did not understand her. Some said they thought that "Nellie," as she was called at times by classmates, would have made a good companion for Emily Dickinson (probably not a compliment). Once, one of the girls in her dormitory heard her complaining, "I was never happy in my life because no one ever loved me."[19]

Although Ellen had a "royal quality," according to one classmate, inwardly she always felt like a poor relation. Her mother had died young, and her father had remarried and produced a second family on whom he showered most of his money and affection. Her full brother, Eugene, also felt deprived and complained that he had to earn his college money by "milking cows and delivering groceries" and, during his four years at Carleton, by acting as "milkmaid, gardener, chore-boy, and man-of-all work" for his uncle, President Strong, and his family.[20]

By odd contrast, none of the nine Veblen farm children had to work their way through school. Nor did they even have to apply for scholarships. Their father was prosperous enough to be able to put his sons and his daughters through college without borrowing money or mortgaging the farm.[21] (He did have to borrow, however, to put Thorstein through his graduate work at Yale.)

Ellen claimed that she "never expected to marry Thorstein." He asked her to marry him when he was eighteen years old and she was sixteen, and she refused. For strong reasons of her own, she may have disliked the idea of marriage altogether; "yet because of his love of me, I felt bound to him in a sense, and did not expect to marry anyone else."[22] Apparently she had no other suitor.

A Stanford friend of Ellen's later reported: "She loved to tell the story of her courtship by Mr. Veblen. It lasted . . . ten years, and she was always the shrinking fearful maiden, and he appeared to me—as she talked—the bold Centaur."[23] Another associate at Stanford, when he heard her story, said, "It was apparent that Mr. Veblen was greatly oversexed, while Mrs. Veblen was undersexed."[24]

After college, Thorstein taught for one year at the Monona Academy in Madison, an ultra-orthodox Lutheran Academy that was, at the time, a "powder keg." Heated theological disputes raged endlessly over the doctrine of predestination.[25] Veblen escaped and went on to graduate work in philosophy and political economy at the new Johns Hopkins University. He was not enthusiastic about Hopkins and soon transferred to Yale, where, in 1884, he got his Ph.D. There he once more concentrated on philosophy; his doctoral dissertation was titled, "Ethical Grounds of a Doctrine of Retribution."[26]

The Carleton classmates might never have married had it not been that, at the end of a two-year stint of teaching high school in Beloit, her hometown, Ellen suffered a nervous breakdown, the first of at least two.[27] Thorstein, meanwhile, had managed to get engaged to a new young woman, probably while he was at Hopkins, and while at Yale, had broken up with her. Ellen claimed that "he did not love [this unknown contender], or ever tell her that he loved" her. "I never knew of it until after we had become engaged three years later."[28]

"The deadly grind of our public school system was too much for Ellen's neurotic hysterical constitution," and, according to Thorstein's sister-in-law, Florence, after the teaching debacle Ellen "never [really] recovered."[29] Thorstein's sister Emily also wrote about Ellen's "very severe nervous break-down" and added, "It is doubtful any man could live with a woman with such nerves and not have troublesome experiences at times."[30]

Physical abnormalities may have caused Nellie to break down. From the age of fourteen she had suffered from an ugly goiter, which she had concealed under her high-collared Victorian dresses. "No treatment had the slightest effect,"[31] she said, and her thyroid problem, which apparently did not bother her at Carleton, became increasingly severe, until finally her body was producing four times the normal amount of thyroid. This drastically affected her personality, and, according to the doctor who treated her later on, explained "why she was so restless and resented her limitations or all limitations. There was an imbalance in the ductless glands that made her rush into anything like an impetuous child, and [she] terrifically resented being thwarted or held back in any situation. She had plenty of intellect, but seemed to lack a balance in the administering of affairs. . . . She was a very peculiar woman. She dwelt wholly in the mind. She was [upset by] any opposition to anything she proposed doing . . . Even as a full-grown woman, she would at times throw herself on the lawn, and kick and cry like a spoiled child when she met opposition."[32] The doctor also called her "domineering." One wonders why Thorstein married her.

Ellen went to Colorado to recuperate. Thorstein got in touch with her and renewed his offer of marriage. This time Ellen accepted. She was in a quandary: she had nowhere to go in life; she was trapped, living at home, as Victorian girls were expected to do, with her difficult family. Her brother "cordially disliked" her, and there had already been rumors, while she was at Carleton, that she suffered from "repression" and "family tyranny."[33]

It may be unfair to assume that Thorstein married her just because he felt sorry for her and thought he should rescue her. However, a letter he wrote to a student, later on, points to that possibility.

5

Tampering with the Sacrament

S oon after he proposed to Ellen Rolfe, the ailing suitor realized that he was
in no position, financially, to marry. Despite wonderful letters of recommendation from Professor John Bates Clark of Carleton College and also
from President Porter of Yale, and despite the fact that in his last year at Yale
Veblen had won the Porter Prize of $250 for the best essay of the year, his
reputation as a maverick was bruited about, and nobody wanted to hire him.

Ellen became outraged that the marriage was not to take place immediately.
She was convinced that "no girl ever had a better right to suppose herself loved
with a wonderfully constant and spontaneous and well-tested love. Nonetheless,
when we had been engaged six months and he told me it would be three years
before we could marry, and made no move to provide the means for our marriage
even at that distant day, I broke the engagement, hurt beyond words . . . at his
delay."[1]

The unemployed scholar and the high-strung ex-schoolteacher then split up
for three more years—three years for Thorstein of lying fallow at his family's
farm. He attempted to find jobs, but his health was not good. He was recovering
from malaria, a common malady in those days. He may also have been recovering from dosages of calomel, a deadly mercury compound much in vogue with
nineteenth-century doctors for the treatment of malaria. Some patients died from
the side effects of this disastrous "therapeutic" intervention, and those who survived faced years of debilitation.[2]

He toughed it out, reading omnivorously, up in the spacious garret of the
family house. Young Thorstein's taste was catholic, everything from penny

25

dreadfuls to hymn books, from Lutheran sermons to novels and poetry. The garret would have been an excellent place to be when he got the shakes from malaria, because it was the warmest place in the house.

In addition to the malaria, he discovered when he was about twenty-nine (1886) "that his heart was inadequate. The doctor had [never] seen a case of such low pressure. He had to take medicine to speed up [the] dangerously slow pulse . . . Later . . . a group of doctors examined him, took a fluoroscope and found his heart about one-third the size required for efficient action" for a man of his build.[3]

Ellen wrote, "If ever a man had a good opportunity to retreat from the engagement even at the last moment, he did, but when he met me again after all the long silence, he completely ignored what I had done and with characteristic assurance came to me as my accepted lover."[4]

In 1888 they were married. Both families were against it. One of Ellen's stepsisters said, "My father did not approve."[5] Thomas Veblen said, "This is the queerest thing I have ever seen. Two sick people marry and expect some good to come of it."[6] Thorstein's younger brother, Ed, was "somewhat peeved at Thorstein for marrying the way he did." He "didn't think much of that performance!" Why, "think what that man could have been and done," he fumed, "if he had had a practical wife who had fed him stuff to make red corpuscles and knocked the conceit out of him." Ed also hoped "he [would have] married enough money to get along and make it possible for him to pursue his literary and scholarly work."[7]

As it happened, Nellie did have a modest income, from some investments her father had settled on each of the four children he had by his first wife.[8] Supposedly, also, her father, who claimed he "fear[ed] any man . . . not a Christian," was considering giving Thorstein a job as an economist with the Santa Fe Railroad.[9]

After a simple ceremony, the couple took up temporary residence at Stacyville, Iowa, the summer home of Ellen's family. Her stepsister, Harriet Rolfe Dagg, wrote that Ellen named the place "The Lilacs," because the rambling white house was nestled among huge lilac bushes. One hundred oaks and maples acted as a hedge around the property. "The Veblens were poor and he in poor health at the time—for that reason my Father had let them use the place—the rest of the family using it only for brief weeks during the summer," said Mrs. Dagg. Various Rolfe relatives called on them during the nice weather. "Mr. Veblen had an easy social grace and he smoked endless cigarettes. Their marriage was casual—much hospitality . . . they had much in common and lived a bohemian life free of surface social restrictions," according to the same half-sister.[10] A niece believed, "They were very happy that summer and were most congenial and delightful together. You can well imagine the treat for one to sit by and enjoy two such minds in their unusual and sparkling repartee, and thousand pities such happiness and comradeship could not have lasted."[11]

Ellen also believed that they were very happy. They had their own garden, a cow, and some chickens. They "botanized," picnicked, and went rowing on a nearby river. Many times she told the story of these three wonderful years. "I can give you no idea of how happy we once were," she wrote later to one of Veblen's ex-students.[12] A college friend also remarked, "Ellen Rolfe told me as a personal experience that the first years of her married life were so entirely soulful and enjoyable that their memory sweetened all the later years."[13] Veblen was busy with a translation of Icelandic stories (Icelandic—Old Norse—literature was a forerunner of Norwegian literature during the years 800 to 1350 A.D.) It was later published as *The Laxdaela Saga.*

In some ways Thorstein was sincerely fond of Ellen. She reported that, a year and a half after they were married, he said to her one day, as if it "were a sweet surprise to him, that he loved me better than when he married me."[14] Ellen took the compliment at face value.

But it soon became apparent that the couple were not perfectly suited to each other. Robert L. Duffus contrasted her mysticism, her love of fantasy, with Veblen's bent toward the hard facts:

> No two persons on earth could have been less alike . . . It was not easy to picture her living with the Veblen I had known, sitting down to two or three meals a day with him, and not only asking him questions but telling him things. There was hardly anything she said that seemed to fit into Veblen's idea of conversation, much less into his idea of lack of conversation. Not even her humor was in his vein; she dealt in playful and sometimes extravagant incongruity, he in careful understatement.[15]

This must at times have become a source of friction. Ellen later told a visiting nephew of a neighbor in Palo Alto that "Veblen was one of the greatest men that ever lived, but cold as a fish."

This nephew "liked Mrs. Veblen and felt a deep sympathy for her but . . . thought it was evident that, with her scattered mentality, she could not possibly have been the right companion for such a man as Veblen. She was a great talker, and I thought, hardly a logical one. She must often have irritated him beyond endurance."[16]

Eve Schütze, who knew them both at the University of Chicago, gave an interview to Dorfman. Although Dorfman's scribbled notes of the interview are not entirely clear, Mrs. Schütze seemed to say that Ellen complained to everyone about Thorstein; he was disturbed by her guests and continual parties; she would not let him work, and tried to get into his mind.[17]

Even during the Stacyville idyll, there may have been lapses from the infinite grace that Ellen pictured. Thorstein's nephew, Helmer Hougen, who was a small child when he knew Uncle Thorstein, recalled Ellen's unheralded visits to their home on the Veblen's "West Farm." He said that Ellen would frequently arrive at the farm, driving her own buckboard, and that she would stay with the family until Thorstein came to urge her to return to him.[18]

Thorstein was asked by a member of his family if he knew what caused her strange behavior. According to his sister-in-law, Florence Veblen, who was reputedly inaccurate and who tended to exaggerate, he replied that she was abnormal physically. Florence also reported that Thorstein's father once remarked, in curt Norwegian, "But she is crazy." And as everyone knew, "Thomas Veblen said nothing lightly."[19]

Probably Ellen and Thorstein's relationship was entirely platonic, for Ellen had more wrong with her than a hyperactive thyroid. After she died, an autopsy report said, "The external form and characteristics of [her] body clearly indicated a condition of infantilism. The form and proportion of the uterus also were infantile. [The ovaries] were extremely small and sclerotic and calcified . . . Vagina and uterus graded into each other, very much the way they do in an early infant. Menstruation must have been abortive, irregular and undoubtedly ceased very early, if it occurred at all."[20]

Thorstein must have found out, abruptly, that a normal sex life with Ellen was impossible. In a later letter to his wife, he stated that their marriage had been an "awful mistake."[21] He deserved, and might have secured, an annulment, but apparently he never sought one. Perhaps Thorstein was too much of a gentleman to wish to air their difficulties in court, and, perhaps, he was also reluctant to admit to his family that they were right when they had opposed his marriage. Still, there were pleasant times. Thorstein and Ellen read Bellamy's *Looking Backward,* and were deeply interested.

In his utopia, Bellamy insisted on equality for women, their right to the vote, child care, communal kitchens, and their right to have jobs or careers like men. He believed women should also have maternity rest periods, both before and after childbirth. Bellamy was looked upon with mild horror by conventional economists, but was a revelation to the Veblens.

Meanwhile a change had come about in the Rolfe family's fortunes. The Santa Fe Railroad came into difficulties in 1889, the year after the Veblens were married. Ellen's uncle resigned as president, and Ellen's father also suffered reverses. As Ed put it, "Misfortune fell upon the Rolfe family so they all had to get out and hustle." The Stacyville idyll was over. Thorstein could no longer look forward to a company job. Brother Ed felt that "those four years on the farm and the [three] years at Stacyville were worse than wasted. [Thorstein], of course, read a great deal, but he did no writing or any constructive work at all. At Stacyville, he did translate *The Laxdaela Saga* which was only published in 1925."[22]

Andrew bestirred himself to find employment for his younger brother. He found an opening at the University of Iowa, but despite excellent recommendations, Thorstein failed to get the position. Andrew found another at St. Olaf College, across town from Carleton College. Here Thorstein was met by an avalanche of questions about his religious attitude. He must state his views about "the Bible, the divinity of Christ, redemption of mankind, the Lutheran Church, and whether [he was] interested in public worship and Sunday School work and so forth."[23]

He thought carefully and gave them more or less this answer:

> The historical content of the Bible must naturally submit to the same criticism as all other historical material without prejudice to scholarship. No one could be more interested in this than the student of social life. With reference to the divinity of Christ [I] agree with what Jesus himself has said in the so-called synoptical gospels, and all later theories should go back to them for proof. Concerning redemption [I] cannot believe that Jesus has atoned for the world, nor that the theory . . . that Christ is the world's proxy is correct. [I] believe that these gospels can be interpreted in a more liberal fashion.[24]

The St. Olaf Lutherans unanimously

> agreed that Dr. Veblen cannot bring our youth nearer to Christ . . . We feel that Dr. Veblen would treat the historical content of the Bible as he would handle an old document that one might find in China. He does not believe that Jesus is true God, for he subscribes to what Jesus himself has said about this in the synoptical gospels and we of course know that we do not there find that Jesus has actually said: I am true God . . . Finally, he does not believe that Jesus has atoned for any sins. Since St. Olaf was founded to combat these principles and since . . . it is well-known that Dr. Veblen holds these views, we believe it [is] impossible to employ him, however honorable and gifted he may otherwise be.[25]

Later, they wrote:

> We cannot use Mr. Veblen because he is not a Christian in faith. This proves the necessity of Christian colleges among our people. Poor Veblen does not see the difference between science and religion. He does not see that all our speculations depend upon premises found upon this planet, but that there must be great truths founded upon facts existing in other planets and places than this earth and that we can get these truths only by revelation.[26]

Poor Veblen. Brilliance of thought is not rewarded in a conformist marketplace.[27] The Veblen family had a conference and decided that T.B.'s best bet was to get out of philosophy, where an independent attitude was dangerous to the ecclesiastical superstructure of academia. Possibly he should get into political economy, which seemed to be the coming thing in universities, and thus avoid revelations from distant planets or moonbeams. Andrew persuaded him to try for one of Cornell's fellowships so that he could get a Ph.D. in the subject. But should he get a fellowship, Thorstein would have nothing much to live on. Ed said, "And that good old man our father, was again called upon for help, and we went through somewhat the same program as in the days [Thorstein] was at Yale."[28]

Thorstein was determined to make the trip to Cornell alone, leaving Ellen at Stacyville. "He went . . . without Mrs. Veblen, much against her wishes," wrote a friend of Ellen's later on.[29] After he succeeded in matriculating, for a whole year he attended classes, and no one knew he was married. Nellie visited a friend in Colorado.

J. Lawrence Laughlin, head of the Economics Department at Cornell, liked to tell the story of when he first met Veblen: One day, an unknown student, dressed in a coonskin cap and wearing corduroys, walked into his office. He was pale and seedy looking. The student announced in a low, uninflected voice: "I am Thorstein Veblen." They had a long conversation. Laughlin was a conventional economist, but he was instantly taken by Veblen's intellect. Cornell gave but four fellowships a year in the social sciences, and their recipients had already been designated, but Laughlin pulled strings and got Thorstein a special grant.[30]

Thorstein was anxious to show what he could do. He produced a paper on a recent book written by Herbert Spencer and some of his followers. The book, *A Plea For Liberty: An Argument Against Socialism and Socialistic Legislation,* was Libertarian in tone, even against government sponsorship of universal free education. The argument of Spencer's group was that man is a self-seeking animal. Under capitalism the self-seekers are held in check by other self-seekers. "In socialism, however, the directing class, acting in a self-seeking manner, as do all human beings, would not have the check provided by other self-seeking groups and individuals, and eventually a despotic empire would arise."[31]

Thorstein's paper seemed vaguely to foreshadow many of the points put forth in his *Theory of the Leisure Class.* He said that the only real token of success in our society is money—the ability to earn, resulting in the possession of a plenitude of dollars. The way to prove that you possessed many dollars was to spend in an obvious manner and spend unremittingly, day after day and year after year. Seeming to be a financial success was even more important than being one. Decency was the ability to spend as much on your housing, clothing, and so on, as your neighbor; even better was, if possible, to spend more. To be well-dressed was more important than keeping warm. The "struggle to keep up appearances" usurped all our energies.

The second part of the paper expresses an inchoate feeling that some form of socialism might possibly put an end to all this envy and emulation. If doing away with competition and free contract would give rise to a system of status, such as that of medieval times—an evil bureaucracy—then hopefully this would not last long. The success of constitutional government among English-speaking people argues that perfection is not needed to make a system workable. The question about socialism is only "whether we have reached such a degree of development as would make an imperfect working of the scheme possible."[32]

The tone was rarefied, high flown—not polemical. In fact, this paper was probably the basis on which Thorstein obtained his second-year fellowship. Before it was definite, Ellen sent a telegram to Thorstein's brother Andrew—which he passed along—stating that she was ill and wanted her husband to come home. Thorstein hesitated, waiting for news of his fellowship, which was to pay next year's crucial $400. He had to be absolutely sure of it before he left.

After another quiet summer in Stacyville, Ellen and Thorstein left for Ithaca. "There," the *Carleton Voice* tells us, "they followed their interest in socialism, studying both American and European socialist thought."[33]

A fellow Cornell student, Andrew Estrem, had become acquainted with Veblen the previous year and looked upon him as "modest, unassuming and plainly dressed. He didn't volunteer much information about himself." One evening Estrem and a friend decided to pay a visit on Veblen. After they knocked on the door, "some hurried movements were heard inside, and then the door opened, and with a gracious smile, Mr. V. introduced us to his wife! That was the first knowledge we had of his being married. The movements heard were caused by a co-operative effort to remove some of the leavings and utensils of a late and frugal supper. Though unexpectedly called upon to be genial, they both acquitted themselves very well."[34]

Later, Ellen wrote to Sarah Hardy Gregory, an ex-student of Veblen's:

> Mr. Veblen was decidedly a country boy . . . even when I married him. The beginning of his disaffection [from me] was that he was ashamed of me, when, after three years of country life, and living solely upon what little money I had, spending all our time together in the most intimate and happy association in a place where I and my family were well-known, and had no need to keep up our respectability by outward appearances, we went away into the world on a fellowship, and thus we have lived ever since, . . . in poverty, working as I never had before, and denying myself everything.

The result was: "My appearance in society was not creditable to him." Ellen had begun to realize that Thorstein's "health was wretched, that it was not in him to look out for the future, and that he was slow and phlegmatic at best" (at least, compared to her growing hyperthyroid superactivity), but that she had "come to love him with all my life."[35]

However, six or seven years later, Veblen wrote to a student who was contemplating marriage that if she was marrying because her love was so strong that she couldn't do otherwise, marriage would mean a full life. But if the student was marrying for any other reason, however disinterested, it would destroy her best qualities. "The sacrament will not bear tampering with. . . . There is nothing . . . that will repay the loss of your life [force]."[36]

As it happened, Veblen's tampering with the sacrament ruined his academic career, endangered his fragile health, and postponed his finding marital happiness for twenty-six years.

6

Student Relations

J. Laurence Laughlin, who brought Veblen with him from Cornell to the University of Chicago, must have been an administrator with foresight and acumen. Though a thoroughly mainstream economist, he seemed to recognize his lowly fellow's subterranean fires and judged them capable of creating, with heat and pressure, the brilliant diamonds of insight and revelation that Veblen eventually produced. He continuously shielded Veblen from Chicago's cranky and power-mad President William Rainey Harper, made Veblen editor of the *Journal of Political Economy* (recognizing that nobody else had the capacity to do the same brilliant job), and encouraged him to teach a course on socialism, which one student said no one else would have been allowed to teach.

There were two factions at the University of Chicago. The first, and largest, was composed of capable, conventional, conservative professors who adjusted well to the comfortable salaries. They did not feel any oppression from President Harper's eternal trinity of faith, oil, and big business. They saw no reason to challenge it and did not want to look too closely at where all the lovely money was coming from.

The second group, a distinct minority, was made up of sprightly intellectuals who responded to the ferment of the 1880s and 1890s. Friedrich Nietzsche, George Bernard Shaw, Walt Whitman, Henrik Ibsen, August Strindberg, Oscar Wilde—all the impudent rascals of the fin de siècle intrigued them, and they had a wide-ranging thirst for, and a desire to delve into, the turmoil they saw around them. They might have been careful about openly siding with the Pullman strikers, or Coxey's armies, but they were intensely aware of all the dangerous topics of the day. They delighted in playing catch-as-catch-can with those in authority and were a source of tremendous irritation to President Harper. He intended to get rid of them all, sooner or later—preferably sooner.

How did these free thinkers happen to be teaching in Rockefeller's sacred enclave? Harper, a biblical scholar, when chosen to head the university, was told to spare no expense to make the University of Chicago unrivaled in the world. He quickly lured away many outstanding scholars from the older colleges. They brought with them their assistants, who had done much of the groundwork that helped to make a name for their bosses higher up on the academic ladder. It was assumed that, since the heavy artillery was safely in the hands of the theologians, the perky intellectuals among the lower echelons could do the overall think tank no real harm.

Laughlin, now head of the Department of Political Economy at $7,000 per year, was content to let Veblen continue on his solitary way, unaligned with any cause or movement and earning a starting salary of $520 yearly.

Isaac Hourwich, a docent in the Department of Political Economy, was sacked first. He was an avowed socialist, and that was reason enough. Also, he had thoroughly investigated one of the two branches of Coxey's Army that had left Chicago for our nation's capital and had found that it was not made up of hoboes, bums, and ignorant foreigners, but of red-blooded Americans who were quite willing to work. This finding was considered outrageous by the powers at Haskell Hall.[1]

A year later, in March 1895, Edward W. Bemis was dropped from the faculty. After being urged to leave Vanderbilt University for a better job at the University of Chicago, he had served as an associate professor in Laughlin's department for three years. Subsequently, he had been abruptly notified by President Harper that the trustees had decided that in four months he would lose his position as a faculty member. Bemis recounted Harper's reasoning thus: "My attitude on public utilities and labor questions was the cause, and [Harper said] that if he cared to talk about the reasons for my dismissal, I could not secure any other college position in the country."

The newspapers took up his cause, and much was written about the injustice done to Professor Bemis. He did get a job between 1897 and 1899, with the Kansas State Agricultural College, but he was unable to find a position in any of the more established universities, and eventually turned to government work connected with public utilities.

> I received no calls for teaching, save as above-mentioned, since I was forced out of the University of Chicago, and for over twenty years have sought none. I have never been a Socialist, or an extremist along any line, but have investigated, and to some degree favored, public ownership of public utilities, and have had a friendly relation with the American labor movement.
>
> My opposition to the efforts of certain Chicago utilities to secure lighting and street railway franchises, while I was at the University of Chicago, and the

public address which I made during the famous Pullman Strike in 1894, wherein I did not endorse the strike but did say that the railroads had [also] often boycotted each other, violated law, etc., as well as had the men, were features assigned by President Harper for the opposition to me, resulting in my dismissal by the trustees of the university.[2]

Veblen, too, obscure as he was, was looked upon with disfavor, because the president could not figure him out. Harper wanted instructors whose lectures at social groups would enhance the university's prestige. Veblen, although he had progressed from fellow to reader to tutor, did not present an imposing image. In fact, John Bates Clark, an old Carleton professor of Thorstein's, while lecturing at the University of Chicago, said, "Veblen is . . . the ablest of the six economists here . . . [but] a quiet mouse-like man, who has such a gift of reticence that one has to force things out of him in order to get any impression of what he is capable of."[3] But this "mouse-like man" was a wily antagonist, and, according to a graduate student, "Nobody influenced Veblen, except possibly to take a contrary view."[4] Another student insisted that "this unassuming manner concealed a character which was firm and a will that was strong. Veblen was a man of real force and determination. There was a dynamic quality in his personality that the casual observer was apt to miss."[5]

Also, Veblen taught a course on socialism. Since there was no talk about such esoteric subjects in the New or Old Testaments, Harper, perhaps, did not see any reason for courses about socialism in the new university. Laughlin did, however, and he wanted Veblen to teach it, because he knew of Veblen's ability to analyze thorny issues objectively.

Laughlin later wrote a letter of recommendation saying that Veblen "has given his course in socialism here with a breadth, depth, and discretion that have always commanded admiration, but never got us into trouble. That is the best test I can give, both of his scholarship and his general good sense. No man in the country is better read than he in this subject."[6]

One day, after Veblen had been teaching for six or seven years and right after *The Theory of the Leisure Class* was published, he received an invitation through the mail to call on President Harper at his earliest convenience. When he got to Harper's inner office, the new author was received with hands outstretched, words of thanks, and fulsome praise. Finally the president got down to the essentials. "But," he said, "Dr. Veblen, much as we appreciate you and your work, I would not stand in the way of your going should you be called to another institution."[7]

Veblen laughed as he told this story to a student ("tittered" was the word used) and did not seem upset in the least. He sat right down and wrote out a letter of resignation. In fact, having heard there was a position open at Stanford, he applied there for a job.[8] Laughlin interceded at this point, and got him a slight raise in salary, so he was persuaded to stay on. According to another student, when this or a similar incident occurred, Thorstein remarked, "Well, if I do go elsewhere, I shall take my pen with me."[9]

On one occasion, President Harper was making a speech about early beliefs compared to present-day religious thinking. "Of course our ideas of a future life are more definite than those of the savages," he assured his listeners. Veblen, who was in the audience, turned to the student sitting next to him and said, "Of course, they aren't!"[10]

Veblen did not trim his sails in view of the hostile winds. Although he was not the type to encourage acolytes, he was continually surrounded by outstandingly intelligent students, some of whom remained close to him the rest of his life. The most striking example was Wesley Clair Mitchell, the noted economist and exponent of business-cycle theory, who doggedly sought him out when he was in trouble, helped him through thin times, and joined with him and others to found the New School for Social Research in New York.

Sarah Hardy, one of those interesting and accomplished coeds who arrived in 1893, said she "admired, no adored, Veblen as a teacher, as did all the graduate students of my day. His wit, his kindness, as well as the compelling magnetism of a great, original mind, endeared him to all the members of the early Chicago colony." Elsewhere, she referred to Veblen as "the emancipator of the mind."[11]

However, it was one thing for Veblen to be teaching a class on socialism objectively, while it was another to be an avowed socialist, and his wife, Ellen, had become just that. "She was a *new thoughter* and [subscribed to] everything new and visionary."[12] She had parties for her socialist friends at their apartment, but Thorstein could rarely be persuaded to attend. When he did make an unavoidable appearance, he clammed up, refusing to follow the party line.[13] "I do not think she received her enthusiasm along this line [i.e. her socialism] from Thorstein," commented her sister, Clara Rolfe Green.[14]

Ellen seemed to be insensitive to Veblen's need to stay independent. She often cornered his students and tried to find out what he *really* thought about socialism, suspecting he was committed but refused to acknowledge it.

A Chicago instructor, Warner Fite (who later taught at Princeton), often spent an hour or more in Thorstein's study in the evenings, and his belief was that "Veblen was the god of all the radicals, and there were few [or] none among the radicals whose intelligence he respected—they amused him."[15]

Veblen was continually at work on essays and notes for the *Journal of Political Economy,* and Ellen constantly interrupted him while he was trying to concentrate. He enjoyed expounding his ideas to his wife, but finally he was ready to write, at which juncture she usually wanted to go on talking. In exasperation, he practically had to push her out of the room, thus hurting her feelings severely, but when the work was done he would come back and get her, "joyfully."[16]

Veblen had a clay statue of some Mexican deity in his room, and, according to an ex-student, he informed one curious visitor that it was the "hay fever god." The student elaborated: "He was afflicted with hay fever and the suggestion was that by paying respect to the image he was trying to appease the god that afflicted him. He was also troubled with indigestion. I remember his saying, 'I wish the Lord would let my stomach alone; I never did anything to him.'"[17]

Thorstein possibly also wished that Ellen would leave his stomach alone. She believed in a diet far in advance of her time, which included lots of raw cabbage, carrots, and tomatoes. The tomatoes particularly disagreed with him. For whatever causes, in later life he developed an ulcer.[18]

Ellen's approach to the wifely arts were sketchy and disorganized as well. Her stepmother told Joseph Dorfman she believed this was what had caused her marital difficulties. A woman who knew Ellen later at Stanford said, "She frequently came to borrow something after ten o'clock in the evening, for she never seemed to manage her house according to any system known to housewives. [But] she was always so interesting that we were glad to see her at any hour."[19]

Following the off-again-on-again courses in botany she had taken at Cornell, Ellen had enrolled at Chicago in courses of Clay Modeling, Textiles, and Elementary Woodwork. In Metal Work and Advanced Woodwork she got As.[20]

She was at loose ends. Thorstein did not take her with him to parties, get-togethers, or on trips to Europe, and she was thus largely left out of his social life. Her friend, Lucia K. Tower, said Thorstein was "noticeably annoyed" when people paid attention to Ellen's vivacious chatter at social gatherings. "She had been quite pretty as a young girl," but now she was so thin her clothes hung on her, "her eyes protruded somewhat," and she evidently had not been able to get rid of her "conspicuous goiter."[21]

Ellen was also shut out of his work. She had been accustomed to discussing his papers with him in advance, to copying manuscripts at his dictation and proofreading them. Now he handed over this sort of work to promising graduate students.

Ellen began to invest some of her modest means in real estate. She bought five acres and built some rental property in Palos Park, which was quite a distance from the university.[22] "It is in the low hills and lovely woods with springs, etc." she later wrote to a friend, "and no more beautiful suburb exists."[23]

She also decided to purchase a farm near Boise, Idaho. Land out there was very cheap. Perhaps it was with the idea of building some kind of dwelling in Idaho that she had taken the courses in metal and woodworking. She was also to purchase windows and doors, and take them out to Idaho.[24]

Throughout the rest of her life, Ellen obsessively bought and sold small pieces of property. She wondered if there was something strange about this. In a letter to her friend Alice Millis she said:

I guess I'll have to be stopped by statute . . . I sometimes wonder what makes me do this . . . I think it is the hope that by some random shot I shall bring to pass home, husband, children and Penates. I buy as the spider weaves . . . [and] perceiving as soon as the thing is my own, that it does not pertain to me, I post the 'For Sale' sign and wander on . . . I don't know but it is time to stop and try to find out what I am doing.[25]

Fortunately, as she had "an eye for charm," many of her purchases turned out to be good investments.

As for children, Ellen seems not to have understood that she could not have any and once imagined herself to be pregnant. Thorstein was reported to be not at all enthusiastic about the idea. She told Dorfman that Thorstein said he did not want any children, and if she were really pregnant she would have to go home and stay there until the pregnancy was over.

In the early 1890s a book by the German economist Ernst Grosse had been translated by Frederick Starr, an anthropologist friend of Thorstein's at the University of Chicago. Thorstein had perhaps already read Grosse's book in the original German—in any case, it may have provoked him into thinking about the subject of women's dress. Grosse's book was called *The Beginnings of Art* (i.e., art as personal decoration or body painting among savages). Grosse compared body painting to the civilized use of rouge in his era. He saw a similarity between native lip-plugs and Victorian earrings. Primitive cultures have no classes, and everyone "dresses" the same. In "class cultures," however, the highest-ranking group sets the styles and the lower orders slavishly copy them. The top echelon then invents something new, to differentiate itself from the masses, and the game goes on.

Laughlin had also written an article called "Economic Effects of Changes in Fashion." Laughlin preferred to look at the beneficial results of constant fashion change — more work for the dressmakers, dress factories, fabric and trim manufacturers, and so on. Published in the *Chautauquan,* it no doubt set Veblen to mulling over a few theories of his own.[26]

In 1894 Veblen's article "The Theory of Women's Dress" was published in *Popular Science Monthly.* According to Thorstein, dress "is an index of the wealth of its owner," not necessarily the woman who wears it, but more likely the husband who pays for it, or the ménage of which she is a part.

Since women start out as chattel, they consume vicariously in honor of their owners, and the more splendid and varied their dress, the more reputable the household. Manners, breeding, and accomplishments also redound to the credit of the master, since acquisition of these finer qualities requires much time and expense, and few can afford to train themselves, their children, or their wives in such style. Costly heirlooms can be worn over the centuries, indicating several generations devoted to wasteful expenditure.

Thorstein appeared to be warming up for *The Theory of the Leisure Class*, especially when he talked about the necessity for fashionable dress to hamper in some way its female wearer. Cinched-in waists and voluminous skirts make it apparent that the victim is incapable of useful activity and must be supported in idleness by her economically superior master.

This line of thought was so original that Veblen began to develop a devoted following; he was becoming almost a hero to certain graduate students and some of his colleagues. Unfortunately, he was not winning much admiration from the people who could further his academic advancement, however.

7

Miss Hardy

One of the students who leaned forward to catch every one of the professor's words on brisk walks about the campus was Miss Sarah Hardy. She had long blond hair, put up in a pompadour. She was not only lovely but brilliant, a great favorite of Laughlin's. She was also ambitious, and although hotly pursued by a rising young California lawyer, Warren Gregory, she loftily claimed, and very convincingly wrote, that she preferred not to marry. She intended instead to become president of Wellesley.

A driven and elusive creature, Sarah was a graduate of the University of California at Berkeley and had received the first scholarship for women given by Phoebe Apperson Hearst. Sarah's mother, a teacher, had graduated from Mount Holyoke, and her father had briefly attended Amherst. They were, however, separated—her father held down a minor judgeship in Hawaii, which paid very little. But Sarah's mother was fiercely ambitious for their child, who had been salutatorian of her class at Berkeley in 1893, and who had come to the University of Chicago on a grant.[1]

Sarah could talk to the professors in the department about the intricacies of economics as well as any of the advanced students, and she was, besides, terribly attractive. She was very like Thorstein in that she always supported the view that was opposite from that which was expected of her.[2]

Laughlin offered her a fellowship at Chicago for $520 a year, but she regretfully turned it down. The pay was too little, she felt; she expected to have to support both herself and her aging mother, and she could probably earn more elsewhere. (Thorstein had been so delighted, only the year before she arrived, to be hired by Chicago for the same amount!)

She had been described by Professor Adolph C. Miller of the Political Economy Department as "quite the most distinguished young lady in the college at present," and "a great career prospect."[3] Miss Hardy, however, was in confusion about her aims in life and what choices she should make.

Her first year at Chicago she wrote to Gregory of having been to the theater occasionally (no doubt taken by beaux), Saturday evening concerts, and two or three parties at Foster Hall (her dormitory), as well as:

> attending recitations, and tramping around the poverty-stricken districts of West and South Chicago into those dreadful places where Bohemians and Poles and Swedes are *existing* on nothing at all—Oh, I have lived more in these past few weeks than in an equal numbers of years at home. How many, many sensations can one crowd into a day even! I come home heart-sick from some of my statistics-tours; the memory of those dark alley-ways and desolate rooms, and the faces of some of those ignorant, patient people haunt me, and then—perhaps the next day, I go to the "*coming-out*" reception of one of Chicago's millionairesses (as I did a few days ago), and see as in a dream, the unimagined beauty and exquisiteness of everything, from the aristocratic girls in their marvelous Worth gowns, to the banks of roses sent to the debutante, and the old masters on the walls.
>
> And I watch and wonder, and come away trying to decide which half of life is real, and where and what I have to do with it all. Do you remember . . . you said you wondered what effect Chicago would have on me, and whether this planet of ours would seem strange to me after a year here? Well, the year isn't over yet, but the queerness of it all, the sense of a different identity almost, is very strong. Hull House, with its practical philanthropy draws me one way; the meetings of our philanthropic Committee (who are starting a University settlement in the Stock-Yards district) keep that half of life prominent, and I'm puzzled with the old, old question. Where do I belong? What shall I do with my life? What right do I have to a good time and pleasant things?[4]

Warren Gregory was not easily discouraged in his pursuit of his blonde goddess. When she wrote that the moment she felt they should not correspond with each other any longer she would definitely tell him so—as she certainly wouldn't want to lead him on—he only paused. In her next letter she might be filled with puzzlement over the length of time it had been since she had heard from her "dear comrade Warren." She was ecstatic that he was coming east to take her to the Columbian fair. After five happy days together doing the White City, as the fairgrounds were called, she wrote in a letter to her mother that she would "probably never see Warren again."[5]

This may have been only a smokescreen, however, as she knew her mother, a bluestocking, did not like Warren because he was a Unitarian, "a clubman," and "he drank." (The rising young lawyer lived and took his meals at the University Club in San Francisco, and had been known to raise a glass or two on a social occasion.)

"Sarah was impressed by Warren because he was earning a certain amount of money," a relative remarked. "Ordinarily she couldn't do things like that [visit the fair on her own], because she was so broke . . . She often said she might not have enough to eat, but she was at least getting an education."[6]

Finally, through heated correspondence, the couple became engaged, but decided to keep it a secret. Sarah Hardy's prospective career as a Wellesley professor would have collapsed had the engagement become known. Her mother would not have collapsed; that was not her manner of dealing with problems, but she might have become bellicose.

It seemed that Sarah had mixed feelings about teaching at Wellesley—indeed, about teaching at all. In a letter to Warren she once expostulated that "the thought of next year [was] worse than the thought of dying." She continued: "Oh, I hate it! I hate books, and Political Economy, and all the life that has led only to this—that I live in utter daily dread of what it has all been a preparation for, i.e., teaching."[7]

And all this while, despite her mixed emotions, she was taking long, long, walks with Assistant Professor Veblen, through the autumn leaves, through the winter snows, through the falling apple blossoms, through the spring rains. Although she had many suitors among the graduate students and was used to the ways of suitors, she seemingly did not suspect that Veblen was a bit too interested in her. On these walks, matters of economics, anthropology, philosophy, or purely academic subjects did not entirely exhaust the agenda. He confided in her his unhappiness with his present lifestyle, and she sympathized. She confided to him her dislike of political economy and the dread of teaching.

"She was a very beautiful woman, a French salon type," said Joseph Dorfman. He felt that she was one of those women "who are not much at talking, but they draw you out."[8]

Ellen had become aware of her husband's walks with Sarah, and was not entirely content with them. Then Veblen showed her the recently published first volume of Cohn's *Science of Finance.* The three years she and Thorstein had been working together on the translation were their "happiest hours." She eagerly looked in the preface, expecting some grateful comment, but there was no mention of her at all. Instead, a certain Sarah McLean Hardy had been given thanks there for her proofreading.[9]

Heartbroken and miserably lonely, Ellen took off immediately by train for her Idaho farm. Later, Sarah wrote Ellen that she too had been "miserably lonely" at Chicago, cut off from her college friends at Berkeley, and thrust into graduate school in the Midwest among strangers. Veblen had been friendly and inspiring, and she had accepted his offer of friendship and long walks, unsuspecting where they would lead. Ellen doubted this. She had never known or believed in such a thing as "a platonic friendship."[10]

After two years in the University of Chicago Graduate School of Political Economy, Sarah very nearly, but not quite, earned her Ph.D. in the field of Money. Because of a two-week bout of influenza in June 1894, she missed some exams and was unable to complete her coursework. She wrote: "Well, these two weeks or so have destroyed three months work. Not being able to take exams means nine months will count as six. Serves me right for having such an inordinately good time."[11] Despite her uncompleted degree, she was offered a job in the fall of 1895 teaching at Wellesley.

Unfortunately, after a few weeks of teaching, Sarah had a complete and mysterious "breakdown." It had been more to please her superambitious mother that she had forced herself to pursue the profession than because of natural inclination.[12]

She had had a premonition that this breakdown might occur. In early September, just before she was to start the year at Wellesley, she had written her fiancé, Warren:

> The blackness [of mood] I know has come from my fear and dread of this next year. As I have told Mother, I would welcome *anything* that might happen to myself to prevent my going to Wellesley. It seems so inexplicable to you? Yes, I suppose so—and to me also. The feeling seemed so unreasonable that I have been held back from *quite* resolving to write Mrs. Irvine and resigning the position . . .
>
> You are entitled to know my feelings, dear, for you are part of my life—I'll summarize:
>
> 1. An innate repugnance for teaching, which I have always felt.
> 2. The certain knowledge that the life of the young, inexperienced teacher during her first years in a place like Wellesley means a very hard, wearing, worrying time.
> 3. A sense of utter brain fag when I try to study Poly Econ or anything akin to it.
> 4. . . . by this year's work I post-pone for two years my happiness. Oh this long, long divorce between my head and my heart! I am so weary of it! I hate Political Economy. I hate teaching, I want to stop thinking, thinking, forever—and live. I want my love, I want to be as other women are.[13]

In a state of collapse she ended up in the hospital. It was there that Thorstein wrote her the first of his revealing letters.[14]

8

"The Wind on the Heath"

Thorstein Veblen to Sarah Hardy, October 28, 1895

Dear Miss Hardy,

It is a long time since anything has hurt me as your letter did today. I had been afraid you were not in trim for heavy work, and that you would undertake more than you ought, but I had not thought of hearing from you in the hospital. Will you write me again, when you have the time and inclination (this does not mean that I wish you to put it off; I should like to hear from you again tomorrow), and let me know how you are getting on? I may be a bold, bad man for asking you to burden yourself with the task of keeping me informed when you have all and more than you ought to do without it, but "I want to know," and what can I do?

. . . I, too, wish I could have a walk and talk with you, whether it should serve to straighten you out in your mind or not. This may be selfish in me, but the (opaque) fact is that I miss you more than it would be well to tell you.

As for dying, I wouldn't think of it. It would be disagreeable to yourself; besides which I should not take it kindly at all, and there are many others of the same mind. I believe I have been at pains to inform you that I once "lay low" for several years, and I have to say that part of the years which I spent to no purpose was some of the most enjoyable times I have had. And the years were not wholly lost either. If it should appear, as the people at the hospital have predicted, that you will have to lie low for two or three years, I venture that you will scarcely regret it in the end. "There's night and day, brother, both sweet things; . . . there's likewise a wind on the heath. Life is very sweet, brother; who would wish to die?" [1]

Very truly yours,
T.B. Veblen [2]

Sarah was touched by the letter and wrote immediately to her fiancé:

Sarah Hardy to Warren Gregory, October 30, 1895

To the Comrade of my heart and life:—
Dear Warren,

I think no sweeter letter was ever written than the one from Dr. Veblen this AM . . . He says in his quaint way, "As for dying, I wouldn't think of it—it would be disagreeable to yourself; besides which I would not take it kindly at all, and there are many others of the same mind." Then a little quotation we used to talk of, and which is just what I need now: "There's night and day, brother, both sweet things; there's likewise a wind on the heath. Life is very sweet, brother, who would wish to die?" Isn't that good philosophy?

In the same letter she admits that

Wellesley is over. That chapter in my life's book will never be written, just a little index, a few headlines, the rest blank. [3]

Sarah evidently continued to consider Thorstein's little quotation, for in a subsequent letter to her fiancé, she reiterated, "Do not think too much about me, for in a year I shall be well perhaps, and I have 'night and day, both sweet things!'" [4] Three weeks later she suggested to Warren that she recuperate in England for the next six or eight months, accompanied by her mother. This would be a good plan, because she hated to return to California a failure. Living in England was at that time cheaper than living in the United States. "I should run no risk of upsetting your plans or distracting you," she wrote, and added: "I should be a week farther from San Francisco, and the postage is more. But it wouldn't be for long—and I don't enjoy that side of it at all." And, possibly, Warren could join her early the next summer; "to turn a disaster into a joy would please my contrary spirit hugely." [5] After all, they had discussed, in letters, the possibility of honeymooning in Europe.

The trip to England did not work out—Sarah's doctor objected. Florida was next considered, and its alternative seemed to be Hawaii. No one, however, could be sure what this will-of-the wisp might propose. "You think I am just going to be docile and do just what you and my respected relatives advise," she wrote Warren, "but I've a great mind not to, just to indicate that I have a mind of my own, even if I am an invalid and feebleminded."[6]

Most of the letters Veblen received from Sarah have disappeared, so one has to guess at their content. In her letters to her mother, Sarah only once or twice mentions Professor Veblen, but often refers to Professor Laughlin, whom she admired, and with whom she was on friendly terms. Her long walks with Veblen were kept from her ultra-proper mother. Sarah did reply promptly to Veblen's previous letter, as is evident by what he writes in his next letter, a week and a half after his first.

Thorstein Veblen to Sarah Hardy, November 10, 1895

Dear Miss Hardy,

I thank you for writing, even though what you have to tell of is so unwelcome news. I wish I could be of use to you in some way, that I could help to make the dreary days pass more lightly.

The unwelcome news was that she was no better.

I know you have many good friends, and that I am unfortunately but a very inferior member of that body, but I trust you will overlook that, too. Will you tell me, too, what is the matter with you? What is the nature of this breakdown? What does the doctor call it?

Veblen next tells her that his socialism class contained all of nine members, instead of the usual three or four, but he ruefully added that most of them had taken all the other courses in the department and so had no other options but to take his course.

As for the proofs of the book on Socialism, which I once in a moment of exaltation talked to you about, you need have no apprehension. As we go over the ground again this fall, it strikes me again that I should like to write something sometime, and I think I see more clearly what I want to say, too. But I shall certainly do nothing about it for another year. I have little time to spare for loafing, and it will be a long time before I shall get to it, if I ever do.

The first volume on the list is The Theory of the Leisure Class, *and I have taken that up in a small way this month. I am putting an hour or two a day on it, and have to neglect my classwork in order to do that. I don't know how long the mood will last. I have written part of the introductory chapter what would perhaps make some twelve or fif- teen small pages. The chrysanthemums are out now, and I have to put in some time with them, to see how they get along. I am a little disappointed in them. They look less bright and delicate than when I saw them with you last year.*

I don't know yet what the chances of my reappointment for next year may be. It is not altogether improbable that I may be dropped from the budget, after the manner of Bemis, when it is made up next month. To make the way plain and smooth, I have struck for higher wages; though I am pretty nearly persuaded that the work I do is worth no more than what I am paid now.

When you write, if you are so kind as to write again, will you tell me how I may reach you, in case I have permission to write.

Very truly yours,
T.B. Veblen[7]

If Sarah answered Veblen's questions about her health, we do not have the letter. But, in an earlier answer to her fiancé, Sarah had mentioned a bad tooth, a backache, being three-quarters blind from an oculist's treatment, the fact that she now had to wear glasses, and a possible upcoming eye operation. She continued, "tonight [I felt] my first misery from my ancient foe dyspepsia (which will evidently keep me up most of the night),—altogether I think I am rather abused! . . . And the worst of it is that I would try and teach last week when I could not think or talk, and the result was utter failure in three of my classes . . . And to begin again day after tomorrow!"[8]

Despite all this Sarah had planned to go on with her teaching, but less than two weeks later she fell seriously ill, and handed in her resignation to Wellesley.

Thorstein Veblen to Sarah Hardy, December 15, 1895

Dear Miss Hardy,

I am sorry to see that you still date your letters from the hospital . . . Do you go to Florida? A certain instinctive sense of disappointment at the announcement that you are arranging to go there argues that I must have been entertaining some unreasoning hope that your next move would be nearer this way, rather than farther away. By the way, you had better not thank me for any imagined kindness. There is (1) nothing in it, and (2) it may encourage me to imagine that I am in some way, not readily comprehensible, a very meritorious person. It further moves me to speak my mind about the matter, and make the awkward admission that the debt of sentiment is all the other way. It might ill become the dignity of my official position to go the whole length, and let you into the secret of what I owe you . . .

The Leisure Class *was, of course, shelved while the Dec.* Journal *took the floor and went through its customary motions. Now (yesterday) the* Journal *is ready to mail. It has been out of my hands for a week, and* The Leisure Class *is on the boards again. It goes without saying that you come in conspicuously under the category, and that your likeness looms up before me constantly as I sit here spinning out the substance of this high theoretical structure. As the writing proceeds, or rather in the attempt to proceed, I find myself embarrassed by an excessive invention of unheard-of economic doctrines more or less remotely pertinent to the main subject in hand; so that after having written what will perhaps make some fifty or sixty pages when revised, I have not yet come in sight of the doctrine of conspicuous waste, which is of course to constitute the substantial nucleus of this writing.*

. . . I am still living within Mrs. Nellis's sphere of influence, in fact in the same place, though not in the same room, as last year. I see none of that cheese this year; I board at a club, where cheese is rare, and of the wrong kind. Mrs. Veblen is farming in Idaho. Her health seems slightly improved, but she does not seem well content . . . My health is about the same kind as it has been, but perhaps a little more of it.

. . . You ask what I did during my years off. That is precisely the point. I did nothing. And as I like that sort of thing I enjoyed it; and enjoyment and profit are pretty nearly synonymous with me.

I wish you a merry Christmas, and I wish you had a sufficiently indolent temperament to let go as cordially as you ought to. May I add that I wish I could help you do it! For I can do that sort of thing well.

Very truly yours,
T.B. Veblen[9]

After the previous letter, Miss Hardy passed through Chicago on her way west to California, where she boarded a steamer for the Hawaiian Islands. There she would join her father, Judge Jacob Hardy, for some months of repose. She and Veblen saw each other briefly, and he accompanied her to the railroad station.

Thorstein Veblen to Sarah Hardy, January 18, 1896

Dear Miss Hardy,

Since I saw you yesterday I have been wrestling with the liveliest regret that has beset me for a good many months past. My stupidity, not to say perversity, prevented my seeing or appreciating until it was too late, the Napoleonic opportunity I had of carrying you off and keeping you to myself for the best part of the afternoon. That I should have hesitated to break a previous engagement in order to meet you at Mrs.

Crane's at luncheon, is, by this time, quite incomprehensible to me. It is not that I ask you to forgive me for having missed my opportunity, but I have to tell you, and beg you to let me do so, as a refuge from my own abject detestation of myself.

I want to tell you also how glad I am to have seen you looking so very well, and apparently feeling so well. I have every hope now that your year of retirement will be not only tolerable, but in a good measure enjoyable, though I still have some misgivings that you are not really as strong as you seem. I hope that yesterday's dissipation had no bad consequences.

I want also to say a word about the Leisure Class, *to which I had no chance to give articulate expression. As I said, the character of this monograph, as near as I can see, is not approximately up to grade. It disappoints me and puzzles me that I am unable to say what I want to, in the way I want to say it. However, I shall go on with it, though it is very doubtful if it will ever be presentable for publication. It is now (the first draft) about half written, or perhaps rather more, and promises to be longer than was originally planned. I expect, D.V. [Deo volente], to complete the rough draft in a month from this time, and shall have to revise and verify and rewrite. After that, and this is what I am coming to, I want permission to send you at least portions of the [manuscript] to get your criticism of it, if it should not be too much of a task. Can you do this for me? Or can you undertake it provisionally? I have, of course, no other claim than that your kindness in the past has established a precedent. You have sown the wind, and are beginning to reap the whirlwind.*

I wish you a happy journey [to Hawaii] and a propitious return, and I beg you to let me hear from you, if you are not displeased with me, before leaving.

Truly yours,
T.B. Veblen[10]

Here Veblen drops the "Very" and says simply "Truly yours," which suddenly seems to express a very personal closure to the letter, although it appears colorless on casual reading.

Thorstein Veblen to Sarah Hardy, January 23, 1896

Dear Miss Hardy,

I beg you to pardon my writing you again in this unprovoked fashion. I have an excuse, however, which will appear before I get through, and if that does not prove sufficient I shall appeal to your goodness in the full confidence of being forgiven on the basis of free grace alone.

... I understand you to say that Professor Laughlin has encouraged you in the notion that you should make some sort of an investigation into the industrial situation in Hawaii ... presumably with a view to "producing something." This was no doubt well-meant advice on his part [but], with all respect, I assure you, it is all wrong.

The only safe way is for you to avoid all work along this line, which you have had too much of for some time past anyway, and which I am inclined to think is more or less tedious to you at the best ... It was precisely this—the strain of the classroom and coming up to an excessively high-strung daily ideal of workmanship—that was the proximate cause of your retirement from Wellesley. It was the strain, rather than the work; though the strain would not have broken you if you had not been fagged out with "practical economics" beforehand—which you will pardon me for saying that you are (to my apprehension) by no means specially fitted for nor inclined to. Therefore, leave everything of that kind out. Don't dare to touch it with the point of your umbrella ... Have to do with nothing that savors of workmanship, especially not in the way of practical economics.

... To begin with the beginning: I have a theory which I wish to propound. I do not know how much, if any or all, of this I have told you before, apart from the few words that passed in the carriage on the way to the station. I am under a vague impression that I have already told you everything I ever knew or thought, but this may not have been included.

... My theory touches the immediate future of the development of economic science, and is not so new or novel as I make it out to be.

He recommends several books on anthropology for perusal in her idle hours. Strangely enough, he sees no hazard to her health from reading extensively in the subject, and relating it to economic theory. He hopes her generation will take the lead in forging a new economics based on modern anthropology and psychology. Economics is to be brought into line with modern evolutionary science, which it has not been hitherto.[11]

He continues:

... These books are easy reading and I have a hope you would enjoy at least part of them. And by the way, do not despise them because they seem irrelevant. Everything seems irrelevant in anthropology if taken by itself, nothing if taken with the rest.

... Be not disturbed in mind, by the way, with apprehension that I am about to write a compendium of this rehabilitated science. It will take a lustier pen than mine to write out even a working scheme, if it is ever done; but it need not be done at all that I know of.

Veblen believes anthropology would make good recreational reading during her convalescence and would be useful no matter what direction the science of economics takes. He suggests that he send some books for her to read in Hawaii.

> *You could return the books to me when called for, or when I see you again. Meanwhile, I could send you another installment if you want more."*[12]

An ex-student's reaction to Veblen's concept of "easy reading" was contained in a letter by George Moffett to Joseph Dorfman:

> *A striking example of his thirst for work, and belief in nothing but work and study, was demonstrated when he gave me references for the next day. The list would have taken most of the day and part of the night. Then, he added that, for recreation, I could take another list and go to the Engineering Library and spend my leisure with them.*
>
> *That was the only course I ever took under him, and I have never followed up a study of this work.*[13]

Veblen's letter to Miss Hardy continues:

> *Will you write me within a day or two and let me know what you have to say; and will you also tell me how you are getting on with your convalescence?*
>
> *I know that I have been bold beyond the limits of conventionality in this, but you will be indulgent because you know that I have a very uncertain grasp of the conventionalities at the best, and I hope that you will not find that I have thrust myself gratuitously and indelicately upon you with all this advice . . . If you find me intolerably officious, will you kindly give me a gentle hint that you have had enough of it, and I shall set myself to the task of bringing about a shrinkage of the supply.*
>
> *Truly yours,*
> *T.B. Veblen*[14]

Thorstein Veblen to Sarah Hardy, February 6, 1986

My dear friend,

> *It was kind of you to let me call you so, and I thank you for this and for all the rest of your letter. It was especially gracious of you to speak so kindly of what I had the presumption to wish you the morning after you left Chicago. I dare say you may have been alarmed at the incoherence and incontinence of that epistle, but you would have been dismayed to know the continence which it cost.*

> *I thank you for undertaking to read [my manuscript] for me. I was not sure but your earlier professions had been more than half in jest, and I was also not sure, until I saw you, whether I ought to ask anything in the way of work, but you looked so well and strong that I have no fear on that score now, and I am anxious to get your criticism if the [manuscript] ever comes to anything. This latter point seems a bit doubtful just now.*
>
> *. . . during the three weeks since I saw you last the entire "Leisure Class" has been in abeyance, having achieved nothing beyond contributing some half-a-dozen sheets of handwriting to the waste basket. It is true, I did count with a good deal of confidence on an affirmative when I asked you for this favor, because I believed you would do me a favor if you could. I can scarcely say, however, that I knew, or even freely suspect [sic] that you would let me designate time and place, for this latter might be found more awkward than you have any apprehension of. There is no guessing what abridgement your stay in the Islands and on the Coast would suffer under a broad construction of this clause, for which I can not help thanking you, after all, more heartily than for all the rest. Have you read a story in William Morris'* Earthly Paradise *called "East of the Sun and West of the Moon"? Lead us not into temptation.*[15]

"East of the Sun" is a 121-page narrative poem that contains, for Victorian times, somewhat purplish passages. The poem speaks of the wandering hands of the lover moving toward a young woman, and "the heaven of her sweet breast." She winds her arms around him, kissing his face, and hanging "above his lovesome pain, desiring him as the spring yearns for the young summer sun."[16] Veblen continues:

> *As for the anthropological reading which I have inveigled you into, I do not know that will be of much direct use; but it should be of some use in the sense of an acquaintance with mankind . . . My own knowledge of anthropological and ethnological lore is very meager and fragmentary, and it is somewhat presumptuous in me to offer advice, but it goes without saying that I shall want to try my hand at all questions that may occur to you, if you will give me a chance.*

He mentions mailing two parcels of books to her. One of the books is in the original French—Mortillet's *Le pré-historique*—and again he cautions her to read only for pleasure.

> *Make no effort to remember any of it. The salient points of classification will fix themselves sufficiently by iteration, and the details are not worth remembering. Do not make work of it; make rest and comfort, that is the rehabilitation of your health, the norm in everything, not to*

be broken over on any pretext. Drop it all, temporarily or permanently, whenever it is in the least degree irksome . . . Whenever any topic suggests itself on which you would like to read more exhaustively, write me and I will send such books as you ask for, or such as I may think you want.

I shall of course have to concede the point of your paying the freight, though I am sorry to do so.

But, he insists, she can pay him back only by letter postage on letters directed to *him*, and "within a reasonable length of time."

It may be selfish in me, but I can not help protesting against the lapse of years which you look forward to before returning to this part of the world. I wish, and always have wished, to see the Coast, even if I can not find a chance to stay there, and the same is true of the Islands, perhaps even more so.

The chance of my achieving it seems very small at present, and as the next best thing to seeing it all (with you, if you will pardon my saying so), I will recklessly ask you to tell me all about it. You have once implied that you like to write to me—perhaps that should be put in the past tense—and this makes me bold to say that I want to hear from you always and on every topic, and let me set conventionality aside for a moment and say that I want to know all about your life down there in that strange world which I may never see.

Yes, in the future world you shall have full liberty to thank me —and I do not know what for—because thanks are sweet, sweetest indeed when undeserved.

Please let me know what is to be your address. I wish, having undertaken your education, to send a couple more books.

Your most sincerely devoted master,
T.B. Veblen[17]

Veblen had once asked Miss Hardy for "a gentle hint" that she had had enough of his constant letters and attentions. He had already received one gentle hint in a previous letter—that she planned to stay away from Chicago for years. And the above letter may indicate that she gave him a second hint, by lagging in correspondence, because he states in this letter: *you have once implied that you like to write to me—perhaps that should be put in the past tense.* Whatever her feelings, Sarah was a properly brought-up Victorian. A close relative assured us she would never have had anything to do with a divorced or married man. And, in the following letter, she gives a not-so-gentle hint, asking the professor whether or not she should marry her young lawyer suitor, and, in fact, indicating that she is about to do so.

9

"The Wind on the Heath Has Fallen Dead"

Thorstein Veblen to Sarah Hardy, February 24, 1896

[Envelope shows address as "Lihue, Kuai, Hawaiian Islands."]

Dear Miss Hardy:

I should scarcely be the one to advise you as to the significance of your approaching marriage. I expect to be divorced about that time. But I will take upon me the ungracious office anyway. If the marriage is entered into because your love of the man compels you, then it means the fullness of life; if for any reason short of that, even from the kindliest and most disinterested motives (I have known one such), then it means death—deterioration and dissipation of what is good and strong in you. The sacrament will not bear tampering with. I know I am mistaken, and I know my sense is not a dispassionate judge in the matter, but I feel— blindly, instinctively, though not without all tangible ground—that the latter may be the case. There is nothing in heaven or earth that will repay the loss of your life.[1]

There must have been some "tangible ground" for Veblen's intuition that Miss Hardy's motive for marrying Warren Gregory was not a passion for Gregory. Sarah had seemingly had, in the past, mixed emotions concerning Warren.

He had proposed to her on short acquaintance before she left Berkeley. In letters she wrote him from the University of Chicago, nevertheless, she insisted that they were just comrades and forbade him to mention love. Once, in answer to his direct question, "Do you love me?" She replied:

Sarah Hardy to Warren Gregory, July 24, 1894

If I had written Sunday as I planned, the answer would have been "no." If I were to write as I feel tonight, it would be 'yes' . . . There was one thing, tho,' that I always thought of, even when I was most sure I loved you, and that was, 'But I don't know him!' Surely love, the best love, is founded not on ignorance or imagination, but on knowledge, and I never have felt as if I really knew you. How can a woman, or a man either, tell whether [a person of] three or four months' acquaintance is the person toward whom the whole 'current of their being sets, not merely for the time being, but for a lifetime'—whether they are growing, and will grow, along the same lines of character and common interests, and grow nearer instead of farther apart? And is that not the secret of a happy marriage, largely? . . . And that feeling of not knowing you has haunted me continually . . .

This letter [of yours] tho! as I read it, brought no spontaneous consent, no instant decision as the other did. You do not know how I distrust myself . . . All during my senior year at college I imagined that I cared for a man who had spoken to me, and then gone away. And yet when other things happened, my coming to [Chicago] and knowing you—it all faded away. It was as if he had never been. Suppose that should happen again! [2]

She says that sometimes she thinks she loves Warren, but sometimes her ambition and pride take over, and she doesn't think of him at all. She considers telling him that she might marry him when she is 25, a year from October. But, on the other hand, maybe she should say goodbye. But how can they? She fears that she would be so lonely.

Was her letter to Veblen, asking him his advice about marriage, just a way of breaking the news to him, or did she still have equivocal feelings about marriage?

Thorstein Veblen to Sarah Hardy, February 24, 1896 (Continued)

Forgive me for what I have done and for what I am about to do. It may be shameless in me to speak as I do; I know it is selfish, and I believe it will pain you, for it means the loss and degradation in your eyes of a friend whom you have thought much of; but it is to be said and I can not help saying it. I love you beyond recall. Ever since the first time I saw you, in the library, you have gone with me as a vision of light and life and divine grace. My life since then has centered about you, and

I have to confess that that is the reason for all my paltry efforts to keep up some kind of contact with you. I had fancied that I might be willing to remain a hanger-on only, but since I saw you this winter that illusion, too, is gone. The wind on the heath is fallen dead. I would turn to you now without circumstance, and without regard for anything, even for your own happiness; there is nothing left but this one elemental fact.

I know how unworthy all this must seem, but I have no other excuse than there is no helping it. Deal not harshly in your judgment, for it is the cry of a lost soul.

I can only hope that this untoward episode will leave at most but a small and vanishing residue of bitterness in your life; I would so gladly that your life should be sweet, and good, and beautiful. And I beg leave to thank you for the light that has fallen across my way in the past, and to say that I know you will forgive me in the end out of the goodness of your heart.

Goodbye,
T.B. Veblen[3]

Now the complimentary close no longer reads "truly yours." Does the "goodbye" mean that Veblen thinks the final word has been spoken? Or did he illogically hope that a "slender, blue-eyed girl" such as Sarah Hardy, carefully raised to abhor the idea of divorce or remarriage, would drop everything and hurry back to him in Chicago?[4]

Thorstein Veblen to Ellen Veblen, March 31, 1896

[Copied by Ellen/sent to Sarah H. Gregory]

Dear Ellen,

I have evil news to tell you, though it may not be altogether news to you. I have to confess to a fondness for Miss Hardy which is no longer to be called by any other name but love. I have come to a conviction that honesty requires me to tell you, and I can see now that I have been deceiving both myself and you about it. She has got into my blood, and there is no help for it. I am sorry to have to speak out, for I know how it will hurt you, and I should be unable to face you with the confession even yet, if it were not for the fact (which I have known for some time) that she is to be married this spring; so that the futility of my confession can, in a way, be set off against the bitter wrong which you have suffered.

During these months, while the conviction has been borne in upon me that I am not your husband in fact, and ought no longer to be so, my feeling toward you has not changed. You are still dear to me, just as you have been—nearer and dearer than anyone else, not even excepting my mother. The new attachment differs in kind, rather than exceeds the old in degree, and you are still the best friend that I have in the world. I want to take care of you as well as I can, and to help make life tolerable for you as far as may be; not out of pity but because I want to, and I beg you not to cut me off from the privilege of doing what I can. I do not ask you to forgive me, for I know that the evil I have done you is beyond forgiveness, but I believe I can still be as good and true a friend and help to you as you can find. But the relation of husband has become untenable, if it has not always been a false one, and the truth of life requires that this false relation should cease in name, as it does not exist in fact.

Do not let the unworthiness of my conduct grieve you, or add bitterness to the evil which my awful mistake has brought upon you; I believe the whole has been beyond human power to help or hinder. Deal gently with me for your own sake, and for your love's sake, and let me still sign myself

Your Thorstein[5]

Ellen wrote to Sarah: "I copy this from a copy and have not the exact date. One day when I was out Mr. Veblen took all the letters he had given me since his confession and also the one I received from you."

Strange that Veblen wrote such a confession to Ellen, when he had known for two months that Miss Hardy was about to marry someone else. One assumes that he did not expect the young student to change her mind, even though he mentioned a probable divorce from Ellen.

The haunting loveliness of a beautiful woman in trouble was not something that Veblen could resist. The more mundane causes of Sarah's conflicts may not have been known to her professor. Besides the eye troubles, back troubles, and indigestion she set forth in her letters to Warren Gregory, she had abundant grounds for feeling aggravated stresses at this point. Her mother, Mary McLean Hardy, made her living by teaching, but Sarah had a morbid fear of becoming a teacher herself. As a child, Sarah was evidently extremely shy and, in a letter to her mother, recalled that she had been "in mortal terror" of the schoolteachers at a grammar school she had briefly attended.[6] Her mother's ambitions for her did not include a marriage to Warren Gregory, and Mary Hardy's pronounced and irrational hostility toward Gregory made Sarah very uncomfortable.

Perhaps the passion Veblen had for Sarah had awakened him to the fact that he had been living a zombie life with Ellen, and no matter what, he had to get out to save his soul. For, at this point, he must have realized that his relationship with Ellen was strangling him. It was not just the fact that physically she was incapable of making love or bearing children. Her mental blathering also was killing him.[7]

Had he cast himself in the role of a mythic hero of Norse epics? In her book *Mythology,* Edith Hamilton says of the Norse gods:

The world of Norse mythology is a strange world . . . No radiancy of joy is in it, no assurance of bliss. It is a grave and solemn place over which hangs the threat of an inevitable doom. The gods know that the day will come when they will be destroyed . . .

The cause the forces of good are fighting to defend against the forces of evil is hopeless. Nevertheless the gods will fight for it to the end.[8]

This seems to apply not only to Veblen's passion, but also to his battle against adversaries in the education hierarchy, and in the world of economics in general.

This is the conception of life which underlies the Norse religion, as somber a conception as the mind of man has ever given birth to. The only sustaining support possible for the human spirit, the one pure unsullied good man can hope to attain, is heroism, and heroism depends on lost causes.[9]

In a lesser man, this would be sufficient to classify him as a "loser." In a genius of heroic mold this is high tragedy. The greatest tragedy here, however, is not so much Shakespearean, Greek, or Norse in nature, but the tragedy of a society that was so close-minded that it was unable to take advantage of the richness of Veblen's provocative ideas, in their complexity and diversity.

Thorstein Veblen to Ellen Veblen, June 1, 1896

[Copied by Ellen and sent to Sarah]

Dear Ellen,

I have hesitated long, perhaps too long already, before asking the wretched favor which I have to ask today. After what I wrote you two months ago, there is, in the nature of the case, no course open to us other than a formal, legal separation; and of course, any move for such a separation must come from your side, for the reason that the blame lies with me, and also because I have no plea on which to ask for a divorce. It may seem cruel, and it certainly feels shameful enough, to ask you to make this move, but I do not see any other way. Therefore, if you are still in Idaho, will you go to Boise City and put your case into the hands of a lawyer there, and let him carry it through. I shall, of course, expect to pay all expenses and can remit whatever amount may be necessary. If you are not in Idaho, or not near enough to return there, then place your case in a lawyer's hands in the state where you are staying, and wait there long enough to satisfy the requirements of residence.

I am persuaded that it is better on all accounts to have this matter formally disposed of as soon as may be; and the only way seems to be that you must do it. I am sorry to ask it of you, for I know how it will hurt you, but I do not see that there is any other way out of it.

Please write me a word when you get this, and let me know where you are, and tell me that I am not asking more than I ought to, and tell me, too, what you intend to do, and whether I will have a chance to see you this summer.

Affectionately,
T.B. Veblen[10]

Ellen R. Veblen to Thorstein Veblen, July 1896

[Copied by Ellen and sent to Sarah]

I have not neglected what seemed necessary to say to you in answer to your letters, but the answers sent through your brother and mine have not been delivered. They were simply as to the impossibility of our meeting again, a request that the name of Ellen should not be used any more, and an assurance I should never take action toward securing a divorce. I shall not be in this part of the country longer. I suppose you can take the action you wish without my co-operation. Mrs. Gregory knows, through me, that you did not wish me any longer to be your wife, even in name, and as to yourself, I shall not in any wise trouble you in the future . . . If I have made any complaint of you it has been to your brother, Andrew, in recent correspondence, and, I fear, in an argument with Miss Willard about "forgiving you and going back and living with you,"—a moderate assurance as to your attitude. I mention this to add that I am infinitely sorry for even thus far sinning against my own changeless feeling of eternal union with the one I loved and married. His sins and weakness are like my own to me, and though they part us absolutely and forever, I can only accept the death it is for me as the natural consequence of a connection with you.

The idea of your family seems to be to keep your action as quiet a possible. If there is any right and wrong in human affairs, which seems a childish question compared to the one whether the race is worth preserving in its hideousness and suffering, the right is certainly on the side of truth and candor.

It is not only for the sake of my dear marriage ring, which I wear every day and shall wear while I live, but it is with indignation that I refuse to take the offensive, and in this far away place.

The law cannot undo what is a fact, and alas! love and shame cannot undo it.

With this let me bid you farewell.
Nellie[11]

Ellen Veblen to Sarah Hardy Gregory, April 1897

[Cover letter accompanying copies of other Veblen correspondence]

Mrs. Gregory:

I enclose some letters which I should like to have you read. Although you ignore that which is behind [you], yet you are one of a trio forevermore. The peace which you wished for us can never come. Not even peace is the end of such a storm. It is ruin. I do not know whether you have known that I returned [to Chicago] in the fall [of 1896]. I wish you to know how I came to do so. Had my husband made this year tolerable for me, or tried to make it so, I could, for the sake of the old love, have borne even what I had to bear in silence, and let my life, love, ideals, ambitions, come to naught, as they must, and time should close over them and bury them without a name. I have lost much before for the sake of that love, but regret, even, was impossible while love and not bitterness was in my heart.

But the last six months have been for me what no human being should bear. Nothing but crime or madness could come out of such a life. My whole self did, indeed, revolt at the idea of merely seeing him again. I could not imagine it either in time or in eternity. It was to make one's very self a lie. The whole universe proclaimed it an impossibility.

Yet I let an impulse instead of my true instinct dictate what I should do, at the moment when my own love and Mr. Veblen's honor were on trial. I trusted him whom I had no right to trust. I thought that not even he would dare to come back to me without having first turned away from the very thought of you. Such was not the case, and I believe he has deliberately treated me this year in such a manner as to compel me to leave him, in which case the odium falls upon me unless all is disclosed.

Perhaps he trusts my love to shield him to the last, even after this last wrong. I cannot yet be sure that every trace of gentleness has been destroyed in me, since I believe I was largely made up of that quality, judging by my own course. But as I now know that my heart has known its last touch of grief, so I also suspect that tenderness will never actuate me again. Even in taking this step—of writing you—I know that I not only take my life in my hands, but that I consent with myself to give him pain, for the first time.

After his confession to me I refused to accept anything from him. As he sees fit to treat me with dishonor, though I was as far as possible from seeking to share his life, I shall, if I leave him, again refuse to allow him to contribute anything to my support. But I have long been thinking that I would not again, as I did in the west last year, by shielding him, expose myself to suspicion and insult.

An occurrence of two or three days ago down town confirmed me. When I was buying goods to take with me on my unutterably lonely venture last year [to Idaho], I bought some doors and windows of a man located near the university. When, after many entreaties, Mr. Veblen condescended to go and look at them, it was in a manner to give that man the impression—true enough—that he cared neither about the deal, nor about me, nor about my lonely undertaking. I quite appreciated even then that the whole matter was disgraceful.

I have met this man twice on the street lately. He seemed surprised to see me back. The last time he said these words in my ear as he hurried past me—"Are you walking the street?" I did not understand so foolish a question, and asked him what he said, and he repeated it and was gone. After some moments it came to me in what manner I had been addressed by a man who knew us and our position. This too, Mrs. Gregory. If Mr. Veblen ever meets this man, he will pretend not to recognize him.

Therefore, if I take any action, it will not be to get a divorce in some distant state where no one knows either of us, where Chicago would never hear of it, and where I should have to make my fame as a woman who had left her husband, but it will be among our friends and ac-quaintances, where I can meet with respect. I will never again endure for his sake what I have in the past, for not even my own family knew that anything was amiss until that letter a year ago. My poor health has been made to cover all that seemed strange, and has been used freely by us both, even though produced by the situation it was supposed to excuse.

I wish you to know that Mr. Veblen's health is entirely broken down. He says often that he will not live through the year. I wish you to know that he, to whom existence was pleasure enough, knows no joy, and I believe no ambition. He speaks of resigning his position here, which means that he will drop out of University life and do no more work.

. . . I shall now have to support myself—in what way I do not know. My search has so far been unsuccessful.

Ellen R. Veblen[12]

Ellen Veblen to Sarah Hardy Gregory [undated, probably April 1897]

Learning towards the last of September [1896] that I was with his parents, Mr. Veblen came to me without warning. He picked me up from where I lay, and took me in his arms. He treated me altogether as his dear wife, and after a time, asked me if we should go and see "our mother." We said not one word about you or the past—we never have—but all that sad, sweet day I was given to understand, by every sign of affection, and, as it were, relief, that the past was the past. More than that I did not require. Happiness there could never be for us again while we endure, but a kind of comfort in one another there could be, because we were certainly set apart from all others, and we had lived together long and were already old—for this has taken every vestige of youth from us both. I trusted entirely to his honor, and came back [to Chicago] as his wife, without any questions and without any promises or pardons.

But from the moment of reaching this city all has been different. Perhaps he only came to me because his brothers said that if his parents learned the truth (they do not know even now), the disgrace of it would kill them. Perhaps he came thinking it would make you happier to learn that we were together. Apparently he took the step for anyone's sake but mine, for I came back to even worse than I went away from.

He says in his letter "if the relation has not always been a false one." No one could be guilty of such sacrilege but he himself. He refers later to his "awful mistake." You may not know, but I do, that this is a reference of like meaning. How little excuse he had for being mistaken in his feelings you may know from the fact that he was my classmate for six years, and told me he loved me "as dearly as he could" when I was only sixteen and he eighteen.

. . . When he warned you against marrying unless love compelled it, his implication was—what you may judge it to be . . .

My own feelings will not permit me to say what I would. When you went from here [to Wellesley], considering what my last year with Mr. Veblen had been, I considered it best to go, too, [to Idaho] and I did not dream that he would so far depart from the wholesome traditions of conjugal fidelity as to seek your love, and I hoped that his heart would turn back to me. I asked him to promise, before I went, that he would not correspond with you, and he promised me. He always either laughed at my jealousy of you or treated me very roughly for it. But it was he, himself, who opened the subject by accusing me of it the night after I got home that fall [1895], when he woke and found me crying. But having become aware of my conviction, you, yourself, can best judge how far he considered my happiness and my rights.

In December, after I went west, he began to address me once more in affectionate terms and once wrote—"Remember the sweet Stacyville days, and keep yourself ready to go back to them." He told me also that he loved me, "and let me add that there is no other." Very suddenly, there came a change, and I felt sure that he had been to see you, or you had been here. It seemed a cruel thing to me, and I lost everything by it.

In March he sent me The Phantom Rickshaw *and left me to draw my own conclusions, hoping, I suppose, that I would express them, and thus give him an opportunity to leave me, "for my jealousy," without needing to make any confession; but I did not do so.*[13]

The Phantom Rickshaw, by Rudyard Kipling, one of Thorstein's favorite authors, was about a man who had been in love with a woman, but now found her tiresome. He told her that he was "sick of her presence, tired of her company, and weary of the sound of her voice."

> *"Jack, Darling!" was her one eternal cuckoo cry: "I'm sure it's all a mistake—a hideous mistake; and we'll be good friends again some day. Please forgive me, Jack, dear."*
>
> *I was the offender and I knew it. That knowledge transformed my pity into passive endurance, and eventually, into blind hate—the same instinct, I suppose, which prompts a man to savagely stamp on the spider he has but half-killed . . .*
>
> *Next year we met again . . . she with her monotonous face and timid attempts at reconciliation, and I with loathing of her in every fibre of my frame . . . I could not have continued pretending to love her when I didn't, could I? It would have been unfair to us both.*
>
> *[Then] we met again . . . The same weary appeals, and the same curt answers from my lips. At least I would make her see how wholly wrong and hopeless were her attempts at resuming the old relationship.*[14]

The woman died, and Jack partly blamed himself for her death because he had been so cruel to her. She became a ghost who haunted him night and day. Through her he lost the girl he loved, his sanity, and finally his life.

Ellen's letter to Mrs. Gregory continues:

> *On the third of April [1896] he sent me a confession of that which he had denied, with cruelties which it would be impossible for you to imagine.*
>
> *Mr. H.K. White came to see Mr. Veblen on the day I left for Idaho. The agony that Mr. Veblen seemed to suffer during that hour, noticeable to me, led me afterwards to ask a question—whether he had discovered that you were engaged to Mr. White. His answer was "I am under the impression that she is." He had led me, once before, to believe that you were engaged to Mr. Robert Hoxie, [a student of Veblen's] in order, I believe, that I should stop protesting against Thorstein's walking with you, etc.*
>
> *When he handed me the first volume of the Cohn [The Science of Finance, published 1895 in Germany, and translated from the German by Veblen], I opened at once to the preface which (I thought from modesty) he had not shown me. He had done what he did [i.e. thanked Sarah Hardy for her help in proofreading, and not mentioned Ellen's help at all], knowing that it would almost kill me. I had written the book all out in manuscript at his dictation. Our happiest hours for*

three years had been spent so. I had also read all the proof once. I closed the book and handed it back without a word, and he left me in anger, and did not come near me or speak to me until the following morning when I went to him, as I must have done if we were ever to speak again.

You in your gaiety, I in my heartbreak, lived our lives of "miserable loneliness." I had never seen a Platonic friendship, and I could but believe that you were drifting toward what I supposed to be your first experience of love. It seems that Mr. Veblen was also deceived, for I can hardly think that so proud a man would have made the confession he did without hope, even if unavowed. I thought he was very wrong to permit himself to fall into and continue in such a temptation, but that it was an almost overwhelming temptation, I could but see. And the sense of his tragical misfortune, and of my horrible fate to be in the way of his happiness, was what most filled my mind in those days.

Since I have known that you did not care for him, this tragedy has seemed, more than ever, all unnecessary to me. When I think of what your fatal friendship has done to us, I feel that you owe him, at least, all that you can give to make his life tolerable. I suppose I love him still in spite of what no one else could forgive, and this fact makes my starved life with him not only ruinous to my self-respect, but maddening. I could be thankful to see him happy with you in any relation whatever. My life is a nightmare to me, and any bettering of his condition could only be a relief. But what actually will come next I cannot foresee. He thinks he can ruin my life with impunity, and that it does not matter, because it is mine. But if I understand myself, I shall not long be passive. And he would not hesitate to take my life.

Mrs. Veblen[15]

Eight years passed after the letter above before Ellen made good her threat that "she would not long be passive." She kept copies of these letters and no doubt made excellent use of them. Much to the delight of the administration, she succeeded in blackening Thorstein's name at the University of Chicago, so much so that he thought it better to look for another job. Three years after that she forced him out of his position as a professor of economics at Stanford. Nine years after that, she prevented him from being hired at Cornell University, although the job was already set up, and only a formality remained to make it a reality. During her campaign to oust Veblen from Stanford, Allyn Young, head of the Economics Department and Veblen's immediate superior, wrote a letter to Professor Herbert J. Davenport of the University of Missouri, in which he spoke of Mrs. Veblen's "ravings." Then, apparently as a prudent afterthought, he lightly crossed the word "ravings" out and used the word "statements" instead.[16]

* * *

Two months after Thorstein wrote her of his hopeless love, Sarah Hardy was married to Warren Gregory, at her father's house in Kauai, Hawaii, in a simple white muslin and lace dress, with a diamond star at her throat and long white kid gloves. The room was decorated with pink and white flowers. She was reportedly delighted to receive presents of silver pieces for her dining table. (If her life had been changed by Veblen's theories, it had not been changed so much that she was willing to give up sterling silver tableware.[17])

Soon thereafter, the couple departed on a wedding trip to Japan. Veblen and Mrs. Gregory remained warm friends the rest of their lives.[18]

10

Chicago, 1896–1899

T
he summer of 1896, Veblen felt the need to get away. He decided to go to England and look up a person whom he had always admired—William Morris.

Unfortunately Morris was in bad shape. After a protracted illness he died that very year. Veblen had perhaps been attracted to Morris because of their common interest in socialism and in Icelandic sagas, and he evidently admired his lengthy poem *Earthly Paradise,* but they were two different beings. Morris, son of an English businessman, and with an Oxford background, was equally adept at creating pre-Raphaelite paintings, avant-garde wallpapers, or "Morris chairs" and was too much of an aesthete for Veblen.

Morris, a blunt type, claimed that "people who do not do their fair share of . . . work are damned thieves." He dressed like a French workman in "a blue suit and a bluer shirt,"[1] sported a curly leonine mane, hung an oriental rug on the ceiling, and shockingly set dishes on a polished bare dining table, but Veblen was not captivated. He also strongly disapproved of Morris's efforts to return to hand-set type on the grounds of "beauty."

In fact, Veblen had sharp things to say about Morris in his *Theory of the Leisure Class,* published two or three years later. In discussing hand-made versus machine-made goods, Veblen says:

> Hence has arisen that exaltation of the defective, of which John Ruskin and William Morris were such eager spokesmen in their time; and on this ground their propaganda of crudity and wasted effort has been taken up and carried forward since their time. And hence also the propaganda for a return to handi-

craft and household industry . . . The manner in which the bias of this growth of taste has worked itself out in production is perhaps most cogently exemplified in the book manufacture with which Morris busied himself during the later years of his life.[2]

When Thorstein came home from England in the fall, he took up his classes and his editorial work with *The Journal of Political Economy* and, despite the fact that his life was a "ruin," according to Ellen, began writing reviews in his usual style.[3]

The only hint that we have that he was depressed was the comment of a student that the professor occasionally gave off a slight aura of having totally given up hope.[4] Although living under the same roof, Thorstein and Ellen must have led completely separate lives.

In July 1897, the university celebrated its fifth anniversary. John D. Rockefeller came—the first time the great man had visited "his" university. There were songs and speeches in his honor, and a parade of the National Guard. God, patriotism, and Rockefeller were the common themes of the many orators. Students sang:

> John D. Rockefeller, wonderful man is he,
> Gives all his spare change to the U. of C.[5]

Veblen could not join in. He had too many reservations about the University of Chicago. "The institution was too new . . . and smelled too much of money," said his brother Ed.[6] Thorstein also disliked the confusion of the city of Chicago, now a melting pot of 1,100,000 people.[7] "He compared it to ancient Rome, and spoke particularly of the architectural jumble," according to one of his students.[8] He was not much fonder of the university's eclectic architecture, describing its gothic halls as "heavy ceiled, ill-lighted lobbies; which might once have served as a mustering place for a body of unruly men-at-arms, but which mean nothing more to the point today . . . than so many inconvenient flag-stones to be crossed in coming and going."[9] He called the fraternities, with their elaborate facades, "temples of snobbery."[10] And, most galling, Veblen knew he was more intelligent than Laughlin and felt he should be given his due, according to Eve Schütze, wife of Professor Martin Schütze (Veblen's colleague and good friend).[11] In 1897, Veblen was still earning only $1,500 a year, while Laughlin, as head of the department, was earning $7,000.

He was also repelled by the gross ugliness of the corps of well-fed sycophants surrounding the entrenched university administration. He later limned the lineaments of their weighty impressiveness:

A flabby habit of body, hypertrophy of the abdomen, varicose veins, particularly of the facial tissues, a blear eye and a coloration suggestive of bile and apoplexy—when this unwholesome bulk is duly wrapped in a conventionally decorous costume, it is accepted rather as a mark of weight and responsibility, and so serves to distinguish the pillars of urbane society.[12]

In mitigation, he pointed out that there was more to it than sheer swinishness. Administrators and their underlings were forced to attend many ceremonial dinners.

"'Indulgence' in ostensibly gluttonous bouts of this kind—banquets, dinners, etc.—is not so much a matter of taste as of astute publicity," because the public admires these elaborate rituals, and their "evidence of wasteful ability to pay," on the part of whoever attends.[13]

Decades later Veblen mused about President Harper: "As is well-known, the first president's share in the management of the university was intimate, masterful and pervasive, in a very high degree; so much so that no secure line of demarcation could be drawn between the administrative policy and the president's personal ruling."[14]

Veblen was not the only one who took exception to the president's "masterfulness." In 1902, Harper determined that the university, which had been founded on the coeducational principle, would be better off with a segregation of the sexes, at least in the lower division. A contemporary newspaper article stated that a committee made up of faculty members had been appointed to report back to the faculty of the lower division. The Alumnae issued a "circular of protest," which said in part:

> The Committee's majority report [favoring segregation] was disapproved by a vote of 19 to 14. After the adjournment of the meeting, President Harper spoke to two members of the faculty, and their votes were then changed from negative to affirmative, making the vote 17 to 16, still against the separation. President Harper himself then voted, and threw out the opposing votes of six other persons. This was done on the ground that they were disqualified because they were on one-year appointments only—a rule of the University, so far as it can be ascertained, never before enforced. The President, then, several hours after adjournment, announced the final vote as 17 to 11 in favor of the separation of the sexes.[15]

The Nation also called Harper's reign "the dictatorship of the president" and bemoaned the fact "that so much power is exercised by the president, and so little by the corps of professors. The professors really make the university, and they ought to determine its educational policy."[16]

Veblen complained that

> the more scantily paid grades of university men . . . have, at the outset, gone into the university presumably from an inclination to scholarly or scientific pursuits; it is not probable that they have been led into this calling by the pecuniary inducements which are slight as compared to the ruling rates of pay for other [equally arduous work]. They have then been apportioned rather

more work as instructors than they can take care of in the most efficient manner, at a rate of pay which is sensibly scant for the standard of (conspicuous) living conventionally imposed on them. They are, by authority, expected to spend time and means in such polite observances, spectacles, and quasi-learned exhibitions as are presumed to enhance the prestige of the university . . . The academic instruction necessarily suffers by this diversion of forces, . . . and the work of inquiry, . . . which is indispensable to their continued efficiency as teachers, is . . . crowded to one side and presently drops out of mind."[17]

An example of the wasteful expenditure expected of impoverished university instructors was the alarming new tendency to wear evening dress to routine social events on the campus. Veblen speaks of the "tolerance" for, and then the "imperative vogue [for], evening dress for men and . . . décolleté for women, as the scholarly vestments proper to occasions of learned solemnity or to the seasons of social amenity within the college circle."[18]

Sarah Hardy had written to her mother that, one evening during her first quarter at the University of Chicago, she had had four callers, "including two senior political econ fellows . . . in *full dress* suits, which is the Harvardian way, I suppose. I felt very crude and westernish beside such Apollos."[19]

But despite the necessity to dress up, these academic get-togethers were not very gay occasions. In a footnote to *The Higher Learning in America* Veblen wrote: "The share and value of the 'faculty wives,' in all this routine of resolute conviviality, is a large topic, an intelligent and veracious account of which could only be a work of naive brutality."[20]

Veblen also quotes from a contemporary lampoon:

> But the grim, grim ladies,
> Oh my brothers!
> They are ladling bitterly,
> They are ladling
> In the work-time of the others,
> In the country of the free.[21]

Another of Veblen's scornful anecdotes exposed the penny-pinching nature of the university authorities: The ventilation of the Hull Biological Laboratory was supplied by a hot-air system. Outside air was steam-heated and piped to every room in the building. Over time, some of the instructors in the science lab began feeling under the weather. After taking sick leave and recuperating, they would return and fall ill again. Finally one of them decided to look into the situation more thoroughly. He explored the basement and found that the administration, in a money-saving effort, had walled off the pipes that led from outside, so that the air, which was being so carefully heated, came partly from a sewer vent.[22]

In 1895, Edward Bemis had told Professor Richard T. Ely of Wisconsin:

"Veblen wants to leave. I wish we could help him to." Perhaps Veblen's desire to leave had something to do with Sarah Hardy's imminent departure for Wellesley, where she was to teach the next fall. Ostensibly, it was because "President Harper has forbidden Veblen (against whom he has no fault to find), from repeating this summer quarter a course on socialism, because the subject might be misunderstood."[23]

Restless as Veblen might have been under the rule of the hard-riding theologian, his days at Chicago were the apex of his academic career. Here, rather than teach the troublesome undergraduates, he was able to teach the more astute graduate students who adored him. Here he wrote *The Theory of the Leisure Class,* and *The Theory of Business Enterprise,* two of his most successful books.[24]

Before he wrote *Leisure Class* Veblen delivered a series of lectures before the graduate club of the university: "The Instinct of Workmanship and the Irksomeness of Labour," "The Beginnings of Ownership" (both of which were published in the *American Journal of Sociology* in 1898), and "The Barbarian Status of Women" (published in the same journal in January 1899). The ownership discussion turned out to be part of the "woman question," as Veblen held that ownership began when the raiding savage captured a woman from a rival tribe, converting her into a slave, with the right to use and abuse her as he wished, and exclude the other tribesmen from the use of his "property." He said that ownership did not begin with the possession of a spear, for instance, because the savage considered his spear, his amulets, his toenail clippings, his footprints, and his reflection in the water to be mere extensions of his personality—hence he was not apt to feel he "owned" them. The same property rights the savage exerted over his woman extended to the fruits of her labor, and the relationship usually slid into a form of "ownership marriage." Veblen contended that, before the concept of ownership arose, the primitive social grouping was a peaceable, co-operative, industrious unit, but this harmony was destroyed when men turned to hunting, fighting, and capturing women. (Was there a parallel for this in the peaceful, idyllic stage in Veblen's own childhood and youth in which the family group spent its time wrestling with the elements instead of with each other?)

He characterizes our present "macho" civilization as being avaricious, emulative, competitive, and mean-spirited. And marriage, for the woman, is only a slightly changed version of the original slave status. In "The Barbarian Status of Women," he wrote:

> . . . the marriage rites of peoples among whom the male head prevails . . . is almost always associated with some survival or reminiscence of wife-capture. In all such case, marriage is, by definition, a ritual of initiation into servitude. In the words of the formula . . . it is the woman's place to love, honor, and obey.[25]

The last of these essays was published in the *Journal of Sociology* only one month before Veblen's first book, *The Theory of the Leisure Class*, was published in February 1899. This turned out to be the book by which he became known.

Veblen once told a student it took him only ten weeks to finish a book, and he didn't use any notes in writing it.[26] However, Veblen had to rewrite *The Leisure Class* several times to make it acceptable to publishers. In fact, in order to get it published at all, Veblen had to put up a guarantee that the publisher would not lose money on the publication.

Many of his startling couplings of contrasting words have gone into the language. The phrase "conspicuous consumption" has become so much a part of the general vocabulary that it is often seen on sports pages of newspapers or heard on television talk shows. Even the concept that the wealthiest class of Chinese bound their women's feet to prove that they need not do any useful work, seems to have a high recognition factor among people who have never heard of Thorstein Veblen.

Obviously, the "vicarious conspicuous leisure" Veblen alluded to in connection with aristocratic women, delicate to the point of incapacity, was easy to accept and remember when it applied to the Chinese. It was not so easy to accept similar charges hurled at American society. Husbands could laugh at the pretensions of American women and make remarks about the corsets, monumental hats, and high heels their leisure-class wives wore. They balked, however, over the concept that these absurdities were a necessary part of a wife's duty to illustrate the success of her spouse. Upper-class women were, in Veblen's eyes, "servants to whom . . . has been delegated the office of putting in evidence their master's ability to pay."[27]

Also, many of the "predators" of the pecuniary culture failed to understand the significance of Veblen's analysis of the male's role in modern society.

Of patriotism he wrote: "The only class which could at all dispute with the hereditary leisure class the honor of an habitual bellicose frame of mind is that of the lower-class delinquents."[28] Of getting ahead in the rat race, he wrote: "Freedom from scruple, from sympathy, honesty and regard for life, may, within fairly wide limits, be said to further the success of the individual in the pecuniary culture. The highly successful men of all times have commonly been of this type."[29] They must follow "a free and unfaltering career of sharp practice."[30]

Property is a trophy of success, scored in the game of ownership. Veblen added that the desire for wealth could never be satisfied. Wealth can never be fairly distributed in a pecuniary society, because the grounds of the desire for it is the drive to outdo others in the accumulation of goods.

A raise in salary results in immediate expenditure for some sort of "necessary conspicuous waste." Most people scrimp in order to appear more splendid in company, while screening their private life from observation. "Through . . . discrimination in favor of visible consumption . . . the domestic life of most classes is relatively shabby, as compared with . . . that overt portion of their life that is carried on before the eyes of observers."[31]

Of sports he wrote: "The addiction to sports in a peculiar . . . degree marks an arrested development of the man's moral nature." There are large elements of make-believe, of "rant and swagger and ostensible mystification," and the "slang of athletics . . . is in great part made up of extremely sanguinary locutions borrowed from the terminology of warfare."[32]

Veblen added that, latterly, "college athletics [have] . . . become a rival of the classics for the primacy in leisure-class education in American and English schools . . . In the German universities the place of athletics and Greek-letter fraternities, as a leisure-class scholarly occupation, has in some measure been supplied by a skilled and graded inebriety and a perfunctory dueling."[33]

Hunters often talk of their love of nature, their need for recreation, and so on. "These ostensible needs could be more readily and fully satisfied without the accomplishment of a systematic effort to take the life of those creatures that make up an essential feature of that 'nature' that is beloved by the sportsman."[34]

When people run out of material ways of asserting their superiority, they can flaunt their conspicuous leisure by showing off a knowledge of dead languages, antiques, or rare breeds of dogs or race horses. These are approved as "serviceable evidence of an unproductive expenditure of time."[35]

Of "devout observances" he had a low opinion. His sister Emily was married to a Lutheran minister who used to read aloud to her from Veblen's works while she washed the dishes. The Reverend Lars Johan Sigurd Olsen must have been dismayed, but he took it all, chin up.

11

A Book to Be Read for Amusement?

With the publication of *The Theory of the Leisure Class,* Veblen soon gained a reputation as the Oscar Wilde of economics. Economists did not take him seriously. A student reported that Ellen claimed Veblen was "very much shocked" to find he was looked upon as a humorist. Veblen himself "cited a German work, *Rhythmik und Arbeit* [then recently published], as proof that work outside the usual lines met with neglect or amused contempt."[1]

John Cummings, formerly Veblen's colleague at Chicago, then an economist at Harvard, wrote an unfavorable review of *The Theory of the Leisure Class.* He later apologized to Joseph Dorfman for this, saying that for reasons not fully comprehended by himself he was not at first able to appreciate Veblen.

Cummings accused himself of being inexcusably dense for initially disliking Veblen's approach to economics and sociology. If he had his review to write over, he would (according to his letter of February 5, 1931) have written it quite differently.[2]

The Theory of the Leisure Class, he noted, had not only begun to influence thinkers in the Economics and Sociology Departments—but also the man in the street. Cummings consoled himself that "[the review] in no way affected our personal relations." He concluded that Veblen probably sighed, shook his head over Cummings's stuffy conventionality, and went on to something else.

According to one student, however, "When the head of the University of Chicago Sociology Department, Albion B. Small, referred to *The Theory of the Leisure Class* as a book to be read for amusement, . . . [Veblen] must have been disturbed."[3]

A few critics liked it. Lester F. Ward was one. Veblen appreciated this, because, as Ward's nephew reported, Ward was the first of the book reviewers who was not enraged and indignant, their icons having been attacked by such an impious assailant.

On the Chicago campus Veblen had to contend with comments such as the statement by a Chicago contemporary, William H. Allen, "I congratulated him and asked if he had thought of having it translated into English." Allen was to have gone with Veblen on a trip to Europe in 1899, which included their meeting in London and again in Dublin, but Veblen mysteriously failed to show.[4] Need we wonder why?

It may have been on this voyage that Veblen, listed in the ship's register as Dr. Veblen (a title he never used), was accosted by a passenger asking what kind of doctor he was. Veblen gravely replied, "Well, I am a horse doctor—but I'd rather you didn't mention it, as I don't want it known."[5]

Ward's favorable review for *The American Journal of Sociology* was doubly appreciated because he *did not* emphasize the book's humorous aspect. In fact, he downplayed it, glossing over Veblen's mordant wit and devilish thrusts, and contending that previous critics had simply read them into it. Ward felt that Veblen's treatise neither advocated any policy, nor attacked any institution, and was "morally colorless."[6] Ward's review reflected the *weltanschauung* of many in America even today, still Calvinistic, and not amused by leisure-class patterns of waste, self-indulgence, self-seeking idleness, and merry, carefree corruption.

Veblen wrote Ward to express his appreciation of the review, saying that it had pleased him more than any other thing that had occurred since the book had been published. He hoped that the praise heaped upon him wouldn't result in making him intolerably conceited. At the same time, Veblen was not unaware of Ward's rather heavy style.

Sarah Hardy, by then Mrs. Warren Gregory, made, in a friendly letter to Veblen, some rather cutting remarks about Ward's treatment. Veblen answered:

> It is not kind of you, and scarcely reverent, to use irony and other allied figures of speech concerning the English of the Patriarch of Sociology in a case where laudable sentiment gets the better of his diction. What you say is true—as it should be—and what you imply is truer still—as is not surprising—when you speak of the magnanimity and positiveness with which Mr. Ward understands the *Leisure Class*. I assure you his review has been a great help to me in that respect. It has brought me to a sobering realization of the very grave import- ance which my writing, and what I now understand to have been my thinking and my insight, have for the spread of knowledge among men.[7]

The conservative William Dean Howells, ex-editor of the *Atlantic Monthly* and one of the most respected of American novelists and critics, wrote an ex- tremely favorable review published in two issues of *Literature*. His enthusiasm helped to make Veblen an overnight sensation, although he interpreted *The Lei-*

sure Class to apply only to the aristocracy and not to the middle classes. This soon became the popular view.

Some thought Veblen's style was impossibly intricate, or "futile, archaic and cumbrous," as one reviewer, D. Collins Wells, of Dartmouth, declared in *The Yale Review.*[8] Others felt that, "like some wine, [it] is strange, if not distasteful, to the beginner, but once familiar, it is heady, bitter and delightful."[9]

Hans Otto Storm, a novelist popular in the 1920s, 1930s, and 1940s, charged that Veblen's style was based on making fun of pompous academic jargon. The writing of conventional economists, according to Storm, consisted of "never using one word where two will do the work, or using a colorful one where a grayish one will take its place." Veblen, however, had learned to combine the usual jargon with his own devilishly ironical meanings, and the received authorities never forgave him for that.[10]

Veblen was, as Lewis Mumford once said, "a stick of dynamite wrapped up to look like a stick of candy."[11]

Thorstein was not entirely discouraged by the reactions to his masterpiece. In a letter to Andrew, he made the comment: "Reviews of *The Leisure Class* are coming in, for the most part quite severe. Opinion seems to be divided as to whether I am a knave or a fool, though there are some who make out that the book is a work of genius, I don't know just how. It is said to sell fairly well."[12]

One student claimed: "The book soon caught on in Chicago, and Veblen told me that one day Dr. Harper took somebody into the press building and showed him the book. Veblen said he was sure that Dr. Harper knew very little of its contents, or he would not be directing the attention of anybody to it."[13]

During the school year of 1899–1900, Veblen took his meals at a boarding house on East Fifty-seventh Street near the university. He sat at one long table with many others, including a French instructress who had written a series of textbooks, one of William Rainey Harper's four personal secretaries, a scientist (well-known at the time), and Carl van Vetchen, then an undergraduate. A young lady at the table said to Veblen, "I have just finished reading your book, *The Theory of the Leisure Class.*" Veblen replied, "I am glad that a second copy of that book has been sold. I had thought I was the only purchaser."[14]

Veblen's living and working arrangements were divided. He had an apartment in "The Beatrice," at 344 East Fifty-Seventh Street. This appeared to be a semi-bohemian apartment or rooming house, in which many of the more interesting and off-beat instructors and their wives found their home.[15]

Evidently he had always eaten lunch, at least, at a boarding house; according to Sarah, for the previous five or six years he had been "the life of a queer, very cheap boarding house on the Midway, where some of us ate for a while."[16]

One student informed us that Veblen had also rented a small separate flat, which he occupied on the four days he taught classes. He must have had little contact with Ellen from Tuesday through Friday, because he ate his breakfast at a nearby lunch room and from there went straight to this 10 A.M. class. Afternoons, people saw him around the Political Economy library, and it was said that he did not begin his serious work until evenings after 8 P.M. He usually stayed at his writing until about 2 A.M. His flat was sparsely furnished, with bookcases made out of packing boxes, a rudimentary table, lamp, and a few chairs, but there he could work freely without Ellen's interference.[17]

Actually, Ellen was having a relatively good period. She had at least partially recovered from the Sarah Hardy interlude and was working on her *Goosenbury Pilgrim* manuscript. She had showed it to President Harper, and "he thought well enough of it to insist that she have it published," which she did in 1902.[18] According to Ellen, Thorstein was most enthusiastic about this children's book, and she quoted him as saying, "When *The Theory of the Leisure Class* is forgotten, yours will be a masterpiece."[19]

She enjoyed the intellectual community of which they were a part, and she was evidently respected at the university. According to her half-sister, Harriet Rolfe Dagg, a Chicago professor once remarked, "When Mrs. Veblen speaks, she has something to say."[20] Besides, Ellen had made friends with Professor and Mrs. Schütze—in his spare time he wrote poems—so did she. She later wrote: "These were the days that were the most promising of my whole life—when I could have done something, and got somewhere, if my life might have gone on smoothly. The Schützes were the greatest inspiration to me—the greatest that ever came my way . . . Oh, it was just the rightest situation twisted all wrong— destroyed. I think they were almost equally important to Mr. Veblen. Indeed, we were so happy in that brief, brief acquaintance."[21]

She does not say what happened, but according to Mrs. Dagg, Veblen's growing fame caused him to be lionized, and this pulled them apart. Afterward, Ellen told an acquaintance that she "regarded [Veblen] as being very attractive to women. In fact . . . women would not let him alone."[22] This notion, whether true or not, was to cause Veblen a mountain of troubles. Ellen's good friend Alice Millis commented that Thorstein's trips abroad were painful to his wife, because, as Ellen later related, they nearly always included some other woman. Ellen was never invited along, and Alice was hazy as to dates and details.[23]

Veblen did not seem to be the type who would get into a frenzy or display angst over disappointing romances. He carried on a normal routine no matter what might have been occurring in his love life. A student who knew him well felt that Thorstein was fond of his wife, Ellen, and, except for possible infidelities, treated her kindly. Long afterwards, Ellen told the student she was still devoted to Veblen.

To this young man it was quite believable that Veblen was attractive to women. One woman told him that she suspected that Veblen had discovered that he had "sex appeal" late in life, and then "made up for lost time."[24]

From such observations, reinforced by remarks of Ellen's friends, one of whom talked of "the melting look in [Thorstein's] eyes he reserved for women he liked,"[25] and from Ellen's well-publicized accusations made to college presidents, there developed the legend of Veblen as a sexual swashbuckler, making up for lost time with hordes of swooning students or professor's wives. Veblen's brother Ed remarked with fraternal bluntness, "Homely and unattractive as he is, it does seem he appeals to some women."[26]

A large part of Veblen's attractiveness was his razor-sharp mind. Ruthmary Penick, Carleton College's librarian and first archivist, and Becky Veblen Meyers went right to the point in a taped interview:

> Meyers: The way I see it, women like a true intellect. They like a man who is *homo sapiens*. They want their children to grow up homo, not beast, or something else.
> Penick: . . . I can attest to that, because he attracted me a long time ago, and he has been dead fifty years.
> Meyers: Did you meet him?
> Penick: No. He attracts me long after he is dead. I can see how he'd attract women when he was alive.[27]

Veblen, one of the first to "discover" Ibsen at Yale, recognized clearly the essential problem of Nora in *A Doll's House*.[28] Nora needed to be treated like an equal partner, not an adorable toy. The critics of the "New Woman" movement contended, angrily, that the American woman was already pampered by her hard-working husband and surrounded by luxuries and "delicate attentions," and they couldn't understand why she was not satisfied.[29]

A French woman novelist, after visiting the United States in the mid-1890s, noticed that this "bird in a golden cage" treatment was having a bad effect on the nerves of American women:

> A German doctor who established himself in America was absolutely dumb-founded by the number and variety of nervous disorders brought to him for treatment. At last he announced the discovery of a new malady . . . American-itis . . . private asylums increase constantly; rest cures are ordered . . . The 'serenity of a little child' is the ideal held up . . . to [female] pupils. One of them told me that by teaching her repose . . . her teacher had put her into such condition that she could roll from top to bottom of the stairs without doing herself any harm.[30]

Veblen wrote, in *The Theory of the Leisure Class,* that the upper- or middle-class women of his time led thwarted lives because of this very pampering, which the critics of the New Woman movement believed should have made them contented and grateful:

> The grievance of the new woman is made up of those things which this typical characterization of the movement urges as reasons why she should be content. She is petted, and is permitted, or even required, to consume largely and conspicuously—vicariously for her husband or other natural guardian. She is

exempted, or debarred, from vulgarly useful employment—in order to perform leisure vicariously for the good repute of her natural (pecuniary) guardian. These offices are the conventional marks of the unfree, at the same time that they are incompatible with the human impulse to purposeful activity.[31]

He noted that society had designated a certain "sphere" for women, that of a satellite to the male. So that questions of civil rights, or women's suffrage, seemed to be "unfeminine," and it was unfeminine for a woman to seek a "self-directing, self-centered life." This was considered a "menace to [the] social order." However, women who were "out of touch with the traditions of status received from the barbarian culture . . . [were] touched with a sense of grievance too vivid to leave them at rest." These women felt "that this whole arrangement . . . [was] somehow a mistake."[32]

> In this "New-Woman" movement . . . there are at least two elements discernible, both of which are of an economic character. These two elements or motives are expressed by the double watchword, "Emancipation" and "Work."
> . . . There is a demand, more or less serious, for emancipation from all relations of status, tutelage or vicarious life.[33]

Women are now "allowed" to be productive in their own right and can escape the necessity of being clotheshorses and perpetual party-givers to prove that their husbands have achieved a status whereby they can support wives who are decorative and idle. But they have not been able to buck their long-designated position as satellite to the male. However the cards are played, women, so far, still end up in a one-down position, juggling their jobs of child-rearing, housekeeping, and office work at a far lower salary and with less credit for their efforts than men.

Veblen asserted that women are endowed with more than their share of the instinct of workmanship, "to which futility of life or of expenditure is obnoxious . . . The impulse is perhaps stronger upon the woman than upon the man to live her life in her own way" and do useful work. A woman's instinct "approves peace and disapproves futility."[34]

> In a sense, then, the new-woman movement marks . . . the perceptible return to a disapproval of futility in human life, and a disapproval of such activities as serve only the individual gain at the cost . . . of other social groups.[35]

Women have not yet won the battle for equality. But Veblen was one of the strongest pro-feminists of the nineteenth century. He obviously liked women, and they were thus drawn toward him. They could feel that he admired them for the qualities that many of them treasured in themselves. Besides which, he seemed to look down upon the swaggerings and posturings of earthlings as from a lofty lookout on Mount Olympus, with an attitude of amused resignation.[36]

Nonetheless, Veblen couldn't count on the finer instincts of the woman he was still tied to, who was bent on preserving that which was serving no useful purpose for anyone but herself—her non-functioning marriage. (Still, divorce in those days cast a pall on the woman, no matter what the merits of the action.)

It was Ellen, in her jealousy and susceptibility to rumors about Thorstein, who destroyed her own "happiness" at Chicago. In her retailing of gossip about a certain Mrs. Triggs, she gave the eager president a way to get rid of a thorn in his flesh. The cunning administrator avoided adverse newspaper publicity by choosing a subtler approach with Veblen than he had with Professor Bemis; he let Veblen know that as long as he stayed at Chicago, he would receive no advancements or further recognition. He could also expect to be "released" momentarily, at the president's convenience. Veblen was trapped.[37]

Thorstein's promising academic career now started on its first long slide downhill. Soon after, he was forced to leave Harper's confines definitively for California. Ellen's "abiding devotion" to her husband, which she continued to proclaim the rest of her life, took on sinister undertones. Thomas Mann's unforgettable character, Tobias Mindernickel, found a way of repeatedly maiming his dog so he could give the animal syrupy love and the finest of veterinary care. This was no less disturbing than Ellen's solicitude. In her "abiding devotion," she knifed his career prospects deftly and definitively, meanwhile crying out, "Oh, my poor Thorstein!"

Not adhering to any British schoolboy code of honor, Ellen had no qualms about "tattling to authorities." She would do it, and do it again.

12

Triggs and Mrs. Triggs

I n 1904, the year that a carefully cultivated scandal involving Veblen and Mrs. Triggs erupted and President Harper gave Veblen his cordial get-lost message, *The Theory of Business Enterprise* was published.

It was unlike any other current book on economic theory. The "unseen hands" of Professor Laughlin and his fellow economists that make everything come out right "in the long run," were shown to be a mirage. Veblen believed in the scientific method, and he examined what was happening in the mines and mills and on the railroads of the day.

What were axioms in Adam Smith's day, when each owner ran his own smithy or mill and supervised every detail, were no longer applicable. The owner-manager had disappeared. The factories, the railroads of the industrial revolution had taken over on an enormous scale. The directors of these enterprises no longer concerned themselves with the quality of goods or services. That was delegated to underlings. Business now was engaged in the flanking movements, spying, stealth, and pouncing necessary to maximize profits.

And then there was sabotage. Veblen took the anti-labor concept and turned it around. The businessmen were sabotaging the efficiency of the machine process by restricting output to raise prices. He concluded that the inevitable consequence of an industrial process run on business principles was depression and war.[1]

Harper may have been encountering the post-construction blues, familiar to college administrators—once the foundations were poured, the urge to donate dried up, and he was hard-pressed for new contributions to glorify his university. *Business Enterprise* seemed to be a direct attack on those commercial titans likely to fund projects dear to the heart of a university administrator. Even though Veblen was considered a "safe" teacher of socialism, his lectures remaining entirely objective, the ideas he expressed in his second book were disturbing. According to a letter Veblen wrote to his friend Jacques Loeb, however, neither his books nor his classroom performance was what was bothering President Harper. Veblen had originally written a section in *Business Enterprise* showing how the worst tactics of modern business maneuverings applied equally well to the corruption of modern university administrations. This had been dropped from the volume, but Veblen proposed publishing it separately. A prospective publisher had sent it to Harper for comment. "The argument," Veblen said, "was, of course, of an entirely impersonal nature, but the president was apparently not pleased with it and seemed to have seen in it some reflection on the regime" at Chicago.[2] A simple firing, as in the case of Professors Hourwich or Bemis, might not be enough to squelch Veblen in perpetuity. Something in the nature of a small auto-da-fé would seem more appropriate. Ready to hand was the Triggs problem. Oscar L. Triggs and Mrs. Triggs.

Several years earlier, Lester F. Ward had warned Veblen indirectly—through a letter written to Professor Triggs, a colleague of Veblen's in the English Department, that "the time was coming [when Veblen would have to] move out of this University . . . and find shelter elsewhere."[3]

Triggs was among the first batch of instructors hired at the opening of the university in 1892. He taught to overflowing classes there for twelve years. He was so popular that it was necessary to find extra-large classrooms to accommodate all who wanted to sit in on his lectures. His background was creditable. After earning a degree at Minnesota, he had completed two years of graduate work at Oxford University and in Berlin and, while teaching, had finished his Ph.D. degree at the University of Chicago.

People flocked to Triggs's classes because he was brilliant and amusing. Perhaps he also made them think. Dismissing the American icon Longfellow with faint praise, he spoke of the good, grey poet's "trite sayings, worn-out metaphors [and] superficial allusions."[4] In the 1890s this was delightful heresy. Triggs's lecture notes, when read today, sound as if they had been written in the 1990s. He was a man perhaps 100 years out of his time.[5]

According to Triggs, many church hymns were "doggerel." God did not care to be praised by the singing of "O, to be nothing, O, to be nothing!" And there was not much originality in the Declaration of Independence. It reflected the French philosophy of the period and was "sophomoric [and] bombastic." Walt Whitman (scorned elsewhere in academia) and Robert Browning were his favorites. As early as 1905 he was praising the practically unknown Carl Sandburg.

Triggs also opined that the University of Chicago hymn was "pretty rotten." The college authorities "got after him about that."[6] Veblen, in a letter to Loeb, called Triggs a friend of his, however, their compatibility extended to their unconventionality and not much more. Triggs was a confirmed socialist in his private life (as many of the more rebellious and independent-minded instructors seemed to be), and, as such, was on the trustees' permanent blacklist. Veblen associated with many socialists during his life, but out of curiosity, not out of partisanship. Partisanship would get in the way of his independence as a thinker. Veblen was no partisan or joiner.[7]

Veblen and Triggs also differed on the relevance of the Arts and Crafts movement. Since his disappointing visit to Morris in England in 1896, Veblen was doubly disdainful of any arty activities. Oscar Triggs was secretary of the Industrial Arts League in Chicago and had written a book on the subject. Thorstein reviewed it for the *Journal of Political Economy* and treated it rather gently. He said Triggs gave "an excellent outline of the work of Carlyle, Ruskin, and Morris." He spoke of Triggs's "facile and engaging manner" of pleading for aid in the movement.

However, Veblen could not on the whole agree with "the Arts and Crafts movement," for he himself ascribed an almost mystical power to the machine culture: "The machine process has come, not so much to stay merely, but to go forward and root out of the workmen's scheme of thought whatever elements are alien to its own technological requirements and discipline. It ubiquitously and unremittingly disciplines the workmen into its way of doing, and therefore into its way of apprehending and appreciating things." The Arts and Crafts movement must fall in line or otherwise "hang as an anemic fad upon the fringe of modern industry."[8]

Veblen's contention was that "business exigencies demand spurious goods, in the sense that the goods must cost less than they appear to, while a democratic culture requires low cost and a large, thoroughly standardized output of goods."[9] He thought that Arts and Crafts, in Chicago at least, might have a salutary effect "in checking the current ugliness of the apparatus of life . . . Archaism and sophistication came of a revulsion against the besetting ugliness [of things as they are]. The absolute dearth of beauty in the philistine present forced them to hark back to the past."[10]

He felt that "a sensuous beauty of line and color" ought to be achievable through machine processes, and he deplored the Arts and Crafts credo that "only outside the machine process is there salvation."[11]

On January 6, 1899, Professor Triggs married Laura Sterette McAdoo and brought his bride back to live at "The Beatrice," at 344 East Fifty-Seventh Street, where the Veblens lived. Triggs had met the young society woman two years before, when he was lecturing on Walt Whitman in Knoxville, Tennessee. An article in her hometown paper called her "one of the brainiest, most brilliant women of this city. A distinguished presence, beauty of an unusual and high type, and that graciousness and charm of manner which is the peculiar birthright of southern women, together with literary attainments of no mean character, have combined to give her an eminent place among the women of Tennessee, and compelled the attention [of] the most exclusive literary circles of Boston and

New York."[12] Laura Sterette McAdoo Triggs "was an intellectual and a stunning looking woman . . . She was the kind of woman that would infallibly cause disaster among men," according to one of Ellen's friends.[13]

Laura belonged to an old, formerly wealthy, southern family. Her ancestors included Confederate generals and owners of large plantations with many slaves. However, after the Civil War, the family had fallen on hard times.

Their "barnlike house [in Milledgeville, Georgia] was sparsely furnished and uninviting." It was very cold in winter. "On frigid days, as the wind swept through the uncarpeted floorboards, the entire family huddled together in the sitting room trying to keep warm."[14]

The McAdoo children, of whom there were seven, wandered through the pine forests, swam in the "mud-red Oconee River," and picked wild plums and black-berries. They went barefoot eight months of the year and wore cast-off clothes. They drifted in and out of school. Their education was sporadic, although their father, William Gibbs McAdoo, who had probably learned law as an apprentice, was a part-time judge in the municipal court and taught his children to read and write.

Laura's father later became an adjunct professor of History, English, and Modern Languages at the University of Tennessee at Knoxville.[15] Although he never attained the position of full professor, one of the perks of his position was that his children could attend the university without paying tuition. Only Laura's brother, William Gibbs McAdoo Jr., took advantage of this; but Laura somehow learned (probably from her father) impeccable French grammar and syntax, which was later remarked upon in French literary circles.

Laura's mother had been an intellectual who wrote two novels, various sketches, poems, stories, and reviews. Her father also wrote essays, book reviews, acrostic sonnets (which he called doggerel) and newspaper editorials. Laura's brother, William Gibbs McAdoo, rose high in government circles, became secretary of the treasury under President Woodrow Wilson, and married the president's daughter, Eileen.

Laura was scheduled to produce articles for *Tomorrow* magazine after her husband became editor in 1905. These articles never appeared, as Laura had fled to France. *Tomorrow* was later associated with the "free love" ideas of Parker Sercombe and was, besides, a highly incendiary little sheet. Triggs himself was an incendiary diagnostician of society's ills, and his facile and shallow radicalism, as shown by his articles in *Tomorrow* magazine, may have been disillusioning to this beauty from the impoverished southern aristocracy. (Her father had often groaned over "journalistic mendacity and exaggeration," had disliked show-offy tendencies of any sort, and had also believed in the gradual emancipation of the slaves, but, when the war came, had fought with the Confederates. He was something of a liberal—but hardly a radical—and he and Laura were very close.)

Thorstein had passed four lonely and frustrating years since the departure of Sarah Hardy. He was still thinking about her. As late as July 1900, he wrote the now Mrs. Gregory: "By the way, I am right, am I not, in catching a note of regret at your being no longer concerned in the *Journal?* Kindly bear in mind that the pages of the *Journal* are always open to you with an expectant and hungering openness!"[16] Ellen continued to refuse to divorce Thorstein, insisting that he stay with her and remain celibate. Perhaps he found something to lift his spirits in Laura Triggs, this new, sweet, sincere, charming, and "beautiful and intelligent woman."[17]

We do not know what, if anything, went on between Thorstein and Laura. They had both been disappointed in their marriages. Perhaps they were simply kindred spirits and confidants. According to Joseph Dorfman, Veblen autographed a first edition of *The Theory of Business Enterprise* (which was published in 1904, five years after they had met): "To Mrs. Laura McAdoo Triggs—with all my heart, Thorstein Veblen."[18] This was an unusual salutation from the reserved Veblen. Also, according to gossip Ellen heard, Mrs. Triggs had been seen coming and going from the "room"—or rather, flat—he occupied when he taught classes.[19] Veblen ridiculed the reports, saying that Mrs. Triggs had attended one of his courses.[20]

Veblen sailed to Europe in the summer of 1904, leaving Ellen, as usual, housebound. According to Veblen's letter, Dr. and Mrs. Triggs and their three-year-old son also went to Europe that summer. Then from somewhere came a report that Veblen had been "seen travelling with Mrs. Triggs."[21]

Veblen wrote:

> Immediately after I had left the country—as I have learned since my return—reports were put in circulation that I had run away with the lady and presumably with the man and the child. Hurried counsel was then taken to dismiss me from the university on the grounds of my having brought the institution into disrepute. No intimation was given me of the proposed action, which after all failed to come to anything because the newspapers refused to print the reports given them. The matter being libellous, the papers refused to print it without some one among their informants taking the responsibility, but these informants who made up the story, being also aware that it was libellous and having nothing to fall back on, were unwilling to vouch for it. So it fell through, leaving nothing but an added degree of ill feeling between the president and me, and such damage to my reputation as these endeavors were calculated to yield.
>
> Under these circumstances I should be glad to leave this place.[22]

The witches' cauldron continued to bubble. Veblen was convinced that the "center of the diffusion . . . [was] apparently the office in Haskell" (i.e., Harper's office). The question was, how had Harper got hold of this telling bit of gossip? Lucia Tower, Ellen's friend, seems to have been the source of some of the contumely, which was passed from Lucia to Ellen and from Ellen directly to the college president.

Ellen's role is revealed in one of her own letters, written a year and a half later. Grieved that her dear friend no longer contacted her, Ellen surmised in a letter she wrote from Oregon on July 3, 1906, that "nothing but an awful misconception" would keep Lucia from replying to her letters. "You probably think I am in an insane asylum somewhere, and you must not write to me." It seems more likely that Lucia might have been upset by Ellen's disloyal tattling, confirmed in Ellen's letter as follows:

> I can think of but one thing. When Mr. Veblen came back from Paris and was brought up and asked to sign a promise to have nothing to do with Mrs. Triggs, he came home and asked me what I had told. I gave him the truth, that I had in answer to President Harper's questions admitted that I had heard one or two specific reports, as for instance, that Mrs. Triggs had been known to call on him in his room and remain until a late hour. Now if you have heard this, and Mr. Veblen has given you trouble about it, know that I neither told him or President Harper *from whom* [author emphasis] I had the report. If Mr. Veblen simply guessed, and confronted you with it as though I had "told" remember always that he is subtle and expert but that I gave him no hint.[23]

Veblen would not sign a statement to have no more to do with Mrs. Triggs as, he said, "he was not in the habit of promising not to do what he was not accustomed to doing."[24] Thorstein's brother Andrew once remarked, "Thorstein was a master at foiling anyone who tried to poke his nose into his affairs or what he chose to consider only his affairs." He called his brother "elusive."[25] Ellen found him increasingly so from now on.

Oscar Triggs was presumably an innocent bystander. In the end, the couple split up, Mrs. Triggs fleeing for Paris with her child and filing for a divorce. As far as can be ascertained, Veblen and Mrs. Triggs did not communicate subsequently nor did they ever see each other again. Professor Triggs was fired from the university.

13

Out of Chicago

It was easier for Harper to oust Triggs than to dismiss Veblen, as Laughlin, Veblen's department head, liked his subordinate, despite their divergent views. The elevated tone that Veblen's scholarly acumen gave the university's *Journal of Political Economy* would be missed. As for Triggs, Harper simply arranged with the head of the English department not to have him rehired.[1]

Triggs claimed that, if the truth were known, there had been a sort of "conspiracy" against him, starting a year or two before he retired. His classroom remarks and his statements outside class were reported in such a manner that, while he thought of himself as a "quiet and reasonable scholar," others began to look upon him as a "freak professor." He could not understand how it happened.[2]

In 1899, Professor Herbert S. Foxwell of Cambridge University, England, wrote to an American colleague, criticizing the firing of Edward W. Bemis by the University of Chicago (see Chapter 6) and saying that British universities allowed their professors to be completely free, that no matter how capricious and eccentric their behavior or speech, they were left alone to teach as they pleased. Cambridge University, in fact, would not recognize a college within its system unless its foundation was totally independent—and it was the teachers themselves (or others equally well qualified) who hired the teachers. "No trustees intervene[d]."[3]

At the University of Chicago, trustees did intervene and so did the college president. The result was that Triggs, "this most popular professor of literature, was driven out of the university" and reportedly became "a common laborer on a California chicken-ranch."[4]

Laura Triggs's fate was even more dramatic. After her divorce she married a Parisian, a certain Dr. Pierre Gagey, who had a flourishing medical practice in Paris and expected to win great financial rewards from his invention of a respirator. The union with Dr. Gagey did not work out any better than the alliance with Professor Triggs, as Gagey soon took on a mistress and, when his invention proved disappointing financially, fell deeply into debt. A few years later Laura met Anatole France, and he became her grand amour.

Biographer Joseph Dorfman claimed that the noted French author "had much in common with Thorstein Veblen."[5] Both were, indeed, erudite iconoclasts, given to irony and sarcasm, willing seriously to consider socialism and communism, irreverent and anti-clerical. Both fell into disfavor after their deaths and have subsequently been neglected. Anatole France had a peasant father who could neither write nor read until he went into the army, when he taught himself to do so. Although Veblen coolly examined the pretenses of the pillars of society and talked much about the needs of the common man, he showed little enthusiasm for rule by the masses, but thought that college-educated engineers might someday save society from the ravages of the businessman. Anatole France, in *Les dieux ont soif,* condemned the French revolutionists; after they seized power they became as avaricious, mendacious, and corrupt as the aristocrats they replaced. Both authors echoed Lord Acton's dictum: "Power tends to corrupt; but absolute power corrupts absolutely."

There was one important difference, however. Famous as he was for his heroic stance on the Dreyfus case, and for his cultivated sympathy for the poor and helpless, France had the philanderer's attitude toward women as prey, which Veblen emphatically did not.

With Laura Gagey, Anatole France had "one of his most serious affairs" following the loss of his celebrated mistress, Léontine, the wife of Arman de Caillavet.[6] After Léontine's death he became depressed and disoriented and launched into a series of romantic escapades. To Laura Gagey he wrote: "My adored one, your letter made my heart beat as if it would break. At last, I will press you in my arms."[7]

"The adored one," a biographer of France wrote scathingly, "was a married woman in her early thirties [she was actually thirty-nine], who had sought out the master who was close to seventy, thrown herself at his head, [and] written him interminable letters breathing a passionate love in every word and syllable. And his pitiless [pitiful?] instability once more had found comfort in her charms. It was absurd—after a while it was also a bore. When she expected him to elope with her, it became tragic . . . she committed suicide."[8] But Laura was experiencing more than pique over an unhappy love affair. Because of implied promises from France she had broken her ties with Gagey. She and her ten-year-old son now had nowhere to turn. Dr. Gagey, who had installed his mistress chez lui, had banished his wife from his house.

"France wrote [pettishly] afterwards, 'I am irritated at my own folly and the importunities to which it has exposed me.' He sums it up after many (other) ventures, 'Great unhappiness follows in the footsteps of these little boredoms.' "[9] But France had not been dilatory in the pursuit of these bothersome little ennuis. At the time he was involved with Laura Gagey, he was carrying on simultaneous affairs with a Danish sex maniac and Leontine's long-time personal maid, the gorgeous and discreet Emma.[10]

Anatole evidently helped Laura, who, according to one French biographer, spoke and wrote French quite well, to prepare a seminar and edit some articles. The two were charmed with each other and met frequently, among other places in the churches Saint-Phillipe-du-Roule and Saint-Germain-des-Prés. While away in Tours, France wrote, "I have escaped for a moment to tell you I do not cease to think of you." Three months later from Bourgogne he continued, "My well-beloved, be content. I have not had an instant of pleasure far from you . . . I love you." In her letter to her adored master, Laura expressed her happiness: "I rejoice that *Les Dieux ont soif* is almost finished. It is a little also mine, this book, which I heard with ecstasy and with great pride in the handsome genius who created it . . . under my eyes." (Her hero at that time was sixty-seven years old but claimed he had the sexual potency of a youth of seventeen. With his immensely long nose and sloping forehead, set off by a frothy white beard and moustache, he looked startlingly like her father, who was nearly fifty when she was born, and thus had related to her more in the guise of a grandfather than as a parent.)

When Anatole France went to Normandy in the summer of 1911, "la belle Floridienne," as he and his friends called Laura, wrote to him every day.[11] On his return to Paris in October, one of his alternate mistresses (the overeager Danoise), also returned from Copenhagen. France let the Danoise know how embarrassed he was by the clinging Laura and his reluctance to break the news to her that he no longer wished to see her. The Danoise was eager to meet Laura, and was willing to take on the burden of telling the American that the great man no longer wished to be bothered with her.[12] In her last note to Anatole, Laura wrote:

> I feel again a cruel lassitude, both moral and physical, which destroys what remains to me of harmony and hope. I hold, oh so lightly to life. It wouldn't take very much to loosen so frail a hold. I do not say this to arouse your pity . . . you made me believe that I helped you live and that, sad myself, you couldn't live without me . . . I believe that if I had a social position equal to my rank and my talents (I affect no false modesty) and if I could receive you at my own house, and meet you at dinners and soirées, I would adjust myself easily to that scheme of life. . . . How should I express myself? You taught me to be afraid of nothing. The essential thing is not feeling myself complete except with another being. That way love has no name nor etiquette. It gives and receives all, is a circle without an end. That is the way I have loved you, guided solely by my instincts and devoid of all calculation.[13]

Laura evidently had dreams of literary fame, nurtured by the life script her father had passed along to her and his other children—a mandate to achieve the distinction that had, except in a minor way, eluded him. Unfortunately, Anatole had already proved with Léontine an inability to relate to someone completely devoted to him. In the end, Laura and the Danoise lost out to Emma, a placid, ailing domestic, passively inured to France's perpetual infidelity, and perhaps a better cook.

If it was true that the unhappy Laura Gagey was the aggressor in the affair with Anatole France, it was also possible that she threw herself at the head of Thorstein Veblen. Judging by his inscription in the book he gave her, Thorstein seemed to have had a deep fondness for the aristocratic Laura, and while she may have returned that fondness, and they may even have had an affair, there was no evidence that either of them had any desire for a permanent bond. Perhaps, as indicated by one of France's biographers, she was overly ambitious and tried to use France and others to launch a literary career in Paris. Similar motives may have drawn her to Veblen, the lion among University of Chicago intellectuals and published author of the shocking *Theory of the Leisure Class* and the eye-opening *Theory of Business Enterprise.*

Whatever the case, poor, impetuous Laura not only caused "disaster among men," as reported, but also reserved the ultimate disaster for herself. When France avoided her, she overdosed on sleeping pills. He followed her funeral cortege all the way to the cemetery at Batignolles. A sad passage.[14]

To continue the soap opera, Ellen, perhaps feeling somewhat ostracized by certain of the faculty wives, took off in late 1904 for the wilds of Oregon. She settled in the town of Hood River for a year and then attempted to get even further from civilization by climbing the slopes of Mt. Hood—sixteen miles up a lonely trail—in order to homestead a timber claim (probably in the summer of 1905). No doubt in the fall she returned to Hood River, as a primitive cabin in the foothills of Mt. Hood would have been uninhabitable in the winter. From her Oregon hideout Ellen wrote Thorstein's sister Mary (Marit) in June 1906:

> If you knew where I was tonight you would, perhaps, not sleep well. But I shall, for I am so deadly tired. So tired that I might easily fall asleep forever, and that is why I wish to write you. I spent about a week, a week ago, on, or rather near, my homestead on top of one of the foothills leading to Mt. Hood. A man who had promised to bring my mail when he came, came and forgot it. It was expected to be important ... I had to take the opportunity to go down with him ... yesterday I began walking from Hood River back. But I got a ride of about five miles. Then I stayed overnight at a farmer's and proceeded this A.M. thus: My kittens were slung over my shoulder in a bag, the cat hung in front done up in my sweater, I carried in my right hand a rather heavy satchel, a very heavy pair of shoes and a Mackintosh. After walking (up the mountain) five miles, I reached my cow [left with a neighbor] and proceeded to put her into the procession. But she had been in a herd and would no longer lead.

It was 12:30 [noon] when I left the man's house and it was five when I reached the next higher ledge and its lone dwelling . . . I . . . worked at forcing a window, finally found the key, I thanked heaven, and got in. I could not have made the other two miles to [my own] cabin and I had not a match, and the woods here are very dangerous, particularly at night. I walked nearly all of that last two miles three times, being obliged to take things piecemeal. I forgot to say I had a strange dog in tow which I am taking up for a safeguard against wild animals. He complicated things. If I left anything behind he stayed to guard it. The cat learned to follow me finally, and [when] I left her behind the dog also stayed to watch her, which effectually prevented her following, so I had to go back for both.

I had no food with me, and what was my joy to find a potato in this house, some butter, coffee, and sugar. Then I milked the cow, and I also found some fine puffballs. Built a fire, found a bed, and now I am going there. Should say that it also rained the last two miles. Ah, the little house by the wayside![15]

Ellen stayed on her timber claim, absolutely alone, for another two and a half months. Her nearest neighbor lived eight miles away. But in her "I gave him no hint" letter to Lucia Tower, sent a month later, it is evident that the wilderness did not keep settlers isolated from gossip; Ellen concludes her discussion of Mrs. Triggs and her husband's waywardness by writing: "The story is now ancient history. I know of a new epoch." The new epoch evidently involved Babe, the woman who was to become Veblen's second wife.

Ellen then writes of her menagerie of animals:

All depend on me as though I were God. I realize if any one of the many things happen to me that could happen, it would mean a lonely unknown death for us all. The nightmare fact that no entreaty of mine can elicit a word from you is one of the poignant sorrows of my life. The mystery of it haunts me perpetually . . . Distress has made me very old and hopeless in this one year. I can hardly bear the thought of being seen by those who have known me.[16]

In 1904, a slightly desperate Veblen, well aware of the difficulties of finding an academic job, applied for a job with the Library of Congress, for which he was vastly overqualified. Despite many glowing letters of recommendation from his colleagues, he did not get the position of "Chief of the Division of Documents." The librarian acknowledged his reputation as a savant, his knowledge of twenty-six languages, his teaching experience, his authorship of two books, and his Ph.D. in philosophy, but said he "needed more of a routine person."[17]

In June 1905, Veblen wrote an article on the uses of credit for the *Journal of Political Economy*. Six months later the editorship of the *Journal* was transferred to John L. Cummings. Veblen was still looking for a more secure situation at another college. In March of 1906, he published his last article for the *Journal,* "The Place of Science in Modern Civilization," which later appeared in the *American Journal of Sociology* and became the leading essay in a book of the same title.[18]

In 1906, Veblen delivered a series of lectures at Harvard during a two-week leave of absence from Chicago. In three different lectures he spoke on "Followers of Karl Marx"; his fourth lecture was devoted to the "Distribution of Socialist Sentiment." Later the *Quarterly Journal of Economics* published these lectures in a slightly different version and they were included in *The Place of Science in Modern Civilization* under a different title, "The Socialist Economics of Karl Marx and His Followers, I and II."

The biggest flaw in Marxism, according to Veblen, is that it does not describe an evolutionary process. When the millennium occurs, Marxists expect that there will be no more private ownership of the means of production for all eternity. Marx, being a Hegelian, is a romantic and does not say what will happen after the millennium. It is the familiar "happily ever after" script.

Another doctrine that is in doubt, Veblen said, is the inevitability of the class struggle. Many nations have declined and died without any perceptible class struggle. "The doctrine that progressive misery must effect a socialistic revolution [is] dubious ... Experience ... teaches that abject misery carries with it deterioration and abject subjection."[19]

Darwin would not have approved of Marx's Hegelian outlook. Evolution could not conceivably have led to a "final ... goal to which all lines of the process should converge and beyond which the process would not go."[20] Besides, "Marx is, always and everywhere, a socialist agitator as well as a theoretical economist."[21] More and more socialists are giving up Marx. "The facts are not bearing ... out [his theories] on certain critical points."[22]

It is in this duo of essays that we also get Veblen's outlook on the future. He wrote:

> Under the Darwinian norm, it must be held that men's reasoning is largely controlled by other than logical, intellectual forces; [that it] is, as much or more, a matter of sentiment ... or an outcome of habit and native propensity, as of calculated material interest. There is, for instance, no warrant in the Darwinian scheme of things for asserting, *a priori,* that the class interests of the working class will bring them to take a stand against the propertied classes. It may as well be that their training in subservience to their employers will bring them again to realize the equity and excellence of the established system of subjection and unequal distribution of wealth. Again, no one, for instance, can tell today what will be the outcome of the present situation in Europe and America. It may be that the working classes will go forward along the line of the socialistic ideals, and enforce a new deal, in which there shall be no economic class discrepancies, no international animosity, no dynastic politics. But then it may also, so far as can be foreseen, equally well happen that the working class, with the rest of the community in Germany, England, or America, will be led by the habit of loyalty, and by their sportsmanlike propensities, to lend themselves enthusiastically to the game of dynastic politics which alone their sportsmanlike rulers consider worthwhile ... It is a question ... not... of logical consistency, but of response to stimulus.[23]

In the letter to Jacques Loeb of February 1905, previously mentioned, Veblen had begun:

> I wish to leave Chicago as soon as I can find a place to work elsewhere, and you might do me the best possible service by speaking to Mr. Jordan in my behalf. There is no university in America that I should prefer to Stanford. Mr. Jordan has in the past expressed the kindliest regard for me, but I believe that, in the present state of the Stanford finances, it would take much urgency to bring him to make me an offer of any kind. Still, he may see his way to do so, and if you will burden yourself with speaking to him, that will be the best possible way in which the matter could be brought to his attention.[24]

Loeb took it upon himself to do so. David Starr Jordan, president of Stanford University, had been interested in Veblen ever since the Macmillan Publishing Company had sent him a copy of *The Theory of the Leisure Class* in March 1899, and had asked him if he would be willing to comment on it. Jordan had formed such a high opinion of Veblen that he later said that Veblen was "the most subtle man in the business. What he cannot reverse, and make appear the opposite of what it purports to be, isn't worth reversing."[25] He had also received Laughlin's glowing endorsement of Veblen and a Veblen inquiry about employment possibilities at Stanford on April 29, 1899. In 1906, however, Veblen's friends believed it was unlikely that Veblen would be offered employment there.

Wesley Clair Mitchell, one of Veblen's star pupils at Chicago (then teaching economics at Berkeley), wrote to Sarah Hardy Gregory that Veblen's appointment might not be easily obtained. Mitchell was certain that Veblen was among those who were being considered for the post, as Loeb and another California professor had got Stanford professor Stillman between them at dinner, and told him of Veblen's capacities. Professor Stillman was supposed to be as "close" to Jordan as any man on the Stanford faculty.

Oddly enough, Jordan's apparent enthusiasm for Veblen might tell against him. The fact that Jordan knew Veblen slightly and had formed a favorable opinion of him, that he was enthusiastic about his books and had been heard to say that he would like their author to teach at Stanford—all this made the situation more uncertain. Jordan, according to Mrs. Loeb, was unpredictable, he rarely behaved as one believed he might. And Jordan was also said to feel, from past experience, that danger lay in allowing "brilliant, but unconventional, men" on the faculty.[26]

But Veblen was undeterred, either by these fears or by the toboggan ride President Harper of Chicago was promising him. On April 9, 1906, he wrote President Jordan that he wanted more money than Jordan had offered. On April 18, the 1906 earthquake struck. Most of Stanford's academic plant (less than five miles from the San Andreas fault) luckily escaped injury. But some of the original, ugly, overelaborate architectural features were destroyed—to the eventual benefit of its architectural symmetry. It was only by heroic measures that the university was able to continue at all.

Jordan was not put off when he read Veblen's letter, which he must have received sometime around the height of the crisis. Veblen had said:

> I am sorry that no more liberal terms are possible at present. I have, of course, thought the matter over ... and my liking for Leland Stanford and for California is no less decided than it has been, but I have come to think that I cannot afford to accept any academic rank lower than the highest assigned to any member of the Department, or any salary less than the highest paid to any member of the Department. I shall be very sorry if this reservation bars me out, but I do not see my way to forego it.[27]

A week later he wrote:

> My acceptance of an inferior grade would be looked on by my friends in the science as something in the nature of a reduction to the ranks. This I cannot afford. I know by experience that such a circumstance would handicap me in my work, and at the same time contribute to my discomfort.
>
> I appreciate that the administrative work of the department, which falls to Mr. Young, may explain his being paid on a more liberal scale than the other members of the department; and with this in mind I should be glad to accept an appointment as associate professor, as you are kind enough to offer, with a salary of $2,500 at the outset. I hope, however that you are willing to add a proviso that the salary be increased to $3,000, beginning with the second year of the tenure.[28]

This was not bad, considering that Veblen had been making $2,000 a year at Chicago. On May 1, 1906, Veblen wrote:

> My acceptance of an appointment at $2,500, without proviso, would mean, to my mind, acceptance of a subordinate rank in the department and this, for reasons indicated, I can not afford ... I venture to suggest that the formal objection to a promise of advancement in the future might be satisfied by making the appointment at the regular salary of $3,000 per year, with the proviso that only $2,500 be paid for the first year."[29]

On May 13, 1906, he wrote to President Jordan: "Your telegram has come to hand with the welcome news that you have been able to arrange for my appointment. I am very glad it has been arranged, and only regret that you should have had an undue amount of bother connected with it."[30] Veblen had triumphed. Even with his back to the wall, his financial demands had been met.[31]

Ellen had been wrong when she wrote Sarah Hardy Gregory that "it was not in [Thorstein] to look out for the future."[32] His correspondence with Jordan showed a skillful and resolute manner of employee bargaining. Everything was set for a rebirth of the phoenix in the Stanford oasis. There the presence of a man of exceptional talent and erudition would lend prestige to a fledgling faculty.

14

The Corner of Indecision

In the year 1904, or thereabouts, Veblen was introduced to the twenty-seven-year-old woman who was to become his second wife, Ann Bradley Bevans. (Actually nobody in her family called her anything but "Babe.") She was married and twenty years younger than Thorstein.

They met at the home of her in-laws, the Bevanses, where the patriarch and giant Homer Bevans, six feet seven inches tall, had long been startling Chicagoans with forceful pronouncements.[1] "I stand for the savage," he often snorted, claiming that "the earth was limitless in elemental forces, . . . [that] only men . . . were vile," and that civilization had made of Chicago "a shambles." Veblen must have been intrigued by such a maverick, reported to be "bold and aggressive to the point of fierceness," and at the same time "the gentlest and most diffident of men." Bevans was 100 percent Welsh and had the defects of his qualities, as Thorstein was wont to say. For decades Bevans had been the principal of various Chicago high schools.

"Once in a warm discussion at a principal's meeting [Homer] had declared, 'I stand for the savage!' Later someone said to him, 'Bevans, you stand for the savage, all right, but your dream of savage splendor always includes a sirloin steak and fixin's at Rector's.' He enjoyed the thrust immensely."[2]

Homer would change all this Chicago vileness by education. Every school should be given half a million dollars. "When asked if this would not bankrupt the city, he replied, 'No. If the city . . . can spend fifty millions for a ditch, if a single man can garner one hundred million from . . . commerce, it is idle to talk of dearth of money!'"[3]

After Homer's son, Tom, and Babe were married, Tom made little effort to ease the shock of Babe's adjustment into the woes of enforced domesticity. Or it may be unfair, a century later, to assess blame in such a categorical fashion on either the high-spirited teachers' college graduate or on the tall, dark, and handsome Tom. A more reasoned summary might be that there was a violation here of the eleventh commandment that only one maverick is allowed per couple.

Babe had come from a warm and interesting family. "Papa" Bradley was an attorney who had won a landmark case: *The People* v. *The Illinois Central Railroad.* The railroad had wangled an exclusive grant to part of Chicago's choice lakefront property from the Chicago City Council. Alexander Stuart Bradley represented the Illinois state attorney general, which contended the deal was an outright steal. However, Bradley early retired from active trial work because of deafness following scarlet fever. His deafness overwhelmed him in his late twenties and hampered his practice of law and the Bradley income. His wife, Harriet Ayer Tolle, then regularly took in roomers, University of Chicago students exclusively, preferring foreign students.

"Mama" Bradley was an amateur herb doctor and a self-proclaimed atheist. Back in her hometown of Fryeburg, Maine, her father and brother had practiced homeopathic medicine (an understandable decision considering the state of allopathic medicine in the nineteenth century), and she practiced the same kind of medicine on her neighbors and on her family.

One of Papa Bradley's distinguished male ancestors had been Senator Fessenden, a member of Lincoln's cabinet. Farther back, female ancestors on both Papa and Mama's side had been accused of witchcraft during the Salem trials.[4] In addition, one of Mama's female ancestors had been jailed for witchcraft in New Hampshire in the 1600s. Babe may have carried some of those feisty genes, as she was given to quixotic behavior and calculated outrageousness.

Fresh out of normal school, ready to prove that anything a man could do a woman could do better, and hoping to save the world by teaching the young the exciting ideas of the new century, her career had been blighted by her impetuous marriage (school boards did not allow married women to teach in those days) and the sudden blessing of two healthy girls to raise.

She thought that most unfair, especially as the young architect husband housed her and their baby in his mother's hayloft while he was away on his first architectural projects. On the other hand she could reflect that if she had taught school, she would have had to remain single, and perhaps, like her sister Mame, live at home with her parents eternally.[5]

Tom was a starving young architect whose low-level assignments with established architects required him to travel hither and thither supervising construction jobs probably designed by his superiors. As her children grew older Babe often followed on the train and, if he stayed long enough to make it worthwhile, set up housekeeping in strange cities. In the Victorian tradition, she had had her two children under dismal circumstances.[6]

Babe's siblings, Mary ("Mame"), Harriet ("Hat"), and Stuart ("Stude"), each had a strong individuality. The schoolteacher Mame, an exotic, fixed up her room in her parents' house like an actress's dressing room with beaded curtains in the doorway. On her wall she had plastered photographs of Sarah Bernhardt and an Arab sheik plus a life-sized poster of Abraham Lincoln with the words: "Brotherhood of all Men. Must have Equal Chance." Hat, on the other hand, was an attractive but ultraconservative stuffed shirtwaist in a liberal family. She was married to Wallace Walter Atwood, a professor of physio-geography at the University of Chicago who later as President of Clark University gained notoriety as an inept bludgeoner of academic freedom. Babe's brother Stude early abandoned the mainstream and took off to build cabins in primitive places.

Babe was Papa Bradley's favorite. In his library, surrounded by cherrywood bookcases with glass doors, and with lovely oriental rugs underfoot, he read to her from Tolstoy, Tennyson, Poe, and the Bible. He liked her fiercely independent nature. He also admired her resourcefulness. Once in Fryeburg she had fought a fire, single-handed, rescuing her bedridden uncle, of whom she was very fond. "She came back with her face all blackened and burnt holes all over her dark wool skirt," her daughter Becky wrote.[7]

Determination and a fiery nature made of Babe's Madonna-like beauty a compelling thing. Although at twelve, she had resembled a blonde, ringletted angel, she became a crack shot, echoing the prowess of the legendary "Calamity Jane." Upon being challenged by her normal school classmates, she shot a hornet's nest "through the thin stem . . . and everyone ran from the swarm" of angry insects.[8]

Still enraged by the injustice of a system that would not allow her to have the career she had prepared for, Babe decided to home-school her daughters. She also became a socialist and a suffragette. In Marie J. Buhle's *Women and American Socialism, 1870–1920,* Buhle points out that some women saw in socialism "the possibility of a literal practice of the Golden Rule."[9] One midwestern woman wrote, in a letter to a newspaper: "I am for Socialism if Socialism is in favor of women. I hope the day will come when we can vote for the laws that govern our lives. I am always a friend to my sex." Josephine Conger, one of the leaders in the socialist movement, wrote, "I am a Socialist, but I am one because I see through the Socialist platform the only possible emancipation of women and children from tyranny and superstition."

Babe "adored Eugene Debs," a union leader of the railway workers in the Pullman strike (1894). She frequently repeated his homily: "If you let anybody lead you, you will certainly be misled. Don't go blindly. Think for yourself." Train conductors were kind to her because she habitually wore a Debs button in her lapel.[10]

Unfortunately, the socialist movement did not meet the expectations of women who hoped for political equality. In San Francisco the appointment of a woman comrade to an important committee caused a man to resign. Afterward the rank and file staged a debate: "Resolved, that women are an important factor in socialism."[11]

An editor of *Comrade* wrote, however:

> At most, [women] are treated with amused indulgence in much the same manner as children are treated. Open, frank, and equal comradeship is very rarely shown toward even the few women who find their way into party organization. If a woman is brave enough to face the ostracism of the rest of her sex and society generally to take the platform in the interest of socialist propaganda—she is permitted—and even encouraged—to do so as a drawing card . . . For the rest, there is toleration rather than welcome for them."[12]

Tom always laughed at Babe's socialistic views. (In fact, her more conservative family members were probably also put off by them.)[13] But he was also bored with the new tied-down, domesticated Babe. Babe, herself, had not really wanted children right away, or perhaps ever, but had had to adapt herself to circumstances.

Later on, Tom wrote bemusedly to one of his daughters in a letter complaining about Babe: "And I recall that a mere job was not the major part of the day's business. Shopping, cooking, [and] washing baby clothes were also routine. And, at the time, I didn't even notice I was doing it."[14] He reflected the still predominant male attitude that the whole of child care should be strictly woman's work—there was nothing swashbuckling about it—and that such activities were taboo occupations for lordly men.

This taboo was defined by Veblen in "The Barbarian Status of Women," written well before he knew Babe. Veblen contended that before there was a stratification of classes among the males, there was a male–female class division that judged women's work (a large proportion of the useful work done, as opposed to the purely honorific and bellicose male activities) humiliating. As a result of the development of rudimentary tools that made "uneventful everyday women's work" more productive, a surplus food supply became available, so that men could indulge in predatory activities. "Merit and propriety rest on an invidious distinction between those who are capable fighters and those who are not."[15] The men fear that if they indulge in routine useful work they will become polluted in some way so that they will lose their status, and "the able-bodied man who is mindful of his virility [will shun] . . . all contamination with the employments that are characteristic of the [weaker] sex . . . The women, their occupations, their food and clothing . . . become ceremonially unclean to the men." And this has lasted in the later cultures as "a sense of the unworthiness . . . of women; so that even now we feel the impropriety of women taking rank with men, . . . in any relation that calls for dignity and ritual competency; as, for instance, in priestly or diplomatic offices, or even in representative civil offices."[16]

To assuage his ennui, handsome Tom Bevans took up the hobby of dressing ladies in harem costumes and taking pictures of them, posed provocatively. In his room, a closet was kept full of costumes suitable for draping his models. Soon Babe discovered that he was not limiting his ennui-chasing activities to photography. He was also "canoodling" a friend of hers. Their marriage was at a breaking point when Thorstein and Babe chanced to meet.

To move out from under a man's roof was, in 1904 or 1905, a scandalous thing to contemplate, yet for the descendant of a "witch," all things were possible.[17] "Veblen called the Bevans' apartment 'the corner of indecision' because they were always trying to make up their minds what to do," a close Chicago associate said.[18]

Babe's new quarters were on Fifty-Seventh Street near the Illinois Central Railroad tracks. There, an impromptu artists' colony had sprung up in a group of abandoned shops that had been built for the Columbian Exposition. "When the trains went over, it was interesting and noisy," wrote Babe's older daughter, Becky Veblen Meyers.[19] Becky and her sister Ann played hopscotch outside the shops, but they often got cinders in their eyes. Inside, soft coal dust was everywhere, and the shop was meagerly heated—at least there were no visible radiators. To keep warm, they "wore wooly undies, woolen stockings and sweaters," and had their warm baths in a round metal washtub. The long narrow shop—with windows in front—possessed a hot plate, water taps, and an enclosed toilet in the rear. There were beds enough but no couch. However, the children spent much of their time at their grandparents' comfortable house, which was within easy walking distance.[20]

Becky called Veblen a "tall, quiet man" and said he dropped by Babe's place from time to time, bringing armloads of books. The first time he stopped in, the children had been quarreling and were crying. "He . . . looked at our faces and said, 'Aha! Just what I need, I have this little bottle, and need some teardrops in it. Could I have just a few?' "[21] The children couldn't squeeze out a single tear.

Babe soon began studying the German socialist movement in German—a gesture bound to intrigue the erudite professor. Her sauciness, spunk, and outspoken advocacy of her humanitarian principles must have been even more compelling.[22]

The growing involvement of Thorstein and Babe was somewhat strained, as Ellen Veblen was certainly aware of her husband's interest in the younger woman. According to Eve Schütze, Ellen claimed that Babe had warningly confronted her with the message that she "wanted to be the mother of a great man's children." Babe, after all, had already produced two lively offspring; Ellen at age forty-five had none.

* * *

Eve Schütze commented, "[Babe] was very beautiful, looked like a Madonna, but was not at all interesting to me . . . I have forgotten whether she ever finally married him." And Veblen "never cared about what other people said, except to agree when they fell in with his thought."[23]

Ellen's own description of Babe was not ungracious: "Mrs. Bevans has blue eyes, and is not small—medium height. Her hair is darkish. Eyes large and beautiful, her face round, expression surprisingly innocent. Figure very correct. Dress unconventional but becoming. She used to affect a sort of close fitting cap perched on the back of her head."[24]

In the summer (probably of 1905), Babe visited her husband's sister, Mrs. Hervey (or Henry) White at "The Warwick" in Woodstock, and Thorstein also visited Woodstock, staying in the same household.[25] Everyone in their circle knew about their affair, and Thorstein's friend Martin Schütze was not pleased about his blatant disregard for the proprieties. The noted feminist, Charlotte Perkins Gilman, author of *Women and Economics,* wrote, "I have met Thorstein Veblen more than once, a dry quizzical man, as I remember, and I marvelled that that amorous little wife-and-mother should have thrown over her family ties and made him sever his, to mate with her. It seemed to me a needless piece of sex extravagance, and it certainly did him great harm in professional standing."[26]

Thorstein and Babe and her children may have spent part of the summers of 1905 and 1906 camping out on Washington Island with Thorstein before he left for California. Located off the coast of Michigan's northern peninsula between Michigan and Green Bay, the island appealed to Thorstein not only because of its freedom from hay fever pollen, but because it had been settled by Icelanders whose language he wished to study (Icelandic was the old Norse of the sagas and the eddas). Babe's daughter Becky wrote that they were hiding out on the island during two or three summers "where [Ellen] couldn't track us down."[27]

Veblen was aware of the potential harm an alliance outside his marriage could do to him at Stanford University and must have come belatedly to a decision to observe the proprieties—at least outwardly. When he bid Babe farewell in the summer of 1906, "forsaking all others" seemed to include Babe at this point.

15

Stanford

One summer day in 1906, Ellen looked up and Thorstein was standing in the doorway of her log cabin on her Hood River timber claim. She was embarrassed because she was dirty and wore overalls. Overalls were a sore point with Victorian women. In the novel *Barren Ground* by Ellen Glasgow, a turn-of-the-century mother and her daughter had the following exchange:

> "You ain't going to wear them [overalls] on the farm, are you?"
> "If I can farm better in them, I'm going to wear them" [the daughter stoutly replied].
> Mrs. Oakley sighed. "Well, I hope nobody will see you."[1]

At the outrageous spectacle, Thorstein collapsed into helpless laughter, while Ellen accepted his sudden reappearance without question. All must be well between them, or he would not have returned to her, and that was all that mattered.[2]

When Veblen had written his former student, Henry Alvin Millis—then an assistant professor of economics at Stanford—that he was coming his way, Millis had asked if he should find him lodgings and would Mrs. Veblen be coming with him? Veblen had replied that he was not sure and not to bother.[3] Perhaps he wasn't even certain that Ellen would agree to accompany him.

Thorstein stayed with Ellen in the cabin for a short time, then together they hiked down the sixteen-mile mountain trail and took the train to California.[4]

When they arrived at the university, Ellen presented a somewhat "bizarre appearance." Her clothes had been lying in a trunk for two years, and she put them on unironed. Professor Millis's wife, Alice, was so taken aback by the couple's "quaint and unusual" look that she found it hard to describe them. Veblen wore a light-colored, shabby suit and an outdated beige fedora hat; Ellen's black skirt was a mass of wrinkles, as was her jacket and cape—"not that she ever dressed or looked like the wife of a professor." The first Mrs. Veblen was, unfortunately, skinny to the point of being wraith-like, and totally without womanly curves. Her skirts almost slid off her hips; her hair was messy; and her hats perched at a strange angle on her disorderly hairdo. Even with the advice of Alice Millis she could not be persuaded to acquire the proper wardrobe for her situation. "But she was so delightful that no one thought of her appearance, i.e., no one who loved her, and many did."[5]

Alice Millis was in the advanced stage of her third pregnancy, and this was immediately the focus of Ellen's attention. Ellen beamed at her "with . . . gracious tenderness" and told her that "she thought [she] was the most beautiful thing she had ever seen!" Such lyricism was Ellen's normal approach. "She would have given her life, I would almost say her soul, to bear a child."[6]

Any thought that this interest in children was just a competitive maneuver stimulated by Babe's desire to have a great man's child would appear ungenerous and hazardous.[7] Ellen's authorship of a book for children, and her later quasi-adoption of two needy youngsters—Henry Cowell, who became a prominent avant-garde pianist-composer, and Evelyn Wells, who developed into an outstanding San Francisco newspaperwoman and writer—appeared genuine and unforced. Both were children of dear friends. Evidently Ellen had a strong maternal impulse, thwarted by her numerous physical disabilities.

At first, the Veblens took modest lodgings near the Millises, but soon arrangements were made to lease "Cedro," which had been built for Ariel Lathrop, the brother of Mrs. Stanford. Since the death of her husband, Mrs. Stanford was the sole representative of the founders of the institution and the *éminence grise* of the university administration. Built in a country area near the campus, Cedro was considered a mansion by some. The one-storied, peaked-roof bungalow was surrounded by a five-acre garden and was entered by a long, gloomy, hedge-enclosed drive. It had a barn and a stable and a chicken house, and "had been quite pretentious with . . . fourteen (I think) acres [altogether]," Alice Millis wrote in a letter to Joseph Dorfman.[8]

The Veblens moved in before the fall quarter of 1906 was over.[9] Ellen must have felt that at last they had come into their own. The situation was similar to that at Stacyville where they were "known" and "important," and where she had been very happy.

They soon collected two score of hens and a couple of roosters, two horses, two cows (one pregnant), plus a bevy of assorted cats.[10] But no dogs. (Thorstein did not like dogs, considering them among the filthiest and most servile of animals, according to his book, *The Theory of the Leisure Class,* and to his stepdaughter Becky.[11])

One contemporary wrote:

> My friendship with Mrs. Veblen began when I was a student at Stanford and she and Mr. Veblen were our near neighbors. I saw Mr. Veblen only as he went to and from the campus—a tall, lean figure on a bicycle. He looked as remote as Odin himself and I thought that he must live in an exalted world and felt the greatest awe for his studious ways. His light usually burned 'til three or four in the morning, but his wife informed me that he was [not studying after all, but] indulging in an orgy of French novels.[12]

Veblen once said that he felt that the French would understand him. Gustave Flaubert, Honoré de Balzac, and Anatole France comprehended the need of human beings for sexual fulfillment. But there was no pro-French tone in the Stanford ambiance. Jordan flatly stated in an address at Bryn (Mawr?) college: "France by her confession is a weak and degenerate nation."[13] And at the new Stanford Chapel, the minister fulsomely regretted the lowering of moral standards in American domestic life. Divorce was particularly regrettable. "If you are tempted to sin," he exhorted, "think of your mother and father."[14] Dr. Jordan reinforced this by stating: "Vice [probably referring to drunkenness] is a waste of energy . . . one third of all the strength of the United States is wasted by vice . . . every vice is charged up to your account and can never be wiped out. Any kind of evil injures a man's health and business."[15]

It soon became apparent to Ellen that her husband was receiving numerous letters from Mrs. Bevans. Ellen's dream of a renewal of the soulful relationship of the quiet years at Stacyville was shattered when she learned that Babe's plans included divorcing Tom and taking the train west to California, specifically to the University of California at Berkeley. There she proposed to take courses in subjects allied to Veblen's work for a year. (The campus at UC Berkeley was only a short train and ferry-boat ride from Stanford.)

Babe's parents, who were probably unaware of her involvement with Veblen, had agreed to take care of their two granddaughters, who were four and six years old. This worked no hardship on the girls as Mama and Papa Bradley had routinely cosseted them. In one of Becky's "Memoirs" she wrote, "I was born to four grandparents." She evidently considered Mama and Papa Bradley as important factors in her eyes as her own parents.

Meanwhile, in Palo Alto, Ellen had decided not even to unpack her crates of belongings after she had discovered to her horror that, as she put it, "Mrs. Bevans had the distinguished honor to be first."[16] (In Veblen's affections?)

Moving to California had put Ellen in close proximity to her old enemy, Sarah Hardy, now Mrs. Warren Gregory and an established fixture of San Francisco and Berkeley society. Ellen had apparently closed out her vituperous letter writing to Mrs. Gregory. She made no attempt to establish further contact, until in January 1907, she wrote Sarah Hardy Gregory from Hood River, where she had a rental house that probably needed attention.[17]

My dear Mrs. Gregory,

    I wish to correct certain possible impressions on your part which would make it more than difficult to meet you. And if I return to Palo Alto, that will doubtless happen in time.[18]
    I should not wish you to feel that I fancied myself still in danger from you. I can fancy myself glad [under the circumstances] if there were foundation in such a fancy.
    Nor should I wish you to be deceived by present appearances [of conjugal amicability?] for it is too terrible a falsehood for me to endure your believing it, whatever others might think. We may be doing the best we can. I should be glad to be thought of as free from the sentiments that have caused me so much pain in the past.[19]

A strange letter, ostensibly friendly, but with all the warmth of a donjon keep, surrounded by moats and shrouded in stone walls, damp moss, lookout towers, a portcullis, and the like.

Veblen quickly got in touch with his former pupil, Wesley Clair Mitchell, now a professor of economics at the University of California at Berkeley.[20] Mitchell was courting and eventually married the beautiful young woman who was Berkeley's first Dean of Women, Lucy Sprague. Miss Sprague, Mitchell, and the Gregorys became the best of friends.

The beauteous Miss Sprague described Warren Gregory as being affable, charming, full of fun, and admiring of and devoted to Sarah. The Gregorys had plenty of money and were extremely generous. They had, at first, lived in their house in San Francisco and owned another, built for Warren's mother, in the Berkeley hills. After the earthquake they felt safer in the East Bay and moved into a third called "La Loma," a "lovely redwood house set in a big rambling garden, with a tennis court and plenty of play space for their four children. And La Loma became one of the chief centers for Berkeley social life. Above anything, Sadie [Sarah] enjoyed a good discussion—she still does. She often had people for dinner. She invited a small group to her house Sunday evenings for supper and a 'talk.'"[21]

Veblen had kept in touch with Sarah throughout the years, and Warren Gregory had also become his friend and a great supporter. Ellen's supposition that she *might* eventually run into Sarah never was put to the test. The spring of 1907 came to be the end of the Cedro experience for Ellen, and all during the Stanford years, when Veblen stayed with the Gregorys or with Mitchell, no mention was made of Mrs. Veblen's accompanying him. It would have been awkward. Although Mrs. Gregory felt her friendship with Veblen had been straightforward, and she had nothing in her past behavior to be ashamed of,[22] Ellen's mercurial temperament would have made her a difficult guest. In her letters, Ellen referred to the Mitchell group as "Mr. Veblen's friends."

President Jordan appreciated having such an erudite scholar as Veblen on his faculty and wholeheartedly admired his intellect. Ellen, as she had previously done with President Harper in Chicago, sought to become better acquainted with the new president. She wrote Jordan delicately suggesting that James Strong, who was retired and living in Southern California, might be prevailed upon to give a speech about his "friendship" with Robert and Elizabeth Barrett Browning. Her exquisite breeding was shown by the fact that, in her letter, she never once mentioned the fact that the ex-president of Carleton College was her uncle.[23]

Veblen was not to write any of his major works while he was at Stanford, but the Shangri-la atmosphere of the 4,000–acre "Stanford Farm" (isolated by miles from the nearest metropolitan area), with its sunny subtropical climate, did not lure him into lotus-land torpor. He busied himself attacking the marginal utility theorists. Professor Edwin R.A. Seligman, editor of Columbia's *Political Science Quarterly,* originally rejected Veblen's "The Limitations of Marginal Utility," feeling it "wasn't practical enough."[24] Fortunately, another journal agreed to publish it.[25] Next Veblen criticized, rather sharply, Professor Irving Fisher's books, *The Rate of Interest* and *Capital and Income,* and wrote a number of other book reviews.[26]

In one of his subsequent reviews, he was again concerned with the importance of women in primitive societies. His old mentor from Carleton College days, John Bates Clark, in his book *The Essentials of Economic Theory,* explained the origin of capital by contending that, from the earliest times (in savagery and lower barbarism), there was a "solitary hunter" who made by his own labor all the goods he used. Not so, said Veblen. He returned to the theme he pursued in his article on the "Beginnings of Ownership," saying that as soon as "mankind reached the human plane . . . [there was] . . . a community of some kind; in which . . . women seem . . . to have been the most consequential factor instead of the man who works for himself."

Veblen then drew upon his examination of the culture of the California Digger Indian, stating that the "capital" they possessed in the form of working tools was insignificant. This capital meant so very little to the Indian society that it could all have been lost with very little hardship.

> What was of "vital concern" to them, indeed, what the life of the group depended on absolutely, was the accumulated wisdom of the squaws, the technology of their economic situation. The loss of the basket, digging stick, and mortar, simply as physical objects, would have signified little, but the conceivable loss of the squaws' knowledge of the soil and seasons, of food and fiber plants, and of mechanical expedients, would have meant the present dispersal and starvation of the community.[27]

Like other followers of Adam Smith, Clark had left the role of women out of the economic picture. Yet, strangely enough, as John P. Diggins wrote: "In many contemporary feminist studies, the name Thorstein Veblen receives hardly more than a passing mention or citation . . . This neglect is regrettable, for there was a time when Veblen came to be regarded as the major cultural critic of the world of masculine domination, the thorn in the side of chauvinism."[28]

When Clark and Veblen met in person, Clark graciously said that when writing his book he should have considered more carefully the views of his former student. Veblen afterward remarked that "Clark was a gentleman."[29] Perhaps, it takes a gentleman to know one, as one of Veblen's University of Missouri students also called Veblen "thoughtful, kindly [and], courteous—a gentleman through and through."[30]

Veblen's article, "Christian Morals and the Competitive System," his last at Stanford, started out with a discussion of ancient Rome and its subjugation of the early Christians. He compared the morals of Christianity with those of a competitive society such as the Roman Empire and pointed out how incompatible they were. Non-resistance, humility, and helpfulness (the Christian virtues) were useful only to the ground-down subject class of an imperialist society (and by indirection to their masters). Veblen then compared present-day business morals with the ethics of the handicraft period that preceded capitalism. Surprisingly, he concluded that while business principles cannot last as a yardstick for human conduct, Christian principles may. He felt that ultimately "the Christian principle of brotherhood should logically continue to gain ground at the expense of the pecuniary morals of competitive business."[31]

Wesley Clair Mitchell was disappointed with the scholarly direction Veblen was taking. He wrote to his old classmate Sarah Hardy Gregory that he agreed with her in wishing that Veblen "would turn to more constructive work." Mitchell objected to Veblen's "speculation" on topics his old professor had treated recently. He felt that this speculative approach left Veblen open to attack. Veblen's work was no longer, as it once had been, "an analytical account of the evolution of economic habits of thought and action." His recent writings seemed to be founded more or less on guesswork, because he simply could not take the time to indicate the basis from which he theorized.

Economic theory was complex, and Mitchell felt baffled by the fact that Veblen had made so little impact on others in his field: "When [they] contest his conclusions I often find that the only real answer lies in doing a lot of work with statistics—work which Veblen has not performed."[32]

It may have been that Mitchell was just laying out for himself what he should do with the ideas that Veblen had generated in him, ideas that, turned into statistics, eventually led him to become the pre-eminent American authority on business cycles.

But part of Mitchell's and Sarah Hardy Gregory's dissatisfaction with their old hero and schoolmaster may have stemmed from their disapproval of his personal life. He was "ruining himself" in his quest for a divorce and his search for marital happiness. Mitchell's proper new acquaintance, Lucy Sprague, whom he married in 1912, may have influenced Mitchell subtly on this point. In her memoirs she tells us that divorce was never mentioned in her family, or in other "good families" in Chicago, as she was growing up. So terrible was divorce considered that if a family friend divorced, he or she was dropped from their circle of acquaintances and never mentioned again. Sarah had similar sentiments on the subject.[33]

Babe was not only getting a divorce, she was using her influence to persuade Thorstein to get one, too, and then to remarry. Besides, she was distinctly peculiar in their eyes—letting passion prevail over preserving her ladylike status, pursuing Thorstein to the West Coast, and recklessly putting his Stanford job and his entire academic future in jeopardy.

According to Joseph Dorfman, Thorstein was supposed to have remarked at some juncture, "What is one to do if a woman moves in on you?" referring to the behavior of Babe.[34] But, according to Duffus's *The Innocents at Cedro,* which told of his year of close association with the professor, Veblen effectively told Babe to leave Cedro after one brief overnight visit, and she left in a bad mood. Nevertheless, there were opportunities for less public meetings. If one reads between the lines of Duffus's account, however, although Babe did not "move in on him," Veblen's time at Stanford was possibly the happiest period of his life. Not the most productive academically, certainly, but considering the whole man, one of the happiest. Stanford had and has something of an unreal atmosphere about it. The architecture is unreal; the weather is unreal; there is nothing much wrong with life around the Stanford Quad at anytime.

This mirage-like Never-Never Land was the ideal place for Veblen and Babe's risky honeymoon, premature and unlicensed as it may have been.

16

Where the Rolling Foothills Rise

Veblen had settled into teaching at Stanford. But many things told against him. For one, his quaint and unusual way of dressing. Although Stanford male undergraduates made a fetish of appearing in non-Ivy League apparel (corduroys, no jackets or ties, and an odd hat called "the plug-ugly") and prided themselves on being called "the Stanford Roughs," they were not attuned to a professor who scorned the habitual professorial raiment.

"The first time I saw him," one student said, "ambling along the Quad with a slouch hat pulled down over his brow, with coat and trousers 'hanging'; with untrimmed hair and moustache creating a general unkempt appearance, I thought he was a tramp."[1]

And while the spirit of the frontier may have liberated a few chosen spirits from stuffy eastern traditions, most of the male students were unenlightened on the "woman question." In the spring of 1908, the Stanford student body voted on whether the women's vote in the Associated Students should be taken away from them. The men—those who bothered to vote at all—voted almost unanimously to take the vote away. But the women came out in force, and their strong negative vote prevailed 300 to 90.[2] Obviously, Stanford men were not ready for Veblen's views on women.

At Stanford, Veblen mainly taught undergraduates, and he was too subtle for many of them.[3] (In order to winnow out the unsuitable students, he asked if prospective class members could read source materials in French or German and whether they had some background in psychology and philosophy.) Nevertheless, he titillated some students. One woman said: "His ideas from *The Theory of*

106

the Leisure Class frequently cropped up in his lectures. Speaking one day on coats-of-arms . . . in the Economic Factors [of Civilization] class, he remarked, 'Why couldn't the Stanfords use the horseshoe and the soup ladle? [Senator Stanford] was at one time a blacksmith and [Mrs. Stanford] ran a boarding house."[4]

A student in Socialism class remembered his course as "about the driest subject I ever attempted to study." Another student commented that, most of the time, "Veblen was over my head," and a third said, "I always felt as if I were listening to one who literally knew everything . . . but I understood precious little of what he actually said."[5]

He had the allegiance of very few students, but two became intensely devoted: William R. Camp and Leon Ardzrooni. Both followed Veblen to the University of Missouri, and Ardzrooni followed him to the New School for Social Research, via Columbia University. Also, a Stanford colleague, Henry W. Rolfe, a professor of Greek, sat in, enthralled, on "Economic Factors of Civilization" nearly every time Veblen taught it. "He was a scholar in ten thousand . . . ," said Rolfe. "His books are [only] footnotes to that great outpouring."[6] Rolfe was Veblen's closest associate, and perhaps friend, on the faculty. "They fed each other's flames. Neither was appreciated by Stanford," Guido Marx, professor of Engineering, wrote Dorfman.[7] Both Rolfe and Veblen were later fired.

Camp, Rolfe, and Veblen studied Homeric society together. On the other hand, not exactly *together*. They did not meet, but Camp selected passages, ran to Rolfe for comments, raced to Veblen for his, and jogged back to Rolfe for further discussion.

According to Duffus, Veblen did not mind having only a few students; he thought that "the ideal situation for a professor . . . was not to have any students at all."[8] Besides, he felt disdain for the "three sacred rituals of academic life— grades, attendance and departmental meetings."[9]

According to Joseph Dorfman, Ernest Sutherland Bates said: "Perhaps one student out of a hundred would have his entire course of life and thought changed by Veblen; the others got nothing from him. He deemed one in a hundred a sufficient proportion."[10]

Robert Duffus, who probably had his life and thought changed as a result of his contact with "the Professor," and who blatantly worshipped the older man, lived with him during one school year (1907–1908). Ellen had moved out in early 1907 and three students, including Duffus and his brother William, moved in the next fall term to help out with the housework and farm. Duffus felt that the great man knew "everything, including what I was thinking. When he said, 'I don't know,' as he almost always did whenever you asked him point blank for a bit of information, I never believed him. He knew, all right."[11]

Veblen was still in his prime. Although fifty years old, his hair was still brown, as was his beard (actually it stayed that way until he died), and his body seemed young, as did his way of expressing himself. Duffus wrote, "He could move as quickly as a cat, and I don't remember that he ever seemed tired."[12] By contrast, at Chicago, contemporaries had said that he was almost always tired or unwell, and that he had never really known what it was to be in good health.

While at Stanford, however, he performed amazing feats of strength. Professor A.J. Newman tells of his climbing a tree to cut off an upper limb, when two or three of his students thought it too difficult and dangerous a job to tackle.[13] Something had inspired him and fired him with new and youthful energy. Could it have been the proximity of Babe Bevans? From 1906 on there seems to have been no other woman in Veblen's life except Babe, and, according to Becky Veblen Meyers, there was no other woman who was in a close relationship with her stepfather until he died.[14]

In the beginning of their affair, possibly Veblen was unable to sort out just how important Babe was, but in August 1907, when she took the initiative of boarding a train bound for California to register for graduate work, Veblen found her proximity and daring irresistible. The University of California, raw and new, already had a reputation as a liberal coeducational establishment with an idyllic setting and climate.[15] The previously mentioned Lucy Sprague, a delicate and fastidious Radcliffe graduate with only a B.A. degree, had been Dean of Women since 1903. When the new dean first became acquainted with her charges, they

> were another shock to me—they were so different from the over-earnest students at Radcliffe. So many of them seemed to have slight intellectual interest. The vast majority were at Berkeley for one of two reasons or both. The first was to have a good time. The second was to get a teacher's certificate in order to earn a livelihood. I made a survey of the women students my first year as dean. Well over 90 percent of the nearly two thousand women were there to get a teachers' certificate. The university, as far as they were concerned, was a normal school with lots of boys around.[16]

Sprague intensely respected knowledge for knowledge's sake, or knowledge gained as a result of idle curiosity. But the girls who attended Berkeley at that time, were, for the most part, from a lower stratum of society than the Radcliffe girls, and many could not afford such intellectual pursuits, even if they had been interested. They had to earn a living.

> The women lived in mixed boarding houses, except the few who lived in sororities or clubs . . . One of my first practical jobs was to visit these boarding houses and make out an approved list [of those suitable to house students]. It was a terrible chore and a difficult one, too, to establish standards where none had been. I met every kind of boarding house landlady known, from meticulous fussy ladies who took a few highly recommended girls into their homes, to florid, blondined ladies who ran houses for prostitutes who periodically turned up registered as students.[17]

Babe was at Berkeley, neither to get a teacher's certificate, nor to meet boys, but she did live in a boarding house—recommended or not. The first semester she took heavy courses in German, philosophy, and economics, earning three Bs and a C. And soon Thorstein found it expedient, quite frequently, to visit Mitchell in Berkeley, and Sarah Hardy Gregory and her husband at their lavish spread, La Loma, at 1906 Greenwood Terrace, in the Berkeley hills near the campus. He often stayed the night in the Mitchell or Gregory household.[18]

Duffus, for one, suspected that Veblen had other than academic interests in these visits. It certainly had been bruited about. But any such extracurricular activities did not monopolize the great man's visits. Many entries in the Mitchell diaries described how he and Veblen had stayed up most of the night discussing economic theory. Duffus guessed that Veblen on his Berkeley visits saw persons other than Mitchell, and that not all of them were men. But the professor invariably returned as calm and self-possessed as when he left for Berkeley. "He did not show any of the symptoms . . . of a man in love."[19]

Thorstein and Ellen had had dinner at the Millises', in 1906, when they first arrived. Later, Alice Millis and Ellen became "best friends." Mrs. Millis knew all the details of Babe's letters, in fact, had read them aloud with Ellen, and was aware of the presence of Babe at Berkeley in the fall of 1907. The news of Babe's arrival could easily have made its way to Mitchell in Berkeley, as he came down frequently to Palo Alto to visit Veblen, Allyn Young (who was head of the Stanford Economics Department), and Alice's husband, an assistant in the economics department.[20] Soon, Lucy Sprague and the Gregorys were involved in worrying about Veblen, and, according to Lucy, "consulted regularly [with Mitchell] about Veblen's many problems."[21]

Veblen did not seem to feel he had any problems. Although otherwise "baffled and tormented" in his life, at Cedro, "he came near to being happy," said Duffus judiciously.

Nothing happened at Cedro that Veblen was not aware of. He kept tabs on the little farm and made periodic inspections of the livestock. He had a rather spooky way of appearing and disappearing like the Cheshire Cat, but this was not out of a desire to be furtive or to surprise anyone. It was just his nature to "walk as soft as a tiger cat," as Elinor Wylie's poem goes.[22] He was constitutionally disinclined to thump and crash about.

Long after Ellen had moved, first to Palo Alto with a friend in the spring of 1907, and then in June, on to Carmel-by-the-Sea, Babe, who arrived by train in California in August 1907, came down to Stanford.[23] Veblen harnessed his horse Beauty to a "two-wheeled cart," and went down to meet her. He did not seem particularly perturbed or ruffled when he left for the station, nor when he came to the dinner table with her.

The live-in student helpers were rather disappointed in the much-talked-about Mrs. Bevans. After all, she had just turned thirty, and they were in their late teens. They did not consider her a raving beauty. "Looking back . . . what troubled me . . . was that she was rather wholesome," said Robert Duffus. "She looked like a young lady a man might marry because he had grown fond of her."

One could not imagine any man throwing himself in the river over her—she was not, in the slightest, a *femme fatale.* "She even looked as though she might really be Veblen's niece, which is what she had told [my brother] William she was."[24]

She seemed quixotic in her conversation. The students felt, somehow, that she might be patronizing them or, possibly, making fun of them. They did not like her much and were startled when Veblen and his erstwhile "niece" retired to his part of the house, and were not seen again until the next morning.

Were they jealous or being clannish? Did they insist that their giant have a matching giantess? Or perhaps Duffus was measuring her by his good friend Ellen's standards. He gives Ellen high praise, in *The Innocents at Cedro,* for being the essence of intuitive, imaginative, and ladylike femininity. Later on, Duffus had extended contact with Ellen, and they attempted to write a sketch together about her ex-husband.[25]

The most pungent conversation Duffus reports he had with Babe was when he was taking her back to the Palo Alto depot. As they jogged along in the cart, she asked how he and the professor got along.

Duffus answered that they got along fine and added that it was "awfully interesting" to hear Veblen's comments. According to Duffus, Babe replied, "Oh, do you think so?" She was silent for a few moments. Duffus could almost feel her smiling in the dark. And then she said, "I don't."[26]

Duffus thought that, throughout history, women "have liked to take great men, and treat them as if they were old fuddy duddies" and felt that Babe "had no apparent reverence for the Professor and his learning."[27] Veblen, however, may have been bored with wide-eyed adulation. He had been known to scorn fawning, left-wing admirers.[28] Besides, the professor had already had the unrefreshing experience of being hero-worshipped by a certain adoring female student, who concealed from him, and possibly from herself, that her true course led to a marriage with Warren Gregory. Babe's saucy, "get real" stance, ninety years or so ahead of her time, evidently appealed.

Later, when William Duffus referred, in Veblen's hearing, to Babe as "the professor's niece," Veblen "fixed him with a cold and tranquil eye" and told him that Babe was *not* his niece.[29] The subject was never mentioned after that.

Veblen also claimed that the passage from the Bible, " 'Remember now thy creator in the days of thy youth, while evil days come not, nor the years draw nigh when thou shalt say, I have no pleasure in them,' had been misread in the Hebrew."[30] He thought it referred to sexual pleasure, sexual potency on the part of the male. (Veblen gave Duffus the impression that the translation had been horribly botched, and Duffus felt sure that Veblen had studied it in the original Hebrew.)

One thing Veblen did, during the time he lived at Cedro, was to put the chicken coop on a wagon and haul it, with a team of horses, five miles up the steep and winding La Honda road. He perched it on top of the ridge that overlooked the ocean on the west side and the valley surrounding the distant southern arm of San Francisco Bay on the east. He had bought an acre of property there that was so slanted that it stood almost on its end; the top of the ridge overlooking grassy fields toward the Pacific, eight miles west, and the Bay side covered with a stand of magnificent redwoods. On top of two mammoth stumps, he had somehow managed to prop Lathrop's chicken coop, which he converted into a rustic cabin. One of the windows faced the ocean, while the land pitched down beneath the cabin at a breath-taking angle to the La Honda road, about thirty feet below, a setting worthy of the most soaring *träume* of *Tristan and Isolde.*

Duffus tells us that Veblen had the cabin set up for light cooking, keeping a few staples up there. The winding dirt road, which ran far below, was not much used. Duffus wrote: "Sometimes he would saddle Beauty, or hitch her to the cart, and jog off. I suppose that was where he went. . . The shack would have been a beautiful spot for two persons, man and woman, who loved each other and wished to be alone." Duffus reasoned that, if Veblen had wanted to get closer to nature, he could have done so on his own fourteen acres. "I do not believe he went up to the hills to worship God, for his universe contained no God. I do not believe that he went up to see chipmunks or the deer, . . . or to study birds."[31]

He may have gone up there to worship Babe.

As part of the Cedro property, the chicken coop rightfully belonged to Mrs. Stanford's brother, Ariel Lathrop, and Veblen had already had a run-in with his landlord. Veblen seemed to take an impish delight in playing "Squirrel Nutkin" with Lathrop. Duffus recounts the story of a shaky suspension bridge over San Francisquito Creek near Cedro. Lathrop had indicated he was worried about its soundness. Veblen sometimes used it to get to the campus, riding Beauty, as it saved him "a mile or two." Veblen reported that Lathrop came out, looked at the bridge, and found hoof prints all around the area. Lathrop believed that a horseback rider had definitely been using it. This was a risky practice, he said, sternly, and ought to be prohibited. "I said I thought so, too," Veblen remarked. Duffus wrote: "[In telling the story, Veblen] looked . . . at us and beamed. I thought, for a moment, he was going to laugh out loud."[32]

In the second February of the year and a half that Thorstein spent at San Ysidro (1908), Babe was evidently cornered by "Mr. Veblen's friends" and urged to leave Berkeley and go home to Chicago. The grounds were that she was endangering his academic position. This we discover from Ellen, who had settled in Carmel, and who kept closely in touch with Alice Millis.

> You know Mrs. Bevans claimed to be going back to Chicago? I do not know whether she really went. It was about the middle of February [1908] . . . Mr. Veblen's friends thought she ought to go. She wept. She did not give him to understand it was ended, but a retreat. How I wish I could look in his real mind. But nobody ever will. Whatever she has done, it had no significance for me. Yet I realize that the horizon is bluer and clearer with her away.[33]

Babe's transcript at the University of California at Berkeley shows that although she was enrolled in five courses in economics, and one in physiology, in the spring semester, 1908, she received no grades at all. Presumably she went home to Chicago. Or did she?

Duffus wrote about a parade he saw in March 1908, in San Francisco, and then waxed poetic about spring at Stanford and San Ysidro, saying that when spring came you could not do a thing: "You didn't give a damn. You wanted it to stay *now,* the present moment, forever. You half believed it would . . . [You] lived in a kind of golden bubble, with Cedro Cottage at the center."[34]

His mental picture of the Veblen of those days was of a benign, non-parental deity, wandering about in a bucolic paradise, inspecting the farm animals, looking at the stars, and reveling in every minor detail of life at Cedro. "I see him *quick and lithe, not touched as yet by any physical frailty . . . Perhaps it was at this time that he had more inclination than before to go into the hills* [author emphasis] . . . I think the rattle of the buggy wheels or the clomp of the hooves had a soothing effect upon him."[35]

Maybe it was the idea of Babe waiting for him at the cabin on the ridge that had the soothing effect on him and his quick and lithe demeanor. Babe, with her sharpshooter expertise, could have augmented the larder with wild game to supplement the staples and water Veblen brought up from below. (He had never succeeded in bringing in a well on the property.)

At the end of the school year, Veblen asked the three students staying with him to help him knock down the globe-trotting chicken coop and haul it with a wagon and a team of horses down the precipitous and winding road to Cedro. Duffus saw the cabin before it was dismantled and found it to be extremely comfortable, masculine, plain, and matter-of-fact in decor.

Duffus and the other students felt a great sadness over Veblen's decision to stop leasing Cedro. Such a beautiful place—one wonders why he gave it up. In early spring 1907, Ellen, angry about the letters Thorstein was receiving from Babe, left Cedro for Palo Alto—a way station to Carmel-by-the-Sea, California. Around the same time (probably shortly after Ellen's departure), Veblen asked the Stanford Board of Trustees to lease the bungalow to him for a term of ten years.[36] He must have been as taken with Cedro as Duffus and the child, Evelyn Wells, were. The Trustees turned him down, hewing to their usual year-to-year renewal policy. The next spring Ellen, not satisfied with the omnipresence of her spies, decided to build a watchtower of her own at his gates. In March, April, and May of 1908, she supervised the building of an arty, board and batten, two-story redwood shanty, with a movable skylight roof in one of the upstairs bedrooms.[37]

Ellen's friend, Alice, wrote that Ellen got a carpenter from the Monterey Peninsula and proceeded to build this house on Sandhill Road (very near to Cedro, where Veblen was still living with the Duffus boys), "on a lot which I *think* she bought before she left Mr. Veblen . . . At best it was questionable taste."[38] In another letter Mrs. Millis comments that Ellen's choice of site "was much remarked on." The two would meet "by chance, but spoke but little. The situation, as you can imagine, was most extraordinary."[39]

Ellen did much of her own construction work on the shack. A working-class socialist acquaintance said:

> As I remember Mrs. Veblen she was a sad, unhappy queer. Could not be idle. Built at least three shacks that we knew of, doing all the work with her own hands—building fireplace and chimney using sand [?] and old bricks that she gathered—mixing her mortar within an old tub or barrel. My husband, being a bricklayer, loved to make fun of her. She always posed as being very poor, but Prof. Veblen told us she was well-provided-for, which we knew afterwards to be true.
>
> We befriended her in a few little ways. She could always sleep here. When she came late, and didn't want to disturb us, she would go in [the] barn and sleep in the hay.[40]

Another of Ellen's Palo Alto friends said:

> She was simply like no one we had ever known, a somewhat pathetic figure—very thin, even emaciated, and at times so exhausted she had scarcely enough strength to make her voice heard across the room . . .
>
> She came to see us once, when [her] skin was nearly all worn off her fingers because she had been building a fireplace, and she had mixed the cement [probably lime mortar] . . . with her bare hands. One of the amazing things about her was these building feats, though she looked, and was, so weak.[41]

The property was extensive, so Veblen could have ridden out the back way without Mrs. Veblen's knowing. Perhaps he did. Nonetheless, having a new "gatehouse," with a gatehousekeeper installed—and constantly on the alert for any signs of Babe—must have been distasteful to him.

17

A Dossier of Positive Statements

If Babe stayed on during the summer, she and Thorstein may have lived in a
tent. He had long before borrowed a tent from a former student (and later a
colleague) at Chicago, Herbert J. Davenport, who was now head of the
Economics Department at the University of Missouri.[1] At the end of the spring
term, 1908, the Cedro livestock had been sold and most of the household accou-
trements given to Ellen. Thorstein, however, who told the students he was going
away, had deposited with a certain local resident a mattress, springs, pillows,
pillowcases, sheets, three laying chickens, a broom, and a dustpan—useful if the
tent was on a platform—to the mystification of Duffus (who was, one suspects,
kept in the dark because he had proven to be a confidant of Ellen).[2] There were
people on the ridge who kept cows and sold milk in that era, so altogether living
up there was not impossible.[3]

Babe, an impulsive, wild spirit, had seen what this loveless marriage was
doing to her idol. Feeling that Thorstein was too gentlemanly to make the
necessary demarche, she conceived the idea that an appeal to reason should
correct an obviously illogical situation. The summer before, while still in Chicago, she had decided to write to Ellen directly. Ellen was, after all, a "New
Thoughter" and a devoted socialist, so she should be able to see the logic of
Babe's position. Ellen would have to admit that her "marriage" was no marriage at all—that Thorstein was, in many respects, woefully deprived. But Ellen
was more guarded than avant-garde. Ellen and her friend Mrs. Millis pored over
Babe's missives and decided that Babe was a cruel, inhuman viper, and was
probably half-crazy to boot.

In June and part of July of 1907, Ellen received daily letters from Babe begging her to give Thorstein up, according to Mrs. Millis. Babe's position was that she and Thorstein were divinely intended for each other, and that if she could help him and encourage him, he would be able to produce even greater works of genius than before. Babe's letters were lengthy, but all harped on the same theme; they urged Ellen to be unselfish enough to release her husband for the greater good of humanity.

Mrs. Millis was extremely fond of Ellen, often praising her to biographer Dorfman—referring to Ellen's sparkling wit and her clipped speech that bore evidence of generations of good breeding.

Ellen's martyr stance, which had been so effective when she played the traitor with President Harper, worked its magic with Mrs. Millis. Ellen's friend could not comprehend any logic or sincerity in Babe's position. She attributed it to an "egotism . . . so colossal and . . . selfishness so unashamed that I was not surprised when she [Babe] became insane in later years. She was already abnormal."[4]

Unfortunately, these letters, meant by Babe to free Thorstein from a marriage in name only, probably were later employed by the Stanford powers to indict Veblen of being unfit to teach at any college or university.

Mrs. Millis had no chance to hear Thorstein's side of the story. In a letter to Dorfman, decades later, she stated that she had been so indignant with Veblen's failure to appreciate his wife that she distanced herself from him and could write very little about him.

Subsequently Ellen followed Mrs. Millis's suggestion to throw most of the letters into her Carmel-by-the-sea fireplace unopened.

In September, 1907, Ellen had something of a religious seizure on the way down to the seaside resort where she had bought a small cottage. She reported to loyal Mrs. Millis that she was "happy, hopeful, anticipatory. I respect life, I am young, I have no fear." As an afterthought she added that this read "perhaps too much like Walt Whitman." She had decided that "materialism is a dreary thing, and the soul demands that it be but half the truth." She continued, "You are aghast, I can see, [but] it seems like the plain beautiful truth about life . . . it doesn't seem like religion, but like a rolling back of the curtain that separates mortality from immortality."[5]

Carmel-by-the-Sea, California, would have been an inspired choice for discussions about mortality and immortality. The village, set up by real estate developers only four or five years earlier, nestled in a grove of pines on the edge of sometimes sparkling blue water crested by white-capped waves. With its wooden sidewalks and a gully down the middle of dusty Ocean Avenue, which, in the rainy season, became a stream bed, it was a very rudimentary version of the Carmel of today. A beautiful trail led from Carmel over the hill to Monterey, and a one-horse wagon doubled as a mail carrier and a stage, making three-hour round trips daily to the latter city. The developers hoped "to attract writers and artists, musicians and college professors," and gave away a few lots free to select artistes. At "least twenty professors [also] maintained summer homes—professors who refused to consort with the Bohemians."[6] S.S. Van Dine, who stayed in the village briefly, reported, "The plumber of Carmel has subscribed to the Harvard Classics, the butcher reads Robert Browning, and the liveryman wears long hair."[7]

Van Dine divided the writers and artists into two distinct categories: The "respectables," who drank mint punch, Scotch highballs, and Riesling, "entertained, and kept Japanese houseboys, and the 'eminently respectables,' who did not drink, went to bed early, and worked hard . . . sunsets and homely virtues for them."[8] He claimed that it was "impossible to be a genius without a necktie that looks like a fat woman's sash"; and that there was a great deal of hair in Carmel—more per capita than any town in America. (Robert Louis Stevenson, Robinson Jeffers, Upton Sinclair, Sinclair Lewis, Lincoln Steffens, Stephen Vincent Benet, and an intermittent Jack London were among the geniuses who were nourished by Carmel.)

How eminently did Ellen fit into Carmel respectability? Apparently pretty well. She proudly informed Alice Millis that her children's book was selling, and that new acquaintances were delighted to welcome her as a real-life author.[9]

Religious ecstasy did not last long for Ellen in 1907. After a brief fling with Christian Science, she stated, "Belief is not for me, has not been for a second. I shall always know . . . that it should be a most blessed thing if . . . an almighty love pervades the universe . . . but I am persistently an evolutionist . . . I am without God and without hope."[10]

In another letter she said, "My poor beloved must suffer. He cannot suffer much. He was made to live in the sun and have no responsibility for anything, and so I must suffer, too."[11] She evidently felt that if she waited long enough, Thorstein might come back. In a letter to another friend, she remarked, "The ocean sends up a long flat wave and then gathers it wearily back with a long drawn sigh tonight, as much as to say, 'Patience, pa—tience.'"[12]

When Thorstein and Ellen had been living together as man and wife, she had written of existing "in poverty, working as I never had before, and denying myself everything."[13] Now, living separated from Thorstein, she harped on the same theme, but at the same time invested sporadically in real estate. In a letter to Lucia Tower she said she was very near to

> sad penury. It is very unscientific to be poor nowadays, and if you are, you are to lie about it . . . I have been at Carmel since July first, have bought a tiny cottage (my father having left me a little insurance, for he, my *dear* father, left us a year ago) and though it is not paid for, I built [another] little cottage in Palo Alto, because I believe there will be something in that, and I desire to carry on the adventure of further living by myself, if possible. In between paying for both places I am kept on rice, so to speak. I may rent this this summer and go up to Palo Alto where friends wish me to be . . .
>
> I look about here and see [Carmel] is a town for (grass) widows [i.e.,

divorcees], perish the name. Most of them have what I lack [money?] but it seems to make no difference in results. Their men are "happily wedded" to "another."[14]

About the same time, Ellen wrote Alice Millis, "Incidentally, I have bought the two corner lots next to mine here from Mrs. Ehrman . . . my purchases since I left Cedro foot up $4,100, sales $2,350. Debt on hand when the two are evened up, $500 or $600." She postulates that her motives for this activity are a result of her "ancestors—or the active idea."[15]

After Christmas, in early 1908, Ellen had written Alice:

> How I hated to leave my fireplace last night, with all the memories gathered near, of childhood, of my dear father, of my sisters and one brother, of my friends, some of the dearest of whom have gone before—where I sometimes long, long to go. My nervous energy is so small. I am so unfit. But the fire and the day and the memories had to go, and with them that sweet feeling of youth . . . [She was fifty years of age.]
>
> I can imagine how unreal and uncanny it must seem to you to be ordering my husband's viands. I am glad that *she* is not ensconced . . . I dreamed, seemingly all last night, of a green-haired and extremely young damsel who had taken my husband's affections. I cut off the hair and bore it about with me in a prodigiously heavy but fascinating beard. She went shaven but conquering.[16]

In the spring she wrote more about philosophy and religion. "I felt all these problems solved when Thorstein loved me and I loved him. There was nothing to it, of course—neither the solution nor the love, but it did the work."[17]

She referred to Mrs. Bevans as "cheap" and "a horrid thing," and she said a friend wondered how a scholarly person (like Thorstein) could care for Babe. Rumors were flying. On March 14, she reported that a friend had learned that Mrs. Bevans had almost rented a cottage in Carmel for the previous Christmas vacation. This would have been bad enough, but Ellen suspected that Thorstein might have planned to visit her there. The friend had dissuaded Babe, warning her that "as she had driven me out of my home and I had taken refuge [in Carmel], she had better leave it to me. Such preposterous horror!"[18]

In a letter to Lucia Tower, Ellen called Mrs. Bevans "a craving nothingness," said Babe had a mother who is "probably proud of the conquest," and a "dreadful sister who would cure anybody of that family." She wrote that Mrs. Bevans had stayed at Berkeley through two terms "until her mother got tired of taking care of her children." She continued: "After this term is out I have no hope but that Mr. Veblen will go to Mrs. Bevans, practically for good. And I call upon stars and angels to prevent! It is not for one to bear . . . I have never seen a better example of the new monster—the female that demands a variety of fathers for her young."[19]

As no stars or angels appeared to help her out, on May 10, 1909, Ellen took the calculated step of writing to President Jordan. Vaguely and elliptically, she referred to her fears and suspicions concerning Veblen's present and previous high crimes and misdemeanors at Stanford and Chicago. On May 11, she received this cautious answer from President Jordan:

Dear Madam:

Permit me to acknowledge your kind letter of May 10th. You will understand that the matter referred to is extremely delicate and difficult in its relation to the University. We know nothing of the facts in question, except certain vague rumors which have reached us from Chicago and from Palo Alto. While on the one hand the University would not for a moment retain in its faculty a person known to be of immoral character, yet on the other hand we must hold everyone innocent until shown to be guilty, and it is quite impossible for the University to undertake investigations without data. If it is necessary for us to know the facts, it is necessary at the same time that we should know them in some other than a general way. I do not know to what statements you refer as "statements made from official sources both here and in Chicago," as neither myself nor the president of the University of Chicago possesses any information on the subject at all, except such as has come from rumors, and we know of no one except yourself who is in a position to indicate what these rumors signify.

You will understand, therefore, why we should give very careful attention to any positive statements, and why we cannot do anything with generalities.

Very truly yours,
David Starr Jordan[20]

Thus encouraged, Ellen began assembling her dossier of "positive statements." After which, she put out feelers toward Thorstein, offering to return to him "on certain conditions." This was to stave off a divorce suit he was preparing, which he was likely to win on the grounds of her extended desertions.

Thorstein was not at all enthusiastic about Ellen's proposal that they be reunited (see the following letter), so she again appealed to President Jordan on June 13, 1909:

Dear Sir:

In view of Mr. Veblen's probable action for desertion, I wrote him recently offering to go back to him on certain conditions. Yesterday, I received the following letter from him:

Dear Madam:

I have your letter of a week ago proposing to return to me. In view of your actions during the past two years, and more

*particularly during the past few weeks, I am unable to believe
that this proposition is made in good faith. I shall not act on it.*

*Sincerely yours,
T.B. Veblen*

*I am anxious to know what knowledge he has of "my action of the
last few weeks," which can only refer to my letter to you. I wrote for the
purpose of suggesting that your knowledge of Mr. Veblen should be
acquired at first hand. I should have been sorry at this particular time to
put him on his guard. He is not a man to testify against himself. If he
has been interviewed in regard to my letter I should be glad to know it,
or whether he has obtained his information in some other way. I have
been and shall be completely handicapped by lack of means. It will be
two years on the 27th of this month since I left home, and I believe that
Mr. Veblen will then attempt "to make the worse appear the better
reason," perhaps with success. In earlier instances I would have permitted this, but the limit has been exceeded. May I see you if you are in
Carmel this week?*

*Very truly,
Ellen R. Veblen*[21]

Perhaps it was at this point that Ellen informed President Jordan that "the wife
of one of Thorstein's friends" (the wife of Tom Bevans?) had been taking graduate work at the University of California the previous year, "until the time when
her husband should get a divorce from her, and Dr. Veblen should become
divorced from his own wife."[22]

This was to be the opening salvo in Ellen's scorched-earth campaign to force
Veblen to return to her.

18

His Last Few Days
of Honor and Competence

In the early fall of 1909, Babe was back with her children in Chicago. (According to Becky, somehow, before this time, her mother had been able to obtain a divorce.[1]) Babe was preparing to take the girls, now eight and six, on the train west. The destination was a log house called "Nowhere," near Grangeville in the mountains of Northern Idaho. It belonged to well-to-do, eccentric, elderly Grandma Bevans, who was no doubt pleased to have someone in the family use it. Squatters were always a danger to an unoccupied house.[2] In Idaho, Babe would be closer to Thorstein and California, but the possibilities of contact, with the indirect train connections, would be remote.[3]

To amuse themselves on the journey, the children cut paper dolls out of a catalogue and made them sail out the train window and into another window farther along. They played with some children who, when they woke up on the train the next day, were broken out with measles. Babe became anxious to get her daughters settled in Grandma Bevans's log house before one of them came down with the disease.

There did, indeed, prove to be a squatter family occupying Nowhere with a large brood of children. Babe moved in nonetheless, establishing a beachhead in the attic, while she dealt efficiently with the squatters. Since Babe warned them about the incipient measles epidemic, they moved out very fast.

Babe "chopped off fir boughs for mattresses," and when the children broke out in rashes and developed fevers, chopped wood for the kitchen cook stove and the heating stove and made gruel for the patients. Also, she had to learn a new skill—milking a cow twice a day. If she wanted groceries, she left the children with neighbors, saddled the palomino mustang, and rode off several miles to Grangeville on horseback, coming back with big, heavy sacks of flour and oatmeal.

But even here there were pitfalls. The mustang "invariably filled his belly with air," so that the saddle slipped sideways and ended up upside down. As soon as the children's measles faded, Becky developed a frighteningly severe case of poison oak and was sicker than she had been previously. Rattlesnakes abounded, one even slithered on the steps leading up to the house. Soon Babe would not bother to shoot any that had less than eight or ten rattles, as she already had a sufficient collection of those. She instructed the children on the contemporary, but now discredited, snake bite procedure: Cut a cross on their flesh with their pocket knives; suck the venom; and use potassium permanganate, which they carried about in little bottles.

Babe had not asked for alimony or child support. She was trying hard to live up to the socialist credo "that a woman is a human being thoroughly capable of refusing any chivalry or concessions offered by men."[4] Circumstances, however, seemed determined to thwart her. When she went for provisions, leaving the children with a kindly grandpa whose grandchildren had often played with hers, he molested Becky. Afterward Babe warned him that if he ever approached their house again, she would shoot him.

In another unsavory incident, several drunken settlers roistered over so-called Rattlesnake Hill one night, one shouting, "The widder woman lives down there—come on—let's go." With raucous yells and laughter they approached the cabin. When Babe found her trusty gun and fired a single shot, a man was heard to yelp, "Right through your hat!" The noisy group changed its collective mind immediately, and scattered in the opposite direction.[5]

The weather got colder. It snowed. Babe found the cow-milking routine so pestiferous that she cut off five or six inches of the cow's switching tail. A hobo came by, and she allowed him to chop firewood and milk the cow in exchange for home-cooked meals. The understanding was, he was to sleep on the porch and keep strictly to the kitchen. (Hoboes should never be turned away without food, she told the children. He might be Big Bill Haywood. Jack London was also once a hobo.)

Veblen had meanwhile moved from Cedro to the Stanford campus in the fall of 1908, taking a room in a professor's house on Alvarado Street.[6] The following spring he applied for a leave of absence for the academic year of 1909–1910—hopefully for two semesters, but at least for one. He was ambitious to study early civilizations in Europe (specifically in Scandinavia) as a background for his "Economic Factors in Civilization" course. This would also get him away from the scrutinizing gaze of Ellen and might allow for a reunion with Babe. President Jordan originally wrote a letter to the Board of Trustees recommending the leave of absence, but withdrew it after submitting it. Ellen had intervened in the meantime.

Mitchell hoped that the Norway trip would work out for his old professor, writing Sarah Gregory (March 30, 1909) that the stimulus of investigating Scandinavian archeology, sagas, and the modern life of the peasantry, with which subjects he was familiar, would be good for him and at the same time oblige him to write about his findings in quite a different way. He would not be able to assume that his readers were as cognizant of the basic facts as he—an assumption which was something of an irritation to Mitchell. This was a continuation of Mitchell's concern that Veblen's work had become too speculative.[7]

On July 1, 1909, Ellen had written her friend Lucia that upon her arrival in Palo Alto she had found "nothing from Mr. V." She had "really expected a [divorce] summons." She added angrily, "in view of all that is rife about me, I shall consider bringing suit myself—against somebody! . . . Nothing of interest in the mail. No more stories accepted or returned. Please don't say anything to my discredit in Carmel—not until things are settled. I know from Mrs. Lawson's late remarks that she has got ahold of the dress complaint. Heretofore she has spoken [in] reproachful wonder about the elegant things she conceived me to possess. She is awfully dangerous, and spreads things so far—being acquainted everywhere." Why was this dangerous? Might it ruin the facade of "sad penury"? Ellen admitted that, when they came to Palo Alto, she really did stock up on clothes to some extent. She added, however, "The public cannot know all the ins and outs of my clothes!"

Then she wailed, "Oh, Lucia—what it has been for me to drop out of everything—and then be so basely 'poor'! Nothing from Mr. V. for over a year . . . I am informed that my claim in Oregon is worth $4,000 cash, and if Mr. V. would only sign [the quit claim deed], I could have a little comfort. All that timber is being bought up now."[8]

In the fall, Ellen's extended agonizing with President Jordan reached crisis stage. On September 9, 1909, David Starr Jordan wrote to Ellen. In his letter, addressed to the Sanitarium El Reposo in Sierra Madre, where she supposedly repaired for "water on the knee," he asked her, "Could you give me the address of Mr. 'Beavens' to whom you referred the other day?"[9] On September 10, 1909, he wrote again:

Dear Mrs. Veblen,

Permit me to acknowledge your kind letter of September 7, with its enclosures [Letters from Babe? Copies of Thorstein's letters to Ellen about Sarah Hardy? Details of Lucia Tower's reports of Laura Triggs's late night visits to Veblen's rooms?] I appreciate most highly your confidence in this matter, and I shall try to do the right thing. I want to express again the deep sympathy I have with you in your most trying circumstances.[10]

This was followed by Jordan's letter to Mrs. Veblen of September 20, 1909, which ran as follows:

Dear Mrs. Veblen,

Professor Bok tells me that Mrs. Bevans left Berkeley something over a year ago. May I ask you if you would regard a letter written by yourself in reference to Mrs. T. [Mrs. Triggs?] as open to inspection of our Advisory Board?[11]

On September 25, 1909, President Jordan wrote again to Mrs. Veblen:

Permit me to acknowledge your kind letter of September 24, with its clear and direct statement of essential facts. I wish to do what is just and right in this matter, toward the University, and toward all concerned. At the same time, I do not see how any advantage accrues to anybody from work, no matter how well done, carried on under false pretences; that is, with the concealment of essential facts.

I am sorry to hear of your continued illness.[12]

On October 6, 1909, President Jordan wrote President Judson of the University of Chicago:

I have been able, with the help of Mrs. Veblen, to find out the truth in detail as to Professor Veblen's relations. He seems unable to resist the *femme mécomprise*. It is fair to say that on my final talk with him, he carried himself in manly fashion, with no attempt at denial or evasion. He has tendered his resignation to take effect at my discretion. This will probably mean with July of next year, for the University cannot condone these matters, much as its officials may feel compassion for the individual.[13]

On October 7, Jordan informed the Board of Trustees that he had received Dr. Veblen's letter of resignation to take effect on July 31, 1910.[14] On October 8 it appears that Veblen was still asking for his leave of absence for the remainder of the year, for Jordan wrote him:

In regard to the matter of leave of absence, it seems to me that before I make formal application, it would be well to consider the matter in all its phases as to whether you really desire it. The main point at issue seems to be that to make this request would involve a somewhat extended explanation of the reason for asking it.[15]

Veblen, nevertheless, wanted his leave of absence, and on October 11, 1909, Veblen wrote Jordan, and hinted at, but avoided dealing with, the full ramifications of Ellen's complex personality.

My dear President Jordan:

As regards the matter of leave of absence, which you are kind enough to refer to me, I shall be glad to be granted such leave for the second semester. I regret the necessity of an explanation that cannot but be distasteful to you as well as to me; but I have particular use for the leisure which such a leave will give me, especially as I shall not have the advantage of a connection with a university after this year . . .

I beg to add a word in reply to your earlier note of the sixth, with which I have hesitated about troubling you. I wish to express my appreciation of the cordial regard you have shown me under trying circumstances, and to thank you for your expressed wish to be of service to me, as well as for the kindly interest you have taken in Mrs. Veblen. Her case is fully as pitiful as you say, but it is more perplexing than you probably appreciate; and I am unfortunately more helpless in it than you think probable. In reply to your suggestion, I have no inclination to "stand on the letter of the bond," beyond what may be required to avoid invalidating the articles of separation, the annulment of which, I am persuaded, would promptly be turned to her own detriment as well as to mine. She has declared her intention, some time past, to make an example of me and bring me to extremities, at any cost to herself, and has pursued that end consistently. I do not doubt that she has taken this course with a good conscience, and it is in some way to be reconciled with her continued devotion, which I believe you have not overstated. But it results that any more from my side is of no effect, or at least of no good effect.

After some hesitation, I avoided speaking of this the other day in the official conference with you, as it could scarcely have official significance; and I speak of it now because it is necessary to an appreciation of the existing condition. I very much regret what seems to me the necessity of troubling you with such matters as these.

Yours very truly,
T.B. Veblen[16]

On October 11, 1909, Jordan wrote Ellen Veblen:

Professor Veblen has tendered his resignation, to take effect at the discretion of the President. This probably means at the end of the year, unless something new should arise. Meanwhile, I have been trying—perhaps with doubtful success—to exert a certain influence in his future career. I may again express my appreciation for your own services in behalf of truth and justice, for nothing can succeed which is running on the basis of deception.[17]

On October 12, 1909, President Jordan wrote to Veblen, acknowledging Veblen's letter of the eleventh and saying that he would make application to the Board "in your behalf for leave of absence for the second semester." Jordan added:

As to the other matter, it is not possible for me to judge. I do not believe that any career can be made successful which involves any degree of concealment of important matters. I believe that your wife has done right in placing the information in her possession in my hands. She is living in Spartan severity, and I am sure that a little unexpected help might be good for her, but that is not for me to say.[18]

On October 15, 1909, President Jordan wrote Veblen again:

I received yesterday (it coming in my absence) a telegram reading as follows: (directed to me)—
  Grangeville, Idaho, October 14.
  Coming to see you. Arrive Frisco Monday morning.

  (Signed) A.F. Bevans.[19]

At this high point in the drama the screen goes blank. There is no subsequent mention of this startling telegram in any of the files at Stanford. Was Veblen able to reach A.F. Bevans (i.e., Babe) with a telegram to Nowhere in time to stop her? Not very likely. Did he intercept her in Oakland at the train depot, on Monday, October 18, before she took the ferry to San Francisco? Even though she thought she could help him, the cause was already lost, and he would have had to explain to her, diplomatically, that her presence on campus could only damage his position further.

On October 16, Jordan sent a copy of Veblen's murky letter of October 11 to the Board of Trustees, asking that it be placed in Veblen's files. (Veblen's letter equaled in opacity the conversation of Aunt Celine, in Proust's *Swann's Way,* who bent so far over backward to be "well-bred" and "delicate" that she considered it uncouth to do more than barely hint at what she wanted to say.[20]) Unfortunately, Jordan read between no lines and only commented that the letter made clear the cause of the associate professor's resignation—solely his domestic situation.

Mitchell wrote Veblen proffering help. Veblen responded, probably sometime in mid-October:

Dear Mitchell,

You are kind enough beyond habit in offering to help me out of a mess, but I have not known how to answer you, and so have let the matter hang. I don't know now, and am writing to say so. It goes without saying that I don't like the present arrangement, and I have no degree of delicacy about letting you undertake an extremely distasteful job in trying to get me out of it. Nor have I any particular hesitancy about airing my private affairs, but unfortunately that is not all of it. The names of some friends of mine who need not have been brought into the case ... would, in all probability, be brought in again if any such move were made as you suggest. These persons, who have no blame or responsibility in my domestic infelicitude, ought not to be punished for the misfortune of having befriended [me] [paper torn] ... to do is to see Mr.

Jordan and find out if it can be arranged that way, for it rests practically in his hands. I take it that you have heard from Mr. Loeb about this. The last question turns on the practicability of keeping these innocent parties out of the case.[21]

On October 21, 1909, Veblen wrote to Davenport, telling him stoically of the turn of events:

I have put off answering your letters, or rather the last of them, because things have been unsettled here, and I wanted to know before writing. I think I know now, and that there won't be any need of further explanation. I have resigned, on request, to take effect not later than the end of the school year. Also, I am fully persuaded that I could not get any kind of appointment at your place, nor indeed at any other university. So I thank you for all your kind efforts in my behalf, and regret that it should all be of no effect. I am sorry, but I have no doubt.

This state of things puts it up to me to tell you something of how it happened, and you will have to read with such patience as you command while I retail private matters that should otherwise have been let alone. As you are probably aware, Mrs. Veblen has, for some time past, had a grievance; or at least she has been in the habit of thinking so, which is just as good. Shortly after you were here, she broke off relations, though unknown to me she had, as it appears, been making preparations for it before we moved to the Cedro. She promised then, and later, to make an example of me, and put me out of the university. Presumably, in the spring, a legal separation, by agreement, not by divorce, was had. Since then she has been here most of the time, and has appeared poverty stricken in the extreme (she took what little property there was in hand when she left me). Nothing serious happened, however, and last spring she finally appealed to Jordan and others in authority by letter to have me inspected and passed on; which again brought no conclusive results. She appears meantime to have written the cabinet in Chicago (probably [Albion?] Small [head of the Sociology Department]), to help do me up, and also to Columbia [University?], perhaps also elsewhere. If she knew of the negotiations at Missouri she would probably have written to [President A. Ross] Hill also, which would explain his change of sentiment; though he could easily have got all the disparagement he wanted from Small or [Thomas Nixon?] Carver [a Harvard professor who had reviewed one of Veblen's books]. During the summer she appealed to Jordan personally, alleging many evil things, true and fancied, and finally got results. From fear of scandal he asked me to resign, which I have done.

In all of this I seem to have been speaking explanation of my own fault, but that is not the intention of it. What I have told is what seems to me to be as much of the facts as is indispensable to an understanding of the outcome; and it is not intended to convey blame or exculpation. Mrs. Veblen has no doubt acted with a good conscience; which is a guarantee that she would not let her purpose be defeated in the future. I understand that it has all been with an eye single (?) to my best good.

I trust you will not let all this disturb you, or lead you to blame anyone unduly, whether me or others, who has been concerned in all this. It is to be said for Jordan, too, that though his decision in the case is foolish, still he means well, he simply lacks backbone.[22]

On October 30, 1909, Jordan wrote Veblen that the Board of Trustees would prefer that the resignation take effect on December 19, 1909, but that the treasurer would pay him the balance of his salary for the year at that time.[23]

On November 3, 1909, Veblen wrote to Mitchell:

> There is nothing doing. The board acted on Jordan's recommendations the other day with the sole effect of advancing the date from the close of the school year to the close of the present semester.
>
> I hear that you are expected to be here at the time of the great game Saturday. I hope you can come on Friday, and stay over Sunday, and that I may see something of you. If you will come here to the house (22 Alvarado), I can arrange for your comfort, or rather for your survival, quite easily.[24]

On November 9, 1909, Veblen wrote again to Davenport:

> I am sorry I gave you the impression that I was trying to excuse myself, but I wanted you to know how complete the finish is, and to let you see that there is nothing doing.
>
> I have been speculating much on your invitation to come to Columbia to live. It is the kindest thing that has come my way for some considerable time, and I should like to do it, for many reasons. But I don't know yet what I can do, and it doesn't seem probable that I will even be able to take advantage of it. I don't know what my movements will be after next month when I leave here. I have very little household stuff, as I sold off or turned over to Mrs. Veblen most of what there was at the Cedro. So that I don't expect to ship anything much, and it would hardly be worthwhile to ship anything at all as far as Missouri. I regret to report also that I have no money on hand to speak [of], and what little there is is not available, I am afraid. Possibl[y] when I see my way out I may have a few hundred, and should be very glad to make a "building loan."[25]

On November 8, 1909, President Jordan wrote Ellen Veblen, at El Reposo, Sierra Madre, California.

> In response to your kind letter of November 5, permit me to say that we have accepted Dr. Veblen's resignation, to take effect on December 20th, and that the Board of Trustees will pay him the balance, $1,600.00, of his salary for the year. So far as we are concerned, of course, this is the end of the matter.
>
> I do not find in Dr. Veblen any willingness to take any responsibility for anything, and such suggestions as I made to him in relation to yourself seem to come to nothing. He ought by all means to share this amount with yourself, but I have no way of making it a condition.
>
> I feel the deepest sympathy with you in your distress, but find myself powerless to accomplish any results other than that of separating the University from all responsibility for his actions.[26]

Two days after this Veblen received a scathing letter from President Jordan, who was doing his best to change what he perceived as a very wrongheaded man's mishandling of his personal affairs.

In a desperate effort to free himself, Veblen had evidently presented Ellen with a "contract of separation," which she had signed, and which he had fondly believed would allow him to lead his own life without further criticism on her part. But he had not got around to paying certain sums due her during the past summer, possibly because of the fury he must have felt about Ellen's conferences with Jordan, and her letter writing of the spring of 1909.

On November 10, 1909, President Jordan wrote to Veblen again:

> I trust that you may pardon me for another suggestion in regard to your personal affairs.
>
> A student returning from Southern California says that Mrs. Veblen is still in bed with water on the knee, and that she is likely to be crippled for a long time, if not permanently. I understand that the interest on her properties and other receipts are adequate for her maintenance only when she is able to help herself.
>
> Mr. Charles tells me further that the contract of separation signed by Mrs. Veblen has no legal value, and that it may be abrogated at any time by either party. In effect, it would seem to be already abrogated by your act in withholding the sums due [her] this summer . . . If brought before a judge, a much larger monthly sum could be assigned.
>
> But irrespective of the law, and irrespective of all personal differences, this seems to me a case of *noblesse oblige*. Of course, I do not know what you may have done for Mrs. Veblen's relief, or what you intend to do. This I know, that you cannot blame her for the break in your academic relations. The facts would have come out sooner or later from other sources, and for these, and for the results that must inevitably follow, you alone are responsible.
>
> I beg your pardon for any impertinence this letter involves.[27]

Two days later, Veblen politely answered Jordan's "impertinent" letter, and one or two paragraphs have significance for this ongoing saga:

> In regard to Mrs. Veblen's circumstances, since you still interest yourself in them, she is not at present hampered for want of ready money, nor by any reluctance on my part to do what I can toward her relief. I may add that the like has been true at any time in the past, although I recognize the difficulty of believing that statement in view of the reports that have reached you.
>
> I thank you again for your kindly interest in Mrs. Veblen's welfare, and trust that you will not again be troubled with troubles such as dictated your very courteous suggestion of the other day.[28]

On December 8, 1909, Jordan wrote Ellen: "Permit me to acknowledge your kind letter of November 13th, which I find on my return from the East. There is nothing more which I can say to Mr. Veblen, and I must leave matters now to take their own course, whatever that may be."[29]

On December 15, 1909, Ellen wrote her friend Alice Millis with lugubrious solicitude:

> I think each day—this is one of my beloved's last few days of honor and competence—he is packing his books and does not know where to send them, is sad and troubled and sick. He has a numbness on one side, and heart very, very slow.[30]

(How she wishes he could see her doctor!)

By December 27, 1909, she sensed the full extent of her Pyrrhic victory, although she described it in terms of "evil days" that "came" without any participation on her part. She had been looking over letters sent by her friend Alice that summer, "before the evil days came." And then she wrote Mrs. Millis, thanking her for sending them:

> It was too good of you and my heart fails me to express what a dear gift it is—I want to cry—but tears are mine no more . . .
> How often I thought on Christmas day . . . of the last Christmas . . . if I could see you, maybe I wouldn't be fatally homesick as I am. My soul crieth out. Oh, the lost dreams, and life fading! I have aged so you wouldn't know me, ever since the ageing process of last summer. [She then speaks of the crutches she must use because of her water on the knee.] . . . I believe I look about 65.[31]

As for Thorstein—was he an arrogant male of the period, who withheld and concealed his assets in order to punish Ellen for her double treacheries? This does not square with our image of him as a profound thinker and exponent of the primary role women took in the development of civilization, and decrier of the subsidiary role allotted them in modern society. Ellen's conduct here does suggest that she was carrying on an elaborate charade to show that her husband was a money-pinching villain who should be punished, and, according to Dorfman, Veblen was "forced to turn over half his salary to his wife" in the final stages of the Stanford break.[32] If he had, however, been contributing substantially to her support all along, why was his response to Jordan stated in such a convoluted fashion?[33] But this much is clear—Veblen was as baffled by, and fearful of, mental instability as most of his contemporaries and felt powerless in the face of Ellen's eccentricities.

Even though Mrs. Millis was aware of Ellen's role in Thorstein's Stanford disaster, she still did not blame her, nor did she appreciate, as Duffus certainly did, the essential incompatibility of their two temperaments. In the 1930s she wrote Dorfman, who had evidently referred to the Veblens as "this curious couple," that she agreed with him that they were curious. But she still thought that they were "ideally" suited to each other. Besides being "impossibly eccentric," they were both "full of curious lore," had "encyclopedic knowledge," and were "alike in looks, in their entire unlikeness to anyone else."[34]

Babe had a distinctly different concept of how to suit Thorstein ideally. After they were married and Veblen was teaching at the University of Missouri, she "spoke [to a Mrs. Sabine] of the unkindness, the unfairness with which she felt he had been treated by persons and those representing institutions. Finally she spoke of his first wife as having treated him badly: 'I don't see how she could treat him so cruelly. I don't see how she could. Because he is simply the sweetest man to live with—the sweetest you could imagine.'"[35]

Mrs. Sabine was a student of Veblen's at the University of Missouri, and, although she knew that some people at Stanford were not in agreement, she was much impressed by the way in which this statement was "passionately and sincerely spoken, in a way that I could not forget."[36]

Veblen had found a champion. His career had been damaged severely in the process, but no one could gainsay that he had gained an agreeable, ready-made family and a fiercely devoted, spirited, and valiant wife.

19

The Station to Nowhere

The Christmas after Veblen was fired was the Christmas he almost lost his life. The plan was that he would take the train to Grangeville, Idaho, bringing along his horse Beauty. He would ride from the station to Nowhere, a few miles away.[1] Unfortunately, the winter snowfall is heavy in the brooding mountainous areas of Northern Idaho. On a high plateau, Grangeville is more than 3,000 feet and is now the gateway to a cluster of ski lifts. Veblen had been expected on Christmas eve, but may have got caught in a "Palouse"—an icy northwesterly gale that blows down from the Arctic. Becky noticed her mother pacing anxiously about the house that evening when Veblen did not arrive and heard her singing: "What is the meaning of the song that rings so clear and loud? Thou nightingale amid the copse, thou lark above the cloud?" and other melancholy ballads.

The falling snow had turned into a murderous blizzard, and when Thorstein finally arrived before dawn on Christmas morning, he collapsed on the doorstep and was hastily put to bed. The local medical man who was sent for was told that the visitor was Babe's brother—otherwise the doctor might have been scandalized. The diagnosis was double pneumonia, complicated by a very weak heart; the prognosis was that Veblen could not possibly live.

All preparations had been made for the most joyous Christmas possible under the dismal academic circumstances. Babe had scoured the woods for a tall and perfect tree and had come home with one that nearly reached the ceiling. The children had decorated it with home-made candles, popcorn, and cranberry strings. Thorstein had added to the excitement by shipping off an advance Christmas present for Babe of assorted chocolate creams in the upper tray of a trunk, and for the children, shoes and moccasins of graduated sizes, good for years to come, in the bottom depths of it.

Veblen had reacted to his Stanford ouster with characteristic reserve. A colleague, Professor Guido Marx, wrote: "I for one never knew that Veblen was to be 'fired' until he announced it as an accomplished fact. I doubt that anyone else on the faculty did, either. I did know some folks were trying to make trouble for him on account of his domestic affairs, but not through him. Remember, he never talked about personal matters."[2]

Veblen had written Jacques Loeb, a former colleague at the University of Chicago: "It is like you to stand by your friends, but your assurance of sympathy and confidence under the circumstances is double welcome to me. I seem to have few friends here."[3]

Veblen had been disappointed in Jordan's reaction to Ellen's onslaught on his character, even though he had never really explained the situation to Stanford's president. Becky wrote: "Veblen expected more understanding and backup from Jordan, [and] didn't forgive him."[4]

On November 14, 1909, Allyn Young wrote of the incident to Herbert G. Davenport at the University of Missouri:

> About a month ago I renewed my efforts to get Veblen promoted to a professorship. President Jordan replied that since my last previous conversation with him about the matter he had secured information about Veblen's domestic affairs of such a nature as to make the promotion impossible. I naturally told Veblen the precise situation. He went to the President, made no attempt to defend himself, and was asked to give in his resignation, to take effect at the pleasure of the President. The result is that Veblen has to go at the end of the semester . . . President Jordan, it seems had talked with Mrs. Veblen, and has taken her statements [the word "ravings" had been crossed out] at face value. I know nothing about the facts in the case. Some of Mrs. Veblen's friends have talked to me, but I have no knowledge of anything that is to Veblen's discredit. Although I may be mistaken, I am inclined to *think* that Veblen has been the victim of a gross piece of injustice. In fact only two things have kept me from handing in my own resignation. One of these is my dependence on my salary for the support of my family, and the other is the conviction that there may be a change of administration at Stanford within a few years.[5]

A year and a half later, Allyn Young did resign from Stanford, saying that the situation was "intolerable in many ways" (essentially what it was when Veblen was fired) and that Millis also was anxious to leave.[6]

Unquestionably, Thorstein's discouragement over his academic future made it hard for him to fight off his pneumonia, but Babe was determined that her idol would survive. She sent her children away, first to neighbors, then to relatives, rolled up her sleeves, and used every method known to homeopathic and conventional nursing.

First she tried mustard plasters, which did not work. Then she ironed his back, which helped, but burned off the skin. Becky said that calomel and steeped lemon were prescribed by the doctor, but permanently ruined and loosened his teeth. "They were never good again."[7]

During the Civil War doctors began dosing the wounded and ailing with emetics. The cure was worse than the disease. One wonders how any already enfeebled patient survived being fed a poisonous mercury compound, considered a cure-all for "fevers, bronchitis, dysentery, pneumonia, hepatitis, inflammations, and laryngitis."[8] This "wonder drug" had been used to induce vomiting since the sixteenth century. "The theory was that the less material in the body, the less chance for disease to feed on it." In very sick patients it was given in huge or "heroic doses . . . Accepted practice was to dose up to the point of salivation, one of the early signs of mercury poisoning. At this point patients customarily experienced very sore gums and lost their teeth, their hair and their voices. Often they could barely swallow, and their tongues swelled to four or five times their normal size and protruded. They extruded a poisonous mucus discharge from their mouths."[9] Those few who recovered from these gargantuan doses had the aftermath effects of "trembling, anxiety, weakness, rheumatic-like pains, chills, restlessness [and] delirium." Ex-patients could not expect to make it through to old age, and their complaints might worsen as they went along. People fulminated against this form of treatment, but their protests were dismissed by the medical establishment. The use of calomel during Thorstein's siege of pneumonia would explain his persistent debility for years after he had recovered from the disease.[10] If it was actually also used earlier, when he had malaria, that would go far to explain Thorstein's later extreme distrust of doctors.

Babe tried everything she could, and kept trying. She had had some nurse's training, and the doctor finally admitted that she had "saved his life by her splendid nursing"—although at great cost to herself. By the time Veblen recovered from the pneumonia–calomel episode, she seemed ten or twenty years older, according to Becky. Later Becky amended this to insist that her mother looked "some forty years older." Babe was like "a ravaged soldier," and Thorstein reminded her of a "living skeleton." He was still in bed, but at last allowed to sit up. Poor, frantic Babe had been so busy "stirring brews, steeping lemons, making gruels and 'rømmegrøt' [a Norwegian mush for invalids]," that she had difficulty in finding the hours required for keeping the fires going, chopping wood, milking the cow, and riding into town on horseback for supplies. Thus she had to send the children away to stay with her brother, and remain alone in the house with Veblen.[11] Becky wrote, "This was a great scandal, although [Thorstein] was so sick nothing intimate could happen."[12]

Babe, henceforth, became a "worn-out woman" in Becky's eyes, never regaining her full youthful beauty, and, judging from photographs taken of him during this period, Thorstein was "all skin and bones."[13]

Nevertheless, Thorstein and Babe had moments of enjoyment during his convalescence. They read Lady Augusta Gregory's plays, Henrik Ibsen, William Butler Yeats, George Bernard Shaw, Henry W. Bates's *The Naturalist on the Amazon,* "some of Babe's socialistic stuff and the Austrian geneticist Gregor Mendel," and so on. Thorstein also dictated to Babe a few thoughts on *The Instinct of Workmanship.*[14] He took over the milking, as well. (Babe, no doubt, gave thanks.)

Thorstein remained a devotee of Yeats's poetry all his life. He was particularly fond of "The Song of Wandering Aengus," which told of a wanderer who caught a "little silver trout" that turned into a "glimmering girl, with apple blossom in her hair." The girl fled, but although the man was already "old from wandering," he determined to follow her, to "kiss her lips and take her hand," and pluck forever "these silver apples of the moon" and "golden apples of the sun."[15]

As soon as he could travel, Thorstein left for Stanford. He was not exactly "old with wandering," not yet. He was only a very frail 53. His current papers and research were still in Palo Alto, and despite his poor health, he had the daunting task of finding some way of earning a living.

He had already applied for positions at various colleges, among them the University of Toronto, which had turned him down. The University of Missouri position was still a question mark. However, there seemed to be the possibility of getting a research grant from some powerful foundation, such as the Carnegie Institution. These wealthy institutions backed various anthropological expeditions, and so Thorstein had set himself, in the fall of 1909, to writing an anthropological-like essay, "The Mutation Theory, the Blond Race and the Aryan Culture," later split into two parts and published as "The Mutation Theory and the Blond Race" and "The Blond Race and the Aryan Culture."[16]

Thus, more than twenty years before the Nazis became obsessed with the supposed superiority of the dolicho-blond type, Veblen was looking into the slippery concept of racial characteristics, emphasizing that irrespective of Darwinian survival concepts, or Mendelian mutation theories, much of what is considered to be physically determined by race is really a consequence of cultural stereotyping.[17]

He finished these essays before he took off for Idaho and after he came back prepared a memorandum, "As to a Proposed Inquiry into Baltic and Cretan Antiquities," appending his essay on the mutation theory. President Jordan backed his application with a letter of recommendation to Carnegie overflowing with such fulsome praise that one wonders if some sense of guilt was not haunting him.

Allyn Young was even more complimentary, calling Veblen "the most gifted man whom I have ever known," while Frank H. Taussig, a Harvard economist, stated that a colleague had once remarked that "Veblen came as near to being a genius as any economist we have; and I am inclined to think the remark was just."[18]

Davenport joined the chorus and let Carnegie know that the University of Missouri was, and had been for some time, eager to have Professor Veblen teach his famous course, "The Economic Factors of Civilization." Warren Gregory added his support. Mitchell wrote that, in half a century, Veblen would be "recognized as the most important figure among economists of this generation." (How wrong he was! Devoted Veblenites are still waiting for that burst of recognition.)

Carnegie did not come through, even though Thorstein's nephew Oswald intervened on his behalf with Woodrow Wilson, who was a trustee. So Veblen accepted the job offer at the University of Missouri that resulted from the efforts of his former student and colleague at the University of Chicago, Herbert J. Davenport, who thus became his boss.[19] He was to start teaching at Missouri in February 1911.

By July 1910, Babe and the children had left Nowhere and had sailed from Portland or Seattle to San Francisco on a creaky ocean steamship. From San Francisco, on July 14, 1910, Becky sent a postcard to her little cousin Rollin Atwood, in Chicago.

Later they made their way to a small, suitable cottage by Pescadero creek, which Veblen had picked out. It was a short horseback ride away from Veblen's property on the crest of the Coast Range, near La Honda road. In Pescadero the Bevanses stayed the winter and spring. It is probable that Thorstein erected a new cabin on top of the mammoth redwood stumps with the "help" of Becky and Ann.

Babe was giving a French lesson every week or two. What she and the children lived on has never been explained. Tom Bevans did not offer support. Perhaps her parents sent her money, or, more probably, Veblen himself underwrote their expenses. "Veblen always found it hard to turn down a friend who needed help," said his stepdaughter. "[He] was inclined to let new clothes or non-essentials go, if a friend was in real need."[20] And these friends certainly were. Possibly Babe was doing work for Veblen all along, copying manuscripts by hand and proofreading, as Becky remembered her doing later, in typescript, when they lived in Kansas.

On August 3, 1910, Veblen wrote Mitchell from Palo Alto that he had received a telegram a week late and had also been hindered from seeing somebody he wanted to get in touch with. He wrote: "The explanation for all this is very simple. You may remember my expressing a hope that I might write something about the Instinct. I arranged to go to work, and directly the hoodoo which rests on that topic became operative. Domestic circumstances, interesting enough in their way, but unprofitable, are all there is time for."[21]

What were the interesting domestic circumstances? Had Ellen come back to Palo Alto temporarily? Were the circumstances of the sort that Mrs. Schütze in Chicago reported when she said that "she [Ellen?] would not let him work?"[22] Was it at this point, too, that Ellen told her husband that "she would get him fired from any place [where] he was working"?[23] Perhaps she was aware that Mrs. Bevans and her children had also come back to California and were living nearby in Pescadero and that the unblessed alliance was continuing.

Winter came; before Christmas, Veblen left for Columbia, Missouri. He and Davenport had always been good friends. Davenport had written him during his last spring at Stanford, "As soon as you fix up something like a definite schedule for summer, let me know what you are going to do. Maybe if we weren't too poor we could get to Alaska together. [Or], if we couldn't do that, we could get into the park somewhere and smoke. Fraternally always . . ."[24]

Now Davenport offered him room and board in his own house. Davenport had married a middle-aged widow from Wisconsin, who had been a very competent teacher and was still teaching an extension course at college level. Veblen was given a magnificent room with a pleasant view. Technically, it was a basement room, because the house was built on a steep hillside; it was a floor below the main entrance, but quite large (fourteen by thirty feet), and airy.

> Perched on the top of a steep slope [Davenport's house, and also Veblen's room] . . . overlooked, from the rear, a wild, wooded 'draw' which stretched southward in the direction of the Missouri River . . . It was a place well suited to a man in need of rest.[25]

Veblen did not stay holed up in the basement, however. According to reports, he was no hermit, but came upstairs and joined discussions—never, himself, saying very much.[26] He also often rambled in the wooded dale below. Except in the coldest weather, he slept outside in a tent erected on a wooden platform. His room had a special door which led to his tent.[27]

Davenport's wife was a great farm-style cook, and Veblen and the Davenports' student helper, Stuart Updegraff, fell into the habit of sneaking around at midnight and raiding her larder of "a piece of mince pie, or some good home-baked sinkers." According to the student helper, she did not mind. She made dozens of mince pies weekly, and they "aged properly in rows and stacks in her pie locker." In fact, she was said to get a great deal of enjoyment out of the men's fondness for her plain Wisconsin fare.[28]

Veblen needed the Davenports' nurturing atmosphere, because he was still far from well. When classes began in February, he and Davenport donned long woolen underwear and walked the mile and a quarter, through heavy snow or blizzards, to the campus. But when Veblen actually reached his classroom, he did not take off his overcoat or rubbers—he felt entirely too chilly.

"There shall ever remain in my mind," said one student, "the impression of a little [?], quiet, soft-spoken man, who presided in a poorly heated classroom, rubbers on his shoes, clad in a warm overcoat and muffler, with a hat on, and hands sunk in the pockets of the great coat, a dozen or so young chaps hanging on each word."[29] Veblen told the students they, too, could keep their overcoats on if they wished.[30]

Veblen was skinny and emaciated, another student reported. He looked as if he were just hanging on. His skin was etched with wrinkles, the pallor of his face was corpse-like, and this was only accentuated by a dark wool muffler wound securely around his neck.[31]

Despite this, Veblen was unquestionably the lion of the campus. The History Department sent their best students and graduates to Veblen's classes—he was considered a better historian than any member of the History Department.[32] A sociology professor told his class that Missouri University had one of the greatest scholars in the United States, and that if he could write a book like *The Theory of the Leisure Class,* he would ask nothing more from life.[33] The students were well aware of Veblen's status. One spoke for them all when she said, "I regarded him with undergraduate awe."[34] Devoted followers William Camp and Leon Ardzrooni from Stanford continued to take graduate work with him here. Ardzrooni also insisted on tagging after him to the Davenports' house in the afternoons, to join him in argumentation and joint wood chopping. Ardzrooni's face grew redder and redder as he shouted louder and louder, but Veblen refused more than an occasional laconic comment.

Head of the department Davenport paints a magical picture of the spell Veblen wove over those who were sympathetic toward him. He admitted that his friend Thorstein was

> not a good teacher, or even a teacher at all in the ordinary sense of the word, lacking all classroom techniques, devices, or strategies.
>
> But his lectures were always in charming literary style and grace—clear, precise and delicately worded. It was admirable book work, although always conversational in manner and never reduced to manuscript. The saving fact was his bubbling wit—that was always drawled out, with all the rest. His students followed him in complete absorption—watching him like the intellectual magician that he was.
>
> I recall that I was once looking through the window of the heavy oak door to his classroom. Not a word was audible to me. You could not even see his lips move. The students sat like mummy figures out of the sleeping palace. But every few minutes all would be shaking in restrained laughter. And still the thing droned on; and the fly in the pane still buzzed—as I surmised—hearing not even that.[35]

20

Miss Havisham Takes the Stand

At the beginning of May 1911, Babe took the two girls and made her way from Pescadero to Berkeley to talk to Mitchell. Mitchell wanted to warn Babe a second time not to jeopardize Veblen's chances of getting back into academia. They talked, "standing by a counter in one of the big university buildings." Mitchell was "debonair and polite."

"Babe was looking worried," according to Becky. "I guess she [was supposed to] promise him that she would not be seeing Toyse again 'til he was divorced."[1]

Thorstein and Babe had been very careful in the fall of 1910. Although not many miles apart, officially they maintained separate residences. After he left for Missouri, Babe and the children must have been lonely. It was a record rainy season, and "they spent lots of time looking out the window."[2] Babe, Becky, and Ann may have come up to Berkeley on their way to the Murphy cattle ranch near Ashland, Oregon, where they were later to meet Thorstein.

Mitchell wrote Mrs. Gregory about their meeting on May 2, 1911, telling her that the previous Wednesday he had received a call from Mrs. Bevans. They had set up an appointment to meet in California Hall. She and her two children had arrived, and Mitchell and Babe conversed for an hour or more, the gist of the conversation being that she had "disposed of" her Idaho property and had taken a small property "in the lovely district between the hills back of Palo Alto and the sea." Veblen had stayed there the previous summer, and his plans were to spend the approaching summer with her there after his lectures were over in June.

Veblen was to be reappointed the coming year at Missouri at a salary of $2,100, although Mitchell, and Veblen's devoted student Camp, were constantly

138

pressing for his reapplication to the Carnegie Institution. But Veblen "exhibit[ed] his characteristic reluctance to take energetic measures."

About Mrs. Bevans, Mitchell added, pungently, "She is just as full of high enthusiasms as you, but looks pitifully ill-kempt. Disregard for appearances seems to be one of her cardinal principles."

There is no description available of Babe's mode of dress for this interview, but we know she did not approve of an Idaho neighbor, "Fancy Fanny," who "dressed like a lady." Babe told the children: "Ladies and gentlemen were parasites. They didn't do any useful work."[3]

Clearly, fastidious Mitchell and the elegant Mrs. Gregory did not hold to the same philosophy. One gets the feeling they did not totally go along with Veblen's involvement with Babe, and, perhaps in a misguided effort to convince them that she was rapidly losing interest in Thorstein, Babe added this saucy sally—faithfully reported by Mitchell to Mrs. Gregory:

> Her chief woe is that she has no intelligent neighbors [in Pescadero] with whom to discuss Socialism, except one charming boy with whom she fears she may fall in love.[4]

In January 1911, Ellen Veblen had written her friend Lucia that she was living in a twelve-by-fourteen-foot hut with an earthen floor, which she had built herself. She wished she had put in a real floor, as with all this rain the tamped earth wasn't working out. She had rented out one of her properties (she lived on her rents), but her Carmel cottage was vacant.[5] She had also partially finished a cabin in the hills behind Palo Alto that past summer (which could have been perilously close to the La Honda and Pescadero retreats). However, because they had been having such a dreadful downpour, she suspected it might have been ruined. She continued:

> Mr. Veblen is in Columbia, Missouri. He once more wishes me to get a divorce. The situation is so complicated that I don't know which way to turn.[6]

It is hard to see why it was so complicated. Was it because Ellen was still stubbornly convinced that if she held out long enough, Thorstein would come back to her?

The close proximity of Ellen's new summer cabin may have made Babe and Thorstein uncomfortable. Perhaps that explains their decision to go to the Murphy cattle ranch in southern Oregon instead. Or, Babe may have been trying to mislead Mitchell about spending the summer in Pescadero, thinking that word might somehow get back to Ellen, and hoping to throw her off the track about their real whereabouts. Becky speaks of this Oregon sojourn as starting in the spring. Thorstein must have joined them in June, after his term was over, bringing with him a tent.[7]

He pitched it near a creek where the four of them were surrounded by "huge basaltic boulders covered with moss and lichen, wild flowers and grasses." They got their milk from the farm. "Babe cooked rice and dried prunes and apricots over a sort of bonfire on flat rocks." The children amused themselves by chasing jackrabbits and riding bareback. They munched on apples and Swedish hardtack, cut their hair short, and dressed in overalls like boys. Thorstein taught them how to chew on wheat tassels in lieu of chewing gum. Although some of the Oregon farmers' wives protested because of their lack of dresses, Babe felt they would be freer that way, arguing that it was a democracy, and "girls were just as good as boys."[8]

"In the summer [the little troupe] packed up the tent and went with the ranchers to the mountains—an endless wagon trip." Fifty years before the decade of the hippies, Thorstein and Babe and the children were living the hippie life— the only one they could afford.[9] But Thorstein was also somehow working intermittently on *The Instinct of Workmanship*—difficult under the circumstances. He finished Chapter 5 in Buck's Prairie, Oregon, the summer of 1911, according to his own notations.[10]

In the fall Thorstein was back teaching at Missouri, while Babe was in Chicago with her parents studying stenography. Learning to type would help her find a job and thus become independent, and, besides, she could type Thorstein's manuscripts. Times were hard, though—there were no jobs to be had in Chicago. In early 1912 she took the children to New York, hoping to get help from ex-husband Tom Bevans. Tom was now involved with a certain Marjorie Hood—eighteen years old, beautiful, pregnant with Tom's child, and with money in her background. "Marjorie liked to go to parks and restaurants, . . . had a flair for . . . clothes, [and] wore them well, unlike Babe's homemade dresses [which were] tailored suffragette-style."[11] Marjorie and Tom had recently married and rented a small apartment. Babe found a cheap room nearby. Jobs were just as scarce in New York as Chicago; Babe tried hard but couldn't find one.

The day came when she and her daughters had only $5 left. Babe invested it in basic foods. She instructed her children to take six olives, one tablespoon of peanut butter, and a ship's biscuit, three times a day, plus all the water they wanted to drink. Becky found this thrilling and romantic; it reminded her of Joseph Conrad's stories. At the end of the month, Babe persuaded her ex-husband to let his girls sleep on his sofa (unfortunately occupied by adults until all hours) and stay in his apartment while she job-hunted. After being treated to a dinner one night at Child's, the children threw up. "Tommy couldn't stand that"; they definitely had to go. Tom's brother, Homer, who played the flute with the New York Symphony, cried, and Babe cried, but Tom was adamant.[12]

Desperate, Babe pleaded with the wife of a Unitarian minister to take care of Becky and Ann. Mrs. Murphy and her husband were fervent philanthropists, who currently sheltered a dozen stranded children, plus a French nursing mother with nowhere to turn. There, the girls would at least get food and a place to sleep, while Babe continued to look for work.

On January 12, 1912, Ellen Veblen, dressed like Dickens's Miss Havisham, took the stand in her divorce action against Thorstein. Her extended absences had made her vulnerable to charges of desertion. After 1903 she had never stayed with Thorstein more than six months at a time. Thorstein could have divorced her on those grounds, so she was finally forced to bow to the inevitable, and consent to sue him for non-support.

The San Jose attorney, Owen Richardson, who represented Thorstein, reported:

> Originally, "the action proposed" reflected rather seriously upon Dr. Veblen's relations with other women, but [I] objected that it would seriously impair his standing and prospects for university work. Eventually a mild complaint, charging mental cruelty resulting from indifference and neglect, was prepared and case heard in Redwood City, decree entered in what was really an ex parte hearing. Mrs. Veblen appeared on the witness stand clad in a quaint white silk dress; she told me after the hearing that she wanted to be divorced in her wedding garment. She seemed to be somewhat affected mentally; inclined, [I] should surmise, from a very short contact with her, toward melancholia.[13]

Ellen's complaint alleged that Thorstein was presently employed at a salary of $3,000 a year (as he had been at Stanford) and could afford to pay her $50 a month alimony.[14] But Ellen's private conferences with the heads of two universities had reduced her husband's market value to the approximately $2,000 a year he was receiving at Missouri, where he was not employed on a permanent basis, but only as a lecturer whose contract was renewable annually.

Ellen wrote her friend Lucia: "After months of parlaying back and forth, I was finally divorced in fifteen minutes and before three men only, on charges of non support!!! ... What a horrible rupture divorce is! Incredible! ... Mr. Veblen, [though] his part of the bargain is to furnish me with $25 a month, probably will not do it."[15] She does not mention that, in an earlier letter to Mrs. Gregory, she had stated that she would accept no money from Veblen under any circumstances.[16]

Thorstein, who had to wait so many years to be freed, commented, laconically, that the process was "purgatory."[17]

Under the terms of California law at this time, Thorstein could not remarry until a full year had elapsed after the entry of the interlocutory decree. However, he waited for a year and a third after that. Babe presumably continued to look for work in New York, but when the first summer came, rushed off to join Thorstein in Taos, New Mexico. They were camping there in a tent—his health was still not good—when Babe was forced to return in haste to New York. The philanthropic Mrs. Murphy had been in a carriage accident and was paralyzed and bedridden; Mrs. Murphy's newborn infant had died in eleven-year-old Becky's arms as a result of the same accident; Becky had contracted a severe case of whooping cough and had blacked out and fallen over the banister; and some unsupervised servants had been looking after the "orphans," who seemed to be existing on a diet of bread and pea soup.

Nine-year-old Ann subsequently blamed her mother severely for their aban-
donment, but Becky, who was more pliable and conforming (and at the same
time more imaginative), took it all in her stride. She had always felt sure that
Babe would return for them eventually, meanwhile, she looked upon their vicis-
situdes as high adventure. While they dined upon pea soup she used to chant
hypnotically, "Now we're eating Mama's roast chicken. Now we're eating
Mama's cream pie," referring to her grandmother Bradley's cooking. The other
children went right along with this play acting.

Babe rescued the girls, taking them back to convalesce with their grandparents. After school was out in 1913, she and Thorstein returned to Chicago to
retrieve them. The four of them spent the summer vacation camping in a remote
retreat (the Mancos Valley, near Mesa Verde), in southwest Colorado. Becky
looked upon that bucolic interval as one of the highlights of her life. Funds were
short, so the ever-resourceful Babe lugged along a 100-pound sack of peanuts for
protein. Sometimes she shot a rabbit to supplement their diet of pinto beans,
peanuts, clabber, vegetables, eggs, and milk.

With two kittens in tow, an abandoned greyhound puppy named "Brutus,"
and a borrowed donkey, "Nellie," who woke them up mornings with a big hee
haw, they slept close to their animals in a vacant workers' shack, then subsequently in someone's empty adobe house, which they were forced to treat for
bedbugs. Babe cooked, and the children scoured the dishes with rushes in a
nearby stream. Thorstein searched for Indian artifacts, made bows and arrows,
and showed the girls how to shoot.

Despite being ravaged by the effects of his illness, Veblen retained his attractiveness to women while at Missouri. According to Stuart Updegraff, Miss Allie
Radford, the sister of novelist Maude Radford Warren—a schoolteacher and not
in her first youth—visited the Davenport household and showed an interest in
Veblen.

Maude and her good friend Mrs. Davenport tried matchmaking behind the
scenes, and Miss Allie was agreeable and made popovers with Veblen—but that
was as far as it went.

Moreover, Mrs. Warren evidently became convinced that Veblen was already
committed to another woman. In answer to a letter from Joseph Dorfman, she
later wrote, "I feel rather sure that Mr. Veblen, after his divorce, if he married at
all meant to marry no one but Mrs. Bevans. She had saved his life once, he said,
when he had double pneumonia, and he always remembered that."[18]

When the fall of 1913 came, and Thorstein returned to teaching, the couple
arranged matters so they would be about 300 miles apart, with direct connections
by train. Babe and the girls had moved to Lindsborg, Kansas, where Ann and
Becky attended fifth and sixth grades.[19] Lindsborg, a pretty town with tree-lined
streets, had been settled mostly by people of Swedish descent. If Thorstein came
from Columbia, Missouri (the tracks of the Missouri, Kansas, and Texas Railroad ran in the gully right next to Davenport's property), and changed at Kansas

City, he could be in Topeka in about four hours. Babe could leave Lindsborg and be in Topeka in two or three hours. Weekends together in Topeka or Kansas City were thus possible. Babe typed all Thorstein's manuscripts; Becky proofread them.

A Missouri student of Veblen's, Matthew Paxton, once met his professor in the old Union Station in Kansas City, where he was changing trains. This may have been a weekend when Veblen was meeting Babe. (In order to get to Topeka from Columbia, passengers had to change trains.) Paxton wrote: "He seemed to remember me, or was polite about it. I spoke of a passage in one of his books, which had always intrigued me, to the effect that football bears the same relation to physical culture as a bullfight does to agriculture. 'One must say something,' [he responded debonairly], and shrugged his shoulders amiably."[20]

In early 1914 Veblen was ousted from the Davenports' comfortable abode by the arrival of a second Davenport offspring, and his hosts' need to use Veblen's quarters for a live-in nursemaid. He then took up residence with Walter W. Stewart, assistant professor of economics, for the rest of the term.[21] Veblen had long been working on *The Instinct of Workmanship*. Chapters 6 and 7 were written in Mancos Valley, and the remainder in Missouri in the fall of 1913. The book was published in 1914.[22] It incorporated a summary of all the different approaches he had used in his "Economic Factors in Civilization," a course he never taught the same way twice.[23]

The work differs from his earlier writing. Perhaps Veblen wanted to make it clear that it was not "to be read for amusement." Soberly, he contrasted early cultures that encouraged craftsmanship and human ingenuity with the present-day pecuniary culture, in which there is a "disesteem of labor" and a respect for people who are able to persuade the populace to pay more for their products than they are really worth.

He felt that the two strongest drives in humanity were the aforesaid "instinct" of workmanship and the parental bent—an urge to protect and cherish the up-coming generation and to pass along to it whatever skills or knowledge one has acquired.

The parental bent inescapably points toward "motherhood, such as has made it in all men's apprehension the type of all kindly and unselfish tendance; at the same time this ubiquitous parental instinct tends constantly to place motherhood in the foreground in all that concerns the common good, in as much as all that is worth while, humanly speaking, has its beginning here."[24]

In the earliest peaceable savage societies, before the barbarian element takes over, Veblen theorizes:

> Matriarchy and maternal ownership [possibly exist] in these usages which antedate the institutions of ownership. [Also the evidence] runs to the effect that the primitive ritual of husbandry, chiefly of a magical character, is in the hands of the women . . . The deities, great and small, are prevailingly female.
> . . . The female deities have two main attributes or characteristics because

of which they come to hold their high place; they are goddesses of fertility in one way or another, and they are mothers of the people.[25]

Descent is also often counted from the female side.

Did Thorstein have some hesitation about permanently allying himself with Babe? Joseph Dorfman reports that one of Veblen's ex-students was convinced that Veblen wanted to be free of marital entanglements. This student worked out a scheme whereby the professor could sidestep them, but after all his trouble, Veblen balked and insisted "that he intended to be married immediately."[26]

If it was his poor health that had made Veblen hesitate, finally he must have felt well enough to take on the dangers of having a wildcat socialist divorcée for a wife. In early summer, 1914, he called Babe at her parents' house in Chicago and asked the very important question, "Are you still willing to marry me?"[27] Despite the fact that Papa Bradley was opposed to the projected alliance (he had put some sort of curse on his daughter if she disobeyed him), Babe excitedly gave her consent. "Yes, she was ready to marry him at any time!"[28]

According to Becky Veblen Meyers, at this moment Babe's brother-in-law, Walter W. Atwood, an ultra-conservative professor of physio-geography at the University of Chicago, came in and overheard the news. Being "one-hundred percent pious [his father had been a minister], and one hundred percent patriotic, and a hundred percent plutocratic," he was very much against any activity that involved Thorstein Veblen.[29] Atwood "did not want a maverick economist associated with his family. He tried to stop her phone call." Babe must have already hung up the phone when thirteen-year-old Becky "heard loud voices [and] silently approached to see him bash Babe on the side of the head with a rifle butt." Babe fell, and "lay on the floor, hands protecting her head."

Becky wrote: "My uncle Wallace used to tell us Indian stories and Eskimo stories. He was good that way, even if he didn't like Toyse. I had always worshipped Wallace before the time when he bashed her head with his gun. I just saw Babe on the floor, trying to protect her head and Wallace standing over her with his rifle and [my Aunt] Harriet, [Babe's sister] saying [or more probably shrieking]: 'You cannot marry Professor Veblen.'" Harriet's conservatism may not have been to the right of her husband, but it was not markedly different.[30]

Becky was sworn to secrecy over this incident. Thorstein was not told. Nor was the Bradley family. Babe did not want to disrupt their affectionate closeness. But the blow was to have its influence on the rest of their lives in many ways.

Thorstein Veblen's birthplace, Cato, Manitowoc County, Wisconsin. *Courtesy of Carleton College Archives.*

Thomas Anderson Veblen, Thorstein Veblen's father, 1877. *Courtesy of Carleton College Archives.*

Kari Bunde Veblen, Thorstein Veblen's mother. *Courtesy of Carleton College Archives.*

Betsy, Marit, and Emily Veblen, c. 1864, before moving to Minnesota. Emily wrote: "And didn't we look fine in our new outfits, [including] hoopskirts, which I loved." *Courtesy of Norwegian Historical Society.*

Architectural rendering of roofed-over basement of the Veblen farmhouse, Nerstrand, Minnesota, where four adults, seven children and a baby spent the winter of 1866–67. *Courtesy of Carleton College Archives.*

Completed Thomas and Kari Veblen farmhouse at Nerstrand, Minnesota. *Courtesy of Carleton College Archives.*

Andrew Veblen, Thorstein's older brother, 1877. *Courtesy of Norwegian Historical Society.*

Emily, a minister's wife and the "smartest" of the Veblen children (according to her college professor) stoutly attacked Thorstein Veblen's detractors. *Courtesy of Carleton College Archives.*

Thomas Anderson Veblen, Thorstein Veblen's father, in his later years. *Courtesy of Carleton College Archives.*

Ellen Rolfe: "Thorstein asked me to marry him when he was eighteen and I was sixteen and I refused." *Courtesy of Carleton College Archives.*

Thorstein Veblen as a young professor ("Homely and unattractive as he is, it does seem that he appeals to some women," according to his brother John Edward Veblen). *Courtesy of Carleton College Archives.*

Ellen Rolfe Veblen. From the age of fourteen she had suffered from an ugly goiter, which she had concealed under high-collared Victorian dresses. *Courtesy of Carleton College Archives.*

Graduate student Sarah Hardy. "A vision of light and life and divine grace." *Courtesy of the Gregory family.*

Thorstein, Orson, Andrew, and John Edward Veblen, c. 1900? *Courtesy of Carleton College Archives.*

Laura McAdoo Triggs, rowing on Lake Placid, New York, c. 1900. *Courtesy of Brice Clagett.*

"Babe" (Ann Bradley), Thorstein Veblen's second wife, as a young girl. *Courtesy of Esther Baran.*

Babe, Becky, and little Ann, c. 1906. *Courtesy of Carleton College Archives.*

Painting of Babe Bradley Bevans by B.J.O. Nordfeldt in her Chicago Artist's Colony days, c. 1905. *Courtesy of Carleton College Archives.*

Thorstein Veblen's ridge cabin, successor to Ariel Lathrop's wandering chicken coop. *Courtesy of Carleton College Archives.*

Grandma Bevan's log cabin at "Nowhere" (Granville), Idaho, where Babe's nursing saved Thorstein Veblen's life. *Courtesy of Carleton College Archives.*

Babe at Nowhere, Idaho, 1909–1910. *Courtesy of Carleton College Archives.*

Thorstein Veblen with family and friends on Washington Island, Wisconsin—probably Hilda Veblen Sims, standing. *Courtesy of Carleton College Archives.*

Ellen Rolfe Veblen, in later years, probably in the 1920s. *Courtesy of Carleton College Archives.*

Thorstein Veblen on the steps of the cabin he built for his study facing Little Lake on Washington Island, Wisconsin, c. 1926. *Courtesy of Carleton College Archives.*

Oswald Veblen, Thorstein's nephew, developer of mathematical systems (e.g., Topology) used in nuclear physics. Professor, Princeton, 1905–1932, and the Institute for Advanced Study, Princeton, 1932–1950. *Courtesy of Carleton College Archives.*

21

Happily Ever After

T he two were married on June 17, 1914, by a Cook County Illinois circuit judge, and left immediately for Norway. They were still in Europe on their honeymoon when World War I broke out at the beginning of August. Babe was not following what Mitchell called her "cardinal principle" of "disregard for appearances" while traveling in Norway and Scotland. For once, she dressed in a fashionable manner and wore a beautiful hat. Declaring herself to be President Wilson's daughter—in a photograph taken at the time she looked stylish enough to be mistaken for that lady—she got them steamer passage home from England a lot sooner than would otherwise have been possible. She was no doubt being protective of Thorstein and his precarious health and worrying about what might happen to him and his job if they were marooned in Europe.[1]

Becky, in speaking of Babe and Thorstein's wedded relationship, said: "I would have said a perfect marriage . . . I mean they were just wonderful together."[2]

But there was something strange about Babe at this juncture. She was only thirty-seven years old, but was beginning to fall apart. To David Riesman, Becky wrote, "My mother had been a bright, strong woman and would have made my stepfather a perfect wife—but her health was broken by the time she married him."[3] In an interview, Becky also said, "She had worn herself out saving different people, including Veblen . . . She was a worn-out woman. So what he married the second time, was a worn-out woman with two little girls."[4]

A year earlier, Babe had started going into the menopause.[5] Since she wanted so much to have "a great man's children," this unusual turn of events in her thirties was devastating.

Her declining health did not at first seem to affect her marriage relationship. According to one of Veblen's Missouri students, Mrs. Winifred Sabine, "Mrs. Veblen (I refer, of course, to his second wife) was devoted to him, happy to type his books and help him in a secretarial way all she could. Their relations seemed very happy indeed. She believed so intensely in the value of his work that she would have done anything to be of service. Her personal feeling for him was equally passionate."[6]

Babe and the girls scrupulously avoided all behavior frowned upon in *The Theory of the Leisure Class.* She saw to it that their clothes were as plain and unadorned as Quaker garb. The girls used what Veblen wrote as their bible and talked in disapproving tones of the way their contemporaries dressed.[7]

They wore long dresses when the style was for short ones and clumpy hiking boots in place of normal shoes. Some of the university people felt this put the twelve- and fourteen-year-olds at a disadvantage. As a result "they became quiet as little mice," and, like their elders, suspicious of those who found it necessary to own an automobile and scornful of those who were amused by the early rinky-tink movies. (But, as Lewis Mumford wrote nine years later, "What sort of person would leave off a good talk for a movie— least of all a 1923 movie!")[8] Student Isador Lubin shanghaied Veblen into attending the highly touted and truly awful *The Birth of a Nation,* and Thorstein's perceptive comment was that it was "the finest example of concentrated misinformation" that he had ever seen. Veblen did not believe in the constant interruptions caused by the newfangled telephone either and felt that most letters would answer themselves if left on one's desk for six months.

According to Walter W. Stewart, and also according to Isador Lubin, Veblen jokingly called Columbia "a woodpecker hole of a town in a rotten stump called Missouri."[9] The girls took up repeating this phrase with many giggles and tauntingly called Missouri "Misery."[10]

On the other hand, Mitchell tells us that Veblen "finds much to like in Missouri, beside the Davenports. The faculty is actually trying to make the fraternity men work, and is discussing the advisability of stopping inter-collegiate athletics— seriously!" The only thing that bothered Veblen was the possibility that the Davenports might leave Missouri, as Cornell had been making vague offers to Davenport.[11]

Veblen's most devastating criticism of Columbia, Missouri, is widely known. It came later in *Absentee Ownership and Business Enterprise in Recent Times:*

> The country town of the great American farming region is the perfect flower of self-help and cupidity standardized on the American plan. Its name may be Spoon River or Gopher Prairie or it may be Emporia or Centralia or Columbia. The pattern is substantially the same, and is repeated several thousand times with a faithful perfection which argues that there is no help for it.[12]

Veblen observed that in the country town, you are caught up in a "scheme of salesmanship seven days a week."[13] Real estate is the major preoccupation and should be ranked with poker as a risky game of chance. The inflated values quoted by country town real estate operators are not to be believed.

The country town distractions did not interfere with his work, however. In 1914, Veblen was "writing furiously" on *Imperial Germany and the Industrial Revolution*, part of the time sitting up in bed, his semi-invalid status not much improved.[14] Other times, after breakfast, he would head up the stairs after addressing the resident cat with: "Well, kitty, it's time to go to work."

Veblen was very fond of cats. He once decided to teach one not to chase birds. Climbing up on a branch with a pea shooter, he would ping the cat in the rear whenever it started to pounce on a bird. "He'd ping it, and then it would always wonder why, and then the next time it did it, it would get another ping, and finally it decided it wasn't worth it," said Veblen's stepgranddaughter, Esther Baran.[15]

Babe was busy typing Thorstein's manuscripts and fixing meals for his favorite students—Ardzrooni frequently came over for supper, and also Max Handman (sociology), Stuart Updegraff, and Isador Lubin. Armenian honey cakes were provided by Ardzrooni, coffee, and kosher matzos were served, and "a lot of Norwegian or Norwegian-style viands of Mrs. Veblen's cooking. Veblen liked flatbrod, and dried goat's milk cheese, *primost,* I think it was called."[16]

Ardzrooni, who was Armenian, was known in the Veblen family as "the prince." A swarthy, barrel-chested little man, he surprised people by his ferocious comments about the need for social change.[17] He amused Veblen, and Ardzrooni's devotion to "the Master" was almost comic. On the other hand, he had a reputation among the women in the family as one who would bear watching.

He wanted much waiting on and requested many favors, according to Becky. For instance, when he had his appendix out, around 1915, he asked Thorstein to be present in the operating room to be sure everything was done correctly. "Veblen tried to stick it out, but when the doctors were sewing up, V. felt faint and to avoid distracting" them, staggered out into the hall, where he fell down, hitting his head on a pipe.[18] Ardzrooni luxuriously convalesced (for weeks in those days) at Veblen's house, and the children ran back and forth with glasses of orange and grape juice and other delicacies.

Outside of entertaining certain students, the Veblens kept to themselves, did not see other people, did not seem to need them. Many of the university staff did not even know he had a wife.[19] Lubin said there were few visitors at the Veblen residence except for curiosity seekers who "wanted to see what [the great man] looked like."[20] Veblen gave them short shrift.

A busybody, who was trying to find Veblen, made his way to his house and noticed somebody leaving. He asked this person if Veblen were at home. Veblen, who was actually the person who had come out of the house, laconically replied, "Well, he was there when I left."[21]

He also did not like politics and once ducked into the woods for an hour or two when another faculty member planned to shepherd him to the polls to vote for a certain local candidate.

Fellow colleague Jacob Warshaw tells us that Veblen's Missouri colleagues, even those who saw him every day at a dining club, were not any better acquainted with him than the general public. Perhaps a score of professors shared a commons with him for breakfast, lunch, and dinner for several years (probably before his remarriage). Warshaw doubted that more than six members knew him well enough to carry on a conversation. The same held true for a discussion club: "They were never able to break through his forbidding reserve."[22]

Nevertheless, Warshaw knew by personal experience that Veblen could be friendly and warm on occasion. When Veblen took his ease in his "loose dressing gown," he looked much more vigorous and energetic than in ordinary day clothes and, "with his drooping mustaches and Nordic features," reminded Warshaw of a Viking warming himself at his own hearth. Warshaw felt this was the best side of Veblen:

> . . . pouring out curious information, throwing off a little malicious gossip which in view of his seclusiveness, he must have picked miraculously out of the air, mixing picturesque slang with brilliant phrases of his own coinage, solicitously watching out for his guests' comfort and in general behaving like a 'regular guy.' An evening with him—when you were fortunate enough to get one—was as good as a French salon or an eighteenth century London Coffee house. When it was over you wished you had had a Boswellian memory and eye.[23]

Veblen did not like people to look over his shoulder while he was reading his newspaper. But this, Warshaw claimed, was probably because he could "read two columns of print simultaneously," and obviously no one could keep pace with him. Warshaw remembered Veblen's smile—he smiled often—and his laugh, "natural and infectuous," which he indulged in many times when they were out walking together "but never, it seems to me, in closed room or in a gathering of people."[24]

The second Mrs. Veblen was, according to a student, full of considerable charm, although "impatient, explosive and very doctrinaire." Babe leaned toward the idea of "violent destruction" and the sweeping away of the old in favor of the "rebuilding that could take place on a clear site."[25] Thorstein, supposedly, rather liked hearing his wife explode and give vent to her irritation, although his stepgranddaughter, Esther Baran, told us that Becky had remarked that the longer Babe lived with Thorstein, the less of a socialist she became.[26]

In 1911, Thorstein had been requested by the managing editor of Columbia University's *Political Science Quarterly* to review two books on socialism. He had answered, "The fact is that the books do not interest me. I take the liberty to add, though it may be of slight interest to you, that in my opinion socialism is a

dead issue. Too dead to be a live topic, and too lately dead for objective historical treatment."[27]

Veblen became known for his unusual prescience. A law professor acquaintance at the University of Missouri remembered having a conversation with him
in 1911 on a certain street corner in Columbia. Veblen prophesied that a Russian
Revolution was imminent and would result in the loss of more heads and blood
than the French Revolution in its most vengeful phase. Veblen also suspected
war would soon be breaking out in Europe.[28]

But that was not all he foresaw. He feared that if the peace after the first
World War were botched (which it was), there might be a second World War in
which Japan, nominally an ally with America in the first war, would join with
Germany, and that Germany and Japan would become war-mongering dynastic
states not unlike the Nazi and fascist states that Germany, Japan, and Italy later
actually became. This he spelled out in his twin books *Imperial Germany and the
Industrial Revolution* and *An Inquiry into the Nature of Peace and the Terms of
Its Perpetuation.* The first book came out in 1915 and the second in 1917.[29]

Veblen felt that even if Germany lost militarily, World War I would have set
back Western civilization in many ways, and he was not sure the setback would
be of short duration.[30]

The kind of peace settlement that was made would determine not only
whether we could look forward to a twenty-year armistice and then a renewal of
hostilities on a more terrible basis, but whether or not we would ever fulfill our
capabilities toward producing a truly bounteous society, which eliminated poverty and homelessness, and offered opportunities to all citizens. A "Pacific
League" (of Nations) must be formed and, in order to change the status-quo-ante,
the allies must reorganize their own societies to give the common man more of a
stake in the benefits of civilization. The alternatives to this would be deadly.

Germany was trumpeting the supposed racial magnificence of the German
people, who had built up a mighty industrial machine in a short period of time.
Veblen pointed out that the German racial stock was about the same as the
British. Also, the Germans had been successful in industrializing their country
quickly because they were able to borrow the set-up from the British, who had
originated it, and were able to install it without the hindrance of early mistakes
made by the originators of the technique.

Veblen had read General Frederick von Bernhardi's startling book, *Germany
and the Next War* (copyrighted in 1912, but published two years later), which
had, for its Chapter 1 subtitles, such horror-provoking gems as "The Right of
Conquest," "War a Moral Obligation," "Beneficent Results of War," "Destruc-
tiveness and Immorality of Peace Aspirations," and "Dangerous Results of Peace
Aspirations in Germany."[31] Veblen considered the book so menacing that he
devoted four or five class sessions to it in the fall of 1914.

He then amazed many of his acquaintances by doing an about-face from his
stance in *The Instinct of Workmanship* to the advocacy of American entry into

World War I. He jolted the many pacifists who expected him to side with them. Max Eastman wrote that his sister brought Veblen to a dinner—and, later, a meeting—held to oppose America's entry into the war. "Veblen looked like a Lapland papoose, and he sat at our table as mum as though made of wood." Although the company offered up *Imperial Germany, Instinct of Workmanship,* and the *Leisure Class,* he did not rise to the bait. Eastman thought he might draw him out with a comment on animism, but "he would hardly as much as grunt in response. We might as well have invited a donkey to dinner."

The eight intellectuals at table ended up having a spirited discussion among themselves. The dinner was half over, when Florence Deshon (Eastman's beautiful beloved) remarked that the roast was perhaps a bit overdone. Veblen perked up over that, and the two of them carried on an extensive tête-à-tête during the rest of the meal, comparing their tastes in food and like trivialities. After dinner, when more people came and the serious discussions commenced, Veblen mummed up again, obviously disbelieving in the necessity of singing for his supper.[32]

Veblen's analysis of what would happen to Western civilization if the bellicose dynastic states weren't squelched had already decided the issue for him.[33] Later, in an article, "Dementia Praecox" (1922), he reversed his position in light of the post-war peace debacle and wrote that pacifists and conscientious objectors had shown what amounted to "excessive sanity" in opposing our entrance into the first great war.[34]

Veblen had repeatedly argued that patriotism was one of the strongest forces promoting war and that its roots were in early barbarism—an anarchic trait that involves the "defeat and humiliation of some competitor." He "was far from optimistic that the beneficial possibilities of industrialism could be realized without the elimination of all vestiges of the patriotic spirit."[35] It was not a feeling of nationalistic chauvinism that was motivating Veblen, but a fear that Western civilization might disappear altogether, unless German barbarism was curbed.

Detestation of patriotism did not affect his partisan feelings for Norway, Isador Lubin noted: "When it came to Norway, he was as great a chauvinist as anybody I ever knew. When he talked about [that country] his face lit up. To the very end [he] spoke of Norway in the most glowing terms."[36]

In *Imperial Germany* there were delicious passages. For instance, Veblen, affecting a tone of great probity, discussed the ways in which Britain used its control of India to keep occupied the scions of its leisure class who otherwise would have nothing to do. "Sports have been a very substantial resource in this gradually maturing British scheme of conspicuous waste . . . It is quite beyond the reach of imagination that any adult male citizen would, of his own motion, go in for the elaborate futilities of British shooting or horse-racing, *e.g.,* or for such a *tour de force* of inanity as polo, or mountain climbing, or expeditions after big game," unless people's sense of proportion had been deadened by generations of such "infantile make-believe."[37]

In 1916, Veblen reworked and finished *The Higher Learning in America,* which he had substantially written just before he left Chicago. Veblen felt that the most important function of a university was to increase human knowledge through its "disinterested pursuit," by scholars indulging their "idle curiosity." This work could be sabotaged by business-oriented administrators (such as the now-deceased Harper, whom Veblen labeled a tool of the "captains of industry," masquerading as a "captain of erudition," who had headed what was, in effect, a "corporation of learning").

The Board of Trustees might as well be eliminated, as it was made up of merchant princes who were unsympathetic to true scholars, and who indulged in "bootless meddling" with academic processes. The university was, in Veblen's mind, made up of graduate students. Few undergraduates had any real interest in studying, anyway, and an "honorable discharge" with a college degree at the end of four years "has become a requisite of gentility."[38]

Missouri's President Hill admired the book and thought it ranked with Veblen's better works, but did not want it to be published, as originally planned, in the University Studies series put out by the University of Missouri.[39] (It might offend other educational leaders.) Ardzrooni called the writing entirely too caustic and told Veblen people would think him insane for publishing it. Jacob Warshaw objected to the overt phrase, "when they assassinated me," referring to events involving Veblen at the University of Chicago. (Veblen still felt that an assassination had taken place, but meekly took the phrase out and even acquiesced to other changes, telling his advisers that he had decided to have it published posthumously.[40] Actually it came out in 1918.)

In the hot Missouri summers Thorstein and family departed for Washington Island. He had originally summered there to escape hay fever when he was at Chicago.[41]

Mrs. Bjarnason, an inhabitant of the island, tells us that Veblen "saw, and fell in love with, a plot of land which lay between Green Bay and a small inland lake . . . where he could see the sunrise over the small lake and the sunset over Green Bay. [There] he wrote and studied in the utmost privacy."[42] He bought property there, and knocked together a couple of rustic cabins near the small lake, one for sleeping and eating, and one for his "study," which remained sacrosanct. Various relatives and friends often joined him.

It was quite a trip from Chicago. One had to take the Goodrich boat *Carolina,* leaving Chicago at 1 P.M., Tuesday, and arriving at the island at 5:30 P.M., Wednesday. As Veblen wrote Lubin: it was "an awkward arrangement, but the best there [was]."[43]

At table he sang songs and told jokes, and was always in very good spirits. For example, the story about 'enery and 'arriet. 'arriet had evidently died, and 'enery asked her spirit:

"Are you 'appy now, 'arriet?"
"Oh yes, 'enery, I'm 'appy."

"Are you 'appier than you was with me?"
"Oh yes, 'enery, I'm 'appier."
"Where are you now, 'arriet?"
"I'm in 'ell, 'enery."[44]

He also quoted from William Morris, "Dreamer of dreams, born out of my due time, Why should I strive to set the crooked straight?"[45] From Yeats, he spoke about "a land where even the old are fair, and even the wise are merry of tongue."[46]

Sometimes he came out with a bit of doggerel, such as:

"The wren can fly, why can't I?
"Isn't my business
As important as his is?"

He had a "merry twinkle when talking to children." Becky reported: "For instance, when his nephew, two-year old Allen Sims, was with us, Allen hadn't seen a beard before, and was tickled at the sight of Toyse's beard. He'd laugh gleefully, look at Toyse, and draw a finger down below his nose and sideways for a moustache. Toyse would imitate the gesture, and both would smile delightedly at each other."[47]

The truth was that Thorstein "was rather an eternal child emotionally. [He possessed] an inexhaustible hopefulness and eagerness, and, of course, a childish curiosity."[48]

But even on Washington Island there were busybodies. A Mrs. Cornell owned a boarding house there. After observing Veblen's way of dressing and living, she couldn't quite place him, financially, and so ventured to inquire, "Professors must make a lot of money, Mr. Veblen, how much money do you make?" Without pausing to take a breath, Veblen shot back, "It's hardly worth mentioning, Mrs. Cornell."[49]

In 1917, Stuart Updegraff, now a graduate back visiting on the Missouri campus, went home to lunch with Veblen at his invitation. The Veblens were currently renting the Davenport house, as Davenport had left for Cornell, where he had been made professor of economics. Meanwhile, Veblen had taken over Davenport's position as leading light of the Economics Department at Missouri. "It was the old familiar place, and the old familiar Thors, but he seemed happier there, sitting at his own fireside, dining with his own doting wife and little stedaughters to wait on him, hand and foot. He cracked funny jokes and kept little Becky and Ann in a gale of giggles all the time, at table."[50] To add to their contentment, and despite the fact that Babe had entered an early menopause and Thorstein was still under par, Babe became pregnant. But, unfortunately, she was taken ill at three to six months, and the miracle baby, a little boy, was born dead at seven months.[51] Thorstein was extremely sad. And, also, the baby's mother was told she "must not have any more children."[52]

Things changed abruptly for the worse. Babe was so distraught she considered killing herself. Thorstein found her with a revolver pressed against her breast. "What would your children think?" he asked, as he took the gun away.

Babe never recovered her health. From then on, Becky and Ann did most of the housework. Ann cooked, Becky cleaned. If Babe made dinner at Washington Island, she rested in a hammock afterward. She suffered perpetually from terrible headaches. Much of the time the girls went shopping there alone.

Nevertheless, Babe wrote Isador Lubin, in the summer of 1917, urging him to come to the Island, warning him that this was really camping, and telling him to bring warm clothes. She added, "In spite of all hardships, this is the best life I know of."[53]

The Veblen family still was managing to be happy on the island together, evidently, although Babe made her older daughter promise that if anything should happen to her—if somehow she could not go on physically—that she, Becky, would do her best to take care of Toyse.[54]

22

World War I Ends

R obert L. Duffus felt that Veblen made a mistake in the war years by
letting himself be drawn into "any program whatsoever," saying he
"was a Jeremiah, or a Voltaire, or a Swift, but not . . . a Lenin, or a
Marx. And certainly not a New Dealer or a Wilson Forward Looker."[1]

But by the end of 1917, Veblen began to feel rather isolated at the University
of Missouri. Davenport had left to teach economics at Cornell by the summer of
1916. Stewart had been offered a professorship at Amherst and departed at the
same time. Max Handman and Stuart Updegraff had moved on. Ardzrooni had
departed for Columbia University. Veblen's friend and esteemed ex-student,
Robert Hoxie (one of the most promising of all the young men whom he had
taught), had committed suicide in 1916. The year after that Lubin was Veblen's
only remaining assistant.[2] In fact, already in 1915, the exodus had begun. Stewart and Davenport had deliberately stayed on an extra year to absorb as much as
they could from the master.[3] And, ironically, Chicago had even offered Stewart
(not Veblen) a job, on the basis of his knowledge of Veblen's work.

Lubin left Missouri in January 1918 to join the Food Administration, and this
seemed to be the last straw. According to ex-student Updegraff, Thorstein felt
"abandoned and forlorn"; he had felt that way ever since the departure of his
good friends.[4] Veblen had been to New York and Washington the previous fall,
hoping to contribute to the framing of the peace proposals by the ad hoc committee set up by President Wilson. Allyn Young, Veblen's champion at Stanford,
was given an important position, that of head of the economic section, but
according to Lubin, "the group didn't want to have anything to do with

Veblen."[5] In his *Nature of Peace,* Veblen had become more forthright and insistent about his major premises. No longer did he envision that the machine process itself would cause changes to come about gradually, and magically, through habituation. Now it seemed necessary forcibly to eliminate the leisure class–absentee ownership scheme and to substitute the technological expert for the captain of finance. This was not a concept the peace planners even wanted to consider, no matter how carefully it was constructed in Veblen's book.

Veblen went back to Columbia, Missouri, with the idea of sticking it out alone. But a month after Lubin left, in January 1918, Veblen returned to Washington to tell him that he, too, was joining the Food Administration.[6] This he did, although he must have been aware of certain negotiations going on at Cornell University that might affect his immediate future.

Loyal Professor Davenport had been working behind the scenes to bring Veblen to Cornell. On March 9, 1918, according to the minutes of the Cornell Board of Trustees Executive Committee, Thorstein B. Veblen was to be appointed a "Professor of Economic Institutions, for the year 1918–1919, at a salary of $3,500," a large part of which was to be donated to the university by an unknown source. A committee composed of the president and the chairman was to work out the details.[7] Veblen was to teach "graduate students, one semester at Missouri, and Cornell the other."[8]

In a little more than a month, however, the Cornell negotiations fell through—most mysteriously. Missouri's President Hill thought it must be the public attacks on *Germany and the Industrial Revolution* that caused Cornell to change its mind. On April 13, 1918, the plan was abruptly, though quietly, dropped.[9] A few words from John Casper Branner, Stanford's second president (retired), were all it took.[10] Branner, a former Cornell student and classmate of David Starr Jordan,[11] had been asked for the usual recommendations by Professor Edwin H. Woodruff, on behalf of Cornell University's President Schurman. Branner backed into the subject as if he did not want to talk about it. In his letter of March 28, 1918, he complained that his Cornell friend had picked out a "mighty disagreeable subject for these disagreeable times," and then, in a general way, attacked people who recommended scholars only on the basis of their academic output and ignored their personalities. Branner lined himself up with those who completely misunderstood *Imperial Germany and the Industrial Revolution,* likening Veblen to the abhorred German historian and politician Treitschke, considered by some to be "the spiritual instigator of World War I." He wound up his letter on other topics.[12]

Later he warmed to the subject and wrote a second letter, embellishing his attack on Veblen. Apparently, Woodruff was worried that Veblen might be a publicity hound who broadcast startling statements in order to attract "newspaper notoriety." Branner said he didn't know about that, but it wasn't necessary to go into it, as Veblen's conduct in the gentlemanly arts was so bad that it wasn't necessary to consider anything else. Branner promoted Ellen to the position of daughter of the president of Carleton College, acknowledged that her husband had been recognized as competent by scholars in his field, but wrote, "scholars are doing mankind no service when they back for a professorship in our colleges a person who is unfit to associate with decent men, to say nothing about decent women, and least of all with young people." Veblen had broken the heart of a woman "of the finest character and breeding ... with brutal deliberation and [driven] her to the verge of insanity or beyond." She now resided "in a hut" close to Stanford, "crushed, broken, and more pathetic than any victim of German brutality in northern France."[13]

Touted as a man of "breadth" and "sound judgment," whose "personal qualities endeared him to everyone,"[14] Branner took at face value the letters that Ellen had showed him. "It was generally understood hereabout that [Veblen] was an advocate of free love, but I paid no attention to the rumors. [And who but Ellen, with her sharing of confidences, large-scale complaining, and prolific letter writing could have earned this reputation for him?] My knowledge of his character is based almost exclusively on a collection of letters that passed between him and his wife before she got a divorce from him. These letters," Branner wrote, "were shown to Jordan and me and they are my warrant for saying that I do not consider [Veblen] proper company for man or beast. I have been told that he has reformed. I do not believe such men reform. They simply change their bases of operations, cover up their moral rottenness, and manage to divert attention from it by the devices practiced by such people. At bottom [Veblen] is a Hun, and he will remain one."[15]

Woodruff thanked Branner for his information, and a week after Branner received his thank-you note and his assurance from Woodruff that the project was going to be dropped, the Cornell appointment was canceled.[16]

In 1931, Stanford's famed developer of IQ tests, Lewis M. Terman, wrote to Veblen's biographer, Joseph Dorfman, that he had talked to the pathologist, Professor A.W. Meyer, about Ellen's autopsy, her infantile sexual development, and the impossibility of her "having had, or given to her husband, a normal sexual life."

Dr. Terman pointed out that the woman Veblen was involved with at Stanford was the woman who later became his second wife. Terman continued:

> To me the significant thing was that although the divorce was losing him his position here, and threatening to ruin his career, Veblen seems never to have said one word that would have helped to explain the situation, and make his own attitude in the affair better understood.
>
> The opinion seems to be still held here, by some of the older faculty group, that Veblen *was* a free-love adherent, and his treatment of Mrs. Veblen was scandalous. I think, therefore, that it is important that Veblen be set right toward the world on this.[17]

Unfortunately, he never was.

The high point of Thorstein's dreary five months' stay in Washington was his run-in with Herbert Hoover, who was the majestic head of this arm of the government. Veblen was sent with Lubin, his subordinate, to investigate grain prices in the Midwest, but Veblen got sick and went home. Lubin daringly proposed that the government should confer with the frighteningly radical International Workers of the World (IWW) to promote better labor relations (basically Veblen's idea). Maybe that way, as Becky commented later, "they would stop striking and get the food supply in."[18] Hoover, however, was outraged. Veblen's paper was returned, with a note stating that the government would *never* deal with the I.W.W. Veblen's answer was to leave Washington. He suspected that, behind the scenes, the food-packing interests were in control of this new government bureau, anyway.

Veblen then moved to New York to become an editor of *The Dial,* an avant-garde political magazine, located in Greenwich Village. The Village was, at that time, a burgeoning center for "century-old ideas for a better life . . . Socialism, Communism, Syndicalism, Anarchism, Ibsenism, Nietzchianism, Shavianism, New Republicanism, Progressivism, Liberalism . . . Feminism, Vegetarianism, free-loveism, nudism—indeed, every conceivable mode of monocular Utopianism . . . That majestic feminist, Henriette Rodman, chaste as the Statue of Liberty, practiced nudism, at least at home, as did Maurice Parmalee, the City College sociologist." Freud's translator, Dr. Abraham A. Brill, "explain[ed] the incestuous Oedipus Complex with shock proof Teutonic deliberation."[19] Everyone believed that the revolution would occur on the day after tomorrow. In this "I can get nirvana for you wholesale" atmosphere, Veblen's articles, calling for a teeth-rattling peace effort and a drastic reorganization of society, stood out for their earnestness, although some people missed his previous quizzical and involved style and felt his articles were now too stridently preachy and not as objective as his other work.[20]

But Thorstein had come into his own and reportedly was the equivalent of the "man of the year" all during 1918. H.L. Mencken became jealous because he encountered Veblen's ideas in practically every magazine he picked up. All the cognoscenti bought and read Veblen's books. William James once had been the "great thinker" in the minds of the weeklies (later edged out by John Dewey); now Veblen was the preferred pundit. "There were Veblenists, Veblen clubs, Veblen remedies for the sorrows of the world," groaned Mencken. "There were even, in Chicago, Veblen girls—perhaps Gibson girls grown middle-aged and despairing."[21]

The Dial sought to serve as an organ of "Reconstruction" (a word of much meaning at the time), concerned with the rebuilding of post–World War I society on a new basis, with "shop committees and industrial councils, and . . . ultimately . . . government ownership."[22] Reconstruction in education meant Dewey's pragmatism. Every form of radical movement was greeted with sympathy and understanding.[23] The board of editors' titular head was John Dewey (then in China), plus Veblen and Helen Marot (an old *Masses* editor, active as a woman's rights crusader and union organizer). Lewis Mumford and others wrote editorials.

Babe and the children joined Thorstein in New York—she had found an apartment on Riverside Drive (rather far from the Village)—and enrolled the girls in high school. "School hadn't started more than a week before the [1918] flu hit us," said Becky, who was then seventeen. She keeled over, was rescued by firemen from a locked bathroom, and was unconscious for several days. Babe came down with a milder version of the same virus.

Ann was given refuge at Mitchell's house in Greenwich Village, and Thorstein stayed at the Columbia Faculty Club. Becky finally awoke, to discover her still ailing mother eager to have her sit up in bed and crane her neck to catch a distant glimpse "of a beautiful young man" (John Reed, famous for his recent *Ten Days that Shook the World)* and a "beautiful young girl" (Louise Bryant), just back from Moscow for a short stay, deep in conversation with Thorstein about the Trotsky take-over of the Russian government ("only four to six deaths . . . due to Trotsky's clever management").[24] Babe, evidently still somewhat unused to such occasions, was whispering, "Becky, wake up! You must see this! This is history!"

A series of Veblen's short articles, originally printed in *The Dial* from October 19, 1918, until January 25, 1919, were reprinted in a book on March 1919, under the title *The Vested Interests and the State of the Industrial Arts.* In a later edition the title was changed to *The Vested Interests and the Common Man.* This small book laid out Veblen's familiar business/industrial dichotomy in a discussion more simplified than usual. It ended by doubting that the common man was menaced by Bolshevism. What did he have to lose? Subsequently, Veblen was to write an essay for *The Dial* with the title "Bolshevism Is a Menace—to Whom?"

Former students from Missouri and elsewhere became alarmed. Such writing was "giving people the misleading idea that [Veblen] was a radical," they chorused.[25]

"Thorstein, his friends and associates . . . had all been happy and hopeful when the Russians tried to gain their freedom by throwing off the Czarists," wrote Becky. "Veblen even thought they had a bare chance to develop a more effective industrial democracy than America . . . He constantly studied the situation . . . He was discouraged when Stalin took the lead there, saying he had always been unscrupulous . . . In '29, about two months before he died, Veblen told Mr. Camp that Stalin was probably the biggest calamity that had yet happened to the world."[26]

Becky and Babe were among the lucky few who survived the lethal 1918 flu bug. They were fairly well recovered and strong enough to participate when Thorstein invited ten guests interested in his work, many of them from *The Dial,* for Thanksgiving dinner. The three women were in the kitchen, Ann making pies, Becky peeling potatoes, and Babe working on the turkey. For no apparent reason, Babe became tense and challenged Becky about her time-lapse potato peeling. Babe had one of her excruciating headaches, a familiar feature of her life since her rough treatment at the hands of her brother-in-law.

Thorstein had told Becky the best part of the potato was right next to the skin, so she was proceeding with due deliberation. But Babe reacted explosively, saying, "I can't stand this—I need a walk." She then rushed out of the apartment. Thorstein hurried in, stuffed the turkey, put it in the oven, and set the table. The ten guests arrived, handsome young Lewis Mumford among them. Late that night Babe returned, saying she had walked by the Hudson River.

The next day she disappeared again. Later, two acquaintances from her old Chicago secretarial school telephoned from Washington, DC. Babe was there, had phoned President Woodrow Wilson, and had tried to get an appointment with him. She was not at all well, and they would see to it that she came home.

When Babe returned, a doctor diagnosed her problems as "the flu," the menopause, and a thyroid dysfunction. This would explain her palpitations, hallucinations, sleeplessness, and headaches. She was usually up writing all night or going for long, solitary walks.[27] Thorstein said he found her recent actions "most uncharacteristic." Babe was given some pills, which she persuaded Becky to flush down the toilet. Actually, she suspected she was pregnant again.

A day or so later Babe took off on a "secret mission." She "had seen" the Kaiser's son in New York, and "felt sure" he was gunning for Thorstein—because of *Imperial Germany and the Industrial Revolution.* Charles Beard, Mitchell, and Davenport were also at risk. She so intended to inform the police.

Three years before in Columbia, Missouri, Babe, may have had the same fantasy in a milder form. Her fears for Veblen's safety seemed also to have influenced her daughters, who were twelve and fourteen years old. Isador Lubin wrote:

> The thing that impressed me about all three of the women was their protective attitude toward Veblen. They felt they had to protect him against something. I could not understand what it was, but it was evident that they were going to see that nothing happened to him. Gradually all three developed a sort of motherly attitude toward me. By the time the year ended, I had a feeling that this attitude toward me was partly due to the fact that I, too, wanted to protect Veblen. But again, I'm not sure what he was being protected against.[28]

However, Lubin knew little or nothing about Veblen's vengeful ex-wife and probably did not realize the gravity of his health problems.

Becky wrote that Babe's major concern in Missouri was that Thorstein might catch pneumonia a second time. "Babe's priority became Thorstein's health. She was determined that he should live to write the things that flooded his mind."[29] But for the moment, now, in New York City, Babe was irrational and in danger. Sending Ann by bus to the Mitchells' on Twelfth Street, Becky and Thorstein followed Babe, as best they could, until "Thorstein's heart gave out. He was in real pain (angina pectoris), and had to sit on a curb and take nitroglycerin.

"Stay with her, " Thorstein instructed his stepdaughter. Becky caught up with Babe and accompanied her to the police station. Soon after, Veblen arrived with Ardzrooni, who eventually escorted Babe by taxi to Bellevue.

Seven months later (on July 31, 1919), Babe was transferred to McLean Hospital in Massachusetts, the girls having been sent to live with the Stewarts in Amherst. Babe preferred not to see her daughters until she was well; they never saw her again after she entered Bellevue.

Wallace W. Atwood, upon the urging of Babe's doctor at Bellevue, escorted Babe from Bellevue to the McLean Hospital. Thorstein was too frail to do so. Atwood wrote Thorstein, saying Babe had "really wanted to see [her husband], but said she couldn't stand the parting again." Although her mind wandered, she was aware of it, and Atwood was encouraged that she realized this, and did not fix on any one idea and cling to it.

In the same summer of 1919, most of the liberalism and left-wingerism of Greenwich Village, and, in fact, of the entire United States, abruptly disappeared. Lewis Mumford says: "My colleagues on *The Dial* were hailed before the Lusk Committee, and examined, under strict oath of secrecy, about the radical activities of the paper. The same committee discovered with horror that the works of Karl Marx and Bernard Shaw could be purchased in ordinary bookstores, and that large groups of people believed that the economic and political basis of the country should be changed." But even before this, according to Mumford, the Socialist Party, which had seemed such a power in 1916, vaporized. The Seattle general strike had occurred in early 1919, after which groups of irate and armed citizens, waving large flags, attacked any and all non-conformists. The Treaty of Versailles, a tremendous blow to those who had hoped for a new society, was signed, and this was followed by the Palmer raids against suspected reds. (Palmer had had his house bombed by a crazed anarchist that spring, and that had set him off.) *"The Dial* was one of the casualties of 1919 . . . Mumford, Robinson, Lovett, Marot, Stearns, Dewey, and Veblen were let go," some of them with only two weeks notice.[30] Then, in November, Warren G. Harding was elected president of the United States, and the era of "liberation" became a memory. The era of "normalcy" had commenced, not to be interrupted until the election of Franklin D. Roosevelt, more than a decade later.

Despite all this, in the fall of 1919, Veblen was to become one of the founders of the liberal, experimental New School for Social Research, along with Charles Beard, James Harvey Robinson, and Wesley C. Mitchell. John Dewey, Harold Laski, and Veblen's former student, Ardzrooni, lectured there as well. Dewey, as director of the School of Education at Chicago, had shared a campus with Veblen in the past. He had gone on to teach at Columbia University, and was already famous as an innovator of non-authoritarian pedagogy.[31] Charles and Mary Beard, the well-known historians, became quite friendly with Veblen, although their opposition to U.S. entry into the war, and their admiration of certain aspects of John Ruskin's philosophy, were points of difference. The New School started out at London Terrace on West Twenty-third Street, and later moved to a handsome modern structure on West Thirteenth Street in the Village.[32]

In the fall of 1920, Babe, still in McLean Hospital, suddenly and unexpectedly died of a pulmonary abscess. "There was also some edema, some swelling around the brain."[33]

Mitchell kept notes in his diary during the time of Mrs. Veblen's illness, as, indeed, he kept notes of all his meetings with Veblen and others throughout his long career:

Sunday, November 17, 1918

Mr. and Mrs. Veblen for midday dinner. Long talk afterwards. Mrs. V violently radical, idealistic.

Friday, November 29, 1918

Mrs. Veblen joined us at lunch and talked . . . until past one. She left the impression that she has specific delusions of persecution. Veblen, Beard, Davenport and myself in danger . . . personal weapons.

Mitchell noted that, on Sunday, December 1, 1918, Veblen came and talked to him and his wife Lucy about his wife's case.

Monday, December 2

Mrs. Charles Beard came at 9:30 to say Mrs. Veblen had left town for Washington and Providence, gone to Washington, then returned to NY and called up the men she thought in danger. Veblen over phone asked me to come up at once. Found Ardzrooni there, Mrs. V very wild. Arranged with Ardzrooni and Mrs. Beard to have physician see her. She became violent towards Ann. Came to house late in the afternoon.

Friday, December 6

Ardzrooni at 3:30 to bring story of Mrs. Veblen to date—now in Bellevue.

On Saturday, December 7, Mitchell called on Veblen and described him as "up from bed, but feeble." The next day, Ardzrooni arrived at noon to tell Mitchell more about Babe, and then left for the hospital.[34]

There are notations about Mitchell's meetings with Veblen on at least ten other occasions during that year, but nothing more about Mrs. Veblen. She died on October 7, 1920, but Mitchell did not mention it. He was in Vermont until October 6, went to New York, then to Washington, and made a brief note that he saw Veblen for the first time later in October, but no other comment.

Becky, who was then entering her second year at the University of Chicago, wrote: "We had just heard that she was better, could come home soon, when [an] emergency telegram said she was dying ... Toyse had brought Ann to start college [after a second year with the Stewart family]. He hurried back, ... and was in time to be with Babe when she died."[35] Babe's mother was also present in her hospital room and was urged by her daughter to carry a message to Becky to be sure to take care of Thorstein.

Veblen reported the death of his beloved to his brother Andrew in a terse, understated manner on October 8, 1920.[36] "Ann died yesterday in the hospital at Waverly [Massachusetts], where she had been for something over a year past, from the effects of abscess of the lung, complicated with symptoms of pneumonia. I have been here with her sister's folks [the Atwoods], going back and forth between Waverly and here. Next week I am to return to New York, where work begins at the New School on the 15th."

Babe's eighty-two-year-old father had a more immediately emotional reaction. He spent days poring over Babe's letters and photos, inscribed her birth and death dates in the family bible ("Born December 27, 1877. She passed away Thursday, October 7, 1920. Kind and gentle to the last. Her last words were 'Goodbye.'"), took to his bed, sobbing, and died. Perhaps he felt guilty for having "put a curse" on his favorite daughter for marrying Veblen.[37]

His granddaughter, Esther Baran, thinks that might have been the case.

23

A Land Where Even the Old Are Fair?

In the summer before Babe died, but while she was still in McLean Hospital, Veblen made a trip to California. By mistake, a real estate agent had included his mountain aerie in the sale of adjoining properties. But, for some unexplained reason, William Camp's sister (who had evidently volunteered to handle his business affairs in California) failed to inform Veblen that she had subsequently arranged to have his title recognized and a minimal rent paid. (Camp had been one of Veblen's most devoted students at Stanford, in fact, his only student in one graduate course called "Thesis," taught in Veblen's last year. Camp, it will be remembered, had taken up the study of Greek with Veblen and Stanford professor Henry Rolfe, and had also followed Veblen to the University of Missouri to continue his graduate work.)

Veblen and Camp's sister drove up to the cabin along with Ardzrooni, Thorstein's sister Emily, his nephew Oswald, and Philip Walter, another close relative.1 Veblen, under the impression that the owner of the land next to his had seized his beloved cabin (the "for sale" sign had not yet been removed), grabbed an axe and began "methodically breaking the windows . . . with a dull intensity like madness." The ever-devoted Ardzrooni broke windows along with him. Shards of glass can still be found in the vicinity. Camp's sister stood aghast, too paralyzed to make any comment. According to Joseph Dorfman, "Everyone got . . . back in the car . . . and in a determined attempt to make conversation, someone enquired, 'And what is going to be the title of your next book, Dr. Veblen?' 'Absentee Ownership,' he answered, and said nothing more on the way home."2

This "dull intensity like madness" had probably been building up in Veblen for some time. Radical movements were collapsing in front of and behind him, and Babe was still in the hospital, not getting any better. The property was doubly important to him, because he had planned to take Babe back to the ridge cabin to recuperate, when she (hopefully) was released from McLean Hospital.[3] And, according to Hans Otto Storm, Veblen, himself, had always had in the back of his mind the plan of returning to California to this cabin in the Redwoods.[4]

In 1919 and 1920 he was paid $6,000 a year at the New School for two years (a total of $12,000, $4,500 of which was contributed by a former student—probably Mitchell). Living frugally, Veblen took some of this nest egg and either loaned it to Ardzrooni or invested it in Ardzrooni's raisin farm.[5] The farm subsequently went bankrupt, and the money was not returned to Veblen or to his heirs. In the 1920s, Veblen also invested in oil stocks and made a profit on some of them. He received similar stocks from a relative in repayment of a debt.[6] Upon Veblen's death, and after the stock market crash, all of his remaining stocks proved to be worthless.

During the less than two years that Babe was in Bellevue and McLean Hospital, Thorstein doggedly continued teaching at the New School. There Blanca Will, the sculptress (and niece of Guido Marx, the Stanford engineering professor), did a bust of him during the early months of 1920.[7]

She later wrote:

> It was a marvelous experience for me, but unfortunately both Veblen and myself were ill at the time . . . We worked very quietly in one of the school rooms under very poor light conditions, but otherwise it was delightful, with the windows facing out into the charming garden-court between the fine simple old buildings which had an alluring old-time flavor.
>
> I don't know whether the setting had an influence or not on the way I did the head. I had been invited to occupy the pleasant guest room while working there, and felt the place strongly so it might have had an influence . . .
>
> I liked Professor Veblen immensely, and got an impression, from quiet daily contact, of profound suffering . . . and of patience and essential kindness that was almost awe-inspiring . . . To tell the truth Veblen made quite a Christ-like impression on me . . . I'm sure he was crucified variously."[8]

Duffus saw Veblen about this time, at lunch with his colleagues at the New School. The vigorous and benign deity of Cedro, wandering around the bucolic paradise and reveling in every minor detail of life, was no more. He ate little, and what he did eat did not appear to please him. The conversation among the professors seemed brilliant to Duffus, but Veblen didn't react.

"Veblen's face throughout wore an expression of deep gloom, almost of despair. Nothing aroused him, or stirred more than a flicker of interest." Duffus at one point asked him a question. He made a sign that he had heard, but refrained from answering.

Duffus then realized he should have remembered that Veblen did not respond to direct questions. But this silence was different; it was portentous.

"[Veblen] was not resenting what anyone said. He was resenting the world. He was resenting himself. One felt not only the old detachment with which we at Cedro had been familiar, but a withdrawal into some private depth of woe."⁹

Duffus does not tell us whether this incident occurred before or after Babe's death, so we do not know whether it was grief over her madness or despair over her death. In any case, it doesn't seem to occur to Duffus that this "private depth of woe" could have had anything to do with the decline or demise of Veblen's second wife.

It doesn't seem to have occurred to other Veblen commentators either. No doubt Wilson's failure to secure a just peace with the Treaty of Versailles, the failure of the New School to rattle the foundations of academia, and the nation's seemingly irreversible turn toward money-mania during the Harding-Coolidge Glittering Twenties were noted, but since Veblen had seen these things coming a long time before, they were no surprise to him.

Horace M. Kallen, who was acquainted with Veblen during his New School days, said:

> I recall how he was stirred by the Bolshevist revolution, . . . with what quiet immovable assurance he anticipated its instant spread. He gave, in the period between 1920 and 1923, an impression of still eager waiting, of watchful readiness. And, when the thing failed to come off, he gave signs of a certain relaxation of will and interest, of a kind of [drive ?] toward death that seemed to grow with the years.¹⁰

Hans Otto Storm, engineer, writer, and brother-in-law of William R. Camp, knew Veblen well during his last days in California and believed that Veblen's life could be encapsulated thus:

> The story of a man . . . earnest, but too lazy with his sharp intelligence to follow after false messiahs, waiting, repressing his enthusiasms, making his genius plod in the queer groove of scholarship, and, incidentally, ironically, getting famous for it, privately hoping all the while for something that he could, without apologies, throw his soul into and which was going to go over—caught up at last by the wild hope of post-war revolution in the West, seeing that revolution fail, retiring quietly into a twilight scholarship, and dying of a broken heart.¹¹

It is hard to give credence to Kallen's or Storm's perspicacity or chronology. In Veblen's September 1919 essay in *The Dial* (republished in *The Engineers and the Price System* with the title "On the Danger of a Revolutionary Overturn"), he correctly predicted that Russia, with its loose-knit and backward industrial system, would be difficult for an invading nation to overpower. Its very lack of centralization gave it the ability to lose one sector of its industry, while the remainder could continue virtually unaffected. For the same reason, Russia would be ineffective as an invader of other nations. Veblen knew, however, that what the Allied powers really feared was that the spirit of Bolshevism would infect the workers in their own countries.[12]

The apprehensions of the European elder statesmen were "not entirely groundless . . . The underlying population" would not have very much to lose from an overturn of the established order. But Veblen perceived that America, with its expanding economy, stood in little danger of any disruption of the status quo.[13]

Veblen's predictions turned out to be correct about the United States. A confirmed rebel, he was undoubtedly affected by the conformist pressures in the 1920s, which discouraged his customary free-ranging attacks on sanctimony and conventionality. The collapse of his *élan vital,* however, must have dated from the loss of Babe and the concomitant worsening of his health, rather than from the turn of world events.

Storm, Kallen, and the others who analyzed Veblen's post-war attitudes placed no importance on the long-suppressed role the second wife played in Veblen's life for thirteen years. The scale of Babe's intellectual contributions to his work is unknown, but she was fully aware of his health difficulties, was determined to give him all the protection and enthusiastic support she could muster, and loved him with a passion.

His writings in *The Dial,* and most of his works of the early 1920s, lack the delicious subtleties of his earlier works, although part of his difficulty with *The Dial* articles may have been an example of the old warning, "Be careful what you wish for, you might get it." The soapbox was not the logical place for an iconoclast whose artistry was reflected best by the snares and traps he laid for the complacent and the unwary.

The Engineers and the Price System, a collection of essays written originally for *The Dial* between April and November of 1919, came out in book form in 1921. A sharpening of Veblen's main theme in *Business Enterprise*—that the control of the nation's industrial plant by business interests inevitably leads to depression—the book became the rage a few years after Veblen's death. In 1932, when President Franklin Delano Roosevelt came to power, depression was so deep that a 100-day bank holiday had to be declared. Farmers were paid to keep prices high by plowing under their crops, while the urban poor stood starving in breadlines. But a reading of the essays today seems to verify Duffus's remark in a letter to Dorfman that Veblen was more of a "Jeremiah" than a builder of systems.

Some of Veblen's contemporary observers were taken in by his use of the words "soviet of technicians," and thought that he must have been bitterly disappointed because bolshevik-like engineers did not take over the country at the close of World War I. Was Lenin also taken in? In 1919, Veblen met with Ludwig C.A.K. Martens, an engineer stationed in New York by a Russian company, whom Lenin had just named the Soviet Union's representative to the United States. The meeting began slowly, according to an anonymous informant, as neither man seemed to want to break the silence. At the end, however, "Veblen turned suddenly from gazing off into space, and began to ask questions. It was like a skilled surgeon wielding a scalpel. He turned Martens inside out; he turned the whole soviet experiment inside out. He got, in the course of possibly an hour or so, all that there was to know. Martens was put at ease at once. He responded beautifully. It was an impressive example of one keen, orderly mind excavating another."[14]

Nonetheless, Veblen knew that American engineers and technicians were "still ... loyal, with something more than a hired man's loyalty, to the established order of commercial profit and absentee ownership," and that "under existing circumstances, there need be no fear, and no hope, of an effectual revolutionary overturn in America, such as would unsettle the established order and unseat those Vested Interests that now control the country's industrial system." [15]

The idea that world events by themselves caused Veblen to go into some drive toward death makes for good theater, but bereavement and loneliness more likely nudged him that way, and the lingering effects of calomel and his incessant smoking did not help.[16] In 1919 an engineer consulting with him at the New School described him as "almost too frail for any kind of contacts."[17]

If there was a twilight of scholarship (his *Vested Interests* [1919–20] and *Absentee Ownership* [1923] seemed at times a bit crepuscular) there were still flashes of wit, particularly when he turned his artillery on religious pomposity.

In *Absentee Ownership and Business Enterprise in Recent Times,* after a sober discussion of the need for advertising and salesmanship in modern business, he appended a sly note saying that the "Propaganda of the Faith is quite the largest, oldest, most magnificent, most unabashed, and most lucrative enterprise in sales-publicity in all Christendom."[18]

Business should look upon religious propaganda as a moral stimulus and pacemaker:

> The whole duty of sales-publicity is to "put it over," as the colloquial phrasing has it ... it should be the high good fortune of the perfect salesman in the secular field to promise everything and deliver nothing ... *Bona Fide* delivery of the listed goods would have to be a tangible performance of quite another complexion, inasmuch as the specifications call for Hell-fire and the Kingdom of Heaven; ... [plus] a broad margin of Purgatory.[19]

The number of people engaged in this "marketing of supernatural intangibles" is more considerable than that engaged in any other calling, except arms, and possibly husbandry.

> Prelates and parsons abound all over the place, in the high, the middle and the low degree ... bishops, deans, canons, abbots and abbesses, rectors, vicars, curates, monks and nuns, elders, deacons and deaconesses, secretaries, clerks and employees of YMCA, Epworth Leagues, Christian Endeavors, etc., bea-

dles, janitors, sextons, Sunday school teachers, missionaries, writers, editors, printers and vendors of sacred literature, in books, periodicals and ephemera. All told—if it were possible—it will be evident that the aggregate of human talent currently consumed in this fabrication of vendible imponderables in the nth dimension, will foot up to a truly massive total, even after making a reasonable allowance, of, say, some thirty-three and one-third per cent, for average mental deficiency in the personnel which devotes itself to this manner of livelihood.[20]

Dorfman said "the writing of *Absentee Ownership* was difficult for Veblen, and he resorted more often than before to Roget's *Thesaurus.*"[21] Lubin heard Veblen remark, in exasperation, "that Roget was the cause of more poor authors and poets than any other person in history."[22] He was also heard to complain, "There are no synonyms in the English language."[23]

The introduction to his *Laxdaela Saga,* written in the mid-1920s (also on familiar anti-clerical ground), is full of the same old fire and brimstone that delighted readers in his earlier works.[24] He attacks the Vikings for their piracy, slaughter, greed, and rapine, and their use of religion to disempower the underlying population:

> That occupation which gave its name and its character to the Viking Age was an enterprise in piracy and slave-trade, which grew steadily more businesslike and more implacable as time went on. It was an enterprise in getting something for nothing by force and fraud at the cost of the party of the second part; much the same, in principle, as the national politics pursued by the statesmen of the present time . . . this business . . . resulted in a cumulative privation and servility on the part of the underlying population. Increasingly, as time passed, the ethics of the strong arm came to prevail among these peoples and to dominate men's ideals and convictions of right and wrong. Insecurity of life and livelihood grew gradually more pronounced and more habitual, until, in the course of centuries of rapine, homicide, and desolation, it became a settled matter of course, and of common sense, that the underlying population had no rights which the captains of the strong arm were bound to respect. And like any other business enterprise that is of a competitive nature, this traffic in piracy was forever driven by its quest of profits to "trade on a thinner equity," to draw more unsparingly on its resources of man-power and appliances and so cut into the margin of its reserves to charge increasingly more than the traffic would bear.[25]

From this analogy of piracy to big business, Veblen moves into a discussion of the effect of the resultant poverty and oppression in promoting a religious climate:

> Increasing squalor and privation on the material side, and an ever increasing habituation to insecurity, fear and servility on the spiritual side, [put] this population . . . in a frame of mind to believe that this world is a vale of tears and that they all were miserable sinners, prostrate and naked in the presence of an unreasoning and unsparing God and his bailiffs.[26]

When Babe went mad, Ardzrooni had wired Lubin to come to New York, which he did in December 1918. Lubin stayed with Veblen through January and part of

February 1919. Then, for a year or more, Ardzrooni took over. An apartment belonging to the New School was provided for them; it was at this point that people talked about Ardzrooni's acting like a valet to his physically incapacitated mentor.

Ardzrooni groveled before Veblen's greatness; on the other hand, he often told negative little anecdotes about him and refused to return any part of his borrowed money. He had the "fan" mentality—something like the mindset of the man who "adored" John Lennon, but eventually shot him.

Ardzrooni, for instance, was responsible for the story that Veblen borrowed an empty sack from a farmer, and returned it replete with hornets. Becky wrote that, considering what she knew of Veblen's mature character and personality, this could never have taken place. She ascribed the story to meanness on Ardzrooni's part, brought out by his conflicts over the money he owed her stepfather which he was not willing to pay. Other anecdotes about Veblen that seem strange or uncharacteristic may have come from the same source, for instance, the unattributed report that Veblen sneered about the offer of the presidency of the American Economic Association, saying: "I was glad to turn it down. They didn't offer it to me when I needed it."[27]

In the early months of 1920, Ardzrooni expressed a fear that he couldn't take care of Veblen adequately. Veblen had become alarmingly debilitated (possibly more heartsick than physically ill). In September, 1920, Veblen had written to Mrs. Gregory and family that he had "a confident hope of seeing you all at least once again . . . BEFORE THE CURTAIN" (his capitalization).

Dr. Alice Broughton, and her housemate, Miss Mildred V. Bennett, mature and efficient ladies, were called upon to shoulder the burden of looking after the great man's health and well-being. Later, the uncle of Herbert J. Davenport roomed and boarded with Veblen in another house, on West Eleventh Street, presided over by Miss Bennett.

Ellen Veblen was still keeping close track of the events in the life of her ex-husband. On March 26, 1922, she wrote to her friend Lucia:

> Mr. Veblen married Ann Bevans in 1914, and she died perhaps a year ago. Strange? He is at 465 West 23rd St., N.Y. Since things began to happen to me, I wrote to him impersonally a few times, telling him. Things began to happen in June. Some children asked me to sit about a table with them to see if it would move. It did. Wonderful things came of it, and at last my hand began to write. I was most solemnly taken to task for my wrong thinking and useless living. And at last came "Come with me," etc., and signed, Jesus Christ. My whole being was convinced and turned toward Him. And then I came in touch with the wonderful messages of Hilarion, the Angel who leads the "John the Baptist" movement, which tells of the near (very near) coming of Christ."[28]

Ellen had been in the religious colony of Halcyon, near Arroyo Grande, California, for just two weeks. Her pet prodigy, Henry Cowell, the avant-garde pianist and composer (who achieved dramatic rumbling sounds on the piano by using his forearms and elbows to ripple over the keys), had become a Halcyon enthusiast, and she had gone there to "rescue him." Now she, in her turn, became a devotee, and wondered why people did not flock there in the thousands. She had written to Upton Sinclair about it and also to Eugene Debs, asking them to consider coming there.

Three years later she wrote another friend: "And why am I in Halcyon, Calif.? Because, instead of being the pagan that I used to be, I have been, for the last three years, just as heartily a Christian Theosophist ... Oh, how glad I am to have reached a satisfactory answer. What a blessing! ... Do write if you don't come ... Mr. V. sends me his books."[29] Mr. V. was also urged to embrace the faith and to receive odd pilgrims from Halcyon who were full of the divine fire.

On November 15, 1924, she sent the following letter to Veblen from Halcyon:

> Dear Thorstein:
>
> Here is a strange request: the man whose folder I enclose wants a recent picture of you—not for the usual reason of vainglory. He wants you to write on the front of it, "To Charles O. Ross," and to sign your name "good and strong ..."
>
> He is a very curious, stimulating, intuitional person—a Russian [who] ... wishes to meet you when you come out. May he? He is a dynamo, but most reserved, and a true son of the woods. If you could make anything of him, you would like him immensely. He is genuine and a man of power. He does *not* understand the Veblen books. Don't expect it. He will understand *you* much better, and in any emergency help you—even save you. He has a curious effect on people's health. For me, he is as good as a thunderstorm—the best thing that can happen to me. My health is perfect, anyway.[30]

In another letter she warns Veblen that he should not stay in New York. Her friends at Halcyon "will not go back to New York. No one should. Disaster will now follow disaster, and I fear for the East Coast. You will leave as soon as circumstances permit, even to a day?"

She continued: "It is all *true,* Thorstein, believe me! There is but one substance, and the Universe is all God. Love everything you can. Love the ground, the air you breathe, each person you meet."

After a similar discourse running to several paragraphs, during which she asserts that everyone on earth has been in existence for millions or trillions of years, she concludes: "The heart thrills at *everything*! Life is sacred, step by step! Be kind, as your nature is to be. The law is thus fulfilled. Know that there are others bending down to you."[31]

Dorfman, who interviewed her before she died, said she was still hoping that Thorstein would come back to her.

The New School underwent a complete reorganization in 1922. Those towering giants, Beard, Mitchell, and Robinson, resigned, leaving Veblen as the last of the "Big Four." Financial support for the institution had evaporated. An article appearing in the *New York Evening Post* indicated that the school was henceforth to be primarily a school of adult education. Rumors that "the school had proved a failure and was going to be shut down," were denied vigorously. Future teaching might include such subjects as chemistry, biology, and physics, and would no longer have radical tendencies.[32] Veblen's salary began to be underwritten by donations from his ex-students and liberal admirers. This was referred to as "The New School Veblen Fund." Veblen struggled on for three or four years on this basis, sometimes teaching, sometimes not.

Around this time a curious incident occurred involving Thorstein and Babe's ultra-conservative brother-in-law, Wallace W. Atwood. Atwood had become president of Clark University in 1920, and his aim was to make Clark "the great center of American geographic and physiographic education."[33]

Geography indeed thrived at Clark under the new president's regime, but at the expense of mathematics, biology, psychology, chemistry, history, and the social sciences. Twelve professors were teaching in the graduate school of geography, but graduate work in mathematics and biology had totally ceased. To appease the bias of Atwood, and his adherence to his "narrow specialty," other departments were also woefully cut down. But this caused consternation only among faculty and students. Atwood achieved national prominence because of an incident involving his attitude toward Thorstein Veblen, as well as his abhorrence of radicals, liberals, or any sort of left-winger.

In March 1922 the Clark Liberal Club announced an upcoming lecture by the well-known socialist professor, Scott Nearing. After giving his reluctant consent, Atwood had shifted the Club's lecture to a smaller hall, as there was to be a geography lecture the same evening. Geography turned out to attract only a handful of people, whereas the controversial Nearing filled his lecture room with an audience of 300, among them Clark faculty members and the distinguished ex-president of the University, Dr. G. Stanley Hall.[34]

Atwood, after emerging from the sparsely attended lecture on his own specialty, dropped into the crowded hall to listen to the last part of the Scott Nearing oration. At that time, "Nearing . . . was speaking on the control of education by the 'vested interests' and quoting freely from the works of Thorstein Veblen."[35] After listening just a few minutes, Atwood declared that the lecture was terminated. "The extraordinary character of the announcement, its bad manners, insolence, and bad faith, led everyone to misunderstand the announcement and the lecture continued," according to a contemporary issue of the *Boston American*.[36]

President Atwood, calling Nearing's speech "disgusting," ordered one of his staff to "stop him" and had the janitor blink, and then turn out, the lights. The audience was left to make its way outside in the dark, one member crying out for his money back.[37]

A big uproar followed. Hundreds of newspapers wrote about the incident, and four of Atwood's professors in the humanities resigned (two of them were offered positions at Harvard and one at Smith College). At a subsequent public meeting of the Liberal Club, one student slapped another in the face, and death threats were received by Atwood and a minister of the Union Church who had praised Atwood for his action.[38]

Atwood excused himself by saying, "If Dr. Nearing took Veblen's book as his theme, he does not understand the author's views. What I heard of Tuesday night's speech had no connection with anything Beblen [*sic*] ever said or wrote."[39] This statement revealed a new facet to Atwood's omnipotence, as an overnight, authentic Veblen scholar.

He continued: "I shall see to it that no more such meetings are held at the University, and if the Liberal Club attempts to conduct them in an outside hall they will have to deal with the United States government—and you may rest assured the government will not hesitate to act."[40]

Nearing's address was supposedly based on *The Theory of the Leisure Class,* but a newspaper reported that the socialist orator believed that the world of the future would be entirely composed of labor groups (i.e., miners, cobblers, metal workers, and tailors), and that his ideas were closer to those already expressed by the International Workers of the World. National boundaries, he said, would disappear—no more England, France, or the United States. Old capitalists would be pensioned off (rather than beheaded). Young, vigorous capitalists would be forced to work very hard.[41] Scott Nearing, recently fired as a professor from the University of Pennsylvania, had become an active socialist politician, and, although he professed great admiration for Veblen's writings, extrapolated unwarranted socialistic meanings from them.

At first Atwood seemed somewhat stunned by the impulsiveness of his conduct, and, the next day, attempted to blunt the violence of the student and faculty protest by appearing apologetic: "I deeply and sincerely regret the dramatic manner in which I interrupted Dr. Nearing." But, after the Worcester Rotary Club burst into cheers upon his appearance there, and a flood of clippings from conservative newspapers across the continent applauded his action, he changed his course. These latter comments outweighed, in his mind, the outrage expressed by academics and liberal newspapers. He announced: "I know that I should have closed that meeting. I do not regret that I have shown, in a positive way, that I disapprove of such influences within . . . the university."[42]

The motto of Clark University was, however, *Fiat Lux* (Let There Be Light), and the will of founder, Jonas Clark, had expressed his desire that "the . . . university, in its practical management, as well as in theory, may be wholly free from every kind of denominational or sectarian control, bias or limitation, and that its doors may be ever open to all classes and persons, whatsoever may be their religious faith or political sympathies or to whatever creed, sect, or party they may belong."[43]

The fiery campus response may have been fueled, in part, by pent-up anger among faculty and students over Atwood's sacrifice of the humanities in order to promote his narrow geographical bias.[44] The beleaguered Atwood subsequently thought it wise to ask his brother-in-law to make a few lectures at Clark. Veblen, however, declined on the grounds of ill health.

24

"I Will Arise and Go Now"

I n 1924, Veblen was tired of teaching at the New School and was "at present taking a sabbatical," according to a letter from Mitchell to Ardzrooni. He was eager to go to England for two years to study British imperialism, but needed funding. A certain Mr. Kaplan had offered to help with a $1,000 annual contribution, and Mitchell would continue to provide $500 each year. Would Ardzrooni be willing to contribute as well?

Mitchell emphasized that this proposed contribution had nothing to do with the Veblen New School Fund. Veblen, he wrote, had just returned from a summer-long vacation on Washington Island in fairly good shape. He had subsequently been through an extended session of dentistry in St. Paul, Minnesota. Mitchell had talked him into giving "a paper at the forthcoming session of the American Economic Association in Chicago on 'The Prospects of Economic Thought in the Calculable Future.'" Veblen's thoughts now seemed to be focused only on this English study, and, "For his happiness as well as for the benefit of the world, I think we should help him get there if we can."[1]

But three months later, in March, Veblen had made no move toward going to England, possibly because of his shaky health, or because the funds collected for that purpose would not cover the costs. The New School director, Alvin Johnson, informed Veblen in March 1925:

> I wrote to Mr. Edward Filene, as you suggested, and have received from him, as his contribution to your fund, $100.
>   As matters stand now, the fund consists of $1200 a year for the two years, contributed by Mr. Kaplan; $1000, appropriated by the Garland Fund; $500,

pledged by Mr. [Joseph H.] Schaffner; $500, by Mr. Mitchell; and this $100, from Mr. Filene. Mr. Filene's secretary does not indicate whether this is a contribution for the entire two years or a first year installment. It is safest to assume that the former is the case.

Of these sums the contributions from Mr. Kaplan and Mr. Mitchell are not contingent on your going to England. The contributions from the Garland Fund, Mr. Schaffner, and Mr. Filene, have been pledged on the assumption that you are going to make this trip and try to put through the study you contemplated. I assume that these people have common sense enough to know that there is always a gamble in a literary enterprise. I have certainly not represented the outcome as a certainty.

In your letter you say that, in any case, you will make a visit to England this year, probably this spring. Could you tell me definitely whether, with the fund as it now stands, you would undertake to spend the two years and make the study? Of course I should continue my efforts to increase the fund, but the process is a slow one, and I am afraid that the interest of the donors will lapse if nothing is done about it soon.[2]

The American Economic Association easily dodged the election of Veblen as its president in 1925 by offering him the presidency on condition he give an acceptance speech. Mitchell and others among the younger economists felt that Veblen should be honored with the presidency even though he was not, and never had been, a member of the organization. Paul H. Douglas had spearheaded the nominating petition to bypass the traditional procedure of nominating by committee. Douglas had said that when he had been a student—and a Veblen enthusiast—he would slyly steal out somewhere with his hero's works and read them voraciously, yet in fear and trembling lest his economics professor discover his crime.[3] He and some of the younger economists had chosen Veblen to be their figurehead in the "palace revolt" within the American Economic Association. Douglas commented that Veblen, who was "to an extraordinary degree an introvert and dreaded public functions, refused [the presidency], and the matter was dropped."[4]

Veblen did not go to England. His thoughts were turning to California and his beloved ridge cabin, where he had planned to take Babe when she was released from McLean Hospital.[5] Also, he had bought from his first wife, Ellen, the "gatehouse" to the old Cedro property, built partly by her own frenzied labors. There were, in fact, three small shanties on that one piece of property, which she had attempted to keep rented.[6]

Since Babe's death, Thorstein had a new, and in some respects, fulfilling role in life, that of sole parent to his stepchildren.7 After Becky had spent a few months with the Stewarts in Amherst, her Auntie Mame had brought her to Chicago to live in her grandparents' old house and to matriculate at the University of Chicago.[8] Ann stayed on alone in the Stewarts' capacious attic dormitory and arrived in Chicago the following fall.

Veblen had visited Amherst often and tried be a "good daddy" to the two girls, but it wasn't always easy. He paid their University of Chicago fees during their college years and took an active role in advising and admonishing them.

The younger stepdaughter, Ann, was not as enthusiastic about her stepfather as Becky, but he tried to be fair. According to Becky, he gave Ann the same amount of college money he gave Becky, even though Ann quit the university after one year and eventually took up nursing. Ann had been understandably upset because her mother had divorced her real father, Tom Bevans, whom Ann was supposed to "take after." She later spent time in New York City trying, without much success, to get to know her father better.[9]

Ann also had periods of estrangement from her older sister, Becky, who was closer to Veblen and took care of him in his old age.

> Ann: I never understood her. She and I just didn't get along at all. She was always reading. I would sit through her reading one Shakespeare play to me, but I'd be darned if I'd sit through another one.[10]

Veblen may not have been as close to the less literate Ann, but he made no attempt to play the heavy parent and pressure her to stay in college or take more courses, according to the correspondence that survives. To her he signed his letters "Veblen," to Becky, he called himself by the pet name "Toyse."

On November 1, 1923, Thorstein wrote Ann:

> I am writing to forward this check for $75.00. The book on *Absentee Ownership* came out today. You should get a copy from the publisher soon.
>
> Veblen[11]

On December 3, 1923, he again wrote Ann:

> Becky's letter and yours have come . . . I am enclosing a couple of checks— $125 all together for current expenses and for registration fees for next quarter, if it will cover that. Let me know if you need any more. Also, I had a sweater sent you . . . the other day. I am quite willing you should do as you like about registering for two courses, or any other number, and will write you a formal statement to that effect if necessary.
>
> Veblen[12]

Earlier Thorstein had written Becky that he had sent her a typewriter and $250 worth of Liberty Bonds for her and Ann's joint use. "Also tell me how your bank account stands and whether you need money."[13]

On October 16, 1923, he wrote Ann: "I am very sorry you waited so long at the station for me that night, but I was glad you were there, on Becky's account, so that she would not have to cross the city alone at night, and I was glad to see you [long] enough to see that you were looking well—better than I have seen [you look] for some time."[14]

On February 13, 1924, he wrote Ann that he was sending two checks for $100 to Chicago, and asked her to let him know if she needed more. On July 12, 1926, he wrote to Becky from Washington Island and began by telling her that Ann would like to hear from her:

> She is feeling hurt about your not having written her or told her whether you like the dress which she sent you for her [*sic*] birthday . . . Also she appears not to have got the check for $15.00. Maybe you did not send it. If so, "Do it now."
> I am not 'appy 'arriet, though it might be worse.
> Toyse[15]

On July 26, in perhaps 1926, Thorstein wrote to Becky from Washington Island:

> . . . Colette [Veblen's grandniece] has been eating too much candy and marshmallows. And [Ralph] Sims [a relative by marriage] and I have all the cigarettes we need. I thank you for the Melachrinos, but it's no use sending any more. I am not quite as lame or tired in my legs, but I get short of breath on less provocation. And what I want to know is whether you count on coming for September. Please let me know. I don't expect to stay if you don't . . . If you need money let me know in time. And don't fail to write to Ann, and tell me all you're doing and all that happens to you and that you are having your dentist's work properly done.
> Toyse
> *And* I thank you for the pictures. Ann's address is 4411 12th Ave., Brooklyn, N.Y. c/o Dr. Wald.[16]

Colette van Fleet reported that Becky and Ann (who were about thirteen to fifteen years her senior) "always wore terribly flat shoes [actually hiking boots], so we were kind of a little bit ashamed of them in Chicago, because they were pretty eccentric young women."[17]

She was also shocked because Becky was dating a Chinese student. "That was pretty, you know, far out!" Colette told her interviewers, Russell Bartley and Sylvia Yoneda, that the girls' appearance may have reflected the fact that "their mother was a rebel," and continues, "I do remember Uncle Thorstein saying to my mother 'I don't know what will happen to them when I die.' He was just very worried about them."[18]

Becky wrote that her mother had wanted her and her sister to become "socialist teachers. She thought socialism would prevail by the time we grew up . . . [Even] though she talked with Thorstein about it . . . and was finally convinced that he knew the world situation and human condition better than she did, it was hard for me to reorient regarding money."[19] In fact, Becky never did reorient. She became such a selfless individual that she was roundly taken advantage of, according to her daughter, Esther Baran.[20]

Miss Mildred Bennett also took it upon herself to advise Veblen on the subject of Ann's problems. Miss Bennett spent two or three "whole summers" with Veblen on Washington Island and, according to Colette, was "the person who knew him best at that time."[21] She and Thorstein also lived under the same roof (her roof) for two or three years in New York. From her correspondence one might judge that Mildred was a boring and fairly conventional person, but in a rather testy letter she suddenly seemed aggrieved because her ex-tenant, Veblen, had not been a faithful correspondent. It was written at the time Thorstein and Becky had left the East Coast for California, on the advice of his physician, who felt that he would not weather another New York winter.

On December 12, 1926, Mildred wrote:

Dear Mr. Veblen,

I answered your letter written in October, but have had no reply, and suspect that I have lost a letter from you, as well as others that I know have strayed. I don't believe you would drop off without telling me you didn't want to write me or hear from me. I don't forget that you have told me I am the best friend you ever had, and I still believe myself as good a friend as I ever was. I can't believe that I could have given to you as I did without reciprocity, and even in spite of recent developments I am still concerned about you.

I have heard through Hilda that you are in Chicago, but I would like to know how you are, and whither going.

May I hear from you soon, and will you be quite frank with me if you wish to stop further connections.[22]

Could there have been a sexual relationship between Mildred Bennett and Thorstein? Her letter sounds like a woman aggrieved because she has been slighted by someone with whom she has been intimate. But it also has a spinsterish tone. If there was an involvement, there is no other insight available, and further speculation seems unprofitable. At this point Thorstein was elderly and frail and Mildred thoroughly middle-aged. Pictures taken of her at Washington Island show she had a lot of wholesomeness going for her. She could have been one of those good-hearted souls who was fulfilling her destiny by taking care of a man whom she rightly considered a national treasure, and it may be she felt that Veblen had unfairly evaporated without giving her a further chance to nurture him.[23]

Veblen's checkbooks for 1924 and 1925 show many entries in favor of Mildred V. Bennett, checks for around $100 each month, probably for room and board. However, in March 1925, he gave her $500, and in February 1926, $1,107.30.[24] The $1,400 or so extra may have been simply a loan. (Veblen delighted in loaning money to relatives and may have considered his sharp-tongued benefactress, the staid Miss Bennett, something in the guise of a relative.) He loaned money to his niece, Hilda, for tuition for teacher training in California; to his niece's husband, Ralph Sims [later the husband of his step-daughter, Ann]; to Harold Veblen; to his brother Orson; and to his brother Ed.[25] Becky said: "Thorstein had money owed him from Orson. He lent Orson money and he chuckled. I remember him chuckling to my mother. Other Veblens thought he was so silly to go off and be a teacher, because if he had gone into business, he would live softer. Yet, he was the one who got to help the business-man, Orson [and later, the businessman, Ed]. Thorstein had to bail Orson out and that really pleased Thorstein."[26]

Thorstein left New York in 1926, stopped in Chicago with his niece Hilda, and summered on Washington Island. He then spent the fall, two months at least, with Lubin in Washington, DC. Lubin wrote: "At that time he had no plans at all for the future. His idea was to go out to California, and stay there until something turned up."[27] He told Becky he was going into "cold storage."[28]

On December 11, 1926, Becky and Veblen arrived in San Diego, where they stayed for four months in a rented house near Thorstein's brother Andrew, who presumably had moved there for the climate. However, Thorstein did not care much for the chilly, dampish winter in San Diego and "was suffering from a persistent and debilitating cold."[29] In late April 1927, he and Becky left for Palo Alto.

Although, in her letter to Riesman, Becky expressed herself as being "delighted" to look after Veblen, in her biography she gives us a picture of her wretchedness over being abruptly transplanted to California. "Veblen's doctor called me when I was in college [graduate school]. He said Veblen was frail and needed to be in a warmer climate. He was living in New York at the time . . . He suffered from angina pectoris. So his doctor wanted me to take him to California and take care of him there . . . So I gave up my marvelous medical research in Chicago . . . I'd been doing research for about seven years [including her four undergraduate years?] and we went to California."[30]

Her daughter, Esther Baran, said Becky was "close to getting a master's degree in microbiology," and she couldn't understand for a long time how her mother could have given it up.[31] After Veblen died, Becky was unable, except briefly, to get back into academic research. Her long lay-off, and the Depression, which started shortly after Veblen's death, apparently made it difficult to re-enter the field. Thereafter, she lived a life close to the poverty line, supporting herself chiefly with baby-sitting jobs.[32]

Becky continued: "We were supposed to move into the Sandhill Road house, but someone had rented it to a woman with a gang of dogs who wouldn't move out. So we had to rent a room from the Storm family (Gracie Storm)."[33]

The tenant and gang-of-dogs-lover was a certain Mrs. Huntoon. Another shack on the property, which Ellen had built for her occasional visits to the Palo Alto area when her main house was rented, was also occupied. Mrs. Huntoon had allowed an old man who paid no rent to live in the shack and had told him he could stay there forever. When Veblen came to realize the full extent of the capture of his property, he collapsed on the doorstep and sat there silently, shaking with bitter laughter.[34] It was ironic that the author of *The Theory of the Leisure Class* and *Absentee Ownership* should be placed in such a position. While the situation dragged on, Veblen took to calling Ellen's old house "The Huntoon Cottage."

Finally, the woman left. Becky recounted: "I sort of cleaned the place up, and we moved in. I didn't do the best job of taking care of him, but I tried."[35] In an interview, she expressed her feelings of guilt: "It was hard to heat the Sandhill Road house when he was there. I should have kept him warmer somehow. I should have done more."[36]

Babe's older daughter had been directed repeatedly by her mother to "take care of Veblen," a parental injunction and later a deathbed mandate that she never considered disobeying, although it did involve such things as going on foot two and a half miles into Palo Alto and returning heavily loaded with groceries. (It was a while before they got a car.) At first the Storms had to drive them to the ridge cabin in their old Ford. But finally, Thorstein bought an Erskine that the Studebaker dealer had used as a demonstrator and Becky became Thorstein's chauffeur.[37]

The ridge cabin was only eight miles from their Sandhill Road house, located on the narrow, multiple switch-backed, "old" La Honda Road, which rose almost 2,000 feet in a short three miles. After they arrived, clothes, groceries, and water had to be carried up to the primitive cabin thirty feet above. And Thorstein, who must meanwhile have been waiting below in the Erskine, would have had to have been helped to struggle slowly up the precipitous incline.

It is unlikely that Thorstein fully realized the sacrifices involved. In a letter to his sister Emily (June 12, 1928), he wrote: "Becky is doing nothing but keeping house for me and one kitten, and I am not doing even that much."[38] Had Becky insisted, however, she probably could have continued with her graduate work, and she did say that Thorstein had stayed on teaching in the east five years longer than he really wanted to, in order to be able to underwrite her studies at the University of Chicago.

William R. Camp's brother-in-law, the writer Hans Otto Storm, helped him repair and prop up the ridge cabin in 1928. Veblen insisted they use redwood in the foundation because of its long-lasting qualities. Storm was surprised that, at age seventy-one, he would worry about such details.[39] To the outsider, Veblen's continued interest in the ridge cabin at a time when intermittent claudication made walking, not to speak of climbing, painful, might have seemed absurd, or even hazardous to his health. But the ridge cabin must have stirred memories in Veblen—of his defiance of convention, of the hauling of Ariel Stanford's chicken coop up the mountain road, of the outwitting of his watchdog-wife on Sandhill Road, of his times alone with the defiant and irreverent Babe. The position of the cabin itself, straddling two giant redwood stumps at the crest of the upthrust Coast Range not far from the San Andreas fault, was to some extent also a form of defiance—a defiance of the law of gravity.

Becky said the ridge cabin "was beautiful, you could see boats go by on the ocean on a clear day . . . We were in La Honda for days on end, but mainly we were in the house on Sandhill."[40]

Becky wrote: "The first thing I wanted when we moved to California was a car. Veblen thought I couldn't drive one—I was too scatterbrained a person to learn to drive. So he was amazed when the man who taught drivers said I was very good. Toyse couldn't believe it. He held tight whenever he went with me driving. I enjoyed driving that [Studebaker] Erskine. Toyse never drove."[41] She continued, "and [he] couldn't walk the two miles from town."[42] She described their life in her "Biography":

> I would come down from La Honda and get food. He'd stay up and keep the stove going . . . Sandhill Road used to get awfully muddy. Once a cold spell came and I couldn't get through. I had to walk down . . . to Palo Alto through the mud to get the food. Usually, though, I would drive down and get food and big piles of books from the library—Stanford and Palo Alto.
>   . . . He had pretty much stopped writing. He wrote something about the environment, but that was about all. He was reading a lot. In his last year he asked me to bring him something by Zane Grey.[43]

Earlier, at the Dr. Alice Broughton–Mildred Bennett menage, he was said to borrow the ladies' murder mysteries and hide them under his mattress. He also told Becky he would like to have written one good novel, saying it would "probably [be] better time spent than trying to teach professors what every laborer had [already] discovered!"[44]

Storm said, "At seventy, he was eager for discussion and he was lonely."[45] Most of his associates from academic days were far away. His brother Orson died June 1, 1928. Ellen had died in 1926.[46] In a letter to his sister Emily, Thorstein coolly assessed his own health: "I am told that I am looking well, but apart from looks I am gradually losing ground; have done so very slowly and steadily since I last saw you—or rather since the succeeding winter."[47]

Sarah Gregory came to see him, probably in the spring of 1928. She wrote about it on April 26 to Mitchell:

> Last Saturday afternoon I drove out along the tree-shaded road which turns off to the right from the Administration Building on the Stanford Campus. After about two miles the road came to an end at the edge of San Francisquito Creek and then Dr. Veblen met me. We strolled across the footbridge, stopping to look away to the blue coast mountains where the creek has its rise, past the gate to a tangled driveway marked 'Cedro,' where Mrs. Stanford used to live, and so to a two-story brown cottage designed and built by Mrs. Veblen, and since her death three years ago, his property. It seemed livable and comfortable.

We sat and talked of many things. Becky, his stepdaughter—a pretty fair-skinned young woman with big frightened blue eyes—came in, and later left to do the Saturday shopping, for which Veblen drew out of his pocket a roll of bills, giving her one.

He looked about as usual, seemed in good spirits, joked and laughed in quite the old way. For reply to queries about his health, he said that about all that bothered him was exhaustion, that he could do nothing without being greatly fatigued — the doctors did not know why. Apparently, he would like to go back to Green Bay, Wisconsin, for the summer months. We talked of their driving across in the Erskine. Becky remarked that he had a "nostalgia" for the Green Bay region. He spoke of "waiting for the clock to strike," which it would do equally in any place—but I think it would be a pleasure for him to be back there in the summer.

Mrs. Gregory talks of giving him $200 for the trip to his cabin by "Little Lake" on Washington Island and asks Mitchell if he might want to contribute $100.[48]

One of Veblen's favorite poems had always been "The Lake Isle of Innisfree" by William Butler Yeats, in which the poet spoke of building a small cabin and living alone in peace by the side of a lake. Yeats was haunted by a continual longing for Innisfree and heard "lake waters lapping . . . in his deep heart's core."[49]

Now it seemed particularly appropriate.

A year or more went by, much in the same fashion. Veblen's health slowly went downhill. One day he called Becky's attention to the fact that he could not see well out of one of his eyes.[50] This bothered him, as he had always had exceptionally keen vision. "I suspect that [somehow] he knew that he had only a day or so to live," said Becky. It may be that he was disturbed by his remembrance that his brother Orson had lost most of his eyesight not long before his death.[51] Soon thereafter, according to Becky, Thorstein "begged his niece [Hilda], and her family [her husband Ralph, and daughter, Colette] who were visiting . . . to stay a few days more . . . perhaps he didn't want me to be left alone at the moment of his death."[52]

The clock eventually struck; the curtain fell. His heart gave out on August 3, 1929, in the Sandhill Road House. He "was taken with a fainting attack," but had whispered to Becky, "Let be," and pressed her hand, which Becky took as a sign that he did not want a doctor. His brother Andrew wrote, "He lived only an hour or a little more; part of the time he was conscious, but did not seem to have much pain." His grandniece, Colette, who was about twelve, became anxious, and her mother, Hilda, called a doctor anyway; Ralph gave him artificial respiration until the doctor came. The doctor was unable to save him, and, as Thorstein made no response to treatment, Becky thought he had already died before the doctor arrived.[53]

A penciled note was found in the drawer of his bedroom. Undated and unsigned, it was as tersely and beautifully written as the most effective of his published writings:

It is also my wish, in case of death, to be cremated . . . as expeditiously and inexpensively as may be, without ritual or ceremony of any kind: that my ashes be thrown loose into the sea or in some sizeable stream running to the sea, that no tombstone, slab, epitaph, effigy, tablet, inscription or monument of any name or nature, be set up in my memory . . . that no obituary, memorial, portrait or biography of me, nor any letters written to or by me be printed or published, or in any way reproduced, copied or circulated.[54]

Veblen justifiably had confidence that the power of his writings would outlast any marble memorials erected in a misguided effort to perpetuate his essence. And he did not want Sarah Gregory or his stepchildren embarrassed by his correspondence. He also undoubtedly would have abhorred the pomposity and distortions found in all ceremonials, and thought it appropriate that the residual molecules of his corporeal being mingle with the elements and form part of the endless cycle of anonymous deaths and births that make up the life of our planet.

This factor in his ending is not what causes Veblen to be such a puzzle to succeeding generations of scholars. The enigma was rooted in his character and makes a consideration of his works and the man himself so fascinating. Guido Marx, his collegue at Stanford and the New School for Social Research, sat that Veblen, at times, looked like:

> . . . a satanically detached surgeon who was engaged in laying bare, with utterly cold technique, the diseased nerve system of a patient for whom he had no personal feeling beyond his interest in the ailment. But, as I got to know him better, I came to the conclusion that this pose was the purely protective armor set up to guard a quiveringly sensitive organism which personally suffered from each and every human wrong and stupidity. If ever there lived a man at whose heart there was a snake constantly gnawing, Veblen was that man.[55]

And Warner Fite, calling him "a tragic figure," elucidated: "He was one of those for whom no place had been provided in the world—he was never at home anywhere."[56] Rick Tilman, however, has commented: "Thorstein Veblen . . . was arguably the most original and penetrating economist and social critic that the United States has produced."[57]

25

After All

A fter wading through the lies and misplaced myths that have hidden the essential Veblen during this century, we have in our present biography unearthed hitherto unknown facts which help to clarify his story. We had long been puzzled that accounts of his life were dull. His writings, the bulk of which are sometimes difficult and obscure, will suddenly reward the reader with ideas so brilliant they seem blinding. These flashes can be unsettling, for they invariably undermine fragile but long cherished beliefs. How could such a wizard's life be dull?

The truth is, his life was not dull. His life was hair-raising. It was awful. His character was "assassinated" at Chicago. His academic career was crippled at Stanford. Medical science destroyed his health with mercury poisoning in Idaho. His second wife, with whom he knew brief happiness, went mad. But through it all, he wrote, brilliantly at times, eccentrically at others. He created gem-like economic and sociological masterpieces (which he often had to guarantee to get published), and earned the right to be considered a national treasure.

He would not abandon a fair maiden in distress, not he. He had first proposed to Ellen at age eighteen, and he married her at the age of thirty. She paid him back by making his life a legend, good for decades of sniggering. With a vengeance worthy of Moriarty's pursuit of Holmes, she tried to destroy Veblen's academic career. She immortalized herself as the devoted "woman scorned," the helpless victim of a cruel and bloodless womanizer. She fed her woeful tale of the stepped-upon aristocrat and out-of-step egghead to all who would listen to her, including William Rainey Harper, David Starr Jordan, John Casper Branner, and Veblen's biographers, Dorfman and Duffus. Ellen's fantasy was fleshed out in Dorfman's full-length biography of Veblen, with the addition of acid comments from Thorstein's younger brother Ed and by assessments of casual acquaintances who completely misunderstood him.

Far from bloodless, Veblen was something of a romantic. His touching and hopeless love (nay, passion) for a brainy, lovely, and sensitive student showed him at his incandescent best. "Under the surface," as Jacob Warshaw, his friend and colleague at the University of Missouri, asserted, "[he] was highly emotional." Perhaps it was as a rescuer in shining armor that he decided to marry his difficult first wife, a college classmate, whose nervous constitution forced her to quit teaching school—with the added drawback of her having to sink back into a family environment that she detested.[1]

Tilman has noted that both Veblen's wives were emotionally ill. Not only that, but Laura McAdoo Triggs Gagey committed suicide.[2] Student Sarah Hardy had a "breakdown," when faced with the reality that her graduate school strivings had prepared her for a career that she had grown to hate. The breakdown was evidently due to her physical makeup, but it did occur at a particularly stressful time for her. Veblen was obviously drawn to women who were brilliant, beautiful, needed rescuing, and were not of the usual complacent or obsequious model for Victorian women. As such, these unusual women may have had many of the same rebuffs as Thorstein encountered: peer jealousy and the scorn of the Philistines for the non-conformist. Victorian society, particularly, attempted to destroy adventurous and innovative women, and pushed many to the brink of instability. "Whom the Gods would destroy, they would first make mad," Seneca said, asserting that there was no great genius without a tincture of madness.[3] And Nietzsche proclaimed that unless there was chaos within, one did not give birth to a dancing star. In his lonely eminence Veblen was perhaps better understood by women who, although they were not in themselves geniuses, could not avoid regarding conventions with skeptical eyes.

Veblen was known as a skeptic, but according to Ardzrooni, he had, in fact, "too much faith."[4] He believed, or perhaps hoped, that the parental bent would eventually prevail, and that a society would be built that depended, not on force and fraud, but on helpfulness and cooperation. In this respect, although he was an agnostic, there was something in common in his thinking with that of the early Christians. In "Christian Morals and the Competitive System," written while he was at Stanford, he stated that while business ethics will not last as principles of behavior, Christian virtues may.[5]

A Darwinian, he rejected the Marxian dialectics and thought in terms of an open-ended system, whose characteristics were no more predictable than the future form of the vermiform appendix. Societies evolved and did not come to a triumphant end, like a college graduation speech. Yet, he seemed drawn toward friends and associates who were socialists and married two women who considered themselves socialists. When questioned as to what he would put in place of the old, rotten, social structure, he remarked that no one asked what should be used as a replacement for cancer or a wart on the nose.[6]

If Veblen had lived two more months, he would have witnessed the October 29 stock market crash and the beginning of the Great Depression, which revived an interest in his views. And if he had lived ten years more, he would have seen the beginning of World War II, with the involvement of Germany and Japan, which he had so amazingly predicted in 1915.

He had also stated that Japan had only a certain window of opportunity, and that its economic superiority over the advanced industrial nations would be temporary, because of "institutional ossification." At this writing, the pundits are now amazed that Japan, for the past few years, has been experiencing financial difficulties, bankruptcies of massive corporations, downsizing, homelessness, and widespread unemployment and social unrest.

Veblen originated the concept of institutional ossification—the idea that the longer an institution lasts, the more it tends to develop rigidities in its ability to adjust to new situations, a theme much belabored some years ago when the news was centered on the inability of American industry to keep pace with the Japanese.

In the face of global warming, Veblen's thoughts are applicable to our current concerns about the exhaustion of natural resources and excess conversion of our energy reserves to support a conspicuously wasteful lifestyle. Like the Viking predators Veblen discussed in *The Laxdaela Saga,* the world is now "trading on a thinner equity."

In 1911, Veblen warned that a European war was imminent. He also believed that a revolution would soon break out in Russia, as mentioned previously. As one who could predict the future, he was uncommonly prescient. But not always—he did admit that his pro-war stance in 1917–1918 was wrong. In 1922 he wrote, "It is evident now, beyond cavil, that no part of Europe is better off for America's having taken part in the great war."[7]

The author of *The Theory of the Leisure Class* has suffered the fate of the messenger who brings bad news. "If you meet [Veblen] on the road, kill him," as the Zen saying (referring to the Buddha) goes.[8] Veblen's critics have had a field day, taking his words out of context, trying to show inconsistencies and confusion in his thinking.[9] But his overall message is clear: We live in a wasteful, dehumanizing society.

Veblen was indeed skeptical about our industrial organization and challenged every premise upon which our society is built—competitiveness, status-seeking, and patriotism, among others. Many disliked him because of his caustic comments about organized religion or his sarcasm about the uselessness of the "kept classes," but it is possible that he was most shunned because of his attitude toward women. He not only attracted women, but he thought women were pivotal to the creation of a healthy society. He used the term "parental bent" and did not exclude the male, but in his *Instinct of Workmanship* he left no doubt that women were the primary figures in socializing the oncoming generation, performing the most essential work in society. Many male movers and shakers could not, and still cannot, forgive him for this.

Nine decades later no down-to-earth economist can quarrel with the accuracy of Veblen's analysis in *The Theory of Business Enterprise*. Wall Street currently leaps with ecstasy when thousands of corporate workers are rewarded for their loyalty with brutal layoffs. The dehumanizing aspects of Big Business maneuvers are even more apparent today than in 1904. But neither Veblen, nor subsequent thinkers, have ever worked out a scheme for changing the system that has a universal appeal.

Veblen may remain buried for another century, but in a world economy run as if we are all in some global Super Bowl race dedicated to tearing our rivals apart limb from limb, this quiet critic eventually will be recognized as a premier American sociologist and economic genius.

He has shown us, by cruel example, how a thinker lived life on his own terms in the rigidly conformist Victorian society, and survived. The story of his turbulent life has been effectively obscured, and his reputation destroyed, but the power of his ideas will not go away.

Appendix

Veblen Correspondence

The letters in this appendix are from the Miscellaneous Collections ("V" folder), Special Collections, University of Chicago.

Thorstein Veblen to Sarah Hardy, August 16, 1895

Dear Miss Hardy,

I sent you some time ago a (somewhat belated) set of proofsheets of Pres. Walker's paper in the Quarterly Journal. *Do you expect to reply in the Sept.* Journal? *If so, it will be necessary to send in copy very soon. Anything that comes in next week, if not more than five or six pages long, can go in. It may be beside the point for me to add that I have now returned to Chicago, and that I hope to get out of Chicago, again for a while very shortly.*

Very truly yours,
T.B. Veblen

Thorstein Veblen to Sarah Hardy, August 23, 1895

Dear Miss Hardy,

The proof sheets were directed to you at Wellesley about July 15.
You could probably do virtually nothing toward an answer to Pres.

Walker between now (Friday P.M.) and the end of the week. So I shall accept your suggestion that you see about an answer if you choose to, by next December.

I am sorry to disconcert and disquiet you with the admission that, contrary to the hope which you have so delicately expressed, there has been more bother than usual this summer, so far.

Very truly yours,
T.B. Veblen

Thorstein Veblen to Sarah Hardy, October 28, 1895

Dear Miss Hardy,

It is a long time since anything has hurt me as your letter did today. I had been afraid you were not in trim for heavy work, and that you would undertake more than you ought, but I had not thought of hearing from you in the hospital. Will you write me again, when you have the time and inclination (this does not mean that I wish you to put it off; I should like to hear from you again tomorrow), and let me know how you are getting on? I may be a bold, bad man for asking you to burden yourself with the task of keeping me informed when you have all and more than you ought to do without it, but "I want to know," and what can I do?

The paper for the Journal, by the way, will take care of itself, to some extent. Professor Laughlin intends to reply to Walker, through the medium of one of the men in his seminary, and he expresses his confident opinion that he can "drive a coach through Walker's paper."

I, too, wish I could have a walk and talk with you, whether it should serve to straighten you out in your mind or not. This may be selfish in me, but the (opaque) fact is that I miss you more than it would be well to tell you.

As for dying, I wouldn't think of it. It would be disagreeable to yourself; besides which I should not take it kindly at all, and there are many others of the same mind. I believe I have been at pains to inform you that I once "lay low" for several years, and I have to say that part of the years which I spent to no purpose was some of the most enjoyable times I have had. And the years were not wholly lost either. If it should appear, as the people at the hospital have predicted that you will have to lie low for two or three years, I venture that you will scarcely regret it in the end. "There's night and day, brother, both sweet things; there's likewise a wind on the heath. Life is very sweet, brother, who would wish to die?"

Very truly yours,
T.B. Veblen

Thorstein Veblen to Sarah Hardy, November 10, 1895

Dear Miss Hardy,

*I thank you for writing, even though what you have to tell of is so
unwelcome news. I wish I could be of use to you in some way, that I
could help to make the dreary days pass more lightly. You speak of
getting something to do. I don't know whether to take that hopefully, as
showing that you feel able to undertake anything, or as meaning simply
that you think you will have to do something. I wish it were for me to
help obviate this necessity, for I am persuaded that you ought to have no
work to do. Will you do me the kindness to tell me—to ask anything,
whether you think I can or ought to have anything to do with it or not?
I know that I am straining a point of courtesy in this question, but you
will overlook that and keep in mind that I mean well. I know you have
many good friends and that I am unfortunately but a very inferior
member of that body, but I trust you will overlook that too. Will you tell
me, too, what is the matter with you? What is the nature of this breakdown? What does the doctor call it?*

*Now, don't answer any of these questions, unless you choose to do so
of your own motion. Let me not put you under obligation to tell unless
you wish to. And do not burden yourself with answering anything if
writing costs you undesirable effort.*

*With regard to your telling Professor Laughlin, I can say that he
knows already, in a general way, that you have not been well, and that
you declined to reply to Walker partly on that account. I have told him
that much. I have also told several of your friends here, who have
inquired about you, probably much all that you told about yourself in
your first letter. Possibly that was something in the nature of a violation of confidence. If so, forgive me, for I knew not what I did. By the
way, I can readily tell Professor Laughlin as much as you choose, if
that should in the least degree relieve you of a burdensome or distasteful effort.*

*I am unable to place the passage of scripture which you cite. It
suggests Kings or Chronicles, but I do not believe there is anything like
it for barbarity in either of those books.*

*As for me, I am teaching (?) Socialism as usual. I don't know
whether I have made my brag to you about the Socialism class or not. It
is this: The class is larger (9) than the average of the graduate classes in
the Department, and it contains all the fellows but one, that one having
had the work already. It may be added, though I should not like this to
go any farther, that these students have already had pretty much all
other courses offered, and so had to take this work to make up the
necessary number of hours. Besides the Socialism, I have still to do with
the* Journal, *as the above letterhead abundantly shows. As for the proofs
of the book on Socialism, which I once in a moment of exaltation talked*

to you about, you need have no apprehension. As we go over the ground again this fall, it strikes me again that I should like to write something sometime, and I think I see more clearly what I want to say, too. But I shall certainly do nothing about it for another year. I have little time to spare for loafing, and it will be a long time before I shall get to it, if I ever do. The first volume on the list is The Theory of the Leisure Class, and I have taken that up in a small way this month. I am putting an hour or two a day on it, and have to neglect my classwork in order to do that. I don't know how long the mood will last. I have written part of the introductory chapter—what would perhaps make some twelve or fifteen small pages. The chrysanthemums are out now, and I have to put in some time with them, to see how they get along. I am a little disappointed in them. They look less bright and delicate than when I saw them with you last year.

I don't know yet what the chances of my reappointment for next year may be. It is not altogether improbable that I may be dropped from the budget, after the manner of Bemis, when it is made up next month. To make the way plain and smooth, I have struck for higher wages; though I am pretty nearly persuaded that the work I do is worth no more than what I am paid now.

When you write, if you are so kind as to write again, will you tell me how I may reach you, in case I have permission to write.

Very truly yours,
T.B. Veblen

Thorstein Veblen to Sarah Hardy, December 15, 1895

Dear Miss Hardy,

I am sorry to see that you still date your letters from the hospital. I have tried to imagine that you might be there in some other capacity than as an invalid this time, but I suppose the dreary facts of the case are against this good natured attempt. Does the situation grow more tolerable as time goes, and do you get stronger? Do you go to Florida? A certain instinctive sense of disappointment at the announcement that you are arranging to go there argues that I must have been entertaining some unreasoning hope that your next move would be nearer this way rather than farther away. By the way, you had better not thank me for any imagined kindness. There is (1) nothing in it, and (2) it may encourage me to imagine that I am in some way, not readily comprehensible, a very meritorious person. It further moves me to speak my mind about the matter and make the awkward admission that the debt of sentiment is all the other way. It might ill become the dignity of my official position to go the whole length and let you into the secret of *what I owe you. It hurts me to think that I should have proved so true a prophet, or that the threat should have come true, and it hurts, too, that I can do nothing to falsify the prediction.*

The Leisure Class was, of course, shelved while the Dec. Journal took the floor and went through its customary motions. Now (yesterday) the Journal is ready to mail. It has been out of my hands for a week, and The Leisure Class is on the boards again. It goes without saying that you come in conspicuously under the category, and that your likeness looms up before me constantly as I sit here spinning out the substance of this high theoretical structure. As the writing proceeds, or rather in the attempt to proceed, I find myself embarrassed by an excessive invention of unheard-of economic doctrines more or less remotely pertinent to the main subject in hand; so that after having written what will perhaps make some fifty or sixty pages when revised, I have not yet come in sight of the doctrine of conspicuous waste, which is of course to constitute the substantial nucleus of this writing. About the three chapters and the bond [?] I don't know. There are difficulties. You ought not now to read anything of so serious a theoretical character. And then I have quite forgotten what scheme of subdivision I may have had in mind when I talked with you about the three chapters. The scheme actually in operation is to write what will at a guess make some thirty pages (12 ms), and then write in a new caption and ostensibly make a new start. Also, I should scarcely be able to revise and complete the three chapters until the whole stands forth in its symmetrical entirety; partly because it would be impossible, and partly because it would be too much bother.

I am still living within Mrs. Nellis's sphere of influence, in fact in the same place, though not in the same room, as last year. I see none of that cheese this year; I board at a club, where cheese is rare and of the wrong kind. Mrs. Veblen is farming in Idaho. Her health seems slightly improved, but she does not seem well content. Mrs. Laughlin is, at a guess, precisely as nice as Professor Laughlin, and Mr. Hill is happy, or at least in sparkling good humor. I volunteer the information that Mr. Closson also married last summer. Mrs. Closson is a German lady, whom I have not met. I don't know if the budget has been made out yet. At any rate nothing has been told me, and I don't know what may be decided about my case. My health is about the same kind as it has been, but perhaps a little more of it.

Miss Felton is in my class and seems to be doing very fair work, but I don't know her very well at all. I shall be glad to give her greetings from you. Mr. Stuart (also in the class) is doing very well. Among other achievements, he has a paper in the current issue of the Journal (of which I make bold to send you a sample copy). "Theronys no more to til."

You ask what I did during my years off. That is precisely the point. I did nothing. And as I like that sort of thing I enjoyed it; and enjoyment and profit are pretty nearly synonymous with me.

I wish you a merry Christmas, and I wish you had a sufficiently

indolent temperament to let go as cordially as you ought to. May I add
that I wish I could help you do it! For I can do that sort of thing well.

Very truly yours,
T.B. Veblen

Thorstein Veblen to Sarah Hardy, January 18, 1895

Dear Miss Hardy,

Since I saw you yesterday I have been wrestling with the liveliest
regret that has beset me for a good many months past. My stupidity not
to say perversity, prevented my seeing or appreciating until it was too
late, the Napoleonic opportunity I had of carrying you off and keeping
you to myself for the best part of the afternoon. That I should have
hesitated to break a previous engagement in order to meet you at Mrs.
Crane's at luncheon is by this time quite incomprehensible to me. It is
not that I ask you to forgive me for having missed my opportunity but I
have to tell you, and beg you to let me do so, as a refuge from my own
abject detestation of myself.

I want to tell you also how glad I am to have seen you looking so very
well and apparently feeling so well. I have every hope now that your year
of retirement will be not only tolerable but in a good measure enjoyable,
though I still have some misgivings that you are not really as strong as
you seem. I hope that yesterday's dissipation has no bad consequences.

I want also to say a word about the Leisure Class, *to which I had no*
chance to give articulate expression. As I said, the character of this
monograph, as near as I can see, is not approximately up to grade. It
disappoints me and puzzles me that I am unable to say what I want to
in the way I want to say it. However, I shall go on with it, though it is
very doubtful if it will ever be presentable for publication. It is now (the
first draft) about half written, or perhaps rather more, and promises to
be longer than was originally planned. I expect, D.V. [Deo Volente], to
complete the rough draft in a month from this time, and shall then have
to revise and verify and rewrite. After that, and this is what I am
coming to, I want permission to send you at least portions of the ms. to
get your criticism of it, if it should not be too much of a task. Can you
do this for me? Or can you undertake it provisionally? I have, of course,
no other claim than that your kindness in the past has established a
precedent. You have sown the wind, and are beginning to reap the
whirlwind.

I wish you a happy journey and a propitious return, and I beg you to
let me hear from you, if you are not displeased with me, before leaving.

Truly yours,
T.B. Veblen

APPENDIX 193

Thorstein Veblen to Sarah Hardy, January 23, 1896

Dear Miss Hardy,

I beg you to pardon my writing you again in this unprovoked fashion. I have an excuse, however, which will appear before I get through, and if that does not prove sufficient I shall appeal to your goodness in the full confidence of being forgiven on the basis of free grace alone. You will also pardon whatever ill taste may appear in my writing you on this dubious stationery [letter written on plain, yellow paper]. I intend to write a long letter and this paper has the easiest surface to get over of any within reach (being selected primarily with that in view, though with a subsidiary consideration of its inexpensiveness). May it reconcile you to it that it is also the particular paper upon which the Science Class emerges, so that it is immediately at hand and [to] resort to it means labor saving on that count also.

Ostensibly, I am going to write you some sage advice touching your health and the measures to be taken to preserve and promote it; at the same time I want to tell you what you ought to do and what you can do safely, to make your leisure time "profitable," seeing that you are, as I infer, bound to make it so anyway; also I want to talk to you, and without this incentive the two first mentioned reasons would have had a speculative interest only.

Assuming then that you need advice, and assuming also the larger assumption that I am at liberty to thrust myself upon you with it: I understood you to say that Professor Laughlin had encouraged you in the notion that you should make some sort of an investigation into the industrial situation in Hawaii in some of its phases, along the line of "practical economics," presumably with a view to "producing something." This was no doubt well meant advice on his part, but with all respect, I assure you it is all wrong. The only safe way for you is to avoid all work along this line, which you have had too much of for some time past anyway, and which I am inclined to think is more or less tedious to you at the best. For both of these reasons—and each is sufficient by itself under the circumstances—it is to be avoided. And even if all this were not so, the strain of working toward any given product would be a drag on you such as you can not and must not afford. It was precisely this—the strain of the classroom and coming up to an excessively high-strung daily ideal of workmanship—that was the proximate cause of your retirement from Wellesley. It was the strain rather than the work; though the strain would not have broken you if you had not been fagged out with "practical economics" beforehand—which you will pardon me for saying that you are (to my apprehension) by no means specially fitted for nor inclined to. Therefore, leave everything of that kind out. Don't dare to touch it with the point of your umbrella. I should be sorely grieved and disappointed to find when you get back that you know anything about the economic situation in the islands. It may be quite irrelevant whether I am grieved or not, but as my own preference is the only principle of conduct with which I am gifted, be indulgent and let me fall back for justification on the only principle which I have got. Have to do with nothing that savors of workmanship, especially not in the way of practical economics. So much for the plan which I infer that you have been deluded into harboring hitherto. We will consider that out of court.

Now as to the constructive part of this scheme. This will require something in the way of preliminary premises, and the like. To begin with the beginning: I have a theory which I wish to propound. I do not know how much, if any or all, of this I have told you before, apart from the few words that passed in the carriage on the way to the station. I am under a vague impression that I have already told you everything I ever knew or thought, but this may not have been included. If it has been told before you can of course save yourself the reading of the present exposition. My theory touches the immediate future of the development of economic science, and it is not so new or novel as I make it out to be. It is to the effect that the work of the generation of economists to which you belong is to consist substantially (so far as that work is to count in the end) in a rehabilitation of the science on modern lines. Economics is to be brought into line with modern evolutionary science, which it has not been hitherto. The point of departure for this rehabilitation, or rather the basis of it, will be the modern anthropological and psychological sciences, perhaps most immediately, for economic theory in the general sense, that folk psychology which is just now taking on a definite form. Starting from this preliminary study of usages, aptitudes, propensities and habits of thought (much of which is already worked out in a more or less available form) the science, taken generally, is to shape itself into a science of the evolution of economic institutions. Detailed theoretical work will of course be in place, as always, and "practical economics" will come in for its share, and these things will have to come into an organic relation with the science, which at present they have not. This theoretical work will have to depend closely on psychological and ethnological data for its premises. This is pretty much all I know about the development of economics in the future, and it is to be admitted that I might not be able to prove even that much in court. Be not disturbed in mind, by the way, with apprehension that I am about to write a compendium of this rehabilitated science. It will take a lustier pen than mine to write out even a working scheme, if it is ever done; but it need not be done at all that I know of.

Now this generalization of the probable fate of economic science in the immediate future may strike you as pretty fantastic, which I shall admit without reserve if you say so, but there is so much of a foundation for it all as that economic speculation and writing is visibly taking on such a cast today. This happens, if nowhere else, in writings of some of the "cranky" economists. It might also be argued that this was the meaning of the movement called the Historical School; but the Historians failed to recognize their vocation and ran off into inanities. On the other hand, the Austrians and their followers in other countries have been groping out instinctively and blindly into the domain of psychology, and trying to find there the premises and justification of their theories, but as they were out of date in their psychology, besides not knowing what they were about, the result has not had the value which it otherwise might. However, and this is to the point even if the rest is not, a reading of some of the books that deal with anthropology in outline would never come amiss whether the growth of the science takes one direction or another. So, if you should find that line of reading interesting you might make a trial of it, provisionally. You see, I go on the supposition that you have done very little of the kind; if I am mistaken, then I take this all back and beg you to consider it erased. It is reading of a different kind from what tired you out last year and last fall, and that is in its favor. And it need not be carried on for a purpose beyond itself, or with a view to systematized knowledge. If you try it at all, do not let it tire you. Go no farther with it than your curiosity will carry you, and never let it degenerate into a task. Drop it without compunction just as soon as you are so inclined. If it does not interest you for its own sake it is of no use to you anyway. My reason for thinking you would be interested may seem a curious one to you. It is chiefly that you look so kindly to Lavengro. [Lavengro: *a novel by George Borrow, permeated with the spirit of "the wind on the heath" and unconventionality.] I believe it takes more or less of a taste for anthropology to like that sort of thing. If you will, I should like to send you two or three elementary books which I have used. (This is the reason for my taking the liberty to write now; so that if I get a favorable answer I could get them to you before you leave California.) These books are easy reading and I have a hope you would enjoy at least part of them. And, by the way, do not despise them because they seem irrelevant; everything seems irrelevant in anthropology if it is taken by itself, nothing if taken with the rest. You could return the books to me when called for or when I see you again. Meanwhile I could send you another installment if you should want more, or if you should want something on any special topic or direction.*

Will you write me within a day or two and let me know what you have to say; and will you also tell me how you are getting on with your convalescence?

I know that I have been bold beyond the limits of conventionality in this, but you will be indulgent because you know that I have a very uncertain grasp of the conventionalities at the best, and I hope that you will not find that I have thrust myself gratuitously and indelicately upon you with all this advice. At the same time do not let the advice influence you against your inclination. If you find me intolerably offi-

cious, will you kindly give me a gentle hint that you have had enough of it, and I shall set myself to the task of bringing about a shrinkage of the supply.

Truly yours,
T.B. Veblen

Thorstein Veblen to Sarah Hardy, February 6, 1896

My dear friend,

It was kind of you to let me call you so, and I thank you for this and for all the rest of your letter. It was especially gracious of you to speak so kindly of what I had the presumption to wish you the morning after you left Chicago. I dare say you may have been alarmed at the incoherence and incontinence of that epistle, but you would have been dismayed to know the continence which it cost. I thank you for undertaking to read [my manuscript] for me. I was not sure but your earlier professions had been more than half in jest, and I was also not sure until I saw you whether I ought to ask anything in the way of work, but you looked so well and strong that I have no fear on that score now, and I am anxious to get your criticism if the ms. ever comes to anything. This latter point seems a bit doubtful just now. And by the way in this connection I have something to retract. You once expressed an unreflecting desire to be subsumed under the category of the leisure class, and I as unreflectingly conceded it. I believe now that that was all a mistake. The foundation of unbelief being the opaque fact, unexplained and incontrovertible, that during the three weeks since I saw you last the entire "Leisure Class" has been in abeyance, having achieved nothing beyond contributing some half-a-dozen sheets of handwriting to the waste basket. It is true, I did count with a good deal of confidence on an affirmative when I asked you for this favor, because I believed you would do me a favor if you could. I can scarcely say, however, that I knew, or even freely suspect[ed], that you would let me designate time and place, for this latter might be found more awkward than you have any apprehension of. There is no guessing what abridgement your stay in the Islands and on the Coast would suffer under a broad construction of this clause, for which I can not help thanking you, after all, more heartily than for all the rest. Have you read a story in William Morris' Earthly Paradise *called "East of the Sun and West of the Moon"? Lead us not into temptation.*
As for the anthropological reading which I have inveigled you into, I do not know that will be of much direct use; but it should be of some use in the sense of an acquaintance with mankind. Not that man as viewed by the anthropologist is any more—perhaps he is less—human than man as we see him in everyday life and in commercial life; but the

anthropological survey should give a view of man in perspective and more in the generic than is ordinarily attained by the classical economist, and should give added breadth and sobriety to the concept of "the economic man." At the same time I have to warn you that I am by no means sure but that the subconscious motive may have been the stronger motive in my obtruding my advice on you in this matter; it may be in great part only that this line of reading is particularly interesting to me. If you find in the event that something of that sort seems to be true, I shall be sorry for having helped you misspend your time, even if, as I am confident, it will help to keep you from brain work of a kind which would be more of a hindrance to your health; for I suppose in that case it would hold that some other line of activity might have been found which would have been more to the purpose in all respects. However, all that can not detract from the immediate gratification which your response gives me—gives to my vanity, perhaps. My own knowledge of anthropological and ethnological lore is very meager and fragmentary, and it is somewhat presumptuous in me to offer advice, but it goes without saying that I shall want to try my hand at all questions that may occur to you, if you will give me a chance.

I have mailed to your address two parcels of books. I found, on looking it up, that the volume which I should have advised you to begin with (Topinard's "Anthropology") is not at hand. I shall be able to send it in a few days however, as it is in town. I would begin with Topinard, follow that with Mortillet (Le pré-historique), follow that with Brinton and Keane. Of the two last, Keane is the most to be relied upon where they differ. As Topinard is not at hand, it will by no means hurt to begin with Brinton and Keane. Make no effort to remember any of it. The salient points of classification will fix themselves sufficiently by iteration, and the details are not worth remembering. Do not make work of it; make rest and comfort, that is the rehabilitation of your health, the norm in everything, not to be broken over on any pretext. Drop it all, temporarily or permanently, whenever it is in the least degree irksome. The book on "Art," by the way, is put in to break the monotony; I think you will find it curious and interesting. Whenever any topic suggests itself on which you would like to read more exhaustively, write me and I will send such books as you ask for or such as I may think you want.

I shall of course have to concede the point of your paying the freight, though I am sorry to do so, as it will hamper me in sending things which I may think would interest you but which you might not wish to pay postage on. It obviously rests with me, however, to say in what manner the remittance shall be made, as I took the initiative in the matter and so am primarily responsible, and as I, further, advance the postage. I have therefore to say that the remittance shall be made only in the form of letter postage, on letters directed to me, and that it shall be paid within a reasonable length of time.

It may be selfish in me, but I can not help protesting against the lapse of years which you look forward to before returning to this part of the world. I wish, and always have wished, to see the Coast, even if I can not find a chance to stay there, and the same is true of the Islands, perhaps even more so.

The chance of my achieving it seems very small at present, and as the next best thing to seeing it all (with you, if you will pardon my saying so) I will recklessly ask you to tell me all about it. You have once implied that you like to write to me—perhaps that should be put in the past tense—and this makes me bold to say that I want to hear from you always and on every topic, and let me set conventionality aside for a moment and say that I want to know all about your life down there in that strange world which I may never see.

Yes, in the future world you shall have full liberty to thank me—and I do not know what for—because thanks are sweet, sweetest indeed when undeserved.

Please let me know what is to be your address. I wish, having under-taken your education, to send a couple more books.

Your most sincerely devoted master,
T.B. Veblen

Thorstein Veblen to Sarah Hardy, February 24, 1896

Dear Miss Hardy:

I should scarcely be the one to advise you as to the significance of your approaching marriage. I expect to be divorced about that time. But I will take upon me the ungracious office anyway. If the marriage is entered into because your love of the man compels you, then it means the fullness of life; if for any reason short of that, even from the kindliest and most disinterested motives (I have known one such), then it means death—deterioration and dissipation of what is good and strong in you. The sacrament will not bear tampering with. I know I am mistaken, and I know my sense is not a dispassionate judge in the matter, but I feel— blindly, instinctively, though not without all tangible ground—that the latter may be the case. There is nothing in heaven or earth that will repay the loss of your life.

Forgive me for what I have done and for what I am about to do. It may be shameless in me to speak as I do; I know it is selfish, and I believe it will pain you, for it means the loss and degradation in your eyes of a friend whom you have thought much of; but it is to be said and I can not help saying it. I love you beyond recall. Ever since the first time I saw you, in the library, you have gone with me as a vision of light and life and divine grace. My life since then has centered about you, and I have to confess that that is the reason for all my paltry efforts to keep up some kind of contact with you. I had fancied that I might be willing to remain a hanger-on only, but since I saw you this winter that illusion, too, is gone. The wind on the heath is fallen dead. I would turn to you now without circumstance, and without regard for anything, even for your own happiness; there is nothing left but this one elemental fact.

I know how unworthy all this must seem, but I have no other excuse than there is no helping it. Deal not harshly in your judgment, for it is the cry of a lost soul.

I can only hope that this untoward episode will leave at most but a small and vanishing residue of bitterness in your life; I would so gladly that your life should be sweet and good and beautiful. And I beg leave to thank you for the light that has fallen across my way in the past, and to say that I know you will forgive me in the end out of the goodness of your heart.

Goodbye,
T.B. Veblen

Thorstein Veblen to Ellen Veblen, March 31, 1896

[Copied by Ellen and sent to Sarah Hardy Gregory]

Dear Ellen,

I have evil news to tell you, though it may not be altogether news to you. I have to confess to a fondness for Miss Hardy which is no longer to be called by any other name but love. I have come to a conviction that honesty requires me to tell you, and I can see now that I have been deceiving both myself and you about it. She has got into my blood, and there is no help for it. I am sorry to have to speak out, for I know how it will hurt you, and I should be unable to face you with the confession even yet, if it were not for the fact (which I have known for some time) that she is to be married this spring; so that the futility of my confession can, in a way, be set off against the bitter wrong which you have suffered.

During these months, while the conviction has been borne in upon me that I am not your husband in fact and ought no longer to be so in name, my feeling toward you has not changed. You are still dear to me, just as you have been—nearer and dearer than anyone else, not even excepting my mother. The new attachment differs in kind, rather than exceeds the old in degree, and you are still the best friend that I have in the world. I want to take care of you as well as I can, and to help make life tolerable for you as far as may be; not out of pity but because I want to, and I beg you not to cut me off from the privilege of doing what I can. I do not ask you to forgive me, for I know that the evil I have done you is beyond forgiveness, but I believe I can still be as good and true a friend and help to you as you can find. But the relation of husband has become untenable, if it has not always been a false one, and the truth of life requires that this false relation should cease in name as it does not exist in fact.

Do not let the unworthiness of my conduct grieve you or add bitterness to the evil which my awful mistake has brought upon you; I believe the whole has been beyond human power to help or hinder. Deal gently with me for your own sake and for your love's sake and let me still sign myself

Your Thorstein

[Ellen wrote to Sarah: "I copy this from a copy and have not the exact date. One day when I was out Mr. Veblen took all the letters he had written me since his confession and also the one I received from you."]

Thorstein Veblen to Ellen Veblen, June 1, 1896

Dear Ellen,

I have hesitated long, perhaps too long already, before asking the wretched favor which I have to ask today. After what I wrote you two months ago, there is in the nature of the case no course open to us other than a formal, legal separation; and of course, any move for such a separation must come from your side, for the reason that the blame lies with me, and also because I have no plea on which to ask for a divorce. It may seem cruel, and it certainly feels shameful enough, to ask you to make this move, but I do not see any other way. Therefore, if you are still in Idaho, will you go to Boise City and put your case into the hands of a lawyer there and let him carry it through. I shall of course expect to pay all expenses and can remit whatever amount may be necessary. If you are not in Idaho, or not near enough to return there, then place your case in a lawyer's hands in the state where you are staying and wait there long enough to satisfy the requirements of residence.

I am persuaded that it is better on all accounts to have this matter formally disposed of as soon as may be; and the only way seems to be that you must do it. I am sorry to ask it of you, for I know how it will hurt you, but I do not see that there is any other way out of it.

Please write me a word when you get this, and let me know where you are, and tell me that I am not asking more than I ought to, and tell me, too, what you intend to do, and whether I will have a chance to see you this summer.

Affectionately,
T.B. Veblen

[Ellen wrote to Sarah: "I append my answer to this request in full, the only letter I wrote him from the time I received his confession."]

Ellen Veblen to Thorstein Veblen

[Copy sent to Sarah Hardy Gregory along with Thorstein's letters]

I have not neglected what seemed necessary to say to you in answer to your letters but the answers sent through your brother and mine have not been delivered. They were simply as to the impossibility of our meeting again, a request that the name of Ellen should not be used any more and an assurance I should never take action toward securing a divorce. I shall not be in this part of the country longer. I suppose you can take the action you wish without my co-operation. Mrs. Gregory knows through me that you did not wish me any longer to be your wife even in name, and as to yourself, I shall not in any wise trouble you in the future. Through my own carelessness, as I find, Miss Willard read a letter I enclosed to her for forwarding. Otherwise the matter is not known outside of my family and yours, except by Mrs. Green, to whom my sister wrote, on a request that she should tell her sometime. I enclose the letter that Miss Willard read and refused to send because of a prejudice in favor of monogamy. If I have made any complaint of you it has been to your brother Andrew in recent correspondence and, I fear, in an argument with Miss Willard about "forgiving you and going back and living with you" a moderate assurance as to your attitude. I mention this to add that I am infinitely sorry for even thus far sinning against my own changeless feeling of eternal union with the one I loved and married. His sins and weakness are like my own to me, and though they part us absolutely and forever, I can only accept the death it is for me as the natural consequence of a connection with you.

The idea of your family seems to be to keep your action as quiet as possible. If there is any right and wrong in human affairs, which seems a childish question compared to the one whether the race is worth preserving in its hideousness and suffering, the right is certainly on the side of truth and candor.

It is not only for the sake of my dear marriage ring, which I wear every day and shall wear while I live, but it is with indignation that I refuse to take the offensive and in this far away place.

The law cannot undo what is a fact and alas! love and shame cannot undo it.

With this let me bid you farewell.

Nellie

Ellen Veblen to Sarah Hardy Gregory, Undated [probably 1897]

Learning towards the last of September [1897] that I was with his parents, Mr. Veblen came to me without warning. He picked me up from where I lay and took me in his arms. He treated me altogether as his dear wife, and after a time, asked me if we should go and see "our mother." We said not one word about you or the past—we never have— but all that sad, sweet day I was given to understand, by every sign of affection, and, as it were, relief, that the past was the past. More than that I did not require. Happiness there could never be for us again while we endure, but a kind of comfort in one another there could be because we were certainly set apart from all others, and we had lived together long and were already old—for this has taken every vestige of youth from us both. I trusted entirely to his honor and came back [to Chicago] as his wife, without any questions and without any promises or pardons. But from the moment of reaching this city all has been different. Perhaps he only came to me because his brothers said that if his parents learned the truth (they do not know even now) the disgrace of it would kill them. Perhaps he came thinking it would make you happier to learn that we were together. Apparently he took the step for anyone's sake but mine, for I came back to even worse than I went away from.

He says in his letter "if the relation has not always been a false one." No one could be guilty of such sacrilege but he himself. He refers later to his "awful mistake." You may not know but I do that this is a reference of like meaning. How little excuse he had for being mistaken in his feelings you may know from the fact that he was my classmate for six years, and told me he loved me "as dearly as he could" when I was only sixteen and he eighteen. I refused him then as I continued to do. I never expected to marry him, yet because of his love of me, I felt bound to him in a sense, and did not expect to marry anyone else. After leaving college he engaged himself to a new acquaintance whom he "did not love nor ever told that he loved." He broke this engagement while at Yale. I never knew of it until after we had become engaged, five years after his graduation from Carleton College [1885]. No girl ever had a better right to suppose herself loved with a wonderfully constant and spontaneous and well-tested love. Nonetheless, when we had been engaged six months and he told me it would be three years before we could marry, and made no move to provide the means for our marriage even at that distant day, I broke the engagement, hurt beyond words to say at his delay. I did this understanding well that his health was wretched, that it was not in him to look out for the future and that he was slow and phlegmatic at best, but though I had then come to love him with all my life, my pride was stronger, I am glad to remember. If ever man had a good opportunity to retreat even at the last moment he did, but when he met me again after all the long silence, he completely ignored what I had done, and with characteristic assurance came to me as my accepted lover. When he warned you against marrying unless love compelled it his implication was—what you may judge it to be. Moreover, when we had been married a year and a half he told me as though it were a sweet surprise to him that he loved me better than when he married me.

My own feelings will not permit me to say what I would. When you

*went from here [to Wellesley] considering what my last year with Mr.
Veblen had been, I considered it best to go, too [to Idaho] and I did not
dream that he would so far depart from the wholesome traditions of
conjugal fidelity as to seek your love, and I hoped that his heart would
turn back to me. I asked him to promise, before I went, that he would not
correspond with you, and he promised me. He always either laughed at
my jealousy of you or treated me very roughly for it. But it was he
himself who opened the subject by accusing me of it the night after I got
home that fall when he woke and found me crying. But having become
aware of my conviction, you yourself can best judge how far he considered my happiness and my rights. In December, after I went West, he
began to address me once more in affectionate terms and once wrote—
"Remember the sweet Stacyville days and keep yourself ready to go back
to them." He told me also that he loved me, "and let me add that there is
no other." Very suddenly there came a change and I felt sure that he had
been to see you or you had been here. It seemed a cruel thing to me, and
I lost everything by it.*

*In March he sent me "The Phantom Rickshaw" and left me to draw
my own conclusions, hoping, I suppose that I would express them, and
thus give him an opportunity to leave me "for my jealousy" without
needing to make any confession; but I did not do so. On the third of
April [1896] he sent me a confession of that which he had denied with
cruelties which it would be impossible for you to imagine.*

*Mr. H.K. White came to see Mr. Veblen on the day I left for Idaho.
The agony that Mr. Veblen seemed to suffer during that hour, noticeable
to me, led me afterwards to ask a question—whether you were engaged
to Mr. White. His answer was "I am under the impression that she is."
He had led me once before to believe that you were engaged to Mr.
[Robert] Hoxie, in order, I believe that I should stop protesting against
his walking with you, etc.*

When he handed me the first volume of the Cohn [Gustave Cohn,
The Science of Finance, *published in Germany in 1895, translated
from the German by Veblen.] I opened at once to the preface which (I
thought from modesty) he had not shown me. He had done what he did
knowing that it would almost kill me. I had written the book all out in
manuscript at his dictation. Our happiest hours for 3 years had been
spent so. I had also read all the proof once. I closed the book and handed
it back without a word and he left me in anger and did not come near
me or speak to me until the following morning when I went to him, as I
must have done if we were ever to speak again.*

*You in your gaiety, I in my heartbreak, lived our lives of "miserable
loneliness." I had never seen a Platonic friendship and I could but
believe that you were unconsciously drifting toward what I supposed to
be your first experience of love. It seems that Mr. Veblen was also
deceived, for I can hardly think that so proud a man would have made
the confession he did without hope, even if unavowed. I thought he was*

very wrong to permit himself to fall into and continue in such a temptation, but that it was an almost overwhelming temptation I could but see. And the sense of his tragical misfortune and of my horrible fate to be in the way of his happiness was what most filled my mind in those days. Since I have known that you did not care for him this tragedy has seemed more than ever all unnecessary to me. When I think of what your fatal friendship has done to us, I feel that you owe him, at least, all that you can give to make his life tolerable. I suppose I love him still in spite of what no one else could forgive, and this fact makes my starved life with him not only ruinous to my self-respect but maddening. I could be thankful to see him happy with you in any relation whatever. My life is a nightmare to me and any bettering of his condition could only be a relief. But what actually will come next I cannot foresee. He thinks he can ruin my life with impunity and that it does not matter—because it is mine. But if I understand myself I shall not long be passive. And he would not hesitate to take my life.

Mrs. Veblen

Ellen Veblen to Sarah Hardy Gregory, April 1897

Mrs. Gregory:—

I enclose some letters which I should like to have you read. Although you ignore that which is behind, yet you are one of a trio forevermore. The peace which you wished for us can never come. Not even peace is the end of such a storm. It is ruin. I do not know whether you have known that I returned [to Chicago] in the fall [of 1896]. I wish you to know how I came to do so. Had my husband made this year tolerable for me, or tried to make it so, I could, for the sake of the old love, have borne even what I had to bear in silence, and let my life, love, ideals, ambitions come to naught, as they must, and time should close over them and bury them without a name. I have lost much before for the sake of that love, but regret, even, was impossible while love and not bitterness was in my heart. But the last six months have been for me what no human being should bear. Nothing but crime or madness could come out of such a life. My whole self did indeed revolt at the idea of merely seeing him again. I could not imagine it either in time or in eternity. It was to make one's very self a lie. The whole universe proclaimed it an impossibility. Yet I let an impulse instead of my true instinct dictate what I should do at the moment when my own love and Mr. Veblen's honor were on trial. I trusted him whom I had no right to trust. I thought that not even he would dare to come back to me without having first turned away from the very thought of you. Such was not the case, and I believe he has deliberately treated me this year in such a manner as to compel me to leave him, in which case the odium falls upon me unless all is disclosed. Perhaps he trusts my love to shield him to the last, even after this last wrong. I cannot yet be sure that every trace of gentleness has been destroyed in me, since I believe I was largely made up of that quality, judging by my own course. But I now know that my heart has known its last touch of grief, so I also suspect that tenderness will never actuate me again. Even in taking this step—of writing you— I know that I not only take my life in my hands, but that I consent with myself to give him pain, for the first time.

After his confession to me I refused to accept anything from him. As he sees fit to treat me with dishonor though I was as far as possible from seeking to share his life I shall, if I leave him, again refuse to allow him to contribute anything to my support. But I have long been thinking that I would not again, as I did in the west last year, by shielding him, expose my self to suspicion and insult. An occurrence of two or three days ago down town confirmed me. When I was buying goods to take with me on my unutterably lonely venture last year, I bought some doors and windows of a man located near the university. When after many entreaties Mr. Veblen condescended to and go and look at them it was in a manner to give that man the impression—true enough—that he cared neither about the deal, nor about me, nor about my lonely undertaking. I quite appreciated even then that the whole matter was disgraceful. I have met this man twice on the street lately. He seemed surprised to see me back. The last time he said these words in my ear as he hurried past me— "Are you walking the street?" I did not understand so foolish a question and asked him what he said, and he repeated it and was gone. After some moments it came to me in what manner I had been addressed by a man who knew us and our position. This too, Mrs. Gregory. If Mr. Veblen ever meets this man he will pretend not to recognize him.

Therefore, if I take any action, it will not be to get a divorce in some distant state where no one knows either of us, where Chicago would never hear of it, and where I should have to make my fame as a woman who had left her husband, but it will be among our friends and acquaintances where I can meet with respect. I will never again endure for his sake what I have in the past, for not even my own family knew that anything was amiss until that letter a year ago. My poor health has been made to cover all that seemed strange and has been used freely by us both, even though produced by the situation it was supposed to excuse.

I wish you to know that Mr. Veblen's health is entirely broken down. He says often that he will not live through the year. I wish you to know that he to whom existence was pleasure enough knows no joy, and I believe no ambition. He speaks of resigning his position here, which means that he will drop out of University life and do no more work.

I can give you no idea of how happy we once were. You yourself could as easily look forward to this as I. Probably far more so, for Mr.

Veblen was decidedly a country boy—even when I married him. The beginning of his disaffection was that he was ashamed of me, when after three years of country life and living solely upon what little money I had, spending all our time together in the most intimate and happy association, in a place where I and my family were well-known and had no need to keep up our respectability by outward appearances, we went away into "the world" on a fellowship, and thus we have lived ever since until the year when I lost him, in poverty, working as I never had before, and denying myself everything. My appearance in society was not creditable to him.

I shall now have to support myself—in what way I do not know. My search has so far been unsuccessful.

Ellen R. Veblen

Draft of Letter from Sarah Hardy Gregory to Thorstein Veblen

[possibly July 4, 1900]

"My," [crossed out] Dear Dr. Veblen:—

Long ago, a wise man taught me the rule "Never do today what you can put off till tomorrow." Therefore, I delayed answering your flattering questions; or acknowledging "Pecuniary Employments" [words illegible] the Journal *and have found it most satisfactory. Will you forgive the triple misdemeanor on my part and lay all the blame on the teacher of the rule?*

Though rude, the chronic procrastinator has no lack of excuses, e.g, the pernicious [words unclear] Americation [words unclear]

Thorstein Veblen to Sarah Hardy Gregory, July 20, 1900

My dear Mrs. Gregory,

Lately, on returning from a tour of inspection of the Rockefeller iron mines north of Lake Superior, I had the pleasure of finding your note of the Fourth waiting for me. You will pardon me if the spirit of indolence moves me to protest against the work of supererogation of your returning the copy of Ward's review which you had honored me with requesting.

Moreover it is not kind of you, and scarcely reverent, to use irony and other allied figures of speech concerning the English of the Patriarch of Sociology in a case where laudable sentiment gets the better of his diction. What you say is true—as it should be—and what you imply is perhaps truer still—as is not surprising—when you speak of the magnanimity and positiveness with which Mr. Ward understands the

Leisure Class. *I assure you his review has been a great help to me in that respect. It has brought me to a sobering realization of the very grave importance which my writing, and what I now understand to have been my thinking and my insight, have for the spread of knowledge among men.*

I am unable to share your view, that the allegation of "too much truth" is to be taken as an accusation. I find myself unable to resent it. It is probably to be construed as a superlative, and that being the case I should like to cross out the exclamation point with which you follow it, as well as the one which punctuates the expression "clear head."

To continue this chapter of corrections, it is not for me to define "too much truth," partly because I disavow responsibility for the expression and partly because my "next book" will have too much else to take care of. The "next book" has been named, as you may have noticed, by Mr. Ward, and also by others before him. It is to be called "The Instinct of Workmanship"—a phrase which, perhaps without your knowing it, I owe to you.

I have no doubt such a volume on the Instinct will be written before long, but I confess, though I should not like it to have it go farther, that I don't know what or what kind of things will go into this new book.

It is needless for me to say how sincerely I thank you, not only for your kindness in writing your congratulations, however, equivocal, but even more for knowing better than the great men who have been good enough to criticize me.

Yours very truly,
T. Veblen

P.S. By the way, I am right, am I not, in catching a note of regret at your being no longer concerned in the Journal? *Kindly bear in mind that the pages of the* Journal *are always open to you with an expectant and hungering openness!*

Thorstein Veblen to Sarah Hardy Gregory, May 29, 1901

Dear Mrs. Gregory

After so long a time I hope you have not forgotten the half-promise of a paper on some of the peculiar industrial or business enterprises of the Coast. I have not urged it in the interval, because you pleaded that you would be busy during the first few months of the fall and winter on account of the moving which was immediately ahead. If it should be feasible now or in the near future for you to help us out with anything of the kind—whether it be fruit, wine, oil, fish, or what not, and whether it be as to industrial methods or results or as to the business management, or both—it would be an act of charity to us and a service to the rest of the race. In any case, I beg you to let me know what chance there is.

There seems at present to be some chance of my making a visit to San Francisco this summer, probably by about the middle of July if at all, and if you should then be in town I might, if I have your permission, find out particularly what you think of the matter and what you would like to do. It is not certain that I shall have the pleasure of seeing either you or your country this summer, even with your permission, but there is at least ground enough to let me hope so.

Kindly convey my regards to Mr. Gregory and let me know how you and your boy have fared through the winter. I was told, by your Mother (to whom I should like to send a word of remembrance), that your health had been quite precarious the previous year, including a severe siege of illness. I hope nothing of the kind has befallen you this year.

I made free, the other day, to send you a copy of a paper of mine, written since I saw you. This I directed to your old address, not being sure of the new. I trust it reached you, not so much because of your interest in it as because of my own.

This also I am directing to your old address, for the same reason as the last.

Yours very truly,
Th. Veblen

Thorstein Veblen to Sarah Hardy Gregory, June 27, 1903

My dear Mrs. Gregory,

Have I been over bold? Had I known that my pamphlet would disturb you and make you less happy it should not have been allowed to do mischief. Yet you save me from much remorse with the remark that the reading has been a pleasure to you. Which encourages me to talk, as you know most things do. Majora horum videbitis, D.V. *[loosely translated: You will see more of this, God willing.] The pamphlet is a chapter out of a prospective book, which has this week gone out to seek a publisher. You may have seen enough to criticize in the pamphlet and in the* Journal *article which you are kind enough to speak of, but the book, I am credibly told, is still more "beyond," or, as my friends which have seen it say, beside the point. Its name is "The Theory of Business Enterprise"—a topic on which I am free to theorize with all the abandon that comes of immunity from the facts.*

I am more interested than you would readily credit in your excursion into English. Still, I am glad to say that so far there is no evidence of your English having suffered from the lessons.

The chance at present seems to be that I shall be in San Francisco some time early in August. If this should come true I should hope to call, if you are in town at that time, and see and hear how things are going with you.

Sincerely yours,
Th. Veblen

Thorstein Veblen to Sarah Hardy Gregory, July 24, 1906

Dear Mrs. Gregory,

As is not unusual with procrastinators, I have been delayed about getting away from here, so that I am thrown out of the chance of making use of your kind invitation to your house this summer. You will pardon the delay in acknowledging your invitation, I know, because you are in the habit of pardoning greater evils. I have not known from day to day, when I might get away. Speak for me as well as you can to Mr. Gregory and to Don. Beth, I take it, does not remember me and is in no way interested. [Donald and Elizabeth were Sarah's children.]

Sincerely yours,
T. Veblen

Thorstein Veblen to Sarah Hardy Gregory, November 13, 1908

Dear Mrs. Gregory,

It was a great shock to learn of Jean's illness. [Jean was Sarah's daughter.] I trust she is well along to good health again by now, and that the strain is over for you. I have had some notion of finding an opportunity to see you during your stay in San Jose, but it has not so turned out. Since coming back I have moved from the Cedro to the campus,—a tedious and long drawn matter, due to the slow and uncertain movements of the Business Office. Otherwise there is nothing to relate.

Lately I have mailed to your Berkeley address a copy of the paper on the Scientific Point of View. I hope soon to see you in good health and spirits.

Sincerely
Th. Veblen

Thorstein Veblen to Sarah Hardy Gregory, September 20, 1920

My dear Mrs. Gregory,

Your invitation to the Farm overtook me after I had made the mistake of coming away from California, and it has gone unacknowledged all this disgraceful time because I promptly got sick again—a sequel of last winter's "Flu." When I went to California last spring I had already made up my mind to intrude on you, but then, in time, came a call to return east and I had to forego it. Still I have a confident hope of seeing you all at least once again BEFORE THE CURTAIN.

Kindly give my best wishes and my thanks to Mr. Gregory, and to Beth and Don, who I hope may still remember me.

I am leaving here this week for New York, where I expect to go on with the lectures at the New School, on a reduced schedule for this Fall. and where I shall be very glad to hear from you again.

Sincerely yours,
Thorstein Veblen

Thorstein Veblen to Sarah Hardy Gregory, May 10, 1928

Dear Mrs. Gregory,

Thank you. I had been looking to see you again soon, but I take it that you no longer count on calling in on your way to the farm, as I once had hoped. Still there is the chance when you get back.

I thank you for the check and for the good will that visibly underlies it, and I count on both to smooth the way to Greenbay.

Sincerely,
Thorstein Veblen

Notes

Chapter 1. Introduction

1. Albert Einstein, "Remarks on Bertrand Russell's Theory of Knowledge," in *The Philosophy of Bertrand Russell,* A. Schilpp (Evanston, 1944), page 179, cited in Lewis S. Feuer, *The Generations of Science* (New York: Basic Books, 1974), page 56.

2. John Dos Passos, *The Big Money* (New York: Harcourt Brace, 1936), page 100.

Chapter 2. University of Chicago Beginnings

1. The University of Chicago opened only a few weeks before the Columbian Exposition. Unidentified newspaper clipping, Dorfman Collection (hereafter DC), Rare Book and Manuscript Library, Columbia University (hereafter CURB&ML).

2. One building of the fair had forty-four acres of floor space covered with an enormous glass skylight; "It could readily contain the United States Capitol, the Great Pyramid, Winchester Cathedral, Madison Square Garden and St. Paul's Cathedral." The Grand Basin, studded with fountains and allegorical statues, opened onto Lake Michigan. Most of the guidebooks of the time seemed convinced that the fair marked the culmination of all history and was comparable to the Golden Age of Greece, the Italian Renaissance, or the reign of Elizabeth I of England. Carl S. Smith, *Chicago and the American Literary Imagination, 1880–1920* (Chicago: University of Chicago Press, 1984), page 141.

3. Henry B. Fuller, a literary figure and scathing critic of the University of Chicago, from clipping in DC, CURB&ML.

4. Madame Blanc (Th. Bentzon, pseudonym), *The Condition of Woman in the United States: A Traveller's Guide* (1895; reprint, Freeport, NY: Books for Libraries Press, 1972; also published in Paris in 1905), page 90.

5. *Ibid.,* page 51.

6. Carl S. Smith, *Chicago and the American Literary Imagination, 1880–1920,* page 147.

7. *Ibid.*

8. Maude Radford Warren, letter to Joseph Dorfman (Veblen's first biographer), September 20 [probably early 1930s], DC, CURB&ML.

9. Joseph Dorfman, *Thorstein Veblen and His America* (Clifton, NJ: Augustus M. Kelley, 1972), page 252, quoting John Cummings.

10. Frances M. Hunt, letter to Joseph Dorfman, March 12, 1930, DC, CURB&ML, Box 62H.

11. Letter from a Mr. Hoover, a Chicago attorney, to Joseph Dorfman, September 30, 1932. Hoover describes Veblen's class as containing only "three or more students," which was unusually small. Not many students had the concentration required; some, who were thrown off because of Veblen's low mumbling delivery, complained that they could not hear the lectures, DC, CURB&ML. According to Becky Veblen Meyers, Veblen's stepdaughter, one of his nostrils was blocked in a childhood accident, and as a result he could not project his voice. Becky Veblen Meyers, "Autobiography," Veblen Collections, Carleton College Archives (hereafter CC).

12. Howard Woolston, letter to Joseph Dorfman, September 11, 1933, DC, CURB&ML, Box 64W.

13. Harriet Bement, letter to Joseph Dorfman, June 23, 1930, DC, CURB&ML.

14. Isador Lubin, "Recollections of Thorstein Veblen," in *The Carleton College Veblen Seminar Essays,* ed. Carlton C. Qualey (New York: Columbia University Press, 1966), pages 131–148.

15. D.G. Mead, letter to Joseph Dorfman, October 5, 1932, DC, CURB&ML. Veblen also took his students to attend socialist meetings and to meet the various socialist speakers who might be visiting Chicago. S.C. Roberts, letter to Joseph Dorfman, September 18, 1932, DC, CURB&ML, Box 62M.

16. The university is non-sectarian, "although one third of its 30 trustees must be Baptists." Encyclopaedia Britannica, 14th ed.

17. Joseph Dorfman, *Thorstein Veblen and His America,* pages 85–86.

18. Olga Glorvik, daughter of Thorstein's sister Hannah, said that the Veblens were well off: "They never suffered, they had plenty to eat . . . Of course, Grandfather Veblen could not sign his name. He signed it with a cross, my mother told me. He could read, yes, but he didn't go to school, other than very little" (Ruthmary Penick, Carleton College librarian, taped interview with Olga Hanson Glorvik, April 2, 1979, CC). Thomas Veblen did, however, attend parochial school until he was fourteen years old, in order to pass the confirmation test. This was probably Sunday School and the instruction possibly was oral. Joseph Dorfman, *Thorstein Veblen and His America,* page 4.

Chapter 3. The Immigrants

1. John Edward Veblen, undated letters to Joseph Dorfman, DC, CURB&ML.

2. Andrew Veblen, letter to Joseph Dorfman, February 20 (or 26 or 28—date unclear), 1930, Minnesota Historical Society (hereafter MHS).

3. Joseph Dorfman, *Thorstein Veblen and His America,* page 174.

4. Mimi Curtin, great-granddaughter of Kari Bunde Veblen and Thomas Veblen, September 7, 1993, letter to Bill Melton about a trip to Norway, CC. She says, "We visited Hurum Stave Church . . . where Kari Bunde and Thomas Anderson

Veflen were married in 1847, just before they emigrated." Possibly they were married earlier in a civil ceremony. "Veflen" became "Veblen" in America.

5. Thorstein Veblen was named after his mother's father, who had been forced to sell his farm in Norway to pay legal fees after being forced into litigation. His mother, Kari, was left an orphan at the age of five, her father having died of grief. Thorstein's paternal grandfather had been forced to sell his farm because of the application of the laws of primogeniture, when a buyer exercised the older son's privilege of recovering the family estate by paying a sum appraised in legal proceedings. But, instead of paying in the previously used silver money agreed upon, the buyer used the new depreciated currency. The grandfather fell to the status of tenant, rather than landowner, an important distinction in Norway. With the small amount of money received, he was unable to buy a new farm. Joseph Dorfman, *Thorstein Veblen and His America,* page 3.

6. Andrew Veblen, letter to Joseph Dorfman, November 9, 1929, MHS.

7. Andrew Veblen, in his "Immigrant Pioneers from Valdris" (MHS, page 13), says it is possible they stopped overnight along the way.

8. Emily Veblen Olsen, "Memoirs," Norwegian Historical Society, St. Olaf College (hereafter NHS), page 1, and Andrew Veblen, "Immigrant Pioneers," page 25.

9. John Edward Veblen, undated letters to Joseph Dorfman, DC, CURB&ML.

10. Emily Veblen Olsen, "Memoirs," page 1, NHS.

11. Veblen pioneered the use of the botanical words "dichotomous," "involute," and "monocotyledonous," in the literature of the social sciences, and, in a sort of enactment of Gresham's law, it is a rare social science Ph.D. thesis that does not have one or two little *involutes,* or *dichotomouses,* deftly installed in a prominent position.

12. John Edward Veblen, undated letters to Joseph Dorfman, DC, CURB&ML.

13. In Sheboygan County they had experienced an unfortunate incident, in which Uncle Haldor was accused of stealing a cow. He was blamed by a miscreant German immigrant, because Haldor could not speak English and defend himself. Thomas and Kari had to go to court to help Haldor clear his name. In his manuscript, "Immigrant Pioneers," Andrew Veblen says they were isolated in Sheboygan County, surrounded by worthy, but stand-offish, Dutch immigrants. They had no playmates aside from themselves, and without traveling a considerable distance, the adults could find no fellow Lutherans or Norwegian compatriots (page 21). In her "Memoirs," Emily writes of the Irish neighbor's children in Manitowoc County, saying: "Being together with them so much, we learned English from them almost as early as we learned Norwegian at home. Thus we grew up bilingually, as it were. As soon as we began school, the learning of English went on, as that language was talked there altogether." Thorstein was only two years younger than Emily, so he participated in all the children's doings.

By the time he entered Carleton, Thorstein was well versed in German and English besides his original Norwegian. There was a legend, fostered by his first wife and perhaps, at times, perversely, by Thorstein himself, that he learned English only after he got to Carleton (Joseph Dorfman, *Thorstein Veblen and His America,* page 35). Ellen may well have tutored him to correct his English, but his brother Andrew strongly objected to the idea that he did not speak it well. Thorstein supposedly told his friend, the well-known painter, B.J.O. Nordfeldt, that "until he was nine or ten his speech was Norwegian, and that Latin came next, on which English was built." Andrew, however, tells us: "[Thorstein] knew every word in the 'National' spelling book, and synonyms and opposites of every word. Long before this, he could not be spelled down on any word in the series of readers and spellers used. It was taken as a mild scandal that he spelled down the teachers." Andrew Veblen, letter to Joseph Dorfman, March 13, 1930, MHS.

Andrew also says that, in Wisconsin, "Thorstein had English-speaking playmates as early as he could toddle one-eighth of a mile to the nearest neighbor; and before that the neighbor's children were daily at our house, or in the yard . . . [He] was sent to school before he filled five years." From the beginning, Thorstein evidently spoke Norwegian and English. He also spoke German, picked up from German neighbors, had a certain working knowledge of Latin, and a smattering of Greek. "When he came to Carleton he spoke as correct and idiomatic English as any of the young people he encountered." Andrew Veblen, letter to Joseph Dorfman, February 28, 1930, MHS.

William Melton, restorer of the Veblen homestead at Nerstrand, Minnesota, says that in the process of removing the deteriorated plaster from the walls of the Veblen farmhouse, they found portions of two newspapers: "One was a Norwegian-language paper printed in Rochester [Minnesota], from 1865 (as I recall). The other was *The Sunday School World,* in the English language, from 1862. Clearer evidence of bilinguality I cannot imagine" (telephone conversation with the authors, June, 1997).

Two of his Carleton classmates reported to Joseph Dorfman on Thorstein's abilities in English. Eugene F. Hunt, in a letter dated January 27, 1930, said he was good in English literature, though sometimes ill prepared in mathematics and the sciences; Henry H. Gladding, in a letter dated March 29, 1930, said of Thorstein and his brother Andrew, "While of Norwegian extraction, their English diction and pronunciation were perfect, but with a faint, elusive, Norse accent, which added to the charm of their conversation." DC, CURB&ML.

14. Emily Veblen Olsen, "Memoirs," page 4, NHS.

15. Mrs. H.T. Hoven, "Pioneer Days in Goodhue County, Minnesota," page 3, DC, CURB&ML.

16. Because he was busy helping his father on the farm during his adolescent years, Andrew did not attend Faribault High School until he was twenty-three years of age. After that he entered Carleton Preparatory, and Carleton College, and did not graduate until he was nearly thirty (Andrew Veblen, letter to Joseph Dorfman, November 9, 1929, MHS). He was the first student to graduate in three years rather than four. Thorstein was the second.

17. Emily Veblen Olsen, "Memoirs," page 3, NHS.

18. *Ibid.,* page 5.

19. Emily Veblen Olsen, "Memoirs," page 6, NHS.

20. Andrew Veblen, "Daybook," MHS, Vol. 44, V395. They moved into the basement "around threshing time," November 23, 1866. Also, letter from Andrew to Joseph Dorfman, May 10, 1931, MHS.

21. There were hand pumps for both the well and the cistern.

22. Andrew wrote: "The basement was built in 1866, and we lived in it in the fall and winter, 1866–7. In the fall of 1865, we quarried building stone for the basement on Section 12, and during the winter hauled it to the building site. The summer, 1866, father built the stone walls himself; and fitted it up as living quarters, and we moved into it, in the fall, 1866, about threshing time, as I remember it" (letter to Joseph Dorfman, May 10, 1931, MHS). Also see Andrew Veblen, summary notes of "Daybook" entries, MHS, Vol. 44, V395.

23. Emily Veblen Olsen, "Memoirs," page 9, NHS.

24. *Ibid.*

25. Andrew Veblen, "Immigrant Pioneers," page 64, MHS.

26. John Edward Veblen, undated letters to Joseph Dorfman, DC, CURB&ML.

27. This took place while the Veblens were still in Wisconsin.

28. Andrew Veblen, "Immigrant Pioneers," pages 64–65, MHS.

29. Lynda McDonnell, "Veblen Redux," *The Region,* Federal Reserve Bank of Minneapolis, December 1993, pages 7–13; and letter from William Melton, June 4, 1997. Also H.T. Hoven commented, "new immigrants came over every year. No one ever dreamed of a quota law in those days," ("Pioneer Days," DC, CURB&ML).

30. These practices were carried on while the Veblens lived in Wisconsin.

31. John Edward Veblen, undated letters to Joseph Dorfman, DC, CURB&ML.

32. Andrew Veblen, "Immigrant Pioneers," page 76, MHS.

33. Census records researched by William Melton.

34. Theodore C. Blegen, "The Norwegian Migration to America," NHS, 1931.

35. Interview of Thorstein Veblen's niece, Olga Glorvik, by Ruthmary Penick, April 2, 1979, CC.

36. Joseph Dorfman, *Thorstein Veblen and His America,* page 13. There was no lack of hazards besides Indians. There was "much drunkenness and fighting" among the settlers. Also, "sometimes the farmers were attacked by highway robbers who took the money they had received from their loads . . . Horse stealing was not rare," Mrs. H.T. Hoven, "Pioneer Days," page 2, DC, CURB&ML. One time, two Lake Steamer captains played at ramming each other's boats on Lake Michigan, with the needless drowning of sixty-eight passengers. Andrew Veblen, "Immigrant Pioneers," page 39, MHS.

37. John Edward Veblen, undated letters to Joseph Dorfman, DC, CURB&ML.

38. Emily Veblen Olsen, "Memoirs," page 6, NHS.

39. John Edward Veblen, undated letters to Joseph Dorfman, DC, CURB&ML.

40. In Minnesota the brothers patronized a local emporium where dime novels in English were on sale. They would buy one for ten cents, and if they returned it they would get five cents off the price of the next one. *Harper's Weekly Magazine* in English was also available. Andrew Veblen, letter to Joseph Dorfman, February 20 (or 26 or 28—date unclear), 1930, MHS.

41. The family called him Tosten until he went to Carleton, at which time his name was Germanized.

42. John Edward Veblen, undated letters to Joseph Dorfman, DC, CURB&ML.

43. *Ibid.*

44. Some of William Melton and Jonathan Larson's remarks were quoted in Lynda McDonnell, "Veblen Redux." Further statements are from letters to the authors. Melton, a mainstream economist, and a specialist in money and banking, has devoted much time, energy, and money to the restoration of the Veblen homestead and research into Veblen family history. His Ph.D. thesis at Harvard applied the optimization model to the Swedish banking system. He is a former chief of the monetary analysis division of the Federal Reserve Bank of New York and is currently vice president of international research for American Express Financial Services in Minneapolis. His father, Rosser Melton, an economics professor at North Texas State University, was a lifelong admirer of Veblen.

45. This was mixed in with his active life as a master craftsman and innovative farmer. Thomas sent to New York State for the "first two horse-power thresher" in his part of Wisconsin and "made a great success of it; he was the first in the

community to put down drains on his farm . . . he operated the first harvester . . . planted the first orchard, . . . was a successful bee-keeper." He also owned the first "platform binder." Andrew Veblen, letter to Joseph Dorfman, February 20 (or 26 or 28—date unclear), 1930, MHS.

46. Florence Veblen, "Reminiscences of Thorstein Veblen by His Brother Orson," *Social Forces* 10, No. 2 (December 1931), CC.

47. *Ibid.,* page 188.

48. Emily, Andrew, and Thorstein graduated from Carleton College.

49. Letter from Joseph Dorfman to Andrew Veblen, September 28, 1926, MHS.

50. John Edward Veblen, undated letters to Joseph Dorfman, DC, CURB&ML. As Thorstein was younger than most of his brothers, he was naturally given the lighter tasks.

51. Florence Veblen, "Reminiscences of Thorstein Veblen by His Brother Orson,'' C.C.

52. John Edward Veblen, undated letter to Joseph Dorfman, DC, CURB&ML.

53. Andrew Veblen, letter to Joseph Dorfman, November 29, 1929, MHS.

54. Becky Veblen Meyers, letter to David Riesman, February 20, 1954, CC.

Chapter 4. Carleton

1. Robert L. Duffus, *The Innocents at Cedro* (Clifton, NJ: Augustus M. Kelley, 1972), page 59.

2. The Reverend B.F. Buck, undated letter to Joseph Dorfman, DC, CURB&ML.

3. Henry Gladding, letter to Joseph Dorfman, March 29, 1930, DC, CURB&ML.

4. John Maurice Clark, "Thorstein Bundy [*sic*] Veblen, Obituary," *American Economic Revue* 19 (December 1929): 742–745.

5. Reverend M. McG. Dana, *The History of the Origin and Growth of Carleton College* (St. Paul, 1879), pages 29–30, cited in Joseph Dorfman, *Thorstein Veblen and His America,* page 18.

6. Hans Otto Storm, letter to Joseph Dorfman, November 6, 1932, DC, CURB&ML.

7. Joseph Dorfman, *Thorstein Veblen and His America,* page 31.

8. Henry H. Gladding, letter to Joseph Dorfman, March 29, 1930, DC, CURB&ML, Box 61G. Both Becky Veblen Meyers and Isador Lubin indicated that later in life he switched to Turkish tobacco. Isador Lubin, "Recollections of Thorstein Veblen," pages 132–148; also, Ruthmary Penick, interview with Becky Veblen Meyers and Ann Sims, 1977, page 4, C.C.

9. W.F. Skilling, "Up and Down Main Street," June 7, 1935, newspaper clipping, DC, CURB&ML, Box 74.

10. *The Carleton Voice,* Centennial Issue, September 1966, CC.

11. Joseph Dorfman, *Thorstein Veblen and His America,* page 32. Thorstein's sister Emily made comments in the margins of Dorfman's biography, filed at the Minnesota Historical Society. She insisted that Thorstein did not call himself a Moravian and went to the distant church in order to improve his German.

12. The title of Thorstein's speech was "Mill's Examination of Hamilton's Philosophy of the Conditioned." The American academic establishment adhered almost

completely to the Scottish Common Sense Philosophy, so this may have been Veblen's first public display of his skill at attacking pomposity adroitly.

13. John M. Clark, "Thorstein Bundy [*sic*] Veblen, Obituary."

14. Joseph Dorfman, *Thorstein Veblen and His America,* page 35.

15. Anonymous letter to Joseph Dorfman, March 5, 1930, DC, CURB&ML, Box 92.

16. James Fuchs, ed., *Ruskin's Views of Social Justice* (New York: Vanguard Press, 1926), pages 8–11.

17. Ellen Veblen, letter to Janet (surname unknown), undated, DC, CURB&ML, Box 64V. In line with her pro-Ruskin views, Ellen felt that Americans definitely needed "saving."

18. Anonymous letter to Joseph Dorfman, DC, CURB&ML.

19. *Ibid.*

20. Although he had made up his mind early on to be a member of the Supreme Court, Ellen's brother wrote that a "complete physical collapse" forced him to quit his law career at age fifty. "Three physicians in consultation" advised him to abandon his profession. He then earned his living for three years by selling "bird's eggs of [his] own collection, and publishing the results of [his] observations with photographic illustrations." Eugene subsequently moved to Oregon. It is not known how he earned a living after that. Eugene Rolfe, letter to editor of the *Carleton Circle,* undated, CC.

21. Norway—in 1905—was the first country in Europe to establish women's suffrage, so it may have been in the liberal Norwegian tradition to give one's daughters equal educational advantages.

22. Ellen Veblen, letter to Sarah Hardy Gregory, 1897, University of Chicago Special Collections (hereafter, UCHISC), Miscellaneous Collections ("V" folder).

23. Undated letter from Mary B. Deirup to Joseph Dorfman, DC, CURB&ML.

24. John Neihardt, letter to Joseph Dorfman, August 29, 1935, DC, CURB&ML.

25. J.R. Christianson, "Thorstein Veblen: Ethnic Roots and Social Criticism of a 'Folk Savant,'" *Norwegian American Studies,* Vol. 34 (Northfield, MN: NHS, 1995). (This was called to our attention by William Melton.) On page 5 Christianson wrote:

> In the years 1880–1881, Monona Academy must have been a terrible place to teach . . . Four years earlier one professor had refused to teach with another, forcing the latter to resign. In the fall of 1883, the same professor refused to celebrate the 400th anniversary of Luther's birth with his colleagues because he did not consider them to be authentic Lutherans. By March of 1885, 'broken in body and soul' this professor abandoned his lecturing in mid-term, unable to carry on in the viciously polarized atmosphere . . . Thorstein Veblen's immediate predecessor . . . resigned with broken health after one year and went to his native Norway to recuperate . . . two others left at the end of next year to regain their health and arm for future battle. Thorstein himself lasted only one year.

26. Wesley Clair Mitchell, "Thorstein Veblen, 1857–1929, Obituary," *Economic Journal* 39 (December 1929): 646–650.

27. Russell Strong, letter to Joseph Dorfman, March 11, 1930, DC, CURB&ML. Evelyn Wells, a San Francisco newpaperwoman and protégé of Ellen Veblen's, tells us that Ellen suffered a second nervous breakdown after the Triggs scandal in 1904, at which time she fled to Evelyn's mother in Ashland, Oregon, as she had fled, in a shattered condition, on several other occasions. Evelyn Wells papers, sent to William

Melton by Clinton F. Wells, January 5, 1955 (this date is probably incorrect, as Mr. Wells's letter mentions a book he received in 1980), CC.

28. Ellen Veblen, letter to Sarah Hardy Gregory, 1897, UCHISC, CC.

29. Florence Veblen, letter to Joseph Dorfman, December 7, 1925, DC, CURB&ML. Andrew Veblen, however, warned against Florence's "various bursts of bombast and perversions of the truth. You cannot rely on anything she says." Andrew Veblen, letter to Joseph Dorfman, September 27, 1926, DC, CURB&ML.

30. Emily Veblen Olsen, annotations to Joseph Dorfman's *Thorstein Veblen and His America,* MHS, page 252 of Dorfman's text.

31. Ellen Veblen, letter to Alice Millis, wife of Professor Henry A. Millis and a close friend of Ellen's, October 17 (probably 1907), DC, CURB&ML.

32. This analysis was made by Dr. M.W. Knapp, doctor for her terminal illness many years later, in a discussion of her autopsy report. Dr. M.W. Knapp, letter to Dr. A.W. Meyer, June 29, 1926, DC, CURB&ML.

33. Anonymous letter from one of Ellen's contemporaries at Carleton College to Joseph Dorfman, March 5, 1930, DC, CURB&ML. Also, letter from Joseph Dorfman to Andrew Veblen, undated. Dorfman states that Eugene Rolfe had refused to tell him anything about Thorstein or his sister Ellen because of his negative attitude toward her, MHS.

Chapter 5. Tampering with the Sacrament

1. Ellen Veblen, letter to Sarah Hardy Gregory, undated (probably fall of 1897 or later), UCHISC, Miscellaneous Collections ("V" folder).

2. Joseph Dorfman, in *Thorstein Veblen and His America* (page 306), reported that Veblen's later poor health might have been due to the calomel treatment he had received while he was "in his thirties." The duration of Veblen's bout with malaria is not clear. Ed reported that Thorstein came back from Yale, after receiving his Ph.D. in 1884, suffering from the malaria that had swept the East Coast in 1883. Ed doubted that it actually was malaria and influenced Dorfman to believe that his brother was simply lazy (page 56). Thorstein would then have been twenty-seven years old. Emily objected to the "lazy" characterization and wrote, "I am sure his health was not good at that time" (Emily Veblen Olsen, annotations to *Thorstein Veblen and His America,* MHS). Andrew also stated that his brother did, indeed, suffer from ill health from 1884 to 1888. Thorstein spent the winter of 1885 in Andrew's house at Iowa State University (Andrew Veblen, letter to Joseph Dorfman, November 29, 1929, DC, CURB&ML). Thorstein married Ellen Rolfe on April 10, 1888, when he was thirty (Andrew Veblen, "Daybooks," MHS, Vol. 44, V395). He was still ill during their first years at Stacyville. For information about subsequent calomel treatments, see Chapter 19.

3. Becky Veblen Meyers, letter to David Riesman, February 20, 1954, CC.

4. Ellen Veblen, letter to Sarah Hardy Gregory, undated (late 1897 or later), UCHISC.

5. Letter to Joseph Dorfman from Harriet Rolfe Dagg, January 12, 1933, DC, CURB&ML.

6. Florence Veblen, "Reminiscences of Thorstein Veblen by His Brother Orson." Also, Joseph Dorfman, *Thorstein Veblen and His America,* page 66.

7. Letters from John Edward Veblen to Joseph Dorfman, one dated April 9, 1930, the other undated, DC, CURB&ML.

8. Letter from Harriet Rolfe Dagg to Joseph Dorfman, March 5, 1933, DC, CURB&ML.

9. Joseph Dorfman, *Thorstein Veblen and His America,* page 66.

10. Harriet Rolfe Dagg, letter to Joseph Dorfman, March 5, 1933, DC, CURB&ML.

11. Letter from Millicent Clute to Joseph Dorfman, undated, DC, CURB&ML.

12. Ellen Veblen, letter to Sarah Hardy Gregory, April 1897, UCHISC, Miscellaneous Collections ("V" folder).

13. Anonymous letter to Joseph Dorfman, March 5 (probably early 1930s), DC, CURB&ML.

14. Ellen Veblen, letter to Sarah Hardy Gregory, April 1897, UCHISC.

15. Robert L. Duffus, *The Innocents at Cedro,* pages 143–145.

16. John Neihardt, letter to Joseph Dorfman, August 29, 1935, DC, CURB&ML.

17. Joseph Dorfman, interview with Mrs. Eve Schütze, October 9, 1930. His apparently hastily written notes are in faint, penciled handwriting and difficult to read; we have reconstructed them (leaving out non-pertinent items) as best we could:

1. [The Schützes] Came to Chicago in 1901.
2. Lived in same apt. building [with Veblen, probably the Beatrice, at 344 Fifty-Seventh Avenue—a building since torn down].
3. [Professor Oscar L.] Triggs reprimanded by president on a number of occasions for saying Longfellow was no poet and [college] hymn pretty rotten and newspapers got after him.
4. Triggs's wife a beautiful woman, intelligent; [Professor Triggs?] taught philosophy, literature in university.
5. [Someone, Veblen?] Seen travelling [with] Mrs. Triggs.
6. [Mrs. Veblen?] Complained to Harper.
7. [Mrs. Veblen?] Complained to everyone about Thorstein.
8. Veblen used to call [Tom and Babe] Bevan's apartment "the corner of indecision" because they were always trying to make up their minds what to do.
9. Veblen never cared about what other people said except to agree when they fell in with his thought.
10. [Veblen?] Disturbed by guests and parties of his wife.
11. She would not let him work; tried to get into his mind.
12. [Veblen ?] Had no use for arts and crafts that they started at the time.
13. Veblen knew he was more intelligent than [Head of the Department] Laughlin and felt he should be given his due.
14. [Veblen? Babe?] Felt aggrieved when [Professor] Schütze did not seem cordial at Woodstock [where Babe and Thorstein were guests of Babe's sister-in-law].
15. Mrs. Bevans said if Schütze stayed at Woodstock she would be uncomfortable.
16. [Professor Herbert G.] Davenport had some doubts about taking Veblen [to teach at Missouri?] due to his escapades.
17. [Veblen's?] Wife had a little money, cheap to live.
18. [Veblen and his wife?] Always fighting.

DC, CURB&ML, Box 72S.

18. Helmer Hougen, *The Carleton Voice,* May 1964, CC, page 9.

19. Florence Veblen, "Reminiscences of Thorstein Veblen by His Brother Orson." An undated letter to Joseph Dorfman from Mildred Bennett, in whose New York apartment Veblen roomed and boarded for several years after the death of his second wife, stated that Florence wrote something about the Veblen family, full of mistakes and misspellings of family names and also negative remarks about Ellen. "Mr. [Andrew] A. Veblen," Bennett wrote, "has no love for Florence" (DC, CURB&ML). Andrew Veblen's letter of February 8, 1932, to Dorfman corroborated this. DC, CURB&ML.

20. Dr. M.W. Knapp's letter to Joseph Dorfman, February 7, 1932, DC, CURB&ML.

21. Thorstein Veblen, letter to Ellen Veblen, March 31, 1896, UCHISC, Miscellaneous Collections ("V" folder).

22. John Edward Veblen, undated letters to Joseph Dorfman, DC, CURB&ML.

23. Thorbjörn N. Möhn, a pillar of the Lutheran Church, letter to T.B. Veblen, concerning a position Thorstein was applying for at Saint Olaf College, July 18, 1890, NHS, Northfield, Minnesota.

24. Paraphrased version of Veblen's letter. Thorbjörn N. Möhn, letter to Reverend Pastor J. Polson, July 30, 1890, NHS.

25. *Ibid.*

26. Thorbjörn N. Möhn, letter to C.J. Rollefson, August 5, 1890, NHS. However, Veblen told John Urie, a student who lived with the Veblens in 1917, that the cosmological scientists base their work on "spiritual assumptions." He cited the scientific concoction of the "luminiferous ether," which supposedly (until killed by Einstein's Relativity Theory) occupied space and transmitted light and energy from the sun to the earth and, according to the same theories, would therefore have a considerable density. Yet the Michelson–Moreley interferometer experiments found that there was no ether effect on the speed of light or the movements of the planets. Veblen concluded "that since even the findings of science were in such illogical shape he preferred to believe that there was some kind of an omnipotent Providence." John H. Urie, letter to Joseph Dorfman, April 24, 1934, DC, CURB&ML.

27. Nevertheless, Thorstein did not hesitate to show his scorn of religious fanatics. Later, when his brother Orson, who had by this time become a trustee of St. Olaf College, asked him to write a recommendation for a friend, Thorstein was told that the administration doubted the applicant's orthodoxy. He promptly wrote the letter requested, asserting that there was no doubt whatever that the man was "too damn orthodox." The applicant got the job. Joseph Dorfman, *Thorstein Veblen and His America,* pages 87–88.

28. John Edward Veblen, undated letter to Joseph Dorfman, DC, CURB&ML.

29. Letter from Lucia K. Tower to Joseph Dorfman, March 23, 1933, DC, CURB&ML.

30. Joseph Dorfman, *Thorstein Veblen and His America,* pages 79–80. Andrew Estrem, a fellow student, heard Veblen announce his triumph and was amazed that Thorstein did not throw his cap in the air and shout, "Hurrah!" But this was not like Thorstein. The fire was all inside, Andrew Estrem, letter to Joseph Dorfman, February 1, 1930, DC, CURB&ML.

31. Joseph Dorfman, *Thorstein Veblen and His America,* page 82.

32. *Ibid.,* page 84, quoting from Thorstein Veblen.

33. *The Carleton Voice,* Vol. 29, No. 5, May 1964, CC.

34. Andrew Estrem, letter to Joseph Dorfman, DC, CURB&ML, see footnote 31.

35. Ellen Veblen, letter to Sarah Hardy Gregory, April, 1897, UCHISC.

36. Thorstein Veblen, letter to Hardy, February 24, 1896, UCHISC, Miscellaneous Collections ("V" folder).

Chapter 6. Student Relations

1. Haskell Hall was the headquarters of the president during W.R. Harper's tenure at the University of Chicago.

2. The university's side of the story, reported in Upton Sinclair's *The Goose-Step,* was that, at the time of his separation from the university, Bemis was not on the regular faculty, but in the university's "extension division," and that "he was offered reappointment."

Sinclair asked Bemis for comments, and Bemis replied:

> My letter which you quote is absolutely correct. No proposition for continuance of my work, half of which was to [be] advanced [by] students within the university walls, was ever made to me.

Upton Sinclair, *The Goose-Step* (Pasadena, CA: Upton Sinclair, 1922, 1923; reprint, New York: Edward and Charles Boni, 1936), pages 244–245.

3. John Bates Clark, letter to Edwin R.A. Seligman, Seligman Correspondence, *Political Science Quarterly* 61 (March 19, 1926).

4. Warner Fite, letter to Joseph Dorfman, July 4, 1930, DC, CURB&ML.

5. C.F. Clayton, letter to Joseph Dorfman, August 13, 1934, DC, CURB&ML, Box 61C.

6. J. Laurence Laughlin, letter to Stanford President David Starr Jordan, April 29, 1899, Department of Special Collections, Stanford University Libraries (hereafter SULSC). The letter began:

> Dr. T.B. Veblen of our staff wishes me to write to you of him. Under the circumstances, my only hesitation is in saying this which might lose him to us. For I must say that he is one of the brainiest, deepest economists we have, with an unusual preparation for his peculiar kind of work. No other man in our department has as strong a hold as he on our graduate students, and his scholarship is broad and deep. Indeed his range is remarkable. His writing, while deep, is fresh and original . . . and he has an unusual facility of expression—due to his early training, perhaps, in philosophy. . . . And he gets a great deal of work out of all his students. Keeps [word obscured] a close relationship with them. Speaking for myself alone I should [hate? (word obscured)] to think of allowing him to go.
>
> But in President Harper's view there is not, just now, income enough to grant Dr. Veblen the promotion which he here deserves. Consequently, he is moved to think he should look elsewhere. I cannot find fault with him in this . . . But I have a hope he will not be tempted away from us until we can honor him as I think he deserves.

7. Delos O. Kinsman (former student of Veblen), letter to Joseph Dorfman, November 18, 1932, DC, CURB&ML.

8. Letter from T.B. Veblen to President Jordan, April 29, 1899, Jordan Papers, SULSC, SC 58 Box 21, Folder 211.

9. I.W. Hawarth, letter to Joseph Dorfman, October 15, 1931, DC, CURB&ML.

10. A.P. Winston, of the University of Texas, to Joseph Dorfman, October 15, 1932, DC, CURB&ML, Box 64W.

11. Letter of Sarah Hardy Gregory to Joseph Dorfman, January 13, 1935, DC, CURB&ML.

12. M.W. Knapp, letter to Arthur William Meyer, M.D., June 29, 1926, DC, CURB&ML.

13. Joseph Dorfman, *Thorstein Veblen and His America,* page 253.

14. Clara Rolfe Green, letter to Joseph Dorfman, undated, DC, CURB&ML.

15. Warner Fite, letter to Joseph Dorfman, July 4, 1930, DC, CURB&ML.

16. Lucia K. Tower, March 23, 1933, letter to Joseph Dorfman, DC, CURB&ML.

17. A.P. Winston, October 15, 1932, letter to Joseph Dorfman, DC, CURB&ML. Veblen went to Washington Island originally to escape pollen, as he was highly susceptible to hay fever. Becky Veblen Meyers, taped interview by Ann Howard, May 29, 1990, CC.

18. Esther Baran, Veblen's step-granddaughter, interview recorded by the authors, April 10, 1994. One of Thorstein's brothers was reportedly so allergic to tomatoes that they made him violently ill.

19. Mary B. Deirup, letter to Joseph Dorfman, undated, DC, CURB&ML.

20. UCHISC, Registrar's Records.

21. Lucia K. Tower, letter to Joseph Dorfman, DC, CURB&ML.

22. The Veblens had first gone to Palos Park to spend time each summer with their mutual friends, the Wellses. Wells was an unusual congregational minister. He was pro-labor and dedicated to pacifism, prohibition, and socialism. According to his daughter Evelyn Wells (Podesta), Veblen asked her mother "to take the neurotic Ellen V. under her wing." When Thorstein's behavior hurt or baffled her, Ellen routinely fled to the sympathetic Mrs. Wells. Wells correspondence, CC.

23. Ellen Veblen, June 13, 1918, letter to Alice Millis, DC, CURB&ML. Alice Millis was the wife of Professor Henry Alvin Millis, a former student of Veblen's at Chicago, and later an economics professor at Stanford and at the University of Chicago.

24. Ellen Veblen, letter to Sarah Hardy Gregory, 1897, UCHISC, Miscellaneous Collections ("V" folder).

25. Ellen Veblen, letter to Alice Millis, September 13, 1907, DC, CURB&ML.

26. *The Chautauquan* was the organ of the literary and scientific circle of the Chautauquan Society of Jamestown, NY, published from 1880 until 1910, when it was absorbed by the Independent.

Chapter 7. Miss Hardy

1. Sarah's mother sometimes lived with her young daughter in a tent in a eucalyptus grove while she taught school, rather than boarding around with people. Sarah's mother defied convention by wearing bloomers, on occasion, while hiking. She had taught Sarah at home, along with three neighbor children, one of whom was the noted architect, Julia Morgan. Early on, Sarah exhibited signs of being a prodigy, and her outstanding performance at Chicago seemed to indicate that her mother's

visions were about to be realized. Interview with anonymous Gregory family member, September 29, 1993, and telephone conversation, September 14, 1997.

2. An example of the fascinating unpredictability of the beautiful graduate student: When she found out that her statistics professor, Isaac Hourwich (later fired as an avowed socialist), was traveling to San Francisco to rescue ten Siberian exiles who were being harassed by the passport division, she gave him a letter of introduction to her suitor, Warren Gregory. Sarah said sarcastically, "Warren will probably bless me for mixing his aristocratic self up in such a matter, but it will be good for him." *Ibid.*

3. Warren Gregory, letter to Sarah Hardy, February 25, 1894, Warren Gregory Papers, 1864–1927 (BANC MSS 91/3C), The Bancroft Library, University of California, Berkeley (hereafter UCBBL). Gregory became an important figure in the San Francisco Bay area. A very successful attorney from an "old" family (the Gregory ranch in Contra Costa County became the town of Walnut Creek), he set up the first Bar Review tests in California and was later made a Regent of the University of California.

4. Sarah Hardy, letter to Warren Gregory, December 28, 1893, Warren Gregory Papers, UCBBL.

5. Interview with anonymous Gregory family member, September 29, 1993, and telephone conversation, September 14, 1997.

6. *Ibid.*

7. Sarah Hardy, letter to Warren Gregory, August 4, 1895, Warren Gregory Papers, UCBBL.

8. Notes by Louis van Elderen of his interview with Dorfman, (DC, CURB&ML, Box 64V). Sarah may have been guarded in her conversation with Dorfman because she had much to guard.

9. The incident is mentioned in Ellen's 1896 letter to Sarah Hardy Gregory. UCHISC, Miscellaneous Collections ("V" folder).

10. *Ibid.*

11. Sarah Hardy, letter to Warren Gregory, June 12, 1894, Warren Gregory Papers, UCBBL.

12. Supposition on the part of Gregory family informant during an interview with the authors on September 29, 1993.

13. Sarah Hardy, letter to Warren Gregory, September 8, 1895, Warren Gregory Papers, UCBBL.

14. Thorstein had written Sarah a few brief letters before, but there was nothing personal in them except the statement in August 1895 that "I am sorry to disquiet you with the admission that, contrary to the hope that you have so delicately expressed, there has been more bother than usual this summer so far."

He may have told Sarah about his conflicts with Ellen. It is unlikely that he was referring to difficulties at the university as, according to our research, Veblen never taught in the summer quarter. UCHISC, Registrar's Records.

Chapter 8. "The Wind on the Heath"

1. George Borrow, *Lavengro, the Scholar, the Gipsy, the Priest* (London: Oxford University Press, 1951), page 181.

2. Thorstein Veblen, letter to Sarah Hardy, October 28, 1895, UCHISC, Miscellaneous Collections ("V" folder). "The Wind on the Heath" had a special meaning

for Veblen and Sarah Hardy. In a later letter (see Appendix, letter of January 23, 1896) Veblen mentions the novel *Lavengro,* by George Borrow [1803–1881], a book that created a sensation in Victorian times (first published in 1851), because it stood for everything that Victorianism wasn't. According to the *Oxford Companion to English Literature,* Sir Paul Harvey, ed. (New York: Oxford University Press, 1937), the author exemplified unconventionality, although he sometimes acted as an agent of the British and Foreign Bible Society in Russia and Spain. Borrow's novels "have a peculiar picaresque quality, graphically presenting a succession of gipsies, rogues, strange characters and adventures of all kinds . . . the whole permeated with the spirit of the 'wind on the heath.'"

3. Sarah Hardy, letter to Warren Gregory, October 30, 1895, Warren Gregory Papers, UCBBL.

4. Sarah Hardy, letter to Warren Gregory, November 2, 1895, Warren Gregory Papers, UCBBL.

5. Sarah Hardy, letter to Warren Gregory, November 20, 1895, Warren Gregory Papers, UCBBL.

6. Sarah Hardy, letter to Warren Gregory, December 18, 1895, Warren Gregory Papers, UCBBL.

7. Thorstein Veblen, letter to Sarah Hardy, November 10, 1895, UCHISC.

8. Sarah Hardy, letter to Warren Gregory, October 14, 1895, Warren Gregory Papers, UCBBL.

9. Thorstein Veblen, letter to Sarah Hardy, December 15, 1895, UCHISC.

10. Thorstein Veblen, letter to Sarah Hardy, January 18, 1896, UCHISC.

11. Thorstein Veblen letter to Sarah Hardy, January 23, 1896, UCHISC. Later (1898–1900) Veblen published a series of articles on this subject in the *Quarterly Journal of Economics.* The first of these was titled: "Why Is Economics Not an Evolutionary Science?" He asserted that physics, chemistry, botany, psychology, anthropology, and ethnology take the evolutionary approach, but academic economics holds (and even now still more or less holds) to its pre-Darwinian stance, natural rights, final causes, the creator, "the unseen hand," and so on.

12. *Ibid.*

13. George Moffett, letter to Joseph Dorfman, October 11, 1932, DC, CURB&ML.

14. Thorstein Veblen, letter to Sarah Hardy, January 23, 1896, UCHISC.

15. Thorstein Veblen, letter to Sarah Hardy, February 6, 1896, UCHISC.

16. William Morris, *Collected Works: The Earthly Paradise: A Poem,* Vol. 5, (London: Longmans, Green, 1910), page 118.

17. Thorstein Veblen, letter to Sarah Hardy, February 6, 1896, UCHISC, Miscellaneous Collections ("V" folder).

Chapter 9. "The Wind on the Heath Has Fallen Dead"

1. Thorstein Veblen, letter to Sarah Hardy, February 24, 1896, UCHISC, Miscellaneous Collections ("V" folder).

2. Sarah Hardy, letter to Warren Gregory, July 24, 1894, Warren Gregory Papers, UCBBL.

3. Thorstein Veblen, letter to Sarah Hardy, February 24, 1896, UCHISC, Miscellaneous Collections ("V" folder).

4. Letter from Wesley Clair Mitchell to Sarah Hardy Gregory, March 23, 1934,

in which Mitchell expresses his fondness for his old college friend, Sarah, in a manner verging on the lyrical: "You can hardly realize what a happy thrill ran through me when I saw your unmistakable handwriting on the two envelopes the other day, or how many happy memories, not only of Veblen, but also of a slender, blue-eyed girl for whom I cherished a secret adoration in the times when she held a fellowship and I was a brand new graduate—you see, I am a bit incoherent still and can't bring my feelings under proper grammatical control." This interesting letter, written about the time Dorfman was publishing his biography, continues: "Your extracts from Veblen's letters seemed to me impeccable in matters of taste. Anyone can entrust his secrets to you with more confidence than he can repose in the confessional. You are so absolutely discreet where your friends are concerned that I have never known whether you hold any secrets at all, beyond those I have confided in your keeping. Veblen is safe in your hands [Sarah Hardy Gregory had excised any reference to Veblen's strong feelings for her in the letters she had sent to Dorfman], and so is everyone else." Letter contributed by Daniel P. Gregory, Sarah's grandson, to CC. Someone, however, had revealed much of the story to Dorfman, who had begun working on his biography of Veblen as a graduate student at Columbia with Mitchell's supervision. In a letter to Maude Radford Warren (who had known Veblen at both the University of Chicago and the University of Missouri), Dorfman inquired about "a lady of social prominence, wealth and distinction" who had "dropped Veblen." Mrs. Warren's reply of September 20 [1930–33?] to Dorfman attested to the nature of his inquiry. DC, CURB&ML, Box 64W.

5. Thorstein Veblen, letter to Ellen Veblen, March 31, 1896, UCHISC, Miscellaneous Collections ("V" folder).

6. Sarah Hardy, letter to Mary McLean Hardy, June 27, 1895, Warren Gregory Papers, UCBBL.

Gregory family members, however, did not feel that her mother's unrelenting pressure was the cardinal factor in Sarah's numerous bouts of illness and eventual breakdown. It was later found that she had suffered all her life from gallbladder problems, and once an operation was performed, in middle age, she regained her energy and remained well thereafter.

Sarah's doctors at Wellesley took her illness seriously and advised her to quit teaching at least for a year. Sarah's recuperation in the Hawaiian Islands allowed her to be near her father, who had been separated from her difficult mother from the time she was seven years old. Anonymous Gregory family member.

7. Perhaps we exaggerate in using the word "blathering." Perhaps not. Rick Tilman, in his book, *Thorstein Veblen and His Critics, 1891–1963* ([Princeton: Princeton University Press, 1991], page 5), cited a revealing quotation from one of Ellen's letters to Thorstein, dated May 16, 1920:

> Think of all that has happened in our lifetime! The Bahai movement, Spiritualism, Theosophy, Christian Science, Darwin, Spencer, Shaw, Mills, James, Edmund Carpenter, Ghandi, Blavatsky, Healers of all sorts, the upheaval of the nation, Bolshevism, Karl Marx, the world war in progress [unintelligible] radio, art, and as I hear, a new ray which renders metal permanently hot. Then, also, the oscilloscope.

Thorstein Veblen Collection, Wisconsin Historical Society (hereafter WHS).

Tilman comments: "History does not record Veblen's reaction to this bizarre juxtaposition of ideas, thinkers, religious movements and inventions."

Ellen was labeled by some as a "New Thoughter," and Veblen, trying to keep his tenuous hold on his assistant professorship at the University of Chicago, and concentrate on his work, had this to say about "New Thoughters" in his book *The Theory of Business Enterprise* ([New York: Scribner's, 1937], page 351, note 1):

> The unpropertied classes employed in business do not take to socialistic vagaries ... [They go for] some excursion into pragmatic romance, such as Social Settlements, Prohibition, Clean Politics, Single Tax, Arts and Crafts, Neighborhood Guilds, Institutional Church, Christian Science, New Thought, or some such cultural thimblerig.

Of course, Ellen did consider herself a socialist when she was at Chicago, but she was also interested in Arts and Crafts, and New Thought, and later for a brief time in Christian Science, and therefore, in Veblen's eyes, was not above thimbleriggery.

8. Edith Hamilton, *Mythology* (Boston: Little, Brown, 1942), pages 443–444.

9. *Ibid.,* page 444.

10. Thorstein Veblen, letter to Ellen Veblen, June 1, 1896, UCHISC.

11. Ellen Veblen, letter to Thorstein Veblen, July 1896, UCHISC. Ellen asserted that this was the only letter she had written to Veblen since his letter of confession.

12. Ellen Veblen, letter to Sarah Hardy Gregory, April 1897, UCHISC.

13. Ellen Veblen, letter to Sarah Hardy Gregory, undated letter, UCHISC.

14. Rudyard Kipling, *The Phantom Rickshaw* (New York: Charles Scribner's Sons, 1911), pages 7–8.

15. Ellen Veblen, letter to Sarah Hardy Gregory, date missing, UCHISC.

16. Allyn Young, letter to Herbert J. Davenport, November 14, 1909, DC, CURB&ML, Box 61.

It is interesting to note that, whether or not Ellen's strange stricture that you "owe him, at least, all that you can give to make his life tolerable" was heeded by Sarah, she did continue from time to time to critique manuscripts for him and maintained a close relationship with him while he was at Stanford. On one occasion, Wesley Clair Mitchell gave Veblen his Stanford Big Game football (rugby) ticket, so he could sit with Sarah. Veblen was her frequent houseguest, staying overnight sometimes at their Berkeley residence, according to Veblen's friend Wesley Clair Mitchell's "diary." Wesley Clair Mitchell Reels (hereafter WCMR), CURB&ML. And in the 1920s, Sarah Hardy Gregory proposed setting up a mutual cash relief fund with Mitchell, so that Veblen could return to his cabin on Washington Island once again. Sarah Hardy Gregory, letter to Wesley Clair Mitchell, April 26 (undated as to year, but Mitchell's reply to her airmail letter is dated April 29, 1928), DC, CURB&ML.

17. This reference to sterling silver tableware does not tell the whole story. Sarah's grandson, Daniel P. Gregory, wrote: "Marriage to a successful attorney made [Sarah] a woman of means, yet she frowned upon signs of 'conspicuous consumption'—though pangs of guilt did not keep her from enjoying first class travel to Europe or belonging to an elegant San Francisco women's club." Daniel P. Gregory, "The Nature of Restraint, William Wurster and His Circle," in *Everyday Modernism: The Houses of William Wurster,* ed. Marc Trieb (Berkeley: San Francisco Museum of Art, University of California Press), page 105.

18. "In later years [Sarah] kept a photograph of [her beloved professor, Veblen]

on her dressing table." Lucy Sprague Mitchell, *Two Lives: The Story of Wesley Clair Mitchell and Myself* (New York: Simon and Schuster, 1953), pages 152–153.

Chapter 10. Chicago, 1896–1899

1. George Bernard Shaw, "Morris as I Knew Him," introduction to *William Morris: Artist, Writer, Socialist,* ed. May Morris (London: Russell and Russell, 1966).

2. Thorstein Veblen, *The Theory of the Leisure Class* (New York: Random House/Modern Library, 1934), page 162.

3. Books he reviewed that year were Enrico Ferri's *Socialism et Science Positive, Darwin, Spencer et Marx,* Richard Calwer's *Einfuhrung in den Socialismus,* and Max Lorenz's *Die Marxistische Socialdemokratie.* He also discussed *Esquisses de litterature politico-economique* by Nikolay C. Bunge, and reviewed a volume of Gustav Schmoller's essays.

4. Jose Ward Hoover, letter to Joseph Dorfman, September 30, 1932, DC, CURB&ML.

5. Thomas W. Goodspeed, *A History of the University of Chicago: The First Quarter Century* (Chicago: University of Chicago Press, 1916), page 397, cited in Joseph Dorfman, *Thorstein Veblen and His America,* page 133.

6. John Edward Veblen, undated letter to Joseph Dorfman, DC, CURB&ML.

7. Madame Blanc, *The Condition of Women in the United States.*

8. Archibald B. Maynard, one of Veblen's graduate students, letter to Joseph Dorfman, DC, CURB&ML, Box 62M.

9. Thorstein Veblen, *The Higher Learning in America* (reprint, New York: Augustus M. Kelley, 1965), page 145. Veblen did not specifically refer to the University of Chicago with this remark, but he did not need to.

10. Robert L. Marquis, North Texas State Teachers' College, letter to Joseph Dorfman, November 19, 1932, DC, CURB&ML.

11. Eve Schütze, interview with Joseph Dorfman, October 9, 1930, DC, CURB&ML.

12. Thorstein Veblen, *The Higher Learning in America,* page 243, note.

13. *Ibid.*

14. *Ibid.*

15. *New York Evening Post,* August 28, 1902, clipping filed in Orrin Leslie Elliott Papers (hereafter OLEP), Container 8, Stanford History Notes (hereafter STWY), SULSC.

16. "The University of Chicago," *The Nation* (September 22, 1892), cited in Joseph Dorfman, *Thorstein Veblen and His America,* page 90.

17. Thorstein Veblen, *The Higher Learning in America,* pages 165–166.

18. Thorstein Veblen, *The Theory of the Leisure Class,* page 372.

19. Sarah Hardy, letter to Mary McLean Hardy, February 25, 1894, Warren Gregory Papers, 1864–1927 (BANC MSS 91/3C), UCBBL.

20. Thorstein Veblen, *The Higher Learning in America,* page 168.

21. "Elizabret Harte Browning, *The Cry of the Heathen Chinee,*" obviously a lampoon on Elizabeth Barrett Browning, "The Cry of the Children," is cited by Veblen in *The Higher Learning in America,* page 168, possibly a bogus footnote to a verse composed by Veblen himself, although the irreverence shown to the original poem and the use of the word "Chinee" seem out of character. Browning's indict-

ment of child labor can be found in *The Home Book of Verse,* selected and arranged by Burton Egbert Stevenson (New York: Holt, Rinehart, and Winston, 1965), pages 283–284.

22. Upton Sinclair, *The Goose-Step,* page 243. See also Thorstein Veblen, *The Higher Learning in America,* page 140, note.

23. Edward Bemis, letter to Richard T. Ely, April 24, 1895, DC, CURB&ML. However, according to Registrar Records in the University of Chicago Special Collections, Veblen never taught during the summer, so Bemis was mistaken about the quarter in question. Russell and Sylvia Yoneda Bartley claim that Veblen spent his summers at Washington Island, Wisconsin, starting as early as the mid- to late 1890s. "Thorstein Veblen on Washington Island, Traces of a Life," *The International Journal of Politics, Culture, and Society* 7, No. 4 (1994): 592.

24. In Chicago he also gathered much of the material for *The Higher Learning in America.*

25. Thorstein Veblen, *Essays in Our Changing Order,* ed. by Leon Ardzrooni (New York: Augustus M. Kelley, 1964), page 58. See discussion in John P. Diggins, *The Bard of Savagery* (New York: Seabury Press, 1978), page 146.

26. A.P. Winston, letter to Joseph Dorfman, February 4, 1933, DC, CURB&ML, Box 64W.

27. Thorstein Veblen, *The Theory of the Leisure Class,* page 182.

28. *Ibid.,* page 247.

29. *Ibid.,* page 223.

30. *Ibid.,* page 228.

31. *Ibid.,* page 112.

32. *Ibid.,* page 256.

33. *Ibid.,* page 397.

34. *Ibid.,* page 257.

35. *Ibid.,* page 45.

Chapter 11. A Book to Be Read for Amusement?

1. Archibald B. Maynard, letter to Joseph Dorfman, February 17, 1933, DC, CURB&ML, Box 62M.

2. John Cummings, letter to Joseph Dorfman, February 5, 1931, DC, CURB&ML, Box 61C.

3. Archibald B. Maynard, letter to Joseph Dorfman, February 17, 1933, DC, CURB&ML.

4. William H. Allen, letter to Joseph Dorfman, DC, CURB&ML, Box 62A.

5. Florence Veblen, "Reminiscences of Thorstein Veblen by His Brother Orson."

6. Joseph Dorfman, *Thorstein Veblen and His America,* page 194, quoting Ward's review of *The Theory of the Leisure Class,* which employs Veblen's phrase from the same book.

7. Thorstein Veblen, letter to Sarah Hardy Gregory, July 20, 1900, UCHISC, Miscellaneous Collections ("V" folder).

8. Joseph Dorfman, *Thorstein Veblen and His America,* page 195.

9. Stuart Chase, foreword to Thorstein Veblen, *The Theory of the Leisure Class* (New York: Random House, 1934).

10. Hans Otto Storm, "The Opaque Facts," a review of Joseph Dorfman's *Thorstein Veblen and His America,* DC, CURB&ML.

11. *San Francisco Chronicle,* July 28, 1944, clipping in the CC.

12. Thorstein Veblen, letter to Andrew Veblen, October 17, 1899, CC.

13. I.W. Hawarth, letter to Joseph Dorfman, DC, CURB&ML.

14. Dora Wells, letter to Joseph Dorfman, DC, CURB&ML, Box 64W.

15. Ellen Veblen's letters, *passim,* and Joseph Dorfman interview with Eve Schütze, October 9, 1938, DC, CURB&ML, Box 72S.

16. Sarah Gregory, undated letter to Joseph Dorfman, DC, CURB&ML, Box 61G.

17. Archibald B. Maynard, February 17, 1933 letter to Joseph Dorfman, DC, CURB&ML.

18. Mary B. Dierup, undated letter to Joseph Dorfman, DC, CURB&ML.

19. Joseph Dorfman, *Thorstein Veblen and His America,* page 253. Robert L. Duffus gives a brief review of *The Goosenbury Pilgrims:* "Mrs. Veblen collected a batch of characters out of Mother Goose and elsewhere—The Three Bears, the King of the Cannibal Islands, Miss Muffet, Wee Willie Winkie, the Crooked Man, Jack the Giant Killer, Robin Hood, and so on . . . the story has flashes of wit and drollery . . . But it has the illogical quality of a dream. No one episode leads into another . . . Ellen Veblen needed to discipline her imagination" (*The Innocents at Cedro* [New York: Macmillan, 1944], page 146). Her rhyme schemes were also lacking, as the opening dedication reads:

> Moon, be pleasant, Moon, be kind,
> Moon, look out of your cheesy rind!
> Take my Pilgrims, take my book!
> Green be the shade of your future luck!

Ellen Veblen, *The Goosenbury Pilgrims* (Boston: Lothrop, 1902).

20. Harriet Rolfe Dagg, letter to Joseph Dorfman, DC, CURB&ML, March 5, 1933.

21. Ellen Veblen, letter to Alice Millis, November 18, 1920, DC, CURB&ML.

22. John Neihardt, letter to Joseph Dorfman, August 29, 1935, DC, CURB&ML, Box 63N.

23. Alice Millis, undated letter to Joseph Dorfman, DC, CURB&ML, Box 63M.

24. Robert L. Duffus, *The Innocents at Cedro,* page 93.

25. Lucia K. Tower, wife of a Chicago professor and a friend and longtime correspondent of Ellen's, undated letter to Joseph Dorfman, DC, CURB&ML.

26. John Edward Veblen, undated letter to Joseph Dorfman, DC, CURB&ML.

27. Interview with Becky Veblen Meyers by Ruthmary Penick, 1977, page 37, CC.

28. Thorstein "read Ibsen, and spread knowledge of him on the Yale Campus." Joseph Dorfman, *Thorstein Veblen and His America,* page 43.

29. Thorstein Veblen, *The Theory of the Leisure Class,* pages 357–358.

30. Madame Blanc, *Condition of Woman in the United States: A Traveller's Guide,* pages 152–155.

31. Thorstein Veblen, *The Theory of the Leisure Class,* page 358.

32. *Ibid.,* pages 355–356.

33. *Ibid.,* page 357.

34. *Ibid.,* pages 353, 358.

35. *Ibid.*, pages 360–361.
36. Robert L. Duffus, *The Innocents at Cedro,* page 58.
37. Veblen, in a letter to Jacques Loeb, October 29, 1905, stated:

> As to my reasons for leaving here. I have never stood well with the president, and have been kept on the staff, rather as a concession to Professor Laughlin, than by the president's own choice. Lately, since last spring, his aversion has grown more steeled, if no stronger; so that I am now staying here on sufferance, and have been given notice that I need look for no recognition or advancement, but may be dropped whenever it can be done without inconvenience. The president's growing dislike is connected with the scandalous gossip which has apparently reached you, being the cause of it rather than the effect. You are right in surmising that the gossip comes from Chicago, the center of diffusion being apparently the office in Haskell.

Jacques Loeb collection, U.S. Library of Congress.

Chapter 12. Triggs and Mrs. Triggs

1. The businessman-run economy also tends toward an archaic militaristic policy to open up new markets abroad. Armed force is necessary to keep these foreign markets safe and orderly for the making of profits (e.g., the Spanish–American War). At the same time, the pomp and circumstance accompanying militarism diverts the minds of the populace from society's problems and the unequal distribution of wealth. But this policy has its dangers. A trend toward "absolute government, dynastic politics, devolution of rights and honors, ecclesiastical authority and popular submission and squalor . . . may easily be carried so far as to sacrifice the profits of the business man." Business enterprise could be in danger both from socialism and a right-wing military dictatorship: "It [is] incompatible with the ascendancy of either" (*The Theory of Business Enterprise,* pages 394–395 and 400). Not until Hitler appeared in Germany could Veblen's brilliance in forecasting the above conflict be recognized.

2. Thorstein Veblen, letter to Jacques Loeb, February 10, 1905, Jacques Loeb Collection, U.S. Library of Congress. Veblen had been close to Loeb when Loeb was conducting his biological experiments at the University of Chicago. Loeb subsequently became a professor at the University of California.

3. Joseph Dorfman, *Thorstein Veblen and His America,* page 255.

4. George H. Shull, lecture notes of Oscar Lovell Triggs's class on American Literature, Autumn Quarter, University of Chicago, 1901–1902, UCHISC.

5. Triggs discussed most poets in less than one lecture, but he talked for four or five days on Whitman, the bête noire of traditionalists, and came back frequently to Whitman when discussing other poets. In a lecture on November 12, 1901, for instance, when discussing Poe, Whitman, and Emerson, he said that Poe was the greatest genius, Emerson the most thoughtful, Whitman best at describing love and was the most comprehensive of the three. Longfellow was more of a teacher than a poet—all his writings were slightly cloaked lecture notes. But Whitman was "the greatest of outdoor poets and his 'Song of the Open Road' was one of the most free and sublime interpretations of nature ever put into ink." *Ibid.*

6. Eve Schütze, interview with Joseph Dorfman, October 9, 1930, DC, CURB&ML.

7. After reading this book in manuscript, Mel Leiman, professor emeritus of economics, New York State University at Binghamton, wrote, "In my opinion, you should subject your comments on Veblen and socialism to closer analysis. Veblen was indeed not a joiner, but I think he was partisan, even though it was in a complicated and somewhat bemused way." See also Robert Griffin, *Thorstein Veblen: Seer of Socialism* (Hamden, CT: Advocate Press, distributed by Roger Books, 1982). This enigma is worth a monograph in itself.

8. Thorstein Veblen, "Arts and Crafts," in *Essays in Our Changing Order,* ed. Leon Ardzrooni (New York: Viking Press, 1934; reprint, Clifton, NJ: Augustus M. Kelley, 1964), page 197.

9. *Ibid.,* page 196.

10. *Ibid.,* page 198.

11. *Ibid.,* pages 195, 198.

12. *Knoxville Journal and Tribune,* January 8, 1899. Calvin M. McClung Historical Collection, Lawson McGhee Library, Knoxville, Tennessee (hereafter LMGL).

13. Lucia K. Tower, letter to Joseph Dorfman, March 23, 1933, DC, CURB&ML, Box 63T.

14. John J. Broessamle, *William Gibbs McAdoo: A Passion for Change, 1863–1917* (Port Washington, NY: Kennikat Press, 1973).

15. Like Veblen, William Gibbs McAdoo Sr. suffered much from the incompetents who inevitably, under the Peter Principle, rise to positions of power as university trustees. After receiving one of a number of disappointments at the hands of the trustees, he growled to his diary:

> Among the body are some ignorant and illiterate men who must need hate anyone of a liberal education and high aims. Some of them bear a personal grudge against me. When I was Attorney General thirty years ago, I refused to favor Brown by corruptly dismissing prosecutions against him; and he has been my enemy ever since that time. Boyd is my enemy, because I employed another (Dr. Deaderick) for my family physician. Gant is my enemy because I failed to fondle his vanity by worshipping his church (Southern Methodist), and himself, instead of God Almighty. For nine long years I have labored faithfully in the University doing more work than any other man—yet never having been a member of the *Faculty* proper.

Diary of William Gibbs McAdoo, February 8, 1886, October 19, 1885–February 22, 1887, LMGL.

16. Thorstein Veblen, letter to Sarah Hardy Gregory, UCHISC, Miscellaneous Collections ("V" folder).

17. Joseph Dorfman, interview with Eve Schütze, October 9, 1930. DC, CURB&ML; diary of William Gibbs McAdoo, July 20, 1876, May 25, 1877, LMGL.

18. Joseph Dorfman, *New Light on Veblen* (Clifton, NJ: Augustus M. Kelley, 1973), page 97.

19. Ellen Veblen, letter to Lucia K. Tower, July 3, 1906, DC, CURB&ML.

20. Thorstein Veblen, letter to Jacques Loeb, February 10, 1905, Loeb Collection, U.S. Library of Congress. Mrs. Triggs's name does not appear in Veblen's class attendance files at the University of Chicago, in which names of students and auditors were recorded. UCHISC, Registrar's Records. Even after the scandal involving Mrs. Triggs and Veblen erupted, and Triggs was fired from his position as Professor of English at the University of Chicago, Triggs wrote enthusiastically about Veblen's

theories in *Tomorrow* magazine. The fact that Triggs felt no rancor toward Veblen seems to bolster Veblen's statement that the whole "Mrs. Triggs scandal" was manufactured. Triggs editorialized as follows:

> The keenest mind at work in the university field in America is that of Professor Thorstein Veblen. Almost alone among economists Professor Veblen writes from the point of view of a fundamental philosophy. His *Theory of the Leisure Class* marked an epoch in the economic interpretation of life because it was absolutely basic in social fact, and therefore beyond controversy. His recent *Theory of Business Enterprise,* published by Scribner's Sons, is the most complete analysis that has yet been made of the working of what is known as 'capitalism' or 'the system' . . . The reader should not fail to note the superb style of the author, his mastery over the phrase, the s[t]ately logic of the sentences, and the occasional flashes of satire.

Tomorrow, February 1905, pages 50–52, U.S. Library of Congress.

21. Joseph Dorfman, interview with Eve Schütze, October 9, 1930, DC, CURB&ML.

22. Thorstein Veblen, letter to Jacques Loeb, February 10, 1905, Loeb Collection, U.S. Library of Congress.

23. Ellen Veblen, letter to Lucia K. Tower. Dorfman in his Veblen biography implies that Ellen's "giving no hint" meant she gave no hint to Harper of Thorstein's supposed peccadillos; however, it is clear from her letter to Lucia that Ellen played a major role in Veblen's undoing at Chicago. Joseph Dorfman, *Thorstein Veblen and His America,* page 259.

24. Joseph Dorfman, *Thorstein Veblen and His America,* page 254. Jacob Warshaw, a friend and colleague at the University of Missouri, surmised that what bothered Veblen most was that he suspected that he was sacrificed at the University of Chicago, not for flouting the Victorian moral code, as they pretended, but for his insistence on being "a scholar and not a salesman for the university" and also because he bullheadedly desired to retain the right to express ideas that might shake up the establishment. Jacob Warshaw, "Recollections of Thorstein Veblen," Jacob Warshaw Papers, 1910–1944, Western Historical Manuscript Collection, Columbia, Missouri (hereafter WHM), Folder 89, No. 36.

25. Andrew Veblen, letter to Joseph Dorfman, November 9, 1929, DC, CURB&ML.

Chapter 13. Out of Chicago

1. The *Chicago Daily News* reported on February 20, 1905, that the secretary of the Board of Trustees had said that public agitation about Dr. Triggs and the "ridicule and criticism heaped upon him unjustly" caused certain members of the Board of Trustees to direct an attack upon him each time that his name came up for reappointment. The article stated, "This, however, does not satisfy Dr. Triggs's friends on the faculty, for his name never reached the board of trustees this year, because Dr. [J.H.] Manley, head of the English department, failed to recommend him." According to the same article President Harper "defended Triggs," from "attacks of irate members of the university board of trustees." It claimed that Manley had said he had had a "toothache" and could not explain his failure to recommend Dr. Triggs.

"The statement of Professor Triggs that brought him most conspicuously before the public," said the *Chicago Daily Tribune* of February 20, 1905, "was his ranking Rockefeller and Pullman with Shakespeare." This caused an immediate uproar. The public must have believed he was indulging in heavy sarcasm. This quip, however, was taken out of context. He had simply stated that "the test of genius is quality of mind, not composition of materials. This age is primarily industrial and the genius of today turns his attention to industrialism, just as the genius of Shakespeare turned to poetic drama."

2. Upton Sinclair, *The Brass Check* (Pasadena, CA: Upton Sinclair, undated), pages 334–335. The Triggs *delenda est* campaign also employed the services of a newspaper reporter who tracked down Triggs for an interview that put him in a strange light. This interview, which appeared in a Chicago newspaper, made note of the fact that in the room next to Triggs's in the community building where he lived (which may have been the Beatrice), hung a pink kimono and some silk stockings. Also his wife was out of town. Readers were left to draw their own conclusions.

3. Edward W. Bemis, "Academic Freedom," *The Independent* (August 17, 1899): 2197–2198.

4. Upton Sinclair, *The Brass Check.*

5. Joseph Dorfman, *New Light on Veblen,* page 97.

6. Léontine-Charlotte Lippman married Albert Arman de Caillavet and is called Madame Arman, Léontine de Caillavet, or Madame de Caillavet by various writers.

7. Jacob Alexrad, *Anatole France: A Life without Illusions* (New York: Harper and Brothers, 1944).

8. *Ibid.* Laura killed herself on December 17, 1911.

9. *Ibid.*

10. In September 1920 he was married to the amply proportioned, but still lovely, Emma Laprevotte.

11. France had been invited to the house of his publisher, Calmann-Lèvy, at Houlgate, in Normandy. The appellation "la belle Floridienne" must have related to the obscure fact that Tennessee was probably part of the America referred to as "La Florida" by Hernan de Soto when he searched the region for cities of gold in 1540.

12. Whether the Danoise did, or did not, pass the news along to Laura Gagey is not certain. Marie-Claire Bancquart surveyed the correspondence between France and Laura and concluded that he had, indeed, led her to expect an enduring relationship, and that he had fooled himself in believing Laura could replace his old mistress. Substitutes for ghosts do not have an easy role to play. He was looking for the complaisant and submissive Madame Arman; she was looking for an indulgent and all-forgiving father. *Anatole France: Un sceptique passionné* (Paris: Calmann-Lévy, 1984), page 318.

13. Jacques Suffel, *Anatole France par lui-même* (Paris: Ecrivains de Toujours, Editions de Seuil), 1954), translated by the authors. Suffel mistakenly described Laura as being thirty-five years of age, but did not exaggerate when he remarked that she spoke French well. He wrote of the thick dark hair framing her face and said she was "assez jolie" (sufficiently pretty). Actually she was distinguished by angular Scottish-Celtic features, but still managed to be lovely. In some respects France's treatment of Laura Gagey was reminiscent of the way France treated Madame Arman, who had promoted his literary career through her influential salons. He had courted Léontine assiduously, and when she fell deeply in love with him, became bored, unfaithful, and treated her badly. She then tried to commit suicide by turning

on the gas, but was rescued in time by a servant. However, she died shortly thereafter from pleurisy, probably as a result of the suicide attempt. France then obsessed over her memory, and declared himself unable to function. For a while it seemed as if Madame Gagey would fill the gap. He began writing again, and *Les Dieux ont soif* is considered by some to be one of his best books—by others one of his worst.

14. Sometime in June 1905, the year after the Triggs scandal occurred, Ellen wrote a mysterious letter to President Harper. Twenty-five years later, its contents could not be fully revealed to Joseph Dorfman when he tried to obtain information about Veblen from the president's office at the University of Chicago. The secretary wrote Dorfman that Mrs. Veblen had told Harper that her husband was in Europe for that second summer, while Veblen claimed to be in Boston waiting to give a lecture before the Massachusetts Reform Club. The secretary continued, however, "Further contents of this letter I am unable to divulge, as they are of a very personal nature." The letter has since disappeared from the university files. UCHISC.

15. Ellen Veblen, letter to Mary Hougen, June 2, 1906, CC. Ellen's friend Alice Millis wrote Joseph Dorfman, July 10, 1936, that in 1904 Ellen had come west to settle for a year in Hood River. Thorstein's interest in Babe became apparent. DC, CURB&ML. The following year Ellen took up the timber claim, perfected as Claim No. 9163, Hood River County Records.

16. Ellen Veblen, letter to Lucia K. Tower, July 3, 1906, DC, CURB&ML.

17. Joseph Dorfman, *Thorstein Veblen and His America,* page 257.

18. Veblen says science is the last court of appeal in our civilization and sets the tone for the whole of western civilization. It gives modern Christendom its authority, its superiority.

There are two approaches to scientific discovery. "Pragmatism"—Veblen takes an obscure meaning of the word, or perhaps his own meaning—has an axe to grind and looks for certain expected results. The alternate approach is "idle curiosity," which happens onto scientific discoveries by accident or serendipity.

Pragmatism, as defined by Veblen, becomes the end-seeking approach. Both pragmatism and the playful, idly curious approach are found in all branches of human inquiry. Idle curiosity simply observes phenomena while pragmatism interprets them to point a lesson or to reinforce an outlook. "What the selective consequences of . . . a protracted regime of pragmatism would be for the temper of the race may be seen in the human flotsam left by the great civilizations of antiquity such as Egypt, India and Persia. Science is not at home among these leavings of barbarism. In these instances . . . the barbarian culture has selectively worked . . . out a scheme of life from which objective, matter-of-fact knowledge is virtually excluded." See the essay, "The Place of Science in Modern Civilization," in the book of the same name (New York: Russell and Russell, 1961), page 23.

19. Thorstein Veblen, *The Place of Science in Modern Civilization,* page 443.

20. *Ibid.,* page 416.

21. *Ibid.,* pages 424–425.

22. *Ibid.,* page 429.

23. *Ibid.,* pages 441–442.

24. Thorstein Veblen, letter to Jacques Loeb, February 10, 1905, Jacques Loeb Collection, U.S. Library of Congress.

25. Joseph Dorfman, *Thorstein Veblen and His America,* page 269.

26. Wesley Clair Mitchell, letter to Sarah Hardy Gregory, December 11, 1905, DC, CURB&ML. Box 62M.

27. Thorstein Veblen, letter to David Starr Jordan, April 9, 1906, SULSC. On April 14, 1906, Allyn Young wrote Jordan from the University of Wisconsin, where he was then employed, that "In case Veblen cannot be secured on reasonable conditions, I would favor [W.C.] Mitchell. He is a thorough and painstaking scholar . . . Mitchell was getting $1800 at California when I last had information from him." Allyn Young had been hired for the following fall as administrative head of the Stanford Economics Department. President Jordan subsequently made the University of California an offer to "interchange Veblen with Mitchell for a term," but the arrangements could not be worked out. A.C. Miller (Berkeley, California), letter to President Jordan, April 17, 1906, SULSC.

28. Thorstein Veblen, letter to David Starr Jordan, April 16, 1906, SULSC.

29. *Ibid.* Also, on May 8, 1906, Veblen followed Jordan's suggestion and wrote that he would be quite willing to begin teaching at Stanford in January 1907.

30. *Ibid.* In his letter of May 19, 1906, Veblen asked Jordan to clarify whether Jordan wanted him to begin teaching in August 1906 or in January 1907 as, if it were to be in January, he would like to take a short trip to England at the beginning of the summer.

31. When Ellen reverted to form at Stanford and Thorstein again felt under attack, he still did not waver in his resolve to maintain his status as a high-salaried professor. His friend Davenport at the University of Missouri had suggested that there might be an opening for him there. Veblen wrote that anything less than a salary of $3,000 would be unacceptable; however, if a slight concession were necessary to get the job, he would leave it to Davenport's discretion (Thorstein Veblen, letter to Herbert J. Davenport, April 14, 1909, DC, CURB&ML). As it turned out, Veblen was paid $1,920 at Missouri in 1913, rising to $2,400 in 1917. He had been earning $3,000 annually at Stanford. Joseph Dorfman, *Thorstein Veblen and His America,* page 306.

32. Ellen Veblen, letter to Sarah Hardy Gregory, April 1897, UCHISC, Miscellaneous Collections ("V" folder).

Chapter 14. The Corner of Indecision

1. Becky Veblen Meyers, letter to David Riesman, February 20, 1954, CC. The Bevans family later became connected by marriage with the van Doren family, and *Life* magazine (October 26, 1959) declared them one of America's most distinguished intellectual clans. Unfortunately, the immediate cause of this write-up was a *cause célèbre.* Charles van Doren, who had amazed the whole country by his prowess in answering the $64,000 Question, fell from grace when it was revealed that the program had fooled the gullible public—it had been feeding van Doren the correct answers all along.

2. R.M. Hitch, "Homer Bevans Memorial," 1908, newspaper clipping from unidentified Chicago newspaper, CC.

3. *Ibid.*

4. Esther Baran, telephone interview with authors, January 2, 1995, and letter to the authors, June 19, 1997.

5. "Women teachers were forced to sign contracts guaranteeing that they would not marry during the term of the contract." "A 1982 Review of *The Barbarian Status of Women,* by Geraldine Mazzei Griffin," in *Thorstein Veblen: Seer of Socialism,* by Robert Griffin (Hamden, CT: Advocate Press, 1982), page 91.

6. Letter from Mama Bradley to her twenty-year-old granddaughter on her birthday (Babe's younger daughter, Ann), February 13, 1923: "Now I was present when you first saw the light of day in that old, dingy hospital, and I don't remember that you looked extremely happy, and why should I wish you any happy returns of that particular day?" CC.

7. Becky Veblen Meyers, handwritten "Autobiography," CC, pages 13–14.

8. *Ibid.,* page 35.

9. Marie J. Buhle, *Women and American Socialism, 1870–1920* (Chicago: University of Illinois Press, 1892).

10. Becky Veblen Meyers, "Autobiography," CC, page 68.

11. Marie J. Buhle, *Women and American Socialism, 1870–1920,* page 137.

12. *Comrade* 11 (October 1903).

13. Telephone conversation with Becky Veblen Meyers and Esther Baran, November 14, 1993.

14. Tom Bevans, letter to [his daughter in] "Oakland," January 25, 1940, CC.

15. Thorstein Veblen, "The Barbarian Status of Women," *Essays in Our Changing Order,* ed. Leon Ardzrooni, page 51.

16. *Ibid.,* pages 51–64.

17. Eventually, Babe left Tom's flat on Ellis Street and moved into an artists' colony. At Tom's flat she had at least enjoyed playing Chopin nocturnes—of which she was very fond—until, upon the complaint of a neighbor who worked nights, Tom abruptly got rid of her piano. She tried to make the best of this by telling acquaintances that it was wrong for some children to have pianos while others had to work in factories. She felt such inequalities keenly, as did Sarah Hardy. (In fact, as Esther Baran has pointed out, there were similarities in philosophies of the two women.) Babe often recited a poem by Elizabeth Barrett Browning about children working from dawn to dusk in the British mines and factories. These phrases Becky never forgot:

> The young lambs are bleating in the meadow, . . .
> But the young, young children, O my brothers,
> They are weeping bitterly!
> They are weeping in the playtime
> Of the others, in the country of the free.

Elizabeth Barrett Browning, "The Cry of the Children," from *The Home Book of Verse,* selected and arranged by Burton Egbert Stevenson (New York: Holt, Rinehart, and Winston, 1965), pages 283–284.

18. Joseph Dorfman's notes of an interview with Eve Schütze, October 9, 1930, DC, CURB&ML. See notes, Chapter 5. The phrase, "the corner of indecision," was a puzzle to Veblen's adopted stepdaughter, Becky Veblen Meyers; and she felt it must refer to the artists' colony in general. The Schützes' explanation seems more probable and convincing.

19. Becky Veblen Meyers, "Memoirs," Julius Ulsson, page 16.

20. One of the well-known characters in the colony was Bror Nordfeldt, an artist of Swedish descent who became famous in the midwest and was considered an extremely able painter, influenced by avant-garde Europeans and the Japanese. Nordfeldt's works are now prominently featured in the collection of the University of Minnesota Museum of Art in Minneapolis. Babe was proud to say that Nordfeldt was a friend of theirs and wrote to the children that they must never forget him. He painted

2. Alice (Mrs. Henry Alvin) Millis, letter to Joseph Dorfman, July 10, 1936, DC, CURB&ML.

3. *Ibid.*

4. Evelyn Wells Podesta had a different tale to tell concerning Ellen Veblen's trek from Oregon to Stanford. According to Podesta, in the summer of 1906, Ellen was staying with the Wells family in Ashland, Oregon, where the family (including three children and an ailing aunt), had settled after leaving the Chicago area. Ellen had fled to her close friends after the Triggs scandal, "as she always fled to Mama [Mrs. Wells] when grief overcame her. There was a nervous breakdown, and she stayed with us and was healing, and we all were having a lovely time. Then Veblen arrived from Chicago. He had a teaching post in Palo Alto. He wanted her there. He wanted us all there."

She gives us two versions of the next sequence of events. "And so Ellen V. left with Veblen, and Mama and her brood followed on the train." The Reverend Mr. Wells, a Congregational minister, followed later in a cattle car where he looked after their three Indian ponies, dog, cat, cow, and pet hen. (Wells had provided himself with a cot and supplies with which to feed himself and the livestock.)

In Evelyn Wells's letter to Carlton Qualey, dated September 26, 1966, she wrote, however, "Veblen had the Stanford offer and asked my parents to bring Mrs. V. to Palo Alto—he had rented Cedro [San Ysidro] Cottage."

In considering the two Wells versions, plus that of Alice Millis, on the arrival of the two Veblens at Stanford, it must be remembered that Evelyn Wells was just entering kindergarten when Ellen Veblen stayed with them at Ashland, so her memories of those events may have been hazy and intermittent. No doubt Ellen Veblen did visit them in Ashland, but perhaps earlier than when Thorstein suddenly appeared to Ellen on the timber claim. Or it is possible that Thorstein and Ellen departed from Ashland for the timber claim, where Ellen had left some of her possessions, and the Wellses followed them on the train later when the Veblens had moved to Cedro. The date of the Veblens' move to Cedro (later in the fall of 1906) also conflicts with the Evelyn Wells version. Miscellaneous papers sent to William Melton [date questionable], by Clinton F. Wells. CC.

5. Alice Millis, undated letter to Professor Joseph Dorfman, DC, CURB&ML.

6. *Ibid.*

7. If Thorstein told her he did not want children, as reported by Ellen to Joseph Dorfman, it may have been to assuage her fears that, because she was unable to have children, their relationship was valueless. Certainly, Veblen was a loving father to Becky and Ann. Becky Veblen Meyers, "Autobiography," CC.

8. Alice Millis, letter to Joseph Dorfman, July 10, 1936, DC, CURB&ML. Also authors' interview with Charles Sims, November 15, 1993. According to Evelyn Wells, who lived at Cedro briefly as a child, the five-acre garden was "intercepted by cypress hedges." She also wrote of "conversations at the table . . . in the long . . . beamed . . . English dining room . . . Anyone would have loved [the place]." Miscellaneous papers sent to William Melton on January 5, 1955, by Clinton F. Wells. The site has been converted to public school grounds.

9. Alice Millis, letter to Joseph Dorfman, June 10, 1936. "At first [the Veblens] took a modest cottage near us, but before the autumn term [of 1906] was over they moved out to Cedro cottage," and Veblen stayed there a year and a half.

10. The Wells family (accompanied by an ailing aunt), old friends from Palos Park, near Chicago, were attempting to keep house for the Veblens at Cedro, and

portraits of Babe and Thorstein (one with a shadowy Becky in the background, was later eliminated from the picture). Unfortunately, Thorstein's portraits hav been lost. Thorstein liked quizzing "Nordy" and the other artists in minute detai their aims and techniques (Becky Veblen Meyers, interview with Ruthmary 1977, CC, page 40). Becky Veblen Meyers mentions only one portrait of Veblen Bartley mentions two. Russell Bartley, "Unexamined Moments in the Life of Th Veblen," paper presented at the second conference of the International Thorstein Association, May 30, 1996, at Carleton College, citing *Nordfeldt the Painter* Deren Coke (Albuquerque: University of New Mexico Press, 1972).

21. Becky Veblen Meyers, "Autobiography," CC, page 18.

22. On occasion, Becky Veblen Meyers said, Thorstein read Babe so Swinburne's poems aloud. One was about the law-and-order man, Apollo, "A god to follow, a beautiful god to behold," who was feared for the punishme meted out, some in the form of illness or pestilence (Becky Veblen Meyers, "A ography," alternate page 82). See Algernon Charles Swinburne, "Hymn to P pine," *Everyman's Book of Victorian Verse,* ed. J.M. Watson (London: J.M. D Sons, 1982), page 209. Originally the preeminent British Victorian poet, Swin fell out of favor because his private life was considered scandalous, and becau his alarming fondness for Baudelaire and the Marquis de Sade. Swinburne w aristocrat who advocated republicanism rather than monarchism and was imp anti-theist. The "Hymn to Proserpine" plays on the conflict between Apollo holder of morals, and Proserpine, part-time mistress of Pluto in the Netherworld contrasts the colorful deities of the ancients with the drabness of Christianity: " hast conquered, O pale Galilean, the world has grown grey from thy breath."

23. Eve Schütze, letter to Joseph Dorfman, August 2, 1930, and interview Dorfman, October 9, 1930, DC, CURB&ML.

24. Ellen Veblen, letter to Alice Millis, October 17 (no year indicated, prob 1907), DC, CURB&ML.

25. Eve Schütze, letter to Joseph Dorfman, August 2, 1930, DC.

26. Charlotte Perkins Gilman, letter to Joseph Dorfman, August 30, 1933, CURB&ML. See Charlotte Perkins Gilman, *Women and Economics* (1898; reprint, York: Harper Torchbooks, 1966. See, also, Gilman's *Herland* (New York: Panth 1979). It is odd that Gilman should have taken such a jaundiced view of Thorstein Babe's alliance, as, long before Gilman met the couple—they must have met ar 1904 or 1905—she had divorced her first husband (taking their only child with her the grounds that the marriage made her very depressed. She then required psychi treatment, which made her even more depressed. In 1900 she had married a man se years her junior with whom she evidently had a satisfactory relationship. The key to waspish attitude toward Thorstein and Babe may have been the words "amorous" "sex extravagance." Gilman did not approve of "the new trend for using sex for rec tional purposes" and felt that sexual activity should be indulged in solely for the purp of procreation, and that it should be up to the woman to decide if and when she wante produce offspring. In her second marriage, she remained childless.

27. Becky Veblen Meyers, "Biography," transcribed by Esther Baran, CC, page 3.

Chapter 15. Stanford

1. Ellen Glasgow, *Barren Ground* (Garden City, NY: Doubleday, Page, 192 page 296.

help run the "farm," but it didn't work out. Too many enfeebled "helpers" were involved. Robert L. Duffus, *The Innocents at Cedro,* page 15. After the break occurred between Ellen and Thorstein, the Wells menage, plus their animals, moved to San Jose. Clinton F. Wells papers. Although they were sympathetic toward Ellen, the family admitted that "she was *hard* on the professor." Becky Veblen Meyers, letter to John P. Diggins, January 17, 1982, CC. The Wilson-Baker family—a mother, a grandmother—and an eleven-year-old girl—became Veblen's new housekeepers. Their stay was of short duration. According to Duffus, the mother considered herself a socialist, and the grandmother believed that "the world was going to the dogs." Again there was "no cash nexus," a family practice often followed on Wisconsin and Minnesota farms. After their departure three students, including the Duffus brothers, cooked and cleaned for Veblen.

11. Becky Veblen Meyers, interview with Paul Veblen, June 10, 1993, page 20, and pages 28–29, CC. Veblen had always been fond of cats and hated dogs, especially since he had been witness to an incident in which a pack of dogs cornered a cat inside a barn and brought it out dead. See also *The Theory of the Leisure Class,* page 141.

12. Mary Deirup, undated letter to Joseph Dorfman, DC, CURB&ML.

13. President Krichner of the San Diego Business and Academic College, letter to David Starr Jordan congratulating him on his address at "Bryn" [Mawr?] College, June 4, 1909, David Starr Jordan correspondence file, SULSC.

14. *Daily Palo Alto* (Stanford's student newspaper), February 17, 1908, SULSC.

15. Speech to a San Francisco business group "On the Strength of Being Clean," *Daily Palo Alto,* February 3, 1908, SULSC.

16. Ellen Veblen, letter to Lucia K. Tower, May 3, 1908, DC, CURB&ML.

17. Surprisingly enough, not only did Ellen own several small houses in California and one in Oregon, she had hung on to the Palos Park property in Chicago. "Hood River and Palos Park houses rented. Mrs. Reed paid $500 on Palo Alto house. Getting out of difficulties," letter from Ellen Veblen to Alice Millis, October 17 (year not given, but probably 1908), DC, CURB&ML.

18. Place names here may be confusing. Early in 1907, however, Ellen moved from Cedro to downtown Palo Alto, before she decided to move on definitively to Carmel-by-the-Sea. At that time the Cedro property was considered a part of Palo Alto although across San Francisquito Creek, which placed it outside the city limits and also in another county. Stanford was also outside the city limits of Palo Alto but considered to be "at Palo Alto," the name of its railroad station. Years later the Cedro property became part of the City of Menlo Park, and Stanford had its own post office designation. In the early days the Stanford student newspaper was named *The Daily Palo Alto* and later became *The Stanford Daily.*

19. This letter, recently conveyed to the CC by Daniel P. Gregory, was brought to our attention by Russell and Sylvia Bartley.

20. Thorstein's visits to his friends were sometimes abrupt and without notice. In Mitchell's letter to Sarah Hardy Gregory, May 17, 1911, he described Veblen's arrival a few days before "without the least warning" (except for a telephone call from San Francisco), and how they had "talked about all things under Heaven in our usual way, and I felt the usual stimulus which he imparts." The next afternoon Veblen vanished as inexplicably as he always did, not telling Mitchell anything about his summer plans. DC, CURB&ML.

21. Lucy Sprague Mitchell, from the chapter, "Our Berkeley Years 1903–1912,"

in *Two Lives: The Story of Wesley Clair Mitchell and Myself* (New York: Simon and Schuster, 1953).

22. Daniel P. Gregory material, CC.

23. Ellen Veblen, undated letter and clipping sent to President David Starr Jordan, David Starr Jordan correspondence file, SULSC.

24. Edwin Seligman, letter to Thorstein Veblen, May 10, 1909, DC, CURB&ML.

25. Thorstein Veblen, "The Limitations of Marginal Utility," *Journal of Political Economy* 17 (November 1909): 620–636, reprinted in *What Veblen Taught*, ed. Wesley C. Mitchell (New York: Viking Press, 1947).

26. Thorstein Veblen, "Fisher's Capital and Income," *Political Science Quarterly* (March 1907): 112–128, and "Fisher's Rate of Interest," *Political Science Quarterly* (June 1909): 296–303. Subsequent reviews included Albert Schatz's *L'Individualisme Economique et Social,* Sidney A. Reeve's *The Cost of Competition, Capital and Income* and his *Economic Phenomena* (see Joseph Dorfman, *Thorstein Veblen and His America,* page 279). Before the Kosmos Club at the University of California at Berkeley, Veblen lectured on "The Evolution of the Scientific Point of View." His article "On the Nature of Capital, Interest, and the Productivity of Capital Goods" was published in *Quarterly Journal of Economics* ([August 22, 1908]: 517–542).

27. Thorstein Veblen, "Professor Clark's Economics," from *The Place of Science in Modern Civilization* (New York: Russell and Russell, 1961), pages 184–185.

28. John P. Diggins, *The Bard of Savagery* (New York: Seabury Press, 1978), page 141.

29. Joseph Dorfman, *Thorstein Veblen and His America,* page 284.

30. C.P. Huse, letter to Joseph Dorfman, July 23, 1934, DC, CURB&ML.

31. Thorstein Veblen, "Christian Morals and the Competitive System," *The Portable Veblen,* ed. Max Lerner (New York: Viking Press, 1948), pages 480–498. This article was a forerunner to the more exciting "Salesmanship and the Churches," also from *The Portable Veblen,* pages 499–506.

32. Wesley Clair Mitchell, letter to Sarah Hardy Gregory, March 30, 1909, DC, CURB&ML, Box 61M.

33. Interview with anonymous Gregory family member, September 29, 1993.

34. Joseph Dorfman, *Thorstein Veblen and His America,* page 295.

Chapter 16. Where the Rolling Foothills Rise

1. Joseph Dorfman, *Thorstein Veblen and His America,* page 274.

2. *Daily Palo Alto,* spring 1908, SULSC.

3. "During his first years at Stanford [Allyn] Young tried to convince Jordan to move into graduate work in economics. Jordan was too much interested in undergraduate studies. At the time he was carrying on a running battle with the trustees, who distrusted the humanities, and wanted to turn the institution into a trade school. Jordan agreed to a limited number of graduate courses, but was unwilling to provide the funds for library acquisitions, visiting speakers, fellowships and additional faculty." Charles P. Blitch, *Allyn Young: The Peripatetic Economist* (London: Macmillan Press, and New York: St. Martin's Press, 1995), page 23.

4. Clarmae Budd Rowley, letter to Joseph Dorfman, September 23, 1932, DC, CURB&ML.

5. Joseph Dorfman, *Thorstein Veblen and His America,* page 274.

6. *Ibid.,* page 275.

7. Guido Marx, letter to Joseph Dorfman, October 21, 1919, DC, CURB&ML.

8. Robert L. Duffus., *The Innocents at Cedro,* page 60.

9. John P. Diggins, *The Bard of Savagery,* page 169.

10. Ernest Sutherland Bates, *Scribner's* (December 1933), quoted in "The Last Man Who Knew Everything," *Carleton Voice* 45, No. 4 (fall 1980).

11. Robert L. Duffus, *The Innocents at Cedro,* page 13.

12. *Ibid.,* page 14.

13. Professor A.P. Winston of the University of Texas, letter to Joseph Dorfman, October 15, 1932, DC, CURB&ML, Box 64W. Reporting Newman's remarks, he adds, "[This] was a time when Veblen was somewhere between 40 and 53 years of age and when for many years he had been regarded as a semi-invalid." Winston had been one of Veblen's students at Chicago.

14. Becky Veblen Meyers, "Memoirs," CC.

15. Mrs. Bevans wrote her daughter Becky a postcard en route to California, August 22, 1907, from Omaha, Nebraska, CC.

16. Lucy Sprague Mitchell, *Two Lives,* pages 194–195.

17. *Ibid.*

18. Wesley Clair Mitchell diary, WCMR, CURB&ML.

19. Robert L. Duffus, *The Innocents at Cedro,* page 94.

20. Charles P. Blitch, *Allyn Young: The Peripatetic Economist,* page 24.

21. Lucy Sprague Mitchell, *Two Lives,* page 153.

22. Elinor Wylie, "The Puritan's Ballad," from *Collected Poems of Elinor Wylie* (New York: Alfred A. Knopf, 1934). Veblen's soft-as-a-paw approach was also noted in Missouri, years later: "Veblen came up to me one day with his quiet, catlike steps." Jacob Warshaw, "Recollections of Thorstein Veblen," Jacob Warshaw Papers, 1910–1944, WHM, Folder 89, No. 36.

23. Alice Millis wrote, "Once, as the boys told me, Mrs. Bivins [*sic*] came down to Cedro, but Mr. Veblen persuaded her to leave at once." Alice Millis, July 10, 1936, letter to Joseph Dorfman, DC, CURB&ML.

24. Robert L. Duffus, *The Innocents at Cedro,* page 95.

25. This apparently didn't jell. Was it perhaps too idealized and sanitized a version of Thorstein and Ellen's life together?

26. Robert L. Duffus, *The Innocents at Cedro,* page 98.

27. *Ibid.,* page 96.

28. Isador Lubin ("Recollections of Thorstein Veblen") reported that Veblen dismissed fans who came to Missouri to see him because he was noted as a "Great Man." Hans Otto Storm, who knew Veblen well after he retired to California in the late 1920s, said: "Veblen was, by choice, the opposite of the type known as a 'grand old man.' As I understand the racket of becoming a public personage, those who arrive at such a state are usually eager for, and cordial to, followers, but are inclined to drop persons who wish, mind against mind, to enter into serious discussion. Veblen was not at all of this taste." Hans Otto Storm, letter to Joseph Dorfman, September 18, 1934, DC, CURB&ML.

29. Robert L. Duffus, *The Innocents at Cedro,* page 98.

30. *Ibid.,* pages 62–63.

31. *Ibid.,* pages 93–94.

32. *Ibid.,* page 67.

33. Ellen Veblen, letter to Alice Millis, March 2, 1908, DC, CURB&ML.

34. Robert L. Duffus, *The Innocents at Cedro,* page 109.

35. *Ibid.,* pages 111–112.

36. David Starr Jordan, letter to Thorstein Veblen, April 29, 1907, SULSC.

37. Ellen Veblen, letter to Lucia K. Tower, May 3, 1908, DC, CURB&ML. She writes that she has been "for three weeks in Palo Alto, building a house to rent (furnished). You know my things came out, but before they got here, I knew Mrs. Bevans had the distinguished honor to be first and they were never uncrated. I shall soon have been in Carmel a year. My Palo Alto life was very brief and awful. Mrs. Bevans came out from Brooklyn [?], I don't know just when, last fall, perhaps, and attended college at Berkeley through two terms."

38. Alice Millis, letter to Joseph Dorfman, July 10, 1936, DC, CURB&ML. Duffus preferred to think that it was Ellen's unquenchable "love" and "faithfulness" to Thorstein that inspired her to move close by. "She evidently wanted to be near Veblen," he wrote. "She wanted to be near the place where he had been" (Robert L. Duffus, *The Innocents at Cedro,* page 144). Unaware of Ellen's role as informant at Chicago and Stanford, Duffus didn't realize that Ellen's purposeful propinquity might be primarily for espionage purposes.

39. Alice Millis, undated letter to Joseph Dorfman, DC, CURB&ML, Box 63M.

40. Virginia Arnott, letter to Joseph Dorfman, March 5, 1933, DC, CURB&ML.

41. Mary B. Deirup, Palo Alto, undated letter to Joseph Dorfman, DC, CURB&ML.

Chapter 17. A Dossier of Positive Statements

1. Thorstein Veblen, letter to Herbert J. Davenport, November 19, 1909, DC, CURB&ML. Veblen wrote: "I forgot, the other day, to mention your tent, which is still here. Shall I send it on, or leave it with the few goods which I expect to leave for later shipment when I know where I am going to ship them? The poles of the tent never came, and I got no accounting for them from the SP [Southern Pacific Railroad] people."

2. Robert L. Duffus, *The Innocents at Cedro,* page 115. On Washington Island and in Columbia, Missouri, Thorstein's tents were always erected on a platform.

3. Ellen Veblen, letter to Lucia K. Tower, January 23, 1912, DC, CURB&ML.

4. Alice Millis, letter to Joseph Dorfman, July 10, 1936, DC, CURB&ML.

5. Ellen Veblen, letter to Alice Millis, September 11, 1907, DC, CURB&ML.

6. Franklin Walker, *The Seacoast of Bohemia* (Salt Lake City: Book Club of California, and Peregrine Smith, 1973).

7. S.S. Van Dine (pseudonym of Willard Huntington Wright, popular mystery writer of the twenties and thirties), article in *Los Angeles Times,* May 22, 1910, quoted by Franklin Walker in *The Seacoast of Bohemia.*

8. *Ibid.*

9. Ellen Veblen, letter to Alice Millis, October 17 (probably 1907), DC, CURB&ML.

10. Ellen Veblen, letter to Alice Millis, September 24, 1907, DC, CURB&ML.

11. Ellen Veblen, letter to Alice Millis, October 17 (probably 1907), DC, CURB&ML.

12. Ellen Veblen, letter to "Janet" from Carmel, undated, DC, CURB&ML.

13. Ellen Veblen, letter to Sarah Hardy Gregory, 1897, UCHISC, Miscellaneous Collections ("V" folder).

14. Ellen Veblen, letter to Lucia K. Tower, May 3, 1908, DC, CURB&ML.

15. Ellen Veblen, letter to Alice Millis, September 13, 1907, DC, CURB&ML.

16. Ellen Veblen, letter to Alice Millis, March 2, 1908, DC, CURB&ML.

17. *Ibid.*

18. Ellen Veblen, letter to Alice Millis, March 14, 1908, DC, CURB&ML.

19. Ellen Veblen, letter to Lucia K. Tower, May 3, 1908, DC, CURB&ML.

20. David Starr Jordan correspondence file, SULSC, SC58–Box 27, Volume 60.

21. *Ibid.*

22. Sylvia and Russell Bartley's research uncovered a nest of three-by-five-inch file cards kept on "The Veblen Case" among the OLEP at Stanford. Elliott compiled the cards while he was working on *Stanford: The First Twenty-five Years,* which, of course, did not mention Veblen at all (OLEP [SC7], Container 8, Stanford History Notes [STWY], SULSC). In a letter to Professor James Haver of Boston, January 21, 1910, Jordan explained that "the whole matter has not involved anything criminal, but it is a kind of Bohemianism which is inconsistent with the requirements of life outside Bohemia." *Ibid.*

Chapter 18. His Last Few Days of Honor and Competence

1. Becky Veblen Meyers, letter to Mason Gaffney, April 4, 1988, and her "Autobiography," page 3, CC.

2. Becky Veblen Meyers, "Autobiography," pages 4 and 20, CC. Mrs. Meyers alternately reported that the date they left for Idaho was in the fall of 1908. They stayed only one year there, and since Thorstein spent the Christmas of 1909 at Nowhere, as well as several months in early 1910 convalescing from pneumonia there, the later date seems more probable. Babe's telegram to President Jordan from Grangeville, on October 14, 1909 (SULSC), appears to confirm the conclusion that, during 1908, Babe was in Chicago getting a divorce from Tom Bevans, and that she and the children spent the fall of 1909 and the spring of 1910 at Nowhere, in Idaho.

3. A letter from Ellen Veblen to Lucia K. Tower (August 16, 1909) states that a student had seen "Veblen's new wife." DC, CURB&ML. The date of the sighting is not indicated. A letter from Mrs. Henry Cowell speaks of Babe's tactless introduction of herself around Palo Alto as "Veblen's wife." This is inconsistent with Babe's behavior around the Duffus boys in 1907–1908, but Mrs. Cowell says this information came from a nephew of Veblen's with whom he spent his declining years [?]. It is not known to whom she was referring. Mrs. Henry Cowell, letter to the librarian at Carleton College, CC.

4. Marie J. Buhle, *Women and American Socialism, 1879–1920* (Chicago: University of Illinois Press, 1981).

5. Becky Veblen Meyers, "Autobiography," page 35.

6. Thorstein Veblen, in a letter to Sarah Gregory (November 13, 1908, DC, CURB&ML), talked of moving from Cedro to the Stanford campus. Duffus, in *The Innocents at Cedro* (page 132), mentioned the fact that he and his brother had laid a carpet in a room Veblen had taken on campus in a professor's house. And in a letter dated November 3, 1909, Veblen invited Mitchell to stay with him on campus at 22 Alvarado Street. WCMR, CURB&ML.

7. Mitchell Collection, CURB&ML.

8. Subsequently, Veblen did sign the timber claim over to Ellen, but it is not possible to ascertain whether Veblen contributed regularly to her support.

9. SULSC, Faculty Files.

10. *Ibid.*

11. *Ibid.* Jordan's reference to Babe as "the wife of a friend of Veblen's," plus Jordan's request concerning "Mrs. T.," indicate that the Stanford administrators had mixed things up but seemed willing to improvise with Ellen's desperate revival of the Triggs *canard,* as Babe had left the University of California the previous year and was in no position to create a scandal *in situ.* (Tom Bevans, so far as we can tell, never was a friend of Veblen.)

12. Branner/Elliott SC7, SULSC, Box 8.

13. University President's Papers 1889–1925, UCHISC.

14. On October 7, 1909, Jordan also wrote to George H. Bose at the University of California: "Prof. Veblen has tendered his resignation, to take effect at the end of the current year. This will put an end to further discussion of the matter, and, as he seems disposed to do his best under difficult circumstances, I can see no special reason why he might not be invited, as suggested by you." SULSC, SC7 Box 8.

15. Elliott Notes, SULSC, SC7 Box 8.

16. *Ibid.,* SC27 Box 4, Folder 10.

17. *Ibid.*

18. SULSC, SC58, Box 18, Volume 61.

19. SULSC, Faculty Files.

20. Marcel Proust, *Remembrance of Things Past,* Vol. 1, *Swann's Way* (New York: Random House, 1934), pages 18–19.

21. Thorstein Veblen, letter to Wesley Clair Mitchell, Stanford University, October 1909, DC, CURB&ML.

22. DC, CURB&ML.

23. Elliott Notes, SULSC, SC7 Box 8.

24. DC, CURB&ML.

25. DC, CURB&ML.

26. SULSC, SC58, Box 20, Vol. 61.

27. SULSC, SC58, Box 30, Letterbook 801.

28. Thorstein Veblen, letter to David Starr Jordan, November 12, 1909, DC, CURB&ML.

29. SULSC, Faculty Files.

30. DC, CURB&ML.

31. DC, CURB&ML.

32. Joseph Dorfman, *Thorstein Veblen and His America,* page 271.

33. It is possible that Thorstein was not honest with Ellen about finances. In a letter to Lucia K. Tower, June 2, 1909, Ellen wrote: "We lived on $400, $500, $600 a year until I went to Idaho. That year (1903) of my absence, Mr. V. jumped to $1,000," DC, CURB&ML. Actually, according to University of Chicago records, Veblen was making $2,000 a year in 1903, and continued earning that sum yearly through 1906. UCHISC, Name Index, Board of Trustee Minutes, 1891–1943. But here again, Ellen may have been poor-mouthing to her friend Lucia.

34. Alice Millis, undated letter to Joseph Dorfman (probably early 1930s), DC, CURB&ML.

35. Winifred S. Sabine, letter to Joseph Dorfman, May 24, 1934, DC, CURB&ML.

36. *Ibid.*

Chapter 19. The Station to Nowhere

1. In her letter to David Riesman of February 20, 1954, Becky Veblen Meyers wrote, "He had come to Idaho, horseback from California," but in her "Autobiography" (page 93B), she wrote that he rode from Grangeville in the fierce storm. He probably came by train and may have hired a horse locally, although, on pages 26 and 27, Becky states that he brought Beauty. CC.

2. Guido Marx, letter to Joseph Dorfman, February 28, 1935, DC, CURB&ML.

3. Thorstein Veblen, letter to Jacques Loeb, October 29, 1909, DC, CURB&ML.

4. Becky Veblen Meyers, letter to Barbara Kevles of the National Educational Television Pathfinder Series, August 20, 1964, and "Biography," page 3 (CC). Jordan, however, seemed to seek some sort of understanding with the man he had fired. After reading Veblen's latest book, Jordan, on August 22, 1917, wrote to him as follows:

> *Dear Sir:*
>
> *I am just reading your book on* The Nature of Peace. *I agree practically with all its statements except those regarding prehistoric man, none of whom I have ever met, at least not under that guise (and so I know nothing about him). I also feel an unholy joy at the subtle and inimitable satire with which you describe the enthusiasms of that group of men which Gelett Burgess recognized as "Bromides." It is a real pleasure, once in a while, to find a Sulphite, a man who can go around "without any mark or brand on him," as Lincoln put it, and occasionally break out in a new spot.*
>
> *Yours very truly,*
> *David Starr Jordan*

DC, CURB&ML, Box 62J.

5. The role of Allyn Young in supporting Veblen at Stanford is amplified in Young's biography, Charles P. Blitch, *Allyn Young: The Peripatetic Economist.* Young recommended that Veblen be promoted to full professorship, in the spring of 1908, and also of 1909. Jordan refused in 1908, but promised to do so in 1909. Young reminded Jordan in September 1909, "but before any action was taken, Veblen was forced to resign" (pages 24–26, DC, CURB&ML, Box 61D).

6. Allyn Young, letter to Wesley Clair Mitchell, April 17, 1911, DC, CURB&ML.

7. Becky Veblen Meyers, "Autobiography," pages 93b and 29.

8. Ruth Adams and Frank Murray, *Minerals Cure or Kill* (New York: Larchmont Books, 1974).

9. See Martha Saxton, *Louisa May: A Modern Biography of Louisa May Alcott* (New York: Avon Books, Houghton Mifflin, 1977), pages 279–80. Sometime between 1915 and 1917, Thorstein told Stuart Updegraff that he "never shaved, and he

said his hair had once started to fall out, but decided not to deciduate or grow, either, any more, so haircuts didn't bother him." Calomel could also have affected, adversely, his already notoriously unhearable voice. Stuart Updegraff, page 27 of manuscript sent to Joseph Dorfman, DC, CURB&ML.

10. Dorfman gave "Veblen's wife" as the source of the remark that Veblen's taking calomel in his early thirties was responsible for his poor health. Joseph Dorfman, *Thorstein Veblen and His America,* page 306. But later Dorfman said he had "wrongly attributed" the remark about calomel to Veblen's second wife. Van Elderen's notes of a conversation with Dorfman, DC, CURB&ML, Box 64V.

11. Babe's brother Stu (then married and with children) lived in Eastern Washington State not far from the Idaho border. Uncle Stu solemnly warned the children, contrary to present-day advice, that if they saw any cougars when they went to the outhouse they were to "look 'em straight in the eye." Evidently, he had heard that this might help to intimidate the beasts and prevent them from springing on them. Becky Veblen Meyers, "Autobiography," page 31.

12. Becky Veblen Meyers, "Biography," page 7.

13. Becky Meyers described her mother as "a woman of great determination, like a firefighter who has seen men die, is weary, but not yet relaxed." She must have been "thinking she had done the impossible—couldn't care what she looked like (no more her Daddy's beautiful Babe)." Becky Veblen Meyers, "Autobiography," page 32 and alternate page 80.

14. "And indeed it was in Nowhere during convalescence that he wrote—or dictated—part of *The Instinct of Workmanship.*" Becky Veblen Meyers, "Autobiography," alternate page 80.

15. W.B. Yeats, "The Song of Wandering Aengus," from *The Faber Book of Children's Verse,* compiled by Janet Adams Smith (London, Faber and Faber, 1953), page 211. These poems and songs are now part of a family tradition. Veblen's step-grandchild, artist Esther Baran, still sings them and makes stained glass–like images evoked by the poetry.

16. *Journal of Race Development* (April 1913): 491–507, and *University of Missouri Bulletin, Science Series* 2, No. 3 (April 1913): 39–57.

17. Cf. Douglas Dowd, *Thorstein Veblen,* Great American Thinkers Series (New York: Washington Square Press, 1966), page 91.

18. Joseph Dorfman, *Thorstein Veblen and His America,* page 299. Frank H. Taussig had written Mitchell on November 16, 1910, suggesting that Veblen might lecture at Harvard on the instinct of workmanship, saying, "Though we should not for a moment think of asking him to lecture here for the mere purpose of helping him out, I, for one, should be glad to do him a good turn if he has enough to say." DC, CURB&ML.

19. In 1897, Herbert G. Davenport attended Veblen's two courses, "The History of Political Economy" and "Socialism," at the University of Chicago, while Davenport was a student working on his Ph.D. and also working as a teaching assistant, teaching one course in "Elementary Theory." He received his Ph.D. in 1899. Davenport came back to Chicago as instructor, assistant professor, and associate professor, from 1902 until 1908. During those years he did not take any additional courses from Veblen. UCHISC, Registrar's Records.

20. Becky Veblen Meyers, letter to David Riesman, February 20, 1954, CC.

21. Thorstein Veblen, letter to Wesley Clair Mitchell, DC, CURB&ML.

22. This reference is to Dorfman's interview on October 9, 1930, with Eve

Schütze, already mentioned in Chapter 5, notes, in which Mrs. Schütze said Ellen [?] "would not let him work—tried to get into his mind." DC, CURB&ML.

23. Becky Veblen Meyers' "Biography," page 3.

24. Herbert Davenport, letter to Thorstein Veblen, April 8, 1909, DC, CURB&ML. Veblen once commented to another student "that his three outstanding 'pupils' were . . . Mitchell, Davenport, and Hoxie," in that order.

25. C.P. Huse, letter to Joseph Dorfman, July 23 (probably 1933), DC, CURB&ML.

26. Herbert J. Day, M.D., Davenport's nephew, letter to Joseph Dorfman, September 21, 1935, DC, CURB&ML. Dr. Day adds: "At that time a certain song became very popular . . . 'You Gotta Quit Kicking My Dog Around' . . . For weeks, a Chicago paper printed [it], each time in a different language. Veblen could read them all, even the Egyptian hieroglyphics. The Icelandic version, he said, was extremely good Icelandic. One day while all this was [going] on, someone dropped an automatic pistol of Veblen's. He said calmly, 'You've got to quit droppin' my gun around.' "

27. Stuart Updegraff, who also roomed in Davenport's house, tells us that during the first year he was in Missouri, Veblen helped Davenport deliver dozens, or maybe scores, of kids (usually in the middle of the night). The theory was that goats would keep the brush, and the pasture behind the house, cleared. This did not work out. The goats were soon eliminated. Besides, as the Chinese immigrant shepherd they had hired to feed and care for the beasts, expressed it: "Too muchee ding-a-ling ba-a-a-a-h!" Updegraff, manuscript and letter sent to Joseph Dorfman (DC, CURB&ML).

28. Stuart Updegraff, undated letter and manuscript sent to Joseph Dorfman, page 22 of manuscript, DC, CURB&ML. Although Veblen shared a shower, sink, and toilet with Updegraff, he made quite a little ceremony out of taking his Saturday night bath in a tub on the second floor. The professor would go back and forth, "in solemn processional, in his black and grey cotton bathrobe, with towels and soap in hand."

A Missouri colleague said that a story often told about Veblen—how he stacked his dishes in a tub until he had used every dish in the house, and then washed them off with a hose, drained them, and left them to dry by themselves—should not have been attributed to Veblen. This was actually the practice of Herbert J. Davenport, his host and landlord in Missouri (Jacob Warshaw, "Recollections of Thorstein Veblen," Jacob Warshaw papers, 1910–1944, WHM, Folder 89, No. 36). But the principle applied equally to both men—perhaps that was one reason they got along so well.

29. D.J. Oven, letter to Joseph Dorfman, October 20, 1932, DC, CURB&ML.

30. Lucinda de L. Templin's version of Veblen in the classroom was strikingly similar: "He was a gaunt-looking individual, and if the weather was cold . . . he would sit down with his heavy overcoat on, a huge woolen muffler wrapped around his neck, a fur cap on with the flaps securely tied under his ears, and with heavy woolen gloves on, and look around the class, and say, in his quiet way, 'If any of you want to keep your wraps on, it will be all right with me.' Then he would begin his lecture, and, apparently, was totally oblivious of the way he was wrapped up." Letter to Joseph Dorfman, September 14, 1932, DC, CURB&ML.

31. Joseph Dorfman, *Thorstein Veblen and His America,* page 313.

32. T.E. Olmstead, interview by Joseph Dorfman, summer of 1932, DC, CURB&ML. See also Joseph Dorfman, *Thorstein Veblen and His America,* page 310.

33. Herbert J. Davenport, undated letter to Leonard (rest of name unknown), DC, CURB&ML, Box 61D.

34. Julia Guyer (Geryer?), letter to Joseph Dorfman, January 23, 1933, DC, CURB&ML. Mrs. Guyer called Veblen's course the high point of her University of Missouri college career: "His ... influence increases as one lives and learns." She described him as a "quiet man, who sat in a rather motionless fashion, and talked in something of a monotone, but out of all this outward calmness would pop the most startling ideas."

35. Herbert J. Davenport, letter to Leonard, DC, CURB&ML, Box 61D. According to a Missouri colleague, Davenport also said that Veblen "talked along monotonously ... Then, suddenly, there opens up a vista through which you look back a thousand or five thousand years" (D.R. Scott, a University of Missouri professor of Statistics and Accounting, letter to Joseph Dorfman, June 9, 1932, DC, CURB&ML, Box 63S). Updegraff tells us that Veblen "was writing *Imperial Germany* during the two semesters I took his 'Economic Factors' course, and of course, he tried out a lot of his stuff on the class before writing it into the book. We were the scant dozen guinea pigs ... His style of lecturing was quite conversational and informal. Sentences not long winded nor ... involved ... as in some of the more ... impossible ... passages in his books." Updegraff, manuscript sent to Joseph Dorfman, page 31, CC.

Chapter 20. Miss Havisham Takes the Stand

1. Becky Veblen Meyers, "Autobiography," page 40, CC. Becky usually refers to her stepfather as "Toyse" (pronounced "Toys"), a Norwegian nickname for Tosten. His grandniece Colette believed that he was not fond of the nickname, especially when she used it. Esther Baran, however, tells us that it was habitually employed by his stepdaughters, by Babe, and also by himself (in self-reference) in family correspondence. Esther Baran, letter to authors, June 19, 1997.

2. Becky Veblen Meyers, "Autobiography," page 42, CC.

3. *Ibid.,* page 38.

4. Wesley Clair Mitchell, letter to Sarah Gregory, May 2, 1911, a typewritten copy of which was sent to Joseph Dorfman by Sarah Hardy Gregory, DC, CURB&ML, Box 62M. Mitchell may have misunderstood Babe's off-hand reference to leaving her mother-in-law's property [Nowhere, Idaho], and assumed it was her property to sell.

5. The money Ellen invested was Rolfe money, part of it settled on her by her father before his death, and some of it left to her in his will.

6. Ellen Veblen, letter to Lucia K. Tower, January 1911, DC, CURB&ML.

7. Becky Veblen Meyers, letter to David Riesman, February 20, 1954, CC.

8. Becky Veblen Meyers, "Autobiography," pages 46–47, CC.

9. Becky Veblen Meyers, letter to David Riesman, February 20, 1954, CC. One incident Becky recounted about Oregon concerned Thorstein's taking a sliver out of her foot (so deftly that Becky became convinced that one of his strongest talents was an aptitude for surgery— and that among other things, he could have become a doctor).

> I jumped off something, landed on a jagged stump (the part that wasn't sawed yet when somebody yelled "timber") and a lot of sliver went into the arch of my foot, deeply. I don't remember yelling, but presently Veblen was there, looking over the wound. I could tell something had to be done—and by

the way he held my foot and scientifically studied the situation, I knew he was the one to do it. May be he used hypnosis. Anyway, when he drew out his little jack-knife, blades as sharp as razors . . . he remarked it would hurt a bit, but I only remember a gentle surgeon . . . no pain!

10. Russell Bartley and Sylvia Yoneda, "Thorstein Veblen on Washington Island: Traces of a Life," page 607, note 15, CC. Veblen's Annotations in his copy of *The Instinct of Workmanship* show that Veblen completed "Chapter V in Mancos Valley, Colorado, in 1912, and the remainder in Columbia, Missouri, in the winter of 1913."

11. Becky Veblen Meyers, "Autobiography," page 56, CC.

12. Becky Veblen Meyers, handwritten "Memoirs," and also her "Autobiography," CC, *passim.* In some anecdotes the children's stay with their father occurs before their stint (on starvation diet) in their furnished rooms.

13. Owen Richardson, letter to Joseph Dorfman, August 14, 1934, DC, CURB&ML, Box 63R. The attorney went on to say: "My impression of Dr. Veblen? He seemed to me to be a man whose research and scholarship set him apart. It was difficult to draw him out; yet when, rather hesitantly and after some urging, he conversed on his life work, his speech was brilliant and scintillating."

14. Complaint filed in Case No. 11205, Ellen R. Veblen v. Thorstein B. Veblen, Superior Court of San Mateo County, Redwood City, California. Final judgment entered February 24, 1913.

15. Joseph Dorfman, *Thorstein Veblen and His America,* page 304. The divorce was granted on the grounds of non-support. The defendant's answer denied that, at any time, Veblen was guilty of cruelty, or that he was earning anything more than $1,000 per year. In later life, after Ellen had given most of her money to Halcyon, her religious community, and needed cash, Veblen helped her out by buying her Sandhill Road property in Menlo Park, California, which he used as a retirement refuge.

16. Ellen Veblen, letter to Sarah Hardy Gregory (April 1897), UCHISC, Miscellaneous Collections ("V" folder).

17. Becky Veblen Meyers, letter to Jack [John] Diggins, January 17, 1982, CC.

18. Maude Radford Warren, letter to Joseph Dorfman, September 20, [1930–33?], DC, CURB&ML, Box 64W.

19. Postcard from Lindsborg, Kansas, from Babe to Mrs. A.S. ("Mama") Bradley, on which Becky wrote, "about 1913—where Ann and I went to 5th and 6th grades." CC.

20. Matthew Paxton, letter to Joseph Dorfman, December 19, 1932, DC, CURB&ML, Box 63P.

21. The Stewart residence was on Stewart Road. After Veblen's marriage he lived in a house on the corner of Hudson and College Avenues, according to D.R. Scott, professor of accounting and statistics at Missouri. According to Charles Hendrick, however, he and Babe and the children lived in a cottage at the corner of College Avenue and Rollins Street ("Veblen Taught Here," *Missouri Alumnus Magazine,* No. 689 [March 1974], WHM). Also D.R. Scott, undated letter to Joseph Dorfman, DC, CURB&ML, Box 72. According to Scott, Davenport's residence was on Lathrop Road.

22. Veblen was not contending that there is such a thing as an genetically transmitted instinct of workmanship, and in his introduction he carefully explained that he was using the term loosely. Around the turn of the century, the word "instinct" was much in vogue. Veblen, in a letter to Sarah Hardy Gregory dated July 20, 1900, said:

"The 'next book' has been named, as you may have noticed, by Mr. Ward, and also by others before him. It is to be called 'The Instinct of Workmanship'—a phrase which, perhaps without your knowing it, I owe to you" (UCHISC, Miscellaneous Collections ["V" folder]). By 1914, however, the argument over whether there was such a thing as an "instinct" of this sort had been well fought out, and Veblen conceded the hollowness of such a concept in his lengthy introduction to the book. However, he was not about to abandon the catch-phrase—not with Sarah Hardy's input still lurking in his memory.

In a letter to Joseph Dorfman, dated March 15, 1935, Clarence E. Ayres, professor of economics at the University of Texas, and an outstanding Veblen disciple, wrote: "I have always insisted that Veblen did not mean to espouse the *instinct psychology.* As a matter of fact, he said so quite definitely. He once asked me in conversation if I had ever noticed his definition of 'instinct,' and when I replied with a grin that I never had, he matched my grin, and remarked that no such definition appears, because, if you define instincts exactly, 'there ain't no such animal.'"

Veblen was well aware of Loeb's experiments distinguishing tropisms and instincts. He kept in close touch with Jacques Loeb, who had chemically induced fertilization of sea urchin ova at the University of Chicago in 1899. Later, the distinguished experimental biologist became a professor of physiology at the University of California, Berkeley. Veblen and Mitchell attended a meeting of the Kosmos Club in Berkeley in October 1907, when Loeb read a paper on instincts. Cf. WCMR, 1907, CURB&ML.

Rick Tilman carefully analyzes Veblen's use of the "instinct" concept and concludes that Veblen sometimes takes a stand on one side of the nature/nurture controversy, sometimes on the other. He concludes: "Suggestions that Veblen was at times more Lamarckian than Darwinian signify that while acquired characteristics are often inherited, this is mostly a matter of cultural inheritance and institutional transmission, not genetic change. Whatever the case, the evolutionary reproduction of institutions posits no fixed end in Veblen's analysis, but a continuous, cumulative process of institutional mutation that will provide no aesthetic or emotional comfort to those seeking social stasis or the arrest of cultural change." Rick Tilman, *The Intellectual Legacy of Thorstein Veblen* (Westport, CT: Greenwood Press, 1996), page 66.

At any rate, Veblen insisted that he was giving the word "instinct" his own meaning. Scholars and critics have a difficult time when they take his words out of the context in which he used them.

23. Joseph Dorfman, *Thorstein Veblen and His America,* page 324.

24. Thorstein Veblen, *The Instinct of Workmanship* (New York: Viking Press, 1914), pages 94–97, *passim.*

25. *Ibid.*

26. Joseph Dorfman, *Thorstein Veblen and His America,* page 304. Mitchell kept a daily journal, apparently on his desk calendar, and every January listed the names and addresses of his friends, including Veblen. But in January 1914, the year Veblen married Babe, Veblen's name was missing from the list. WCMR, 1914, CURB&ML.

Mitchell was teaching at Columbia University while Dorfman was working there on his Ph.D. dissertation, which later became the monumental Veblen biography. Mitchell's bias against Babe seems to make itself felt in Dorfman's book. Although

Mitchell was a great admirer of Veblen, and helped raise funds for his continued teaching at the New School for Social Research, Lewis Mumford wrote, "It was hard to detect any direct influence of Veblen, either in outlook or method" in the latter-day Mitchell. Lewis Mumford, *Sketches from Life* (New York: Dial Press, 1982), page 220.

When Dorfman was being interviewed by Louis van Elderen, a Dutch sociologist who visited the biographer on September 26, 1979, Dorfman stated that it was Hoxie who had "wanted to help Veblen" avoid the second marriage. Hoxie was conveniently dead (he killed himself in 1916) and could not dispute this. DC, CURB&ML, Box 64V and author's conversation with van Elderen, May 30, 1996..

27. Becky Veblen Meyers, "Memoirs," pages 4–5, CC, and "Biography," CC.

28. *Ibid.*

29. Upton Sinclair, *The Goose-Step,* page 293. Variations of this story have Babe phoning Thorstein from her sister Harriet's house, built back to back with the Bradleys' three-story concrete residence at 5450 Ridgewood Court, Hyde Park, near the University of Chicago; she spoke with Atwood as she was going out the front door. Authors' interview with Esther Baran, July 10, 1994.

30. Becky Veblen Meyers, "Biography," page 6, CC.

Chapter 21. Happily Ever After

1. Ann Sims, Ruthmary Penick interview with Ann and her sister Becky, 1977, CC, page 53.

2. Becky Veblen Meyers and Esther Baran, taped interview with Paul Veblen, June 10, 1992, CC, page 6.

3. Becky Veblen Meyers, letter to David Riesman, February 20, 1954, CC, page 5.

4. Becky Veblen Meyers, interview with Ruthmary Penick, 1977, CC, page 45.

5. Authors' interview with Esther Baran, July 10, 1994.

6. Winifred S. Sabine, letter to Joseph Dorfman, May 24, 1934, DC, CURB&ML, Box 63S.

7. Isador Lubin, "Recollections of Thorstein Veblen," pages 131–148.

8. Lewis Mumford, *Sketches from Life,* page 216.

9. Joseph Dorfman, *Thorstein Veblen and His America,* page 306. Also Isador Lubin, letter to Joseph Dorfman, January 28, 1932, DC, CURB&ML, Box 62L.

10. Becky Veblen Meyers, "Autobiography," page 78, CC.

11. Wesley Clair Mitchell, letter to Sarah Gregory, May 17, 1911, DC, CURB&ML. Mitchell mentioned that Veblen was still hoping that new funds given by Carnegie to the Institution for the Advancement of Science might enable him, Veblen, to receive the grant he had been applying for while waiting out his University of Missouri appointment.

12. Thorstein Veblen, *Absentee Ownership and Business Enterprise in Recent Times* (New York: B.W. Huebsch, 1923; reprint, New York: Augustus M. Kelley, 1964), page 142.

13. *Ibid.,* page 159.

14. Becky Veblen Meyers, "Autobiography," page 80.

15. Esther Baran and Becky Veblen Meyers, interview by Paul Veblen, *supra,* page 28, CC.

252 NOTES TO CHAPTER 21

16. Stuart Updegraff, manuscript accompanying his September 26, 1935, letter to Joseph Dorfman, DC, CURB&ML, page 28.

17. Robert L. Duffus, *The Innocents at Cedro,* page 154.

18. Becky Veblen Meyers, letter to David Riesman, February 20, 1954, CC.

19. Max F. Meyer, letter to Joseph Dorfman, August 5, 1934, DC, CURB&ML.

20. Isador Lubin, "Recollections of Thorstein Veblen."

21. Ann Sims, Ruthmary Penick interview, CC, page 52.

22. Jacob Warshaw, "Recollections of Thorstein Veblen," Jacob Warshaw Papers, 1910–1944, WHM, page 3.

23. *Ibid,* pages 3–4.

24. *Ibid,* page 4.

25. Winifred S. Sabine, letter to Joseph Dorfman, May 24, 1934, DC, CURB&ML.

26. Esther Baran, authors' interview, July 10, 1994. Babe enjoyed arguing about socialism with Dr. Olmstead's wife too, but finally Veblen got tired of the eternal struggle and remarked that there were plenty of books in the library to justify both their sides. Joseph Dorfman, interview with Mrs. Olmstead, summer, 1932, DC, CURB&ML.

27. Thorstein Veblen, letter to Parker Thomas Moon, August 11, 1911, DC, CURB&ML.

28. Grover C. Hosford, letter to Joseph Dorfman, August 27, 1932, DC, CURB&ML, Box 62H.

29. In an article titled "The Opportunity of Japan" (*Journal of Race Development* 6 [July 1915]), he spelled out even more clearly his fears of the potential for future Japanese aggression.

30. "Whatever may be the nominal balance of profit and loss in the way of what is called the 'fortunes of war,' the net consequences will be much the same; and these consequences can not but be of the nature of retardation to Western civilization in those respects that mark it as Western and modern" (Thorstein Veblen, *Imperial Germany and the Industrial Revolution* [New York: Macmillan, 1915], page 261). See also Douglas Dowd, *Thorstein Veblen* (New York: Washington Square Press—Great American Thinker Series, 1966), pages 92–99.

31. General Friedrich von Bernhardi, *Germany and the Next War* (New York: Longmans, Green, 1914).

32. Max Eastman, *Love and Revolution* (New York: Random House, 1964), page 67.

33. Veblen's objective approach to the German question thoroughly confused the bureaucrats. The censors of the Post Office prohibited the mailing of both *Imperial Germany* and *The Nature of Peace.* At the same time the government's Committee on Public Information was urging their use in combating German propaganda. Isador Lubin, letter to Joseph Dorfman, May 3, 1934, DC, CURB&ML.

34. Thorstein Veblen, *Essays in Our Changing Order,* ed. Leon Ardzrooni, page 427.

35. Douglas Dowd, *Thorstein Veblen,* page 99.

36. Isador Lubin, "Recollections of Thorstein Veblen." Lubin is probably using the word "chauvinistic" here for humorous effect, as it implies a bellicosity or jingoism that seems out of place in a more sober assessment of Veblen's feelings for Norway.

37. Thorstein Veblen, *Imperial Germany and the Industrial Revolution,* pages 137–138.

38. Thorstein Veblen, *The Higher Learning in America,* pages 66, 88, and 101.

39. Joseph Dorfman, *Thorstein Veblen and His America,* page 353. Veblen said

President Hill was the best college president he knew, but commented wryly that the best of men, after ten years as a college president, become highly undesirable characters (pages 306–307).

40. Jacob Warshaw, "Recollections of Veblen," page 6. See also Jacob Warshaw, "A Few Footnotes to Dorfman's *Veblen,*" pages 7–8, Jacob Warshaw Papers, 1910–1944, WHM, Folder 89, No. 36.

41. Becky Veblen Meyers, interview with Ruthmary Penick, 1977, CC, page 53.

42. Mrs. K. Bjarnason, letter to Joseph Dorfman, September 16, 1934, DC, CURB&ML. Some of Veblen's discussions about the early anarchic cultures in North Germany, in *Imperial Germany and the Industrial Revolution,* reflect his previous fascination with the Icelandic sagas. See the account of his Washington Island years in Russell Bartley's and Sylvia E. Yoneda's "Thorstein Veblen on Washington Island: Traces of a Life," pages 589–613.

43. Thorstein Veblen, letter to Isador Lubin, July 12, 1917, DC, CURB&ML, Box 62L.

44. Becky Veblen Meyers, "Autobiography," page 60, CC.

45. Alexander W. Allison et al., eds., *The Norton Anthology of Poetry,* 3rd ed. (New York: W.W. Norton, 1983), page 832.

46. W.B. Yeats, "The Land of Heart's Desire," a one-act play from *Collected Plays of W.B. Yeats* (New York: Macmillan, 1990).

47. Becky Veblen Meyers, "Autobiography," page 104, CC.

48. Esther V. Gunnerson, "Washington Island's Thorstein Veblen," page 4, CC. A case in point was when a child asked Veblen what his initials "T.B." stood for. Veblen answered, "Teddy Bear," and the little girl confidently called him that from then on. Robert L. Duffus, *The Innocents at Cedro,* page 19.

49. Becky Veblen Meyers, "Autobiography," page 85, CC.

50. Stuart Updegraff, page 28 of typed manuscript. As John P. Diggins points out in *The Bard of Savagery* (page 162), it seems strange that a man so intent on the liberation of women should allow himself to be waited on, "hand and foot," by willing females. However, the role of servitor to Veblen was not a unisex role, as when Veblen was in New York, Ardzrooni appeared to some as if he were acting as a butler to his master. Besides, casual observers had no way of knowing the extent of Veblen's actual physical disabilities. Some did not believe he was physically impaired in any way and thought he was shamming, not appreciating the fact that a man suffering from severe allergies could appear to be physically fit at one time, and grievously ill at another. (One of his allergies may very well have been to Turkish tobacco.) Becky tells us he had a weak heart, and, after his pneumonia and the calomel treatments, Veblen remained feebler than most of his contemporaries realized. Colette Sims van Fleet, his grandniece, when talking about the Washington Island days, reports: "I always had the feeling that he wasn't well, and I can still remember . . . one of the rituals was that [after] he sat back in his chair, somebody would [have to] pull him up by his hands to help him up." Colette Sims van Fleet, interview with Jeff Moriarty, May 9, 1993, CC.

51. Joseph Dorfman's notes of a conversation with, or communication from Albert T.E. Olmstead, summer 1932, DC, CURB&ML.

52. Becky Veblen Meyers, "Autobiography," page 100, CC.

53. Ann B. Veblen ("Babe"), letter to Isador Lubin, June 29, 1917, DC, CURB&ML.

54. Becky Veblen Meyers, "Autobiography," page 90, CC.

Chapter 22. World War I Ends

1. Robert L. Duffus, letter to Joseph Dorfman, December 16, 1935, DC, CURB&ML.

2. Isador Lubin, letter to Joseph Dorfman, January 28, 1932, DC, CURB&ML. In the letter Lubin comments on an early draft of Dorfman's Veblen manuscript.

3. Joseph Dorfman, *Thorstein Veblen and His America,* page 354.

4. Stuart Updegraff, undated letter and manuscript sent to Joseph Dorfman, DC, CURB&ML.

5. Isador Lubin, letter to Joseph Dorfman, January 28, 1932, DC, CURB&ML.

6. Soon after he arrived in Washington, DC, a sign was put on his door, "Dr. Thorstein B. Veblen." Veblen, the dead-pan comedy artist (so signified by Lewis Mumford), told Lubin to get the sign off the door, saying that the only reason he came to the Food Administration "was to get rid of the title 'Doctor.' " Mumford thought Veblen "a humorist," whose drollery was based on a wooden facial expression, combined with elephantinely elaborate sentence structure. Lewis Mumford, *Findings and Keepings* (New York: Harcourt Brace, 1975), pages 209–210.

7. Joseph Dorfman, *Thorstein Veblen and His America,* page 383.

8. *Ibid.,* page 373.

9. *Ibid.,* page 383.

10. This note, sequestered in the Special Collections at Stanford University, was discovered, after persistent archival sleuthing, by Russell and Sylvia Bartley, its contents to be discussed by the Bartleys in a forthcoming article in the *International Journal of Politics, Culture, and Society.*

11. Orrin Leslie Elliot, *Stanford University: The First Twenty Five Years* (Stanford: Stanford University Press, 1937), page 563.

12. John Casper Branner, letter to Professor Edwin H. Woodruff, March 28, 1918, Faculty Files, Letter No. 155, SULSC, John Casper Branner papers, private collection.

13. John Casper Branner, letter to Professor Edwin H. Woodruff, March 28, 1918, Faculty Files, Letter No. 156, SULSC. Also, Orrin Leslie Elliott files, SC7, Container 8, Stanford History Notes (STWY), SULSC.

14. Orrin Leslie Elliott, *Stanford University: The First Twenty Five Years,* page 563.

15. John Caspar Branner, letter to Edwin H. Woodruff, March 28, 1918, Faculty Files, Letter No. 156, SULSC.

16. One is reminded of Veblen's letter to Davenport during the Stanford crisis (October 21, 1909) concerning his wife, Ellen, about whom he wrote: "She appears . . . to have written the cabinet in Chicago (probably Small), to help do me up, and also to Columbia [University], perhaps, also, elsewhere. If she knew of the negotiations at Missouri, she would probably have written to Hill, also." DC, CURB&ML.

17. Joseph Dorfman, and to some extent Robert L. Duffus, were so careful not to identify any one woman as being involved with Thorstein, that they made it seem as if there might be many—thus, the wild misconceptions of all the subsequent innocent writers (all appreciative of Veblen except for Riesman), who based their opinions on Dorfman's and Duffus's writings. Legend had it that, at Stanford, coeds would visit Veblen's "log [sic] cabin," and stay on for more than tea and conversation (see John P. Diggins, *The Bard of Savagery,* page 169. There is no documentation for this. There was also the well-worn "joke," that President Elliot of Harvard advised Veblen

that he was doubtful of hiring him, because he feared for the faculty wives. Veblen supposedly replied that Elliot should not worry, because he, Veblen, had "tried them all, and they were no good." A variation on this bit of apocrypha has the Chicago faculty wives similarly maligned.

Becky, who was close to him for thirty years, wrote that "people who called [him] a philanderer just didn't know him" (Becky Veblen Meyers, "Autobiography," page 105). "He was, in his way of life as in his writing, meticulously careful, neat, considerate and responsible, as far as his frail health permitted" (Becky Veblen Meyers, letter to Barbara Kevles of the National Educational Television, Pathfinder Series, August 20, 1964, CC). So the legend of the sexy economist dies hard, if it dies at all. Economists, particularly, may be reluctant to take leave of it. The stories of sexy professors are a dime a dozen, but tales of sexy economics professors are rare.

18. Becky Veblen Meyers, "Autobiography," page 74, CC.

19. Lewis Mumford, *Sketches from Life: An Autobiography,* page 217.

20. Veblen's thoughtful style could still be found in many an article, and one of his most noteworthy of this period is his article, "The Intellectual Pre-eminence of Jews in Modern Europe." It could have been a description of Veblen himself—"a disturber of the intellectual peace, . . . a wanderer in the intellectual no-man's-land, . . . a skeptic by force of circumstances over which he has no control." Veblen's thesis was that the Jews have great acuity as outside observers—alienated from their own culture, and belonging nowhere, but able to see clearly the drawbacks and inconsistencies of gentile institutions. The Zionists believed that, if they had a homeland, they could be even more brilliant and admirable—but Veblen thought their outsider position was their source of power. *Political Science Quarterly* 34 (March 1919), reprinted in *Essays in Our Changing Order,* ed. Leon Ardzrooni, pages 219–231.

21. "The Last Man Who Knew Everything," *The Carleton Voice* 45, No. 4 (fall 1980), CC.

22. Lewis Mumford, *Sketches from Life: An Autobiography,* page 218.

23. *Ibid.,* page 213.

24. Becky Veblen Meyers, "Memoirs," page 9, CC.

25. Joseph Dorfman, *Thorstein Veblen and His America,* page 422.

26. Becky Veblen Meyers, letter to David Riesman, February 20, 1954, page 6, CC.

27. Strangely enough, Babe was writing anxiously about planned parenthood. She feared it would be used by the government against the poor.

28. Isador Lubin, "Recollections of Thorstein Veblen," pages 131–148, *passim.*

29. Becky Veblen Meyers, "Autobiography," page 81, CC.

30. Donald L. Miller, *Lewis Mumford: A Life* (New York, Weidenfeld and Nicolson, 1989), page 112.

31. Beard, Robinson, and Mitchell resigned from Columbia University to start the new institution. Dewey continued on at Columbia, but lectured at the New School. Because Veblen attacked the concept of pragmatism, and Dewey was renowned as a developer of one of the leading schools of Pragmatism, it would be easy to conclude that there might have been a conflict between them. Veblen, however, was not attacking the philosophy of educational pragmatism per se, but college administrators who wanted to be "practical" and turn universities into glorified trade schools.

Veblen, after hearing an attack on Dewey by a behavioristic psychologist, responded, "He will never know as much as Dewey and [William] James forgot" (Joseph Dorfman, *Thorstein Veblen and His America,* page 450). Dewey, at Chicago, was one of the few faculty members who praised *The Theory of the Leisure Class* and, in the 1930s, used Veblen's distinction between industry and business enterprise in an article on the Depression (*The New Republic*, April 27, 1932). Dewey "always found Veblen's own articles very stimulating, and some of his distinctions, like that between the technological side of industry and its 'business' aspect, . . . quite fundamental in [his own] thinking ever since [he] became acquainted with them" (Joseph Dorfman, *Thorstein Veblen and His America,* page 450). A more detailed exposition of the differences between Veblen and Dewey can be found in the chapter titled "Veblen and American Pragmatism: The Case of John Dewey," in Rick Tilman's *The Intellectual Legacy of Thorstein Veblen* (Westport, CT: Greenwood Press, 1996), pages 109–141.

32. Alvin Johnson, *A Pioneer's Progress: An Autobiography of Alvin Johnson.* (Johnson was director of the NSSR.) (New York: Viking Press, 1952), page 277.

33. Esther Baran, interview with the authors, July 10, 1994, discussing Babe's autopsy report released to her. In a letter to the authors dated May 11, 1994, Bill Melton, restorer of the Veblen farm and facilitator of several Veblen research efforts, reported, "Babe's massive lung infection may have stemmed from the forced feedings to which she was subjected. Russ [Russell Bartley] had a physician at UCLA (a relative of his, I think he said) have a look at the autopsy report, and the conclusion was that there was no evidence that Babe had been injured by a beating on the head. The edema was generalized (not localized), and the logical result of the shut-off of oxygen that occurred in the brain as Babe's lungs were overcome by infection. Russ concludes that the 'bashing' story is probably true, but the meningitis story [a theory of Becky's] must have been Becky's reasonable conjecture, on the basis of what she knew."

34. Wesley C. Mitchell's Journal, WCMR, Mitchell Collection, CURB&ML.

35. Becky Veblen Meyers, "Autobiography," page 99.

36. Thorstein Veblen, letter to Andrew Veblen, October 8, 1920, DC, CURB&ML. His brother Ed insisted, "He [Thorstein] wants all and sundry to think he is so phlegmatic and impersonal as to be scarcely human, but you take it from me, he is all human." John Edward Veblen, undated letter to Joseph Dorfman, DC, CURB&ML.

37. Esther Baran, interview with the authors, July 10, 1994. In her March 18, 1982, letter to John P. Diggins, Becky Veblen Meyers wrote about Babe's "own adoring Papa Bradley—I heard him tell her that if she married this man [Veblen], he would put his 'dying curse' on her." CC.

Chapter 23. A Land Where Even the Old Are Fair?

1. Joseph Dorfman, *Thorstein Veblen and His America*, page 455, and Emily Veblen Olsen's Annotations thereto, MHS.

2. Joseph Dorfman, *Thorstein Veblen and His America,* pages 455–456.

3. Becky Veblen Meyers, letter to John P. Diggins, February 26, 1982, CC, Box 4, Folder 13. Less than a year earlier, Veblen had received a letter from Grace Camp, October 3, 1918, (CC), which read:

> I went down to Redwood [City] in the afternoon. At last, the expected thing has occurred. Your name is off the tax list, and they calmly said that your half acre does not exist—talked around for about an hour with four different individuals, including the new tax collector . . . Everyone was very gracious,

but, . . . of course, an individual is rather helpless in such a situation. . . . They have a new map . . . which they show with great gusto and pride, thoroughly up to date, but with no Veblen property indicated.

One wonders why Miss Camp did not inform Veblen of the property's changed status during the more than half-hour ride from Menlo Park to the mountain aerie. Perhaps one should not pull too many threads in examining the fine embroidery of this story, a prime anecdote of the Veblen legend. It is possible that Grace did tell him that the matter was now settled in his favor, but the sight of the "For Sale" sign convinced Veblen that she had been duped, or that Grace stayed in the car, on the La Honda road far below, during the glass-shattering.

4. Hans Otto Storm, letter to Joseph Dorfman, November 6, 1932, DC, CURB&ML.

5. In a letter to David Riesman, Becky Veblen Meyers wrote (February 20, 1984, page 6, CC) that the amount of the loan was $10,000, while her sister Ann, in their 1977 interview with Ruthmary Penick, page 53, said the amount was $1,000 (CC). However, Thorstein's will states that $10,000, not $1,000, was to be left to Becky Veblen Meyers and paid by money owed by Ardzrooni. Esther Baran told the authors (phone call, May 5, 1996) that Ardzrooni later recouped his losses with the raisin farm and became very well heeled, but never paid Becky the $10,000.

6. Veblen sent broker Donald W. Stewart $100 in 1925 and $1,000 in 1926 to invest in International Oils, Limited. In 1927 he sent $1,400 more. He also sent broker Ethel Williams (Black Gold Products) $630 in 1925 and $420 in 1926. In a black metal box found among Veblen's effects after his death was a letter from Harold Veblen, enclosing documents of oil drilling rights, forwarded as partial repayment of a loan made to him by Thorstein (CC). Veblen also bought some oil stock upon the advice of Dr. Broughton and, in this instance, came out ahead. Joseph Dorfman, *Thorstein Veblen and His America,* page 485.

7. On October 21, 1919, Veblen wrote Guido Marx, professor of Machine Design in the School of Engineering at Stanford University, urging him to teach at the New School for Social Research for a semester: "It is an intimate part of the ambitions of the New School to come into touch with the technical men who have to do with the country's industry and know something about the state of things and the needs of industry." Marx replied that he was excited about the prospect, as he was aware of what Veblen was trying to do. He said he read *The Dial* regularly with intense enjoyment. Marx was surprised that his wife, "with all her keen intelligence and sense of humor," did not appreciate Veblen's involved style. Marx suspected he knew the reason for this style (perhaps to confuse the Philistines) and wrote: "If I could tell you that I think I am onto your curves, you would at once invent some new form of literary spit-ball just to show me my mistake, so I won't say it. However, how do you expect to keep out of jail if you toss such easy, straight ones as the Oct. 4th *Dial*?"

Dorfman asked Marx how he happened to commission the Blanca Will sculpture, and Marx wrote that he had enjoyed his association with the faculty and his students at the New School so much that he felt he had been paid for a "stimulating vacation." Since his niece was coming to New York to have some bronze casting done, he decided to induce her to do the bust. He contributed his salary at the New School to do so. Guido Marx, letter to Joseph Dorfman, February 1, 1934, DC, CURB&ML, Box 62M (also, SULSC, SC129, Box 5, Folio 4).

8. Blanca Will, letter to Joseph Dorfman, March 8, 1934, DC, CURB&ML, Box 64.

9. Robert L. Duffus, *The Innocents at Cedro,* page 154.

10. Undated clipping from unknown newspaper, DC, CURB&ML, Box 62J.

11. Hans Otto Storm, "The Opaque Facts," a review of Joseph Dorfman's biography of Veblen, DC, CURB&ML. Storm graduated from Stanford with a B.A. in engineering, became an expert in radio-telegraph engineering, and constructed new radio stations in Sayville, New York, in Nicaragua, and Peru. He was ordered out of Peru in 1939 because Peruvian authorities were enraged by his book, *Pity the Tyrant* (New York and Toronto: Longmans, Green & Co., 1937). Storm was author of three other books: *Full Measure* (New York: Macmillan, 1929); *Made in U.S.A.* (New York and Toronto: Longmans, Green & Co., 1939); and *Count Ten* (New York and Toronto: Longmans, Green & Co., 1940). He was accidentally electrocuted in 1941 at the age of forty-six, when testing Trans-Pacific transmission equipment for the Globe Wireless Company, of which he was chief engineer. Thorstein Veblen was one of his strongest intellectual and literary influences.

12. Indeed, Lenin's justification for Russia's signing the Treaty of Brest-Litovsk with Germany in 1918 was that widespread workers' revolts in Europe would protect Russia.

13. Veblen was actually disturbed, during the early part of the Russian Revolution, when the Bolsheviks grabbed power from the Kerensky Regime, especially after the Treaty of Brest-Litovsk was signed. He felt that this might result in Germany's winning the war. Joseph Dorfman, *Thorstein Veblen and His America,* page 372.

14. Eliot Janeway (*The Economics of Chaos: On Revitalizing the American Economy* [New York: Truman Talley Books, E.P. Dutton, 1989], page 80) implies that Lenin was aware of Veblen's American Blütetzeit. See also Joseph Dorfman's account (based on the testimony of an anonymous informant), in *Thorstein Veblen and His America,* pages 426–427. Becky reported that at the University of Chicago she took Russian "in 1922 or so, when I was to go with V. to Russia (Lenin had invited him, but Stalin cancelled it)" (Becky Veblen Meyers, letter to John P. Diggins, January [25 or] 27, 1982, CC). Veblen also started to learn Russian, with the intention of going to the Soviet Union in 1924, to find out "what's what there" (Becky Veblen Meyers, letter to David Riesman, February 20, 1984, page 4, CC. By 1925, according to letters from Mitchell and Alvin Johnson (see Chapter 24), Veblen's European trip was to be centered on Great Britain.

15. Thorstein Veblen, *The Engineers and the Price System* (New York: Viking Press, 1926), page 138. Veblen concluded the chapter with the statement: "There is nothing in the situation that should reasonably flutter the sensibilities of the Guardians [of the Vested Interests] or of that massive body of well-to-do citizens who make up the rank and file of absentee owners, just yet" (page 169). One does get a feeling of heavy irony and menace from his frequent repetition of the phrase "just yet."

16. Veblen's New York physician gave Becky the following advice about Veblen's intermittent claudication: "A very experienced doctor of Clinical Medicine told us during my graduate study in Europe (Vienna) . . . [that] since . . . smoking increased such pain in the legs, . . . he advises [patients] to give up smoking." Dr. Gross tempered this by saying that Veblen did not have to give it up entirely, only perhaps for a week after a bout of leg pain. Becky wrote that her stepfather tried to give up smoking, but could not—however, he did cut down. Benjamin Gross, M.D., letter to Becky Veblen, November 23, 1928; also, Becky Veblen Meyers, "Autobiography," page 43, both in CC.

17. Morris L. Cooke, director of Philadelphia Public Works, quoted by Joseph Dorfman, in *Thorstein Veblen and His America,* page 455.

18. Thorstein Veblen, *Absentee Ownership and Business Enterprise in Recent Times* (New York: Viking Press reprint, Sentry Press, 1964), page 319.

19. *Ibid.,* pages 321–322.

20. *Ibid.,* pages 324–325.

21. Joseph Dorfman, *Thorstein Veblen and His America,* page 467.

22. Isador Lubin, September 17, 1931 letter to Joseph Dorfman, DC, CURB&ML.

23. A.G. Kenagy, letter to Joseph Dorfman, September 8, 1932, DC, CURB&ML.

24. The bulk of the actual translation from the Icelandic was, of course, accomplished during his three-year honeymoon with Ellen at Stacyville in the 1880s.

25. Thorstein Veblen, *The Laxdaela Saga* (New York: B.W. Huebsch, 1925), pages ix–x. Despite Lubin's contention that Veblen was a Norwegian "chauvinist," it is evident that Veblen's feelings for Norway did not color his depiction of these Norwegian and Icelandic free-booters. William Ellery Leonard, an Icelandic scholar at the University of Wisconsin, was full of praise for Veblen's translation: "As imaginatively vital a transfer from language to language as can well be. . . Is Veblen, by any chance, himself an Icelander? If I'd seen the manuscript, I'd have suggested jarl for earl . . . but I trust this won't ruin the sale." William Ellery Leonard, review from unknown periodical, DC, CURB&ML, Box 62L.

In his introduction Veblen makes the point that the saga has ethnographic significance, because it deals with the Viking period. The sagas themselves center around the "blood feud," which was "then a matter of course, and of common sense, about the merits of which no question was entertained—no more than the merits of national patriotism are questioned in our time. It is only in late and spurious tales, dating from after the infiltration of the medieval chivalric romances into the Scandinavian counties, that other interests or principles of conduct have come to supplant the blood-feud as the finally dominant note."

Veblen's ability as a literary critic was shown here in his comments about the Icelandic text:

> By comparison with the common run of sagas, the received text of the Laxdaela is a somewhat prosy narrative, cumbered with many tawdry embellishments and affectations of style and occasional intrusive passages of devout bombast. The indications are fairly clear that the version of the text which has come down to the present, has come through the hands of a painstaking editor-author whose qualifications were of a clerkly order, rather than anything in the way of literary sense, and whose penchant for fine writing would not allow him to let well enough alone. . . . So that, e.g., Kjartan Olafson comes to be depicted as a sanctimonious acolyte given to prayer, fasting, and pious verbiage; instead of being a wilful, spoiled child, vain and sulky, of a romantic temper and endowed with exceptional physical beauty, such as the run of the story proclaims him. Whereas Gudrun, a beautiful vixen, passionate, headstrong, self-seeking, and mendacious, is dutifully crowned with the distinction of having been the first nun and anchorite of Iceland and having meritoriously carried penance and abnegations to the outer limit of endurance.

Thorstein Veblen, *The Laxdaela Saga,* pages xiii–xiv.

26. *Ibid.,* page x.

27. Becky Veblen Meyers, however, heard Veblen "decline the American Economic Association presidency because he was really too done up. He'd have liked it when [he was] strong enuf [*sic*] to do some good." Letter to John P. Diggins, January 17, 1982, CC.

28. Ellen Veblen, letter to Lucia (Tower) Keene, DC, CURB&ML, Box 63V.

29. Ellen Veblen, letter to Annie Sargent Bemis, May 22, 1925, DC, CURB&ML, Box 64V.

30. Ellen Veblen, letter to Thorstein Veblen, November 15, 1924, CC.

31. Ellen Veblen, undated letter to Thorstein Veblen (date on envelope: September 16, 1923), CC.

32. Undated article, CC.

33. Upton Sinclair, *The Goose-Step,* pages 293–294.

34. Ex-president G. Stanley Hall was a most unusual man. Among other things, he was inspired to bring five world-famous psychoanalysts to Clark in 1909: Abraham A. Brill, Ernest Jones, Sandor Ferenczi, Sigmund Freud, and Carl Jung. The five made speeches about their work. Scientists from many other universities attended, and the famous analysts were given honorary degrees.

35. Testimony of the president of the Clark University Liberal Club before the investigating committee of the American Association of University Professors. Joseph Dorfman, *Thorstein Veblen and His America,* page 464.

36. *The Boston American* (March 18, 1926), clipping in Clark University Archives.

37. *New York Student* (April 19, 1922), and *The Gazette* (March 15, 1922), clippings in Clark University Archives.

38. William A. Koelsch, *Clark University: A Narrative History* (Worcester, MA: Clark University Press, 1987), pages 132–133 and 162. He wrote, "The Nearing incident proved disastrous to Clark and to Atwood's reputation in and outside the institution . . . A group of Pacific Coast alumni petitioned the trustees for Atwood's removal, a sentiment which was to be joined by alumni elsewhere, and by the graduating class of 1923." But Atwood hung in there. In that same year a sixty-year-old physics professor committed suicide for fear of losing his job in Atwood's relentless downgrading of math, chemistry, physics, and the humanities. Harry Elmer Barnes and three more faculty members announced their resignations, and "by the time of Atwood's [forced] retirement in 1946, the University was in shambles."

39. The Worcester *Telegram* (March 16, 1922), clippings in Clark University Archives.

40. *Ibid.*

41. *Boston Post* (March 26, 1922), clippings in Clark University Archives.

42. Upton Sinclair, *The Goose-Step,* page 298.

43. *New York Student* (April 19, 1922), clipping in Clark University Archives.

44. The students were further incensed because in a speech their president later made claiming he believed in freedom of speech, he asserted that he had a right and duty to decide what was proper for students to hear, and that he would exercise that right even more stringently in the future. *Boston Post* (March 20, 1922), clippings in Clark University Archives.

Chapter 24. "I Will Arise and Go Now"

1. Letter from Wesley Clair Mitchell to Leon Ardzrooni, December 9, 1924, DC, CURB&ML, Box M38.

2. Alvin Johnson, letter to Thorstein Veblen, March 1925, DC, CURB&ML.

3. A.F. Larson, letter to Joseph Dorfman, October 29, 1932, DC, CURB&ML, Box 62L. Larson, of the sociology department, William Woods College, indicates that Douglas made this statement at a luncheon given in his honor at the University of California. Larson mistakenly believed that Douglas was a student at the University of Chicago. Actually, Douglas attended Bowdoin, Columbia, and Harvard, and taught at Chicago (1920–1925), long after Veblen had departed.

4. It may be ascribing too much cunning to the old guard on the nominating committee to assume that they knew Veblen would not accept their conditional offer of the presidency. Probably Veblen was advised of the infighting on the committee and declined the offer on the ground that it was not a wholehearted gesture. Douglas said, "I think [however], from certain comments that Veblen made to friends of mine, that he was pleased by the fact that so many members of the association wanted him, and with the fact that it at least had been offered to him." Paul H. Douglas, letter to Joseph Dorfman, May 18, 1932, DC, CURB&ML, Box 61D. See also, Joseph Dorfman, *Thorstein Veblen and His America,* pages 491–492.

5. Becky Veblen Meyers, letter to John P. Diggins, February 26, 1982, CC, Box 4, Folder 13.

6. On June 18, 1923, Ellen had written to Thorstein: "[I] hung on to [the] house near Cedro with the idea that you might like it sometime. Can't do it much longer." On August 13, 1923, she wrote that she was willing to sell him the house, plus a three-room cabin in the rear, with a bath and "auto shed." The house was worth at least $2,000 (lots cost $725 in 1907), and it rented monthly for $15. Thorstein sent her a check for $500—the remaining $1,500 would follow. He had seen the place from the road, "three years ago," and that was evidently enough for him. CC.

7. Robert L. Duffus saw Veblen at Amherst in July 1919. His stepchildren were with him, and although Babe was either in Bellevue or McLean Hospital (she was transferred to McLean on July 31, 1919), "he seemed happy [with the children] and almost contented." He was more talkative than usual, which Duffus took as a good sign. At that point, too, Veblen may have thought that Babe would recover. The meeting was with Walter W. Stewart, Isador Lubin, Leo Wolman, and Walton Hamilton, who joined with Veblen in trying to get a grant—a project that never came off. Robert L. Duffus, *The Innocents at Cedro*, page 152.

8. Becky Veblen Meyers, "Autobiography," page 99, CC.

9. Becky Veblen Meyers, "Biography," page 5, CC. Charles Sims, Ann's adopted son, wrote: "Becky and Ann were similar in many ways. They both showed little interest in money, or valuables, or convention. . .They both worked hard to keep Veblen's work in print." He felt that his mother, Ann, "had the same respect and admiration for Veblen as that shown by Becky." Charles Sims, letter to authors, August 17, 1997, CC.

10. Ruthmary Penick, interview with Becky and Ann, 1977, page 60, CC.

11. Thorstein Veblen, letter to Ann Veblen, November 1, 1923, CC.

12. Thorstein Veblen, letter to Ann Veblen, December 3, 1923, CC.

262 NOTES TO CHAPTER 24

13. Thorstein Veblen, letter to Miss Becky Bradley (Becky Veblen Meyers), January 20 (probably 1920), CC.

14. Thorstein Veblen, letter to Ann Veblen, October 16, 1923, CC.

15. *Ibid.*

16. *Ibid.*

17. Esther Gunnerson, in her monograph, "Washington Island's Thorstein Veblen," repeated, as part of the islanders' history, the observation that the Veblen girls dressed in out-of-fashion long skirts, plain blouses, and clumsy boys' shoes, ordered from mail-order houses. She mistakenly believed this mode of dress was at Veblen's insistence. Gunnerson recounted the tale that the girls once changed clothes on a ferryboat, and upon reaching their destination, emerged wearing outfits of the latest style. In view of the fact that the girls were so devoted to their mother's ideas, there is reason to question the accuracy of this bit of Vebleniana. Page 8, CC.

18. Colette van Fleet, interview with Russell Bartley and Sylvia Yoneda, July 23, 1993, CC.

19. Becky Veblen Meyers, "Autobiography," alternate page 61, CC.

20. Authors' interviews with Esther Baran, July 10, 1994, and Charles Sims, February 13, 1994.

21. Colette van Fleet, interview with Russell Bartley and Sylvia Yoneda, pages 3 and 9, CC.

22. Mildred Bennett, letter to Thorstein Veblen, December 12, 1926, CC.

23. Becky Veblen Meyers, in tapes made by Ann Howard, May 29, 1990, describes Mildred Bennett as a "New York friend who had been trying, with another woman, to take the place of his wife in the sense that he got fed right." CC.

24. Checkbooks in CC.

25. In June 1927, Hilda wrote her uncle Thorstein that his $300 check had come Saturday, and that as soon as she got a teaching job and received her salary, she would make a point to repay it (CC). Veblen sent Ralph Sims $475 and $200 in 1928; Harold Veblen received $350, $200, $300, and $100 from Thorstein in 1927. Ed Veblen's letter to Thorstein (September 9, 1926) indicated that he had failed as a builder in San Diego and had borrowed money from Thorstein, which he hoped soon to pay back. He wrote: "I was surprised at the way you responded. It was a case of getting help just when help was needed . . . Anyway, I will return your money as soon as I get in the habit of making it again . . . I will not be entirely destitute when I get my San Diego affairs settled up, but almost" (CC). Thorstein also sent Orson Veblen $2,500 to help him out of a bad spot (Florence Andrews Noble Veblen, letter to her sister, Eva Andrews Leonard, May 23, 1922, CC, File 278). Thorstein was happy to take a promissory note from Orson secured by a mortgage, even though it almost cleaned out his bank account—that, and his salary, were all he owned at that time, he wrote. Ed also asked Thorstein for $500 to $5,000 on May 2, 1929—"any amount would help (CC)." Previously, on February 27, 1927, he had written Thorstein thanking him for an unspecified amount, saying, "You seem to be luckier than some of us." CC.

26. Becky Veblen Meyers, "Autobiography," page 34, CC.

27. Isador Lubin, letter to Joseph Dorfman, April 21, 1934, DC, CURB&ML.

28. Paul Veblen, interview with Becky Veblen Meyers, CC, page 14.

29. Thorstein Veblen, letter to Isador Lubin, February 22, 1927, DC, CURB&ML.

30. Becky Veblen Meyers, "Biography," page 4, CC.

31. Esther Baran, telephone conversation with the authors, March 5, 1994.

32. According to Mrs. Baran, Becky remembered the difficult time her mother had simultaneously holding a job and caring for her children, and liked to work for women in similar predicaments.

33. Becky Veblen Meyers, "Biography," page 4, CC.

34. Becky Veblen Meyers, letter to John P. Diggins, January 17, 1972, CC.

35. Becky Veblen Meyers, "Biography," page 4, CC.

36. Becky Veblen Meyers, interview with Ruthmary Penick, 1977, CC, page 42.

37. Becky Veblen Meyers, letter to John P. Diggins, January 17, 1962, CC.

38. Thorstein Veblen, letter to his sister Emily Veblen Olson, MHS. Thorstein seemed to be reproaching himself for his inability to be "up and doing"; Andrew, too, was stricken by twinges of guilt when he was unable to accomplish things. In a letter to Thorstein (June 2, 1927), Andrew wrote, "I am still pursuing the idleness cure; I am good-for-nothing. Perhaps I am more scared [about his physical condition] than I ought to be. I am afraid I worked too hard in my efforts to keep our yard from getting to be a reproach to my state of decency, as judged by conventional standards—this, superimposed on my terrible experience with the dentists, was probably what was too much for me." MHS.

39. Hans Otto Storm, letter to Joseph Dorfman, November 6, 1932, DC, CURB&ML, Box 63S.

40. Becky Veblen Meyers, letter to David Riesman, February 20, 1954, CC. Becky also mentions that they both were homesick during this period. Becky Veblen Meyers, "Biography," page 4, CC.

41. Becky Veblen Meyers, "Biography," page 4, CC.

42. Becky Veblen Meyers, letter to David Riesman, February 20, 1954, CC.

43. Becky Veblen Meyers, letter to Barbara Kevles of Pathfinders, May 26, 1990, CC. Also, Becky's "Biography," page 4, CC.

44. Becky Veblen Meyers, letter to Barbara Kevles, CC.

45. Hans Otto Storm, November 6, 1932, letter to Joseph Dorfman, DC, CURB&ML, Box 63S.

46. At the end of her life "[Ellen] became very much of a mystic and had visions—perhaps I should say hallucinations, which were much more real to her than the world of reality." Mary Dierup, undated letter to Joseph Dorfman, DC, CURB&ML. Ellen left Halcyon before she died, "and went to [Evelyn Wells's] mother's house in San Jose to spend her last days." Evelyn Wells, November 26, 1966, CC.

47. Thorstein Veblen, letter to Emily Veblen Olsen, June 12, 1928, MHS.

48. Sarah H. Gregory, letter to Wesley Clair Mitchell, April 26 (or 28?), 1928, DC, CURB&ML, Box 61. Mitchell answered that he would prefer to give his usual stipend of $500, annually, through the New School, as Veblen might be counting on it (Wesley Clair Mitchell, letter to Sarah Gregory, April 29, 1928, CC). Also, in Florence Veblen's letter to Thorstein (March 11, 1928), Florence had written that she and Orson were "very sorry to know you are losing ground. Orson, too, is losing ground." CC, File 277a.

49. William Butler Yeats, "The Lake Isle of Innisfree," *Modern American and Modern British Poetry,* ed. Louis Untermeyer (New York: Harcourt Brace, 1955), pages 470–471.

50. Becky Veblen Meyers, "Autobiography," CC, page 61. Also, Mrs. R.E. Fisher, letter to Joseph Dorfman DC, CURB&ML, February 15, 1932, reported that

while she was visiting at the ridge cabin shortly before Veblen's death, Veblen said he had begun to hear dead relatives speak to him in Norwegian as plainly as if they were actually in the cabin. According to Becky, Mrs. Fisher had only a slight acquaintance with Veblen, and he undoubtedly would have scorned the idea of Norwegian ghosts. As Hans Otto Storm wrote to Dorfman, "For all forms of mysticism [Veblen] expressed a profound contempt, not an anger at it, as at misdirected intellect, but a contempt for the thing as meaningless nonsense." (Letter to Joseph Dorfman, November 6, 1932, DC CURB&ML, Box 63S.) One wonders how much of Mrs. Fisher's quotation was derived from Veblen, and how much from a distillation of other near-death reports. See Joseph Dorfman, *Thorstein Veblen and His America,* pages 503–504, for his account of Mrs. Fisher's anecdote. Becky wrote that not long before his death Veblen performed an exacting veterinary operation:

> A month or so before Veblen's death we took our [cat] up to the ridge shanty . . . [she] showed up, wounded . . . some idiot with a gun saw a speck of white and fired at it blindly. Our white kitty went straight to [Veblen]. He put her gently on his knees. Her eyes said she knew he would fix her up. While he mumbled curses . . . he studied the numerous flecks of red where the buck shots went in . . . he worked patiently on kitty, who was also patient and plucky, most of the morning . . . finally he said he thought the shot was all out. The cat had a slight limp for a while, but recovered.

Becky Veblen Meyers, letter to David Riesman, February 20, 1954, CC.

51. Florence Veblen, in letters to Thorstein (January 23 and March 11, 1928), described Orson's pitiful loss of sight. She wrote, "I have not given up hope that Orson's eyes can be helped if we find the right physician. The specialists we saw in Great Falls last summer said nothing could be done . . . 'senile atrophy' came on suddenly" CC.

52. Becky Veblen Meyers "Autobiography," alternate page 61, CC.

53. Andrew Veblen, letter to Edward Bemis, October 4, 1929, Andrew Veblen Papers, MHS. Also letters from Becky Veblen Meyers to John P. Diggins, January 17 and February 26, 1982, CC.

54. Joseph Dorfman, *Thorstein Veblen and His America*, page 504.

55. Guido Marx, biographical sketch of Veblen, SULC SC129, Box 2, Fol. 6. Of course, the complexity within Veblen's character is not the whole story, which includes the complex characters who interacted with him. For example: Dorfman said to Dutch sociologist Louis van Elderen that he though Veblen was no more sexually inclined "than any other person. I think the problem was his wife . . . but I do not wish to blame her." DC, CURB&ML Box 64V. And there was Ellen's brother, Eugene Strong Rolfe, who, on January 7, 1930, predicted that Dorfman's biography "would do that very rascally thing [of representing] my sister, Ellen Rolfe Veblen, as hopelessly insane and a clog upon . . . her husband . . . this pestiferous Dorfman . . . might be a blackmailer . . . we had better all of us caraefully ignore him." Letter to the editor of *The Carleton Circle,* Alumnae File, 277-D-4-23, Ellen Strong Rolfe, Class of 1881, CC.

56. Warner Fite, letter to Joseph Dorfman, July 4, 1930, DC, CURB&ML, Box 61F.

57. Rick Tilman, *Thorstein Veblen and His Critics, 1891–1963* (Princeton: Princeton University Press, 1992), page ix.

Chapter 25. After All

1. Dr. Stephen B. Karpman, a San Francisco psychiatrist, described the rescuer personality as one who is involved in a "Drama Triangle." The two players in the triangle alternate roles as rescuer, victim, and persecutor. The rescuer sometimes switches to persecutor; the victim can become a rescuer; and the original rescuer may turn into a victim. See Stephen B. Karpman, "Fairy Tales and Script Drama Analysis," *Transactional Analysis Bulletin* 7, No. 25 (January 1968): 18, and "Script Drama Analysis," *Transactional Analysis Bulletin* 7, No. 26 (April 1968); and Muriel James and Dorothy Jongeward, *Born to Win* (Reading, MA: Addison-Wesley, 1971), page 87.

2. Laura McAdoo Triggs Gagey had shown in her youth some signs of emotional stress. As a child she walked in her sleep and had one episode of hyperventilation when she was ten years old. Her father entered this in his diary on February 6, 1881:

> Oh, the tortures of yesterday and today! Laura is fearfully ill of some nervous malady. Dr. Tiedeman has been frequently to see her; has tried many remedies; yet she is now—at 6:45 PM—almost in convulsions. Yes, quite; for at intervals of about ten seconds she fetches three to six convulsions, catching of her breath very much resembling a rapid groan, the middle one being the loudest, and her hands are clenched. But she has no fever; and in momentary intervals between these rapid paroxysms, she is ready for conversation on any topic . . . I greatly fear she may go into violent convulsions. I fear congestion or lesion of the brain—death. In fact, I do not see how she can get well . . . I am losing hope of saving the dear child's life. She is wonderfully bright and always was intellectually precocious. Would that I could die for her!

On February 7, 1881, he wrote, "Convulsions reappeared . . . Dr. Boynton pronounced it St. Vitus dance." On February 8, 1881, finally the doctors gave her calomel.

Laura may simply have been badly frightened by her father's melancholy and his preoccupation with death. An examination of her father's diaries shows he haunted his local cemetery, sometimes with Laura:

> June 3, 1880: Laura and I walked to the cemetery and strolled about . . . Near eleven I was awakened by a noise. Laura *walking* about the hall in her sleep.

> January 3, 1881: Walked in the cemetery and back in the afternoon. Visited my lot; gazed on the spot where my dust must soon lie.

> November 24, 1885: I am not well; I have a cough and my left lung is pertinaceously weak. It is the beginning of the end. But the beginning of life is *the beginning of the end.*

> September 20, 1886: I have agonizing discouragement[s] which would not gain the slightest relief from being recorded here—which compel me to long for death as the sole method of their ending. I went yesterday and looked at my cemetery plot, longing to lie there in peace.

October 1, 1886: [Many people he knows are dying] ... The day has been a very solemn and gloomy one for me. What is left on earth for me but to die? God knows best. I will *endure until He calls me.*

October 7, 1886: A day of impossible concentration of attention on any subject. Thus glides away the last currents [*sic*] of my life.

December 19, 1886: Little Maze, a white girl in our neighborhood, died just before day.

December 20, 1886: I stepped into the little house occupied by the Maze family; saw Lillie Maze's corpse ... she was young, poor, ignorant; is not her death happy for her?

January 18, 1887: The whole day has been spent in vain endeavors. The day is typical of my whole life. Tonight, on the table near me, is a heap of old diary volumes going back more than thirty years. The record is one of vain endeavor.

Despite the gloomy tone underlying the journals, McAdoo was in reasonably good health and lived until 1894—seven more years. He died at age 73. He was, however, plagued by a steady loss of status beginning with defeat of the Confederacy. He was an unusually gifted individual, whose aristocratic background only hampered him in fitting in with those who sat in the seats of the mighty. William Gibbs McAdoo, Senior, Diaries (LMGL).

  3. Seneca, *De Tranquillitate Animi,* page 17, quoted from John Bartlett, *Familiar Quotations* (Boston: Little, Brown, 1906).

  4. Leon Ardzrooni, letter to B.W. Huebsch, April 12, 1936, DC, CURB&ML.

  5. *International Journal of Ethics* (January 1910): 168–185. This article was reprinted in Max Lerner, ed., *The Portable Veblen* (New York: Viking Press, 1948), pages 480–498.

  6. Becky Veblen Meyers, letter to John P. Diggins, February 26, 1982, CC, Box 4, Folder 13.

  7. Thorstein Veblen, "Dementia Praecox," in *Essays in Our Changing Order,* ed. Leon Ardzrooni, page 423.

  8. Sheldon Kopp, *If You Meet the Buddha on the Road, Kill Him* (Palo Alto, CA: Science and Behavior Books, 1972, Reprints—New York: Bantam Books). Kopp's point, of course, is not that Buddha is the bearer of bad news, but that it is only by rejecting the received truths of the masters that we can create pertinent truths applicable to our present predicaments. This is essentially the same message that Veblen is giving us—that we must discard the institutionalized truths of the economic soothsayers if we are ever to get out of the predatory push to thinner equities and a dehumanized world.

  9. Rick Tilman (*The Intellectual Legacy of Thorstein Veblen* [Westport, CT: Greenwood Press, 1996] and *Thorstein Veblen and His Critics, 1891–1963* [Princeton: Princeton University Press, 1991]) carefully destroys the relevance of such critics. Snippets of attention are still given Veblen in the mazed world of contemporary economic thought. The stately economic journals, bastions of orthodoxy, have published serious articles on "Veblen effects" along with the usual scis-

soring of supply and demand curves and solemn geometric apologies for the fact that people splurge on certain name-brand extravagances just because they are recognizably expensive. And the late Eliot Janeway, a Time-Life-Fortune alumnus and stock market seer, in his valedictory book, *The Economics of Chaos* (1989), contended that Veblen's economic heresies, though unacknowledged, energized the New Deal reformers, and were indirectly responsible for our present-day welfare capitalism. He felt that many M.B.A. candidates, preparing for well-paying careers of "trained ignorance," would be surprised to recognize the sum total that Veblen had contributed to their training, though "few would have heard of him."

Bibliography

Adams, Ruth, and Frank Murray. *Minerals Cure or Kill.* New York: Larchmont Books, 1974.

Alexrad, Jacob. *Anatole France: A Life Without Illusions.* New York: Harper and Brothers, 1944.

Allison, Alexander W. et al., eds. *The Norton Anthology of Poetry,* 3rd edition. New York: W.W. Norton, 1983.

Ardzrooni, Leon, ed. *Essays in Our Changing Order.* New York: Augustus M. Kelley, 1964.

Bancquart, Marie-Claire. *Anatole France: Un sceptique passionné.* Paris: Calmann-Lévy, 1984.

Bartley, Russell, and Sylvia Yoneda Bartley. "Thorstein Veblen on Washington Island: Traces of a Life." *International Journal of Politics, Culture, and Society* 7, No. 4 (1994).

Bemis, Edward W. "Academic Freedom." *The Independent,* August 17, 1899.

Bentzon, Th. (Mme. Blanc, pseudonym). *The Condition of Woman in the United States: A Traveller's Guide.* Reprint of a 1895 edition, also published in Paris in 1905. Freeport, NY: Books for Libraries Press, 1972.

Blegen, Theodore C. "The Norwegian Migration to America." Norwegian-American Historical Association, St. Olaf College, 1931.

Blitch, Charles P. *Allyn Young: The Peripatetic Economist.* London: Macmillan Press and New York: St. Martin's Press, 1995.

Borrow, George, *Lavengro, the Scholar, the Gipsy, the Priest.* London: Oxford University Press, 1951.

Broessamle, John J. *William Gibbs McAdoo: A Passion for Change, 1863–1917.* Port Washington, NY: Kennikat Press, 1973.

Browning, Elizabeth Barrett. "The Cry of the Children." In *The Home Book of Verse,* selected and arranged by Burton Egbert Stevenson. New York: Holt, Rinehart, and Winston, 1965.

Buhle, Marie J. *Women and American Socialism, 1870–1920.* Chicago: University of Illinois Press, 1892.

Christianson, J.R. "Thorstein Veblen: Ethnic Roots and Social Criticism of a 'Folk Savant.' " *Norwegian American Studies* 34. Northfield: Norwegian-American Historical Association, 1995.

Coke, van Deren. *Nordfeldt the Painter.* Albuquerque: University of New Mexico Press, 1972.

Dickens, Charles. *Great Expectations.* New York: George Routledge and Sons, 1850.

Diggins, John P. *The Bard of Savagery.* New York: Seabury Press, 1978.

Dorfman, Joseph. *New Light on Veblen.* Clifton, NJ: Augustus M. Kelley, 1973.

————. *Thorstein Veblen and His America.* Clifton, NJ: Augustus M. Kelley, 1972.

Dos Passos, John. *The Big Money.* New York: Harcourt Brace, 1936.

Dowd, Douglas. *Thorstein Veblen.* Great American Thinkers Series. New York: Washington Square Press, 1966.

Duffus, Robert L. *The Innocents at Cedro.* Clifton, NJ: Augustus M. Kelley, 1972.

Eastman, Max. *Love and Revolution.* New York: Random House, 1964.

Edith Hamilton. *Mythology.* Boston: Little, Brown, 1942.

Einstein, Albert. "Remarks on Bertrand Russell's Theory of Knowledge." In *The Philosophy of Bertrand Russell.* Evanston: A. Schilpp, 1944, page 179. Cited in *The Generations of Science* by Lewis S. Feuer (New York: Basic Books, 1974).

Elliott, Orrin Leslie. *Stanford: The First Twenty-five Years.* Stanford: Stanford University Press, 1937.

Feuer, Lewis S. *The Generations of Science.* New York: Basic Books, 1974.

Fuchs, James, ed. Introduction to *Ruskin's Views of Social Justice.* New York: Vanguard Press, 1926.

Glasgow, Ellen. *Barren Ground.* Garden City, NY: Doubleday, Page, 1925.

Goodspeed, Thomas W. *A History of the University of Chicago, the First Quarter Century.* Chicago: University of Chicago Press, 1916.

Griffin, Geraldine Mazzei. A 1982 review of "The Barbarian Status of Women." In *Thorstein Veblen: Seer of Socialism* by Robert Griffin. Hamden, CT: Advocate Press, distributed by Roger Books, 1982.

Griffin, Robert. *Thorstein Veblen: Seer of Socialism.* Hamden, CT: Advocate Press, distributed by Roger Books, 1982.

James, Muriel, and Dorothy Jongeward. *Born to Win.* Reading, MA: Addison-Wesley, 1971.

Janeway, Eliot. *The Economics of Chaos: On Revitalizing the American Economy.* New York: Truman Talley Books, E.P. Dutton, 1989.

Johnson, Alvin. *A Pioneer's Progress: An Autobiography of Alvin Johnson,* foreword by Max Lerner. New York: Viking Press, 1952.

Karpman, Stephen B. "Fairy Tales and Script Drama Analysis." *Transactional Analysis Bulletin* 7, No. 25 (January 1968), page 18.

————. "Script Drama Analysis," *Transactional Analysis Bulletin* 7, No. 26 (April 1968).

Kipling, Rudyard. *The Phantom Rickshaw.* New York: Charles Scribner's Sons, 1911.

Kopp, Sheldon. *If You Meet the Buddha on the Road, Kill Him.* Palo Alto, CA: Science and Behavior Books, 1972; New York: Bantam Books, reprint.

Lerner, Max, ed. *The Portable Veblen.* New York: Viking Press, 1948.

Lubin, Isador. "Recollections of Thorstein Veblen." *The Carleton College Veblen Seminar Essays,* edited by Carlton C. Qualey. New York: Columbia University Press, 1968.

Mann, Thomas. *Stories of Three Decades.* New York: Alfred A. Knopf, 1951.

McDonnell, Lynda. "Veblen Redux." *The Region.* Federal Reserve Bank of Minneapolis, December 1993, pages 7–13.

Meyers, Becky Veblen. "Autobiography." Veblen Collections, Carleton College Archives.

————. "Biography." Transcribed by Esther Baran. Veblen Collections, Carleton College Archives.

————. "Memoirs." Veblen Collection, Carleton College Archives.

Miller, Donald L. *Lewis Mumford: A Life.* New York: Weidenfeld and Nicolson, 1989.

Mitchell, Lucy Sprague. *Two Lives: The Story of Wesley Clair Mitchell and Myself.* New York: Simon and Schuster, 1953.

Mitchell, Wesley C., ed. *What Veblen Taught.* New York: Viking Press, 1947.

Morris, May, ed. *William Morris: Artist, Writer, Socialist.* London: Russell and Russell, 1966.

Morris, William. *Collected Works: The Earthly Paradise, A Poem,* Vol. 5. London: Longmans, Green, 1910.

Mumford, Lewis. *Findings and Keepings.* New York: Harcourt Brace, 1975.

————. *Sketches from Life.* New York: Dial Press, 1982.

Murray, Frank, and Ruth Adams. *Minerals Cure or Kill.* New York: Larchmont Books, 1974.

Olsen, Emily Veblen. "Memoirs." Norwegian Historical Society, St. Olaf College.

Proust, Marcel. *Remembrance of Things Past,* Volume 1. New York: Random House, 1934.

Qualey, Carlton C., ed. *Carleton College Veblen Seminar Essays.* New York: Columbia University Press, 1966.

Saxton, Martha. *Louisa May: A Modern Biography of Louisa May Alcott.* New York: Avon Books, Houghton Mifflin, 1977.

Shaw, George Bernard. "Morris as I Knew Him." Introduction in *William Morris: Artist, Writer, Socialist,* edited by May Morris. London: Russell and Russell, 1966.

Sinclair, Upton. *The Brass Check.* Pasadena, CA: Upton Sinclair, undated.

————. *The Goose-Step.* Pasadena, CA: Upton Sinclair, 1922, 1923. New York: Edward and Charles Boni, 1936.

Smith, Janet Adams, ed. *The Faber Book of Children's Verse.* London: Faber and Faber, 1953.

Smith, Carl S. *Chicago and the American Literary Imagination, 1880–1920.* Chicago: University of Chicago Press, 1984.

Stevenson, Burton Egbert, ed. *The Home Book of Verse.* New York: Holt, Rinehart, and Winston, 1965.

Suffel, Jacques. *Anatole France par lui-même.* Paris: Ecrivains de Toujours, Editions de Seuil.

Swinburne, Algernon Charles. "Hymn to Prosperpine." In *Everyman's Book of Victorian Verse,* edited by J.M. Watson. London: J.M. Dent, 1982, page 209.

Tilman, Rick. *The Intellectual Legacy of Thorstein Veblen.* Westport, CT: Greenwood Press, 1996.

————. *A Veblen Treasury,* Armonk, NY: M.E. Sharpe, 1993.

————. *Thorstein Veblen and His Critics, 1891–1963.* Princeton, NJ: Princeton University Press, 1991.

Untermeyer, Louis, ed. *Modern American and Modern British Poetry.* New York: Harcourt Brace, 1955.

Veblen, Andrew. "Immigrant Pioneers from Valdris." Minnesota Historical Society.

————. "Daybook." Minnesota Historical Society.

Veblen, Ellen. *The Goosenbury Pilgrims.* Boston: Lothrop, 1902.

Veblen, Florence. "Reminiscences of Thorstein Veblen by His Brother Orson." *Social Forces* 10, No. 2 (December 1931).

Veblen, Thorstein. *Absentee Ownership and Business Enterprise in Recent Times.* New York: B.W. Huebsch, 1923; reprint, New York: Augustus M. Kelley, 1964.

————. "The Barbarian Status of Women." *American Journal of Sociology* (January 1899), pages 352–365.

————. "The Beginnings of Ownership." *American Journal of Sociology* (January 1899), pages 352–365.

————. "The Blond Race and the Aryan Culture." *University of Missouri Bulletin, Science Series* 2, No. 3 (April 1913).

————. "Dementia Praecox." *Freeman,* June 21, 1922, pages 127–132.

————. "Christian Morals and the Competitive System." *International Journal of Ethics* 20 (January 1910); republished in *Essays in Our Changing Order,* edited by Leon Ardzrooni. New York: Augustus M. Kelley, 1964; republished in *The Portable Veblen* edited by Max Lerner. New York: Viking Press, 1948.

————. "Dementia Praecox." In *Essays in Our Changing Order,* edited by Leon Ardzrooni. New York: Augustus M. Kelley, 1964.

————. *The Engineers and the Price System.* New York: Viking Press, 1926.

————. *The Higher Learning in America.* New York: Augustus M. Kelley, reprint, 1965.

————. *Imperial Germany and the Industrial Revolution.* New York: Macmillan, 1915.

————. *An Inquiry into the Nature of Peace and the Terms of Its Perpetuation.* New York: Macmillan, 1917.

————. *The Instinct of Workmanship.* New York: Viking Press, 1914.

————. *The Laxdaela Saga.* New York: B.W. Huebsch, 1925.

————. "The Limitations of Marginal Utility." *The Journal of Political Economy* 17 (November 1909), pages 620–636. Republished in *What Veblen Taught,* edited by Wesley C. Mitchell (New York: Viking Press, 1947).

————. "The Mutation Theory and the Blond Race." *Journal of Race Development* (April 1913), pages 491–507.

————. "On the Nature of Capital, Interest, and the Productivity of Capital Goods." *The Quarterly Journal of Economics* 22 (August 1908), pages 517–542; republished in *The Place of Science in Modern Civilization: And Other Essays.* New York: Huebsch 1919; New York: Russell and Russell, 1961.

————. "The Opportunity of Japan." *The Journal of Race Development* 6 (July 1915), pages 23–38.

————. *The Place of Science in Modern Civilization.* New York: Russell and Russell, 1961.

————. "The Socialist Economics of Karl Marx and His Followers I." *The Quarterly Journal of Economics* 20 (August 1906), pages 578–595.

————. "The Socialist Economics of Karl Marx and His Followers II." *The Quarterly Journal of Economics* 21 (February 1907), pages 299–322.

————. *The Theory of Business Enterprise.* New York: Scribner's, 1937.

————. *The Theory of the Leisure Class.* New York: Random House/Modern Library, 1934.

————. "The Theory of Women's Dress." *Popular Science Monthly* (November 1894), pages 198–205.

————. *The Vested Interests and the State of the Industrial Arts.* New York: B.W. Huebsch, 1919; reprinted in 1920 as *The Vested Interests and the Common Man.*

————."Why Is Economics Not an Evolutionary Science?" *Quarterly Journal of Economics* 12 (July 1898); republished in *The Place of Science in Modern Civilization.*

von Bernhardi, General Friedrich. *Germany and the Next War.* New York: Longmans, Green, 1914.

Walker, Franklin. *The Seacoast of Bohemia.* Salt Lake City: Book Club of California and Peregrine Smith, 1973.

Warshaw, Jacob. "Recollections of Thorstein Veblen." Jacob Warshaw Papers, 1910–1944. Western Historical Manuscript Collection, Columbia, Missouri, Folder 89, #36.

Wylie, Elinor. "The Puritan's Ballad." In *Collected Poems of Elinor Wylie,* edited by William Rose Benét. New York: Alfred A. Knopf, 1934.

Yeats, W.B. "The Land of Heart's Desire." A one act play in *Collected Plays of W.B. Yeats,* edited by Lady Augusta Gregory. New York: Macmillan, 1990.

Index

About the Authors

Elizabeth Watkins Jorgensen was born and grew up in the Pacific Northwest. She first heard about Thorstein Veblen in her freshman citizenship course at Stanford; ideas from *The Theory of the Leisure Class* immediately permeated her thinking. After receiving her B.A. at Stanford she spent the next six years attending various art schools, among them the New York Art Students' League, the San Francisco Institute of Fine Arts, and the Corcoran Gallery's School of Art in Washington, DC. Specializing in painting offbeat portraits, she searched for people's innermost characteristics—more closely related to biography than one would imagine.

Henry Irvin Jorgensen was also impressed by Thorstein Veblen's point of view in his freshman year at Stanford but not so much as he was by Elizabeth, whom he met on the last day of his senior year. After earning an M.A. in economics at Columbia University, choosing Professor Dorfman as his mentor because of Dorfman's biography of Veblen, and after a sufficient amount of economic toil for the federal government, Jorgensen returned to Stanford for an L.L.B. and then practiced small-town and small-county law.

The Jorgensens previously co-authored *Eric Berne: Mastergamesman,* a biography of the unorthodox psychiatrist and author of *Games People Play,* both books published by Grove Press.